IT SECURITY

INDIAN INSTITUTE OF BANKING & FINANCE

- **Updated by Dr. Pradeep Kumar, Professor, Information Technology and System Area, IIM Lucknow**
- **Vetted by Dr. Deepak Kumar Tomar, Professor, HOD, Computer Science & Engineering Department, The Maulana Azad National Institute of Technology, Bhopal (MANIT Bhopal)**

Edition : 2024

Price : ₹ 435

Published by :
Taxmann Publications (P.) Ltd.

Sales & Marketing :
59/32, New Rohtak Road, New Delhi-110 005 India
Phone : +91-11-45562222
Website : www.taxmann.com
E-mail : sales@taxmann.com

Mumbai
35, Bodke Building, Ground Floor M.G. Road,
Opp. Railway Station, Mulund (W), Mumbai - 400 080
Mob. +91-9322247686, 9619668669, 7045453844/45/51
E-mail : sales.mumbai@taxmann.com; nileshbhanushali@taxmann.com

Regd. Office :
21/35, West Punjabi Bagh, New Delhi-110 026 India

Printed at :
Tan Prints (India) Pvt. Ltd.
44 Km. Mile Stone, National Highway, Rohtak Road,
Village Rohad, Distt. Jhajjar (Haryana) India
E-mail : sales@tanprints.com

FOREWORD

It is with great pleasure and pride, IIBF is presenting this comprehensive book on the "IT Security". In an era defined by rapid technological advancements, the importance of robust IT Security practices assumes utmost importance. It gives me immense satisfaction to see the institution take the leading role in shaping the future of banking and finance professionals through this certification program on a contemporary topic. In today's interconnected world, where digital innovations continue to redefine the landscape of financial services, the need for a secure and resilient IT infrastructure is paramount. The Certificate Examination on IT Security is a testament to IIBF's commitment to equip banking and finance professionals with the knowledge and skills necessary to navigate the complexities of the digital age.

This book serves as a comprehensive guide, offering in-depth insights into the various facets of IT Security, form the fundamentals of Cyber Security principles to the intricacies of Risk Management in a digital environment.

The authors, experts in the field, have meticulously crafted this book to provide a clear and concise understanding of the challenges and opportunities inherent in securing sensitive information involving the financial sector.

I place on record the dedication of the Subject Matter Experts in creating a curriculum that not only meets the high academic standards but also addresses the real-world challenges faced by the professionals in the banking and finance sector. The concepts under pinning IT Security which have been explained in a lucid manner will enable the learner to understand the intricacies involved in the subject.

As we navigate the ever-evolving landscape of digital finance, the role of IT Security professionals becomes increasingly critical. The Certificate Examination on IT Security, facilitated by this comprehensive course, stands as a beacon, guiding professionals towards a secure and resilient future.

I extend my best wishes to all the candidates who intend to undertake this certification and I am confident that the knowledge gained from this course will not only empower them in their professional journey but also contribute to the overall security and integrity of the financial systems they serve.

We welcome suggestions for improvement of the courseware.

Mumbai | **Biswa Ketan Das**

2024 | **Chief Executive Officer**

RECOMMENDED READING

The Institute has prepared comprehensive courseware in the form of study kit to facilitate preparation for the examination without intervention of the teacher. An attempt has been made to cover fully the syllabus prescribed for the subject. The presentation of topics may not always be in the same sequence as given in the syllabus.

Candidates are also expected to take note of all the latest developments relating to the subject covered in the syllabus by referring to Financial Papers, Economic Journals, Latest Books, Publications and relevant websites.

SYLLABUS

MODULE A - IT SECURITY OVERVIEW

Unit 1: Introduction to Information Security - Data and Information, Information Classification, Need to Know, Information Security, Other Applicable Attributes of Information Security, Physical Security, Logical Security, Advantages of organization's information security programme, Disadvantages of organization's information security programme, Goals of Information security, Types of information security, The services of information security.

Unit 2: Corporate IT Security Policies - Meaning of Corporate IT Security, Need for a Corporate IT Security Policy, Legal Requirements, Essential Features of Corporate IT Security Policy, Physical Security Policy, Methodology of Framing an IT Security Policy, Awareness Initiatives, Aspects of security measurement.

Unit 3: Organisational Security and Risk Management - Organisational Security, Public Sector Organisation, Right to Information Act, 2005, Risk Metrics, Downstream Liability, Risk Management in Banking, Classifications of security attacks in IT security, The information security attacks.

Unit 4: Security Governance - Concepts, Policies, Framework, Key Responsibility Areas, Security Governance in Public Sector Undertakings, Security Governance in Banks, Compliance to Policies is a Must in Any Organization, Monitoring.

Unit 5: Physical and Environmental Security - Concepts, Physical Security Equipment, Intrusion Prevention Systems (IPSs), Environmental Security.

Unit 6: Hardware Security - Hardware, Network Related Devices Like Routers, Switches, Hubs.

Unit 7: Software and Operational Security - Concepts, Cloud Computing, Operational Security, Banking, Telecom Industry, IT Industry, BPO and KPO Industries, User Level Controls, Software Security Techniques.

Unit 8: Security Standards and Best Practices - ISO 27000 Standards, ISO – ISMS, Benefits of ISO 27001, Cobit-Control Objectives in IT, CIA triad - Confidentiality, Integrity, Availability, Importance of Confidentiality, Components of Confidentiality, Different types of Confidentialities.

MODULE B - IT SECURITY CONTROLS

Unit 9: Asset Classification and Controls - Asset Classification and Control, Protection of Information Assets, Control of Hardware Equipment, Traditional Methods to Control Hardware Assets, Control of Software Assets, OSI Model.

Unit 10: Physical and Environmental Security Controls - Physical Security Layer-Concepts, Environment Controls, Lighting, e-Waste.

Unit 11: Software Security Controls - Operating Systems (OS), Windows Security, Databases, Application Level Security, Mobile Banking, Internet Banking, Credit Cards.

Unit 12: Network Controls - Concepts, Controls in a Layered Network, VLANs, Protocols used in Network, Intrusion Detection System (IDS), Firewalls, Unified Threat Management, The Information Management Security, Advantages of information management security.

Unit 13: Controls in Software Development and Maintenance - Software Security-Concepts, Software Development, Cloud Computing, Big Data.

Module C - IT SECURITY THREATS

Unit 14: Security Threats Overview - Threats, Cyber Espionage, Cyber Terrorism.

Unit 15: Prevention and Detection of Software Attacks - Viruses and Malwares-Malware, Controls.

Unit 16: Incident Management - Objectives of Incident Response, Action Methodology, Processes Running, Awareness.

Unit 17: Fault Tolerant Systems - High Availability (HA), Services Oriented Architecture (SOA), The primary aspects of Service-Oriented Architecture.

Unit 18: Business Continuity and Disaster Recovery Management - Downtime, Phase I, Backups, Who Should Call 'Disaster'? Phase II, Phase III.

Module D - IS AUDIT AND REGULATORY COMPLIANCE

Unit 19: Information Systems Audit - History of EDP Audit in Banks, IS Auditor, External v. Internal IS Auditor, Audit Methodologies, Types of Audits, Planning Phase, Report Presentation, Audit Policy, Cobit and Framework, Audit Reports.

Unit 20: Regulatory mechanism in Indian Banks - RBI as the Regulator, RBI'S Regulatory Initiatives Taken so far, Gopalakrishna Working Group, Compliance in Banks, Penal Powers of RBI, RBI's Regulatory Mechanism Already in Place, RBI, SEBI, TRAI, IRDAI, Legal Enactments.

CONTENTS

MODULE

IT SECURITY OVERVIEW

1

C H A P T E R

Introduction to Information Security

OBJECTIVES

Upon the completion of this chapter, readers should be able to understand the meaning and definition of information, data and security, components of information, the concept of security and rules governing the classification of information. A brief introduction is also given on areas relating to physical security, logical security such as Network Access, Software Access and Application Access. These are discussed in-depth in the later chapters.

1.1 Introduction

In common parlance, the words 'data' and 'information' are used interchangeably, though technically, there is a subtle distinction between the two. What we input into a computer is referred to as data, and what the computer stores is also data. Our software programs and other utility software provides the information we need as output after processing the stored data. Therefore, data is typically considered the raw form of information, which requires processing to be used in a particular desired manner. In other words, processed data is generally referred to as information.

The Indian Information Technology Act, 2000 (IT Act, 2000) defines data as:

'A representation of information, knowledge, facts, concepts or instructions which are being prepared or have been prepared in a formalized manner, and is intended to be processed, is being processed or has been processed in a computer system or computer network, and may be in any form (including computer printouts, magnetic or optical storage media, punched cards, punched tapes) or stored internally in the memory of the computer'. [Section 2(o)]

Though data is considered to be the first stage of information, sometimes the output or a piece of stored information or a print-out can also be called data. Therefore, it is quite clear that data does not necessarily mean the numbers and characters stored in the system but in a broader sense it refers to all that is stored in whichever form like music files, audio files, video files or in any internal medium like a hard-disk, a memory chip in the computer or an external medium like floppy, CD, DVD, Pen-drive etc.

The word 'processing' assumes significance when distinguishing data from information. Processed data is normally called information. Information is the data presented in the format required for use or

other forms of analysis as part of Management Information System. In a computerised environment, information also includes all forms of data, in any format stored in the system, like audio files, video files, information in a network device, information while in transmission or stored in an external device.

1.2 Data and Information

Though technically, there is only a thin layer of distinction between data and information as explained above, in this chapter the word 'information' is used to refer to processed data and as far as storage in a computerized information is concerned and security ramifications are concerned, the word 'information' also includes 'data' unless otherwise specifically excluded in the context. The I.T. Amendment Act, 2008 has widened the definition of 'information' by including the words 'data', 'message' and 'text' within its ambit and the word 'information' is given an inclusive definition by bringing in 'image, sound, voice, codes, computer programmes, software and databases' as part of the definition.

Information Asset

Before we go into the subject of Information Security, it is better to know *what* to secure. Information Asset is the computer component where information is stored or passes through and the loss or non-availability of which may result in loss of facts of a business. Hence it can be a hardware gadget or software where information lies. It could be a network device, a hard-disk, a storage device, a pen-drive or a print-out, or just a communication channel where information traverses and is not stored. Securing the information asset is the first step in Information Security. Threats to information assets could be from

- outside as an external factor or event or
- human failures or
- systemic failures or
- just from factors beyond the control of an organisation.

Identification of an Information Asset is the preliminary and basic task before going ahead with the study of Information Security.

After identifying what exactly constitutes an information asset, we have to identify the parties or entities associated with an information asset. Every information asset has three persons associated with it: Owner, Custodian and User.

Owner of an information asset is the person or entity who has created or acquired the asset or who is legally the owner of the asset. For instance, in a typical bank set-up, the branch In-charge has the overall responsibility of all the physical records and ledgers in a bank and hence he is the owner. In a computerized set-up the branch manager is the owner of entire data relating to his branch. Of course, in the modern day Core Banking Solution adopted by all commercial banks in India and most of the co-operative banks, the issue of ownership of data is a little tricky. It is interesting to record here that even amongst many tech savvy bank officers, there seems to be a lack of clarity on who is the owner of CBS data.

With the obliteration of the concept of branch banking (*i.e.,* no bank branch holds data), many bank officials appear to be under a misconceived notion that the data centre or the IT Department is the owner of the data. In CBS, there is a common database maintained at the Primary Data Centre (the primary data centre has the first level back-up and a secondary data centre also referred to as a Disaster Recovery Centre has the next level of backup) and the ownership is anyway with the person who created the data.

To put it in simple terms, unlike in the earlier non-computerised or partially computerized days, when the ledgers and registers were kept at the branch and the branch had a (perhaps a comfortable) feeling that the data is with him/her and all are under control in the premises, now in the CBS set up, the data is actually kept thousands of miles away but the ownership of the data still vests with the branch.

It would be wiser to understand that the entire branch data is not just one lot (like segmented or bifurcated branch data or register) but is a part of the whole data of Current Account, Customer data, Loans ledger, etc. out of which, every row in the data or the table (*i.e.,* a record in the file) may have a different owner depending upon who actually input that particular row (*i.e.,* record) in the RDBMS (Relational Database Management System). The database mandatorily stores the user id of the official who has input the data record *i.e.,* row and in most cases, and also the one who has verified or approved it. Therefore, ownership of the data vests with these officials who may sometimes not even belong to the branch where the customer has the account.

This situation is quite understandable especially in the context of CBS, where the branch concept is declining and there is going to be no longer a 'branch customer' and only a 'bank customer'. Perhaps in the upcoming days, customer may not even need to fill in the branch column (in an application form or in a credit challan/requisition slip) which could be left blank or just filled in as 'virtual' or 'digital'. In short, the question of ownership of CBS data is often considered to be intricate.

Custodian of the information asset is the person who takes care of the database. Normally the system administrators are the custodians, since they are responsible for maintaining the external media when they take backup of the systems and when they keep safe custody of the backup tapes or DVDs or other media. Sometimes, such administrators also handle some transactions and are given limited powers to access and input some data in the database when they perform the role of users besides being the system administrators or custodians.

Typically, all bank employees who have access to an information asset are users. Interestingly, even non-employees can be users of a bank's computer resources or an information asset in a bank in instances such as auditors who have access to a limited menu in a CBS system for viewing or a vendor who has a very limited access to the hardware resource or system related information in the bank.

Even internet banking customers for the time they are logged into a bank's computer system and customers using the terminals provided at branches for viewing their accounts, are all users for the respective areas of operation within the limited access control privileges assigned to them. Hence in that capacity they are responsible for the resources they are utilizing and are bound by the rules and regulations of the bank like Information Systems Security Policy and other related policies. *All these policies are discussed in detail in Chapter 4.*

1.3 Information Classification

Having studied *what* constitutes information and the role of different entities in an information asset, let us now study the nature and importance of information classification. We have to secure *only* that information that is needed to be kept and preserved. Hence, information is to be properly identified and classified.

Information Asset Classification is itself a very important ingredient of IT Security, because, it is at the stage of Asset Classification that an asset is given the importance and categorization that would impact its treatment as an asset. Standards such as ISO 27000 emphasise the importance of Asset Classification and it often becomes one of the early steps in the process of preparation for ISMS certification. Lack of classification or inadequate classification or improper classification will largely impact the IT security environment in the organization.

In practice, it is often observed that in most of the organizations, employees are not aware and in many cases even those at top management level especially the non-IT managers are not aware of the importance of any information. It has become quite common in organizations these days to

send a mail to a select group in the top management and when one of the managerial personnel in the group wants a part of the information to be passed on to a lower level employee, he may at times simply forward the mail, without passing on the relevant and smaller part of the action point in the mail, without knowing the seriousness of the other information contained in the mail and the classification of such information.

For instance, a level 'C' employee in top management or a Director level employee who will be privy to some discussion or minutes of a particular meeting, should not pass on the minutes to his lower level employee even though that part of the minutes warrants some action to be taken by the employee who reports to him. Instead he has to give suitable instructions only without enclosing the entire minutes of the meeting.

Here, it should be kept in mind always that it is the information owner who does the information classification and decides the criticality or confidentiality of the information and not the other stakeholders. Through information security policy or other broader rules in this regard, a wider perspective will be drafted by the Information Security Committee represented by the Chief Information Security Officer, it is anyway, the owner who does the classification and decides the amount of criticality that the information or data should be treated with.

Information may be classified based on its Criticality, Confidentiality, Availability and Purpose.

Criticality: information may be classified as Most Critical, Critical and Least Critical or Insignificant. What is available in the public domain, what can be recreated easily and what is quite easy to get may be called least critical and that which is more difficult, on these parameters, is called Critical and Most Critical.

Confidentiality: information may be classified as Most Confidential or Private, Confidential and Least or simply as High, Medium and Low. Here again, what is confidential to one group of users may not be confidential to the other group. For instance, the HR data of an organisation's employees may be treated as confidential to all employees but not within the HR department who need the data for their routine processing like salary, leave etc. Some information may be private to one individual and confidential to that particular employee alone and never to be revealed to anyone else. Confidentiality itself may again be classified as High, Medium and Low depending upon the nature of secrecy involved in it. Some information may be confidential based on time. For instance, exam results or any public information will be confidential only until the time of its official release or official uploading in the web-site for public viewing and not later. Such time-dependent secrecy, however, has also to be classified and treated with utmost confidence till it is made public.

Availability: Information may also be classified on the basis of its availability depending upon the nature it is stored. If the information is available in only one source and no further copy is available nor can be taken, then such information should be classified as topmost critical. For instance, an old document, an old video film or the negative of an old photo taken in a public function for which copies are not available is supposed to be classified as topmost critical.

Purpose: Depending upon the purpose for which the information is being gathered, it may be classified as Highly Critical, Medium or Low. If a crucial MIS decision is to be taken based on data obtained from different sources or from different systems, then the data may be available freely, but the report or the information so processed or presented or the note being prepared based on the data gains confidentiality. Such information may have to be treated as High, Medium or Low depending upon the nature of confidentiality vested with it and the information presented by it.

1.4 Need to Know

Information should always be made available on a need to know basis. Availability of information should be on the basis of need and not as a matter of routine. For instance, information taken from a data warehousing application may be made available to the actual users or the functional users depending upon their need to use the information as part of their routine official work. Top management, however, should have free access to a variety of information for its MIS purposes.

Need to know basis actually implies that employees in the organization are provided with the particular information and facts which are required to enable them perform their role in the organization and that information or fact is provided at the appropriate time and circumstances only and not otherwise.

Hence, Need to Know basis encompasses other basic principles of information security like Access Control, Access privileges, Availability, Authentication etc., about which we will discuss in the following paragraphs.

Information classification should be made on Need to Know basis. Based on the classification, right at the point of creation of the information and such classification should be maintained until the information reaches the archives and loses the significance of labelling of categorisation marked in it. Issues relating to Software Access Control and the availability of information based on Need to Know basis for a particular class of users, are being dealt with separately in the chapter on Access Control.

1.5 Information Security

After having studied *what* constitutes information and the nature of criticality and confidentiality, let us now examine the concept of security.

Security is the state of being protected from attacks and threats and other unauthorized access to an information. To understand security, we have to look at *what* needs to be secured, from *whom, when* and *where.* An objective study into these aspects will reveal the entire structure of Information Security. Information Security can be broadly said to be the quality or state of being protected from unauthorized access and potential losses. Security is basically about protection of information assets. While it is generally understood that hundred percent security cannot be achieved, effort should always be in place to achieve the idealistic goal of cent percent.

Pillars of Information security

Information security typically relies on several fundamental principles called pillars. Information is widely considered to have three main attributes. Information security lies fundamentally in ensuring these qualities without compromising any of these. The three such pillars of Information Security are *Confidentiality, Integrity* and *Availability.*

Confidentiality

Confidentiality as in normal parlance is the quality of secrecy in information. Security and secrecy has always been closely related. Though the terms *privacy* and *secrecy* are also used to denote confidentiality, there is a technological difference between these two terms on one hand and confidentiality on the other. While *privacy* is considered to be the protection of personal data, the term *secrecy* is normally used to denote protection of data belonging to an organisation. Whereas confidentiality is the state of keeping an information asset secret and disclosing it to authorised persons only. It is an assurance that the information is shared only among authorised persons or organisations.

Confidentiality does not only mean hiding an information but also not making it available for viewing or copying or any other kind of access whatsoever other than through an authorised process. As was explained in the earlier part of this chapter, classification on the basis of confidentiality may differ from one information asset to another. Confidentiality of information asset is a dynamic concept and not static. What is confidential today may cease to be so tomorrow. What is confidential for one group of employees in an organisation may not be so for the other. However, confidentiality as an attribute of information security depends on the classification of the asset as decided by the owner of the asset.

Integrity

Integrity refers to detection and correction of modification including an intentional modification or a transmission error which has changed the data in transmission. Integrity controls in data give an assurance to the user that the data stored and retrieved is authentic and can be relied upon completely and is adequately accurate for the purpose it is used. Such controls also assure the user that the data stored cannot be altered other than through an authorised process of data entry and such other access to database.

Data should be maintained in the same manner as it was created and should not be accessible in an unauthorized manner for any kind of manipulation. No one should be allowed to tamper with the data or information from the time of its creation until the time of its ultimate destruction and it should remain the same throughout its entire life-cycle. Integrity is, this 'non-tamperability' of data or the state of information asset that it is exactly remaining in the same state it is supposed to be. If an information asset is prone to be tampered or is stored in a system which is vulnerable, easy for unauthorized access and manipulation then the asset is said to fail its attribute of integrity. In other words, data integrity is said to exist when the data in the system is the same as in the source and has not been exposed to accidental or deliberate attempt of destruction or alteration.

Integrity of information should be maintained not only in the computer system with proper controls, but also when it is in transit in a communication channel from one system to another and is stored elsewhere and retrieved. Integrity should be maintained on any number of retrievals and accesses to the system and not be hampered by any amount of attacks to the system. Consistency of data at different levels is often considered to be synonymous with data integrity.

Availability

On the face of it, availability may appear to be a simple term. But *availability* actually means that the information asset is available to the authorized user in an authentic manner when required and not available to any other users at any point of time. For instance, a bank official advising the account balance in a customer's account at the bank counter is an example of *availability.* The same official not informing the customer his account balance or advising the balance through a letter sent to him which may reach him at a later date only, is a breach of the attribute of *availability.* Hence availability can be said to be the property of an information asset of being accessible and usable when required by an authorized entity.

Ensuring *availability* of data has always been a serious concern of information security managers and system administrators in any organisation. Attackers normally target an information system with the objective of making it either not available to the rightful users or making it easily available to all unauthorized users too. Attackers or intruders prevent authorized access to resources or send huge network data to a system and delay the process in time-critical operations and thus deny its service to authorised users. Such an attack often called *Denial of Service* attack results in breach of the attribute of availability.

1.6 Other Applicable Attributes of Information Security

In addition to the three traditional areas or pillars of information security as above, modern day security professionals often include some additional attributes as ingredients of information security, like Non-repudiation, Accountability, and Reliability. Let us discuss these in a nutshell.

Non-repudiation refers to the state of an information asset that makes the sender or the creator of the asset own the responsibility of such sending or creation and does not give any room for disowning it. In physical form, when one signs a letter or sends a hand-written communication, such hand-writing makes him own the task of writing or sending. He will not be allowed to repudiate or deny that he wrote it or sent it. In an electronic communication too, such a requirement does exist

and it is but essential that the data entry operator of an asset or originator of the communication should be made to own it and should not be allowed to disown it. Usage of electronic signature in an electronic record or electronic communication is commonly used to bind the person who created the data or sent it and make him responsible for it.

To elucidate the concept with practical banking examples, if in an RTGS (Real Time Gross Settlement) or other electronic funds remittances, imagine a situation, when a sender of remittance disowns the act of sending or the receiver after having received it, denies having received the message. Or, in a CBS database, a record (*i.e.,* a row in the RDBMS) in the data which the data shows as having been entered by the particular user or the official and such user or the official disowns having entered the data, stating that he is in a branch hundreds or thousands of kilometers away.

In all such cases, it is strength of the data or the system to prove that the data was actually input or sent or accessed or received by the actual user. This is an important pillar of information security. In a non-computerized environment, the user or the official's signature or initials would be the biggest evidence making his denial impossible which in a computerized environment, is the role of Non-Repudiation.

Accountability of information asset is the attribute of such audit information, to be kept selectively so that actions affecting security can be traced to the particular entity who breached it. Accountability presupposes a proper identity of authorised users and their records and availability of proper audit trail. Audit trail is the log or history of all system activities in chronological order, providing documentary evidence of processing that the data has been undergoing in its path of transformation from its inception right upto the final report generation and permanent storage. Accountability, therefore, is considered to be an off-shoot of non-repudiation and should be flawless in information security. Especially in the event of an attack to data security strong accountability ensures that the management has proper control and is able to identify the users who accessed the data at every stage.

Authenticity may be broadly defined as conformance to the fact and therefore worthy of trust, reliance, or belief. Being authentic is the quality of being absolutely true and in fact, not fraudulent or counterfeit and being worthy of belief, 'in absolute fact', not fraudulent or counterfeit. In information security, it is the assurance that a message, transaction, or other exchange of information is from the source it claims to be from. Authenticity involves proof of identity.

Authenticity is verified through a process of authentication, which is a very popular word in information security parlance. Very often we hear words like One Factor Authentication, Two Factor Authentication, etc. The process of authentication usually involves more than one "proof" of identity when such proof could be something a user knows, like a password. Authentication is the process of verifying a user who he claims to be. A user can prove his identity by producing his card and swiping it in a device by which the authentication is by a One Factor Authentication of 'what he has'. The gadget or the device or the credit/debit that is produced for swiping is the authentication device of One Factor Authentication. In addition to such physical possession of the device, suppose the user inputs a password or a number after entering his user id, such authentication is said to be based on 'what he knows'. Hence in ATM transactions it is always a Two Factor Authentication of what the user has (*i.e.,* the ATM card) plus the ATM PIN *i.e.,* 'what he knows'.

Suppose the authentication is done through a process of biometric verification after the user id is input or the card is swiped, then it is said to be based on 'Who the user *is' i.e.,* a biological factor of the user, say his fingerprint scans or retina or palm or hand geometry scans or such physical parts of the body to confirm that he is the user he claims to be.

Reliability is another attribute of information security that focuses on dependability. This assumes significance especially in the event of a crisis or a disaster when an information is retrieved and is wholly relied upon and used. In such an event, if the information sought lacks dependability or is unreliable, then the entire process of security will fail. Hence, reliability has a bearing on the related

areas of a computer system like safety giving an assurance to its users that the information can be relied upon even in times of an emergency in a safety-critical application. For instance, in the case of a non-computerised environment, it is an assurance that data extracted from say, a physical record is a reliable copy of the original one and can be acted upon.

Resilience: Resilience involves the ability of an organization to withstand and recover from security incidents, disruptions, or failures. It includes proactive measures such as risk management, incident response planning, and business continuity management to minimize the impact of security breaches or disasters and ensure the organization can continue to operate effectively. The organizations, including Banks, by addressing these pillars comprehensively, can establish a robust information security posture that protects their assets from various threats and risks.

1.7 Physical Security

Information Security has two layers *viz.* Physical Security and Logical Security and a successful implementation of security depends upon proper usage of both of these. Physical Security is the most fundamental security layer for any information asset. The moment an information asset is created in a physical form like purchase of a computer, arrival or installation of a hardware system or a network device, its physical upkeep assumes significance and the physical security steps related to the asset should be in place.

Physical Security can be enforced by having protective compound walls and barriers with posting of security guards, ensuring frisking of visitors, installation of CCTVs in critical and public areas and even having one or more additional layers to reach a critical physical area like a Network Operation Centre or a Core Banking-Data Centre or a Server Room. Physical Security is dealt with in a detailed manner in Chapter 5.

1.8 Logical Security

While physical security is about a user's physical entry to a system or an information asset, logical security is about a user's access to data or information in a system through a computer system either in the same premises or from a far off location through computer network. It cannot be debated which of these - physical or logical - is crucial and important. It depends upon the nature of application and the nature of information asset.

For a network-centric application wherein nothing is stored physically in front-end computer system or Workstation or node, physical security issues may be less important and logical security is more important. For instance, in a bank-branch which is part of core banking, physical security for the resources in a branch, say the PC work-stations or nodes are not so crucial like logical security since loss of the physical resources may not impact the core banking solution resources, but breach of logical security from a local branch to the centralized resources may have disastrous impact.

In such an environment, the physical security would largely confine to the physical assets in the branch like the computers or the network devices (since no significant or valuable data or software is stored at the branches) and of course non-electronic assets like cash, jewels and furniture that are part of the branch books and are thus valuable and important.

Logical Security: Every computer resource can be accessed by reaching it through a physical contact and attacked. Just like physical threats to a computer resource, there are also logical threats through logical accesses. When a computer resource in the form of an information stored in a hard-disk or any other device, is accessed through computer resources like key-board or a mouse either on-site or through a remote location or through a network, such access is called a logical access. Such logical access can be through a proper user id of a front-end system as part of the application and the database.

If such access is attempted in an unauthorised manner or with authorisation manner to carry out an unauthenticated transaction, then such access should be denied and proper log of such attempt should be maintained. Logical Security is an essential element of information security. Detailed study of logical security is covered in Chapters 6 and 7 and controls for such security are also detailed in the later chapters.

Access Control restrictions should be in place for the success of any information security implementation. Top management and the security managers should be aware of what access is to be given to which user — either physical or logical — and the related control measures should be put in place.

Access Privileges are a subset of Access Control Management in which the security managers decide upto what level of access is to be given to the user. For instance, in a banking environment, the data entry operators or the clerical staff members are given access to perform data entry jobs by recording an entry including debiting an account, but their access normally stops there (unless the system specifically permits them to do a limited supervisory job like teller functions) and after such posting of the debit, say a cheque, the privilege of passing it and releasing the corresponding credit like cash payment, etc. is vested with a supervisory official. Such an arrangement is called Access Privilege.

- Role of Supervisory Official: Similarly, a normal supervisory official will have powers to pass cheques but not to grant an overdraft. Powers of an overdraft in a Current Account will normally be given to a senior manager or the branch In-charge or other officers nominated for the purpose by the branch or by whatever is the process as prescribed by the bank in its Manual of Instructions or Work Manual or its Systems document, by whatever name called. Not defining or adhering to such a system will be called breach of privilege.

An important principle underlining Access Privileges is the Maker Checker principle which is compulsorily adhered to in most banking applications (*i.e.*, software programs running in banks). Data entry is normally made by one staff member and it is checked by another preferably by a supervisor or a person of higher hierarchical ranking called the checker and then the record is saved in the system. Application software is normally designed to ensure proper maker and checker principle in all operations and breach is normally not possible. The system normally records the user details who has entered the data (*i.e.*, the maker) and the supervisory user who has passed it (or approved it *i.e.*, the checker) and every transaction carries the time stamp along with these details. Maker-Checker principle also ensures proper access control mechanism especially in Software Access Control and Logical Access Control and enhances the security strength of the system.

The terms IT Security and computer security are often used interchangeably, though a discerning security specialist may like to distinguish between these two words as IT Security is more technology based and computer security is more user based on the use of a computer or other devices that can be defined as computer. However, for the purpose of our understanding, the terms refer to the entire spectrum of Information Technology including application and support systems and the protection afforded to an automated information system in order to attain the applicable objectives of preserving the pillars of information security as stated above in all computer related resources including all kinds of hardware, software, firmware and telecommunications.

It would be quite relevant here to also use the phrases "Cyber Security", "Computer Security" and "Information Security". While for a common usage, all the three may be used interchangeably, for an expert in the area and for an information security professional, there is a clear difference. Information Security refers to the privacy and security of information in the system, say the hardware or the software or application (commonly referred to as just "apps" these days) or even the network and the entire gamut of computer systems. Cyber Security is more with reference to the security in the cyber space especially in a network or while the data is in transit or part of some communication say in e-commerce or an electronic funds remittance or a social networking site wherein communication is the essence. Computer Security may be generally referred to in the context of the data and information privacy and security stored in the computer and all those devices what may be broadly called a computer.

1.9 Advantages of organization's information security programme

Improved security: by identifying and classifying sensitive information, organizations can better protect their most critical assets from unauthorized access or disclosure.

Compliance: many regulatory and industry standards, such as hipaa and pci-dss, require organizations to implement information classification and data protection measures.

Improved efficiency: by clearly identifying and labelling information, employees can quickly and easily determine the appropriate handling and access requirements for different types of data.

Better risk management: by understanding the potential impact of a data breach or unauthorized disclosure, organizations can prioritize resources and develop more effective incident response plans.

Cost savings: by implementing appropriate security controls for different types of information, organizations can avoid unnecessary spending on security measures that may not be needed for less sensitive data.

Improved incident response: by having a clear understanding of the criticality of specific data, organizations can respond to security incidents in a more effective and efficient manner.

1.10 Disadvantages of organization's information security programme

Complexity: developing and maintaining an information classification system can be complex and time-consuming, especially for large organizations with a diverse range of data types.

Cost: implementing and maintaining an information classification system can be costly, especially if it requires new hardware or software.

Resistance to change: some employees may resist the implementation of an information classification system, especially if it requires them to change their usual work habits.

Lack of flexibility: information classification systems can be rigid and inflexible, making it difficult to adapt to changing business needs or new types of data.

False sense of security: implementing an information classification system may give organizations a false sense of security, leading them to overlook other important security controls and best practices.

Maintenance: information classification should be reviewed and updated frequently, if not it can become outdated and ineffective.

1.11 Goals of Information security

The goals of information security delve deeper into the intricacies of safeguarding information assets, addressing emerging threats, and ensuring compliance with industry standards and regulations. The goals of information security, includes:

Risk Management: A key goal of information security is to implement robust risk management practices. This involves identifying, assessing, and prioritizing risks to information assets based on their potential impact and likelihood of occurrence. Advanced risk assessment methodologies, such as quantitative risk analysis and probabilistic modelling, are employed to quantify risks accurately.

Threat Detection and Response: Information security aims to detect and respond to cybersecurity threats effectively. Advanced threat detection technologies, including machine learning, artificial intelligence, and behavioural analytics, are utilized to identify suspicious activities and potential security breaches in real-time. Incident response plans are developed and tested to ensure a rapid and coordinated response to security incidents.

Security Architecture and Design: Another focus area will be on designing and implementing secure architectures and systems. This involves applying security principles such as defense-in-depth, least privilege, and separation of duties to architect resilient and secure IT infrastructures. Advanced cryptographic techniques and secure protocols are employed to protect data in transit and at rest.

Compliance and Governance: Ensuring compliance with industry regulations, legal requirements, and organizational policies is a critical goal of information security. Information Security professionals are responsible for establishing robust governance frameworks, implementing controls, and conducting regular audits to verify compliance with standards such as ISO 27001, NIST, GDPR, and HIPAA.

Security Awareness and Training: Information security aims to cultivate a culture of security awareness and knowledge sharing within organizations. Information security professionals develop and deliver advanced training programs, workshops, and awareness campaigns to educate employees about cybersecurity risks, best practices, and their role in safeguarding information assets.

Secure Software Development: The focus will be on integrating security into the Software Development Lifecycle (SDLC). This involves conducting secure code reviews, implementing secure coding practices, and leveraging automated security testing tools to identify and remediate vulnerabilities in software applications before deployment.

Continuous Monitoring and Improvement: Information security revolves around to establish continuous monitoring capabilities to detect and mitigate security threats proactively. The Information security professionals implement Security Information and Event Management (SIEM) systems, Security Orchestration, Automation, and Response (SOAR) platforms, and conduct regular security assessments and penetration testing to identify areas for improvement.

Cybersecurity Research and Innovation: Information security professionals contribute to cybersecurity research and innovation by exploring new technologies, developing novel security solutions, and advancing the state-of-the-art in cybersecurity practices. They collaborate with academia, industry partners, and government agencies to address emerging threats and challenges in the field of information security.

Mitigation of Risks: The organizations, by pursuing these goals, can establish a mature and comprehensive approach to information security that effectively mitigates risks, protects critical assets, and fosters innovation and growth.

1.12 Types of information security

Information security encompasses various types or domains, each focusing on specific aspects of protecting information assets from unauthorized access, disclosure, alteration, and destruction. The types of information security can be classified based on the nature of the assets being protected or the techniques employed to safeguard them. Let us discuss some common types of information security.

Network Security: Network security focuses on protecting the integrity, confidentiality, and availability of data transmitted over computer networks. It involves implementing measures such as firewalls, Intrusion Detection Systems (IDS), Intrusion Prevention Systems (IPS), Virtual Private Networks (VPNs), and secure network protocols to safeguard network infrastructure and communications.

Application Security: Application security aims to prevent vulnerabilities and secure software applications against malicious attacks and unauthorized access. It involves implementing secure coding practices, conducting code reviews, performing application security testing (e.g., penetration testing, code scanning), and deploying Web Application Firewalls (WAFs) to mitigate risks associated with software vulnerabilities.

Cloud Security: Cloud security focuses on protecting data, applications, and infrastructure deployed in cloud computing environments. It involves implementing security controls such as encryption,

access controls, Identity and Access Management (IAM), and security monitoring to ensure the confidentiality, integrity, and availability of cloud-based resources.

Endpoint Security: Endpoint security means, securing end-user devices such as desktops, laptops, smartphones, and tablets from security threats. It involves deploying Endpoint Protection Platforms (EPP), antivirus software, Host-based Intrusion Detection Systems (HIDS), and endpoint encryption solutions to defend against malware, ransomware, and other endpoint-related risks.

Data Security: Data security concentrates on protecting the confidentiality, integrity, and availability of data throughout its lifecycle. It involves implementing data encryption, access controls, Data Loss Prevention (DLP) solutions, data masking, and data classification to safeguard sensitive information from unauthorized access, disclosure, or theft.

Physical Security: Physical security refers to protecting information assets, IT infrastructure, and facilities from physical threats such as theft, vandalism, natural disasters, and unauthorized access. It involves implementing security measures such as access controls, surveillance systems, biometric authentication, security guards, and environmental controls (e.g., temperature and humidity monitoring) to mitigate physical security risks.

Incident Response and Management: Incident response and management starts from focusing on detecting, responding to, and recovering from security incidents effectively. It involves developing incident response plans, establishing incident response teams, implementing incident detection and analysis tools, and conducting post-incident reviews to minimize the impact of security breaches and restore normal operations.

Identity and Access Management (IAM): IAM revolves around managing user identities, roles, and access rights to ensure that only authorized individuals can access resources and data. It involves implementing authentication mechanisms (e.g., passwords, multi-factor authentication), authorization controls, and identity governance solutions to enforce least privilege access and prevent unauthorized access to sensitive information.

Comprehensive security protection: These types of information security are interconnected and complementary to each other, working together to establish a comprehensive security posture that protects organizations' information assets from a wide range of threats and vulnerabilities.

1.13 The services of information security

Information security services encompass a broad range of offerings designed to help organizations protect their information assets, mitigate security risks, and ensure compliance with regulatory requirements. These services are typically provided by specialized cybersecurity firms, Managed Security Service Providers (MSSPs), or internal security teams within organizations. Some common services offered in the field of information security are:

Risk Assessment and Management: This service involves identifying, evaluating, and prioritising security risks to an organization's information assets. It includes conducting comprehensive risk assessments, vulnerability assessments, and threat modelling exercises to identify potential threats and vulnerabilities, assess their potential impact, and develop risk mitigation strategies.

Security Consulting and Advisory: Security consulting services provide expert advice and guidance to organizations on developing, implementing, and maintaining effective information security programs. Consultants help organizations assess their security posture, develop security policies and procedures, conduct security awareness training, and navigate compliance requirements.

Penetration Testing and Ethical Hacking: Penetration testing services involve simulating real-world cyber-attacks to identify security weaknesses in an organization's systems, networks, and applications. Ethical hackers, also known as penetration testers, attempt to exploit vulnerabilities and assess the effectiveness of existing security controls. The results are used to remediate vulnerabilities and improve overall security posture.

Managed Security Services (MSS): Managed security service providers offer a range of outsourced security services to help organizations enhance their security capabilities. These services may include 24/7 security monitoring, threat detection and response, incident response management, vulnerability management, and security device management (e.g., firewall and intrusion detection/ prevention systems).

Security Awareness Training: Security awareness training services help organizations educate employees about cybersecurity best practices, threats, and their role in protecting sensitive information. Training programs may include online courses, workshops, phishing simulations, and other interactive learning experiences designed to raise awareness and promote a culture of security within the organization.

Incident Response and Forensics: Incident response services help organizations prepare for, respond to, and recover from security incidents such as data breaches, cyberattacks, and insider threats. Incident responders assist with developing incident response plans, establishing incident response teams, coordinating response efforts, and conducting forensic investigations to determine the root cause of security incidents and prevent future occurrences.

Compliance and Regulatory Services: Compliance services assist organizations in meeting industry-specific regulatory requirements and standards such as GDPR, HIPAA, PCI DSS, and ISO 27001. Consultants provide guidance on interpreting regulatory requirements, conducting compliance assessments, developing compliance frameworks, and implementing controls to ensure adherence to applicable regulations.

Security Architecture and Design: Security architecture services focuses on organizations design and implement secure IT architectures, systems, and applications. Security architects assess existing architectures, develop security requirements, design security solutions, and oversee the implementation of security controls to protect against evolving threats and vulnerabilities.

Identity and Access Management (IAM): IAM services revolves around managing user identities, roles, and access rights to ensure that only authorized individuals can access resources and data. IAM consultants help organizations implement IAM solutions, develop access control policies, and enforce least privilege access to minimize the risk of unauthorized access and data breaches.

Data Protection and Encryption: Data protection services help organizations safeguard sensitive information through encryption, tokenization, and other data protection techniques. Consultants assess data security risks, develop data protection strategies, implement encryption technologies, and ensure compliance with data privacy regulations to protect sensitive data from unauthorized access and disclosure.

Enhancing Cybersecurity Posture: These are just a few examples of the many information security services available to organisations seeking to enhance their cybersecurity posture and protect their valuable information assets. Depending on their specific needs and priorities, organisations may engage with service providers to address specific security challenges and achieve their cybersecurity goals.

Know Your Progress

Data is normally considered to be the raw format and processed data is called information. Information also includes data in any format like audio files, video files, digital formats stored in a computer

or other electronic device or even print-outs. Information can be classified depending upon the confidentiality, criticality and other factors. Classification of information is important to decide how the information is to be treated and the level of security it should be given. Information classification thus occupies prime space and is considered to be the first step in the study of information security.

Information is to be secured against physical threats, attacks in a computer system may take place either directly or through a network or by other forces. Security of information lies in safeguarding its confidentiality, integrity and availability. Information should be confidential, wherever it needs to be, and should ensure integrity guarding itself against any tampering and unauthorised access and remaining in the same state right from its creation to its ultimate destruction in an authorized manner. Besides these three factors, there are also other factors like Non-Repudiation which should make the owner of information own it without letting him deny its creation and Authentication, Accountability, etc.

Information should be protected against physical threats and attacks. Physical Control measures include protecting the computer resources with physical barriers like security guards, Entry Access restrictions, bio-metric restrictions, etc. Logical Access should also be monitored and controlled wherever necessary by ensuring that only those who are authorized to access the computer resources are accessing it and are only doing those functions that they are specifically authorised to do.

Key Words

Data	Information	Security	Confidentiality
Integrity	Availability	Non-Repudiation	Authorisation
Authentication	Access Control	Access Privileges	

Questions

1. Which of the following statement is correct?

a. Data is a subset of information.

b. Information is a subset of Information Security.

c. Information includes data and therefore only information needs to be secured.

d. Processed data for use by management is normally called information.

2. The three pillars of information security are:

a. Confidentiality, Integrity and Accountability

b. Confidentiality, Integrity and Availability

c. Secrecy, Integrity and Security

d. Confidentiality, Availability and Accountability

3. Denial of Service Attack is considered to be a breach of ______________ in information security.

a. Confidentiality

b. Authenticity

c. Availability

d. Integrity

4. History of all computer transactions in a chronological order is called______________.

a. Audit Trail

b. System Trial

   c. End of Day Routine
   d. Transactions Summary

5. Unauthorised access to a computer resource through a computer network is called _______.
   a. a breach of the Access Privilege mechanism.
   b. an effective control measure in Logical Access system.
   c. a weakness in the Logical Access Control Management.
   d. a breach of the Logical Access Control.

6. Non-Repudiation refers to_______________________________.
   a. the state of Denial of Service in which the sender cannot deny his responsibility
   b. the state of information in Denial of Service benefit is given to the sender
   c. an information which makes the sender or the receiver own the responsibility in an electronic communication
   d. a state of information asset that binds the sender or owner of a communication and which he cannot disown.

7. The Maker-Checker principle is a typical software in banks ensures that_____________.
   a. all entries in the bank are checked thoroughly before they 'make' the way into the system
   b. data entry made by one person is passed (or authorised/approved) by another official
   c. every transaction is made by the operator and checked by him immediately and then only saved in the system
   d. the entire software in the bank is made and checked repeatedly before they are used in the bank's transaction.

8. Custodian when performing their duty as back-up and system managers are given rights to access data of banks. (True/False)

9. Integrity of information is to be maintained right from the point data is entered. (True/False)

10. Since banks have many branches spread out geographically, logical security in banks is always considered to be more critical and important than physical security. (True/False)

Answers

1. *d*	6. *d*
2. *b*	7. *b*
3. *c*	8. False
4. *a*	9. True
5. *a*	10. False

2

CHAPTER

Corporate IT Security Policies

OBJECTIVES

After reading this chapter, you will get an idea of what Corporate IT Security is and how a Policy for Corporate IT Security is drafted. The governing principles which are to be followed while drafting an IT Security Policy for an organization like a bank or a corporate undertaking are presented here. The responsibilities of an organization with regard to IT Security *vis-a-vis* the individual users and employee's responsibilities in IT Security are also discussed.

2.1 Meaning of Corporate IT Security

IT Security is not the responsibility of an individual alone. It is a popular misconception that IT Security is in the domain of the top management. Though top management involvement and concern on IT Security is of utmost importance for the successful planning and execution of all IT Security initiatives, it is always the collective responsibility of employees across different cadres. The drive and thrust, however, should come from the top management.

Just like an individual safeguarding his assets, a corporate entity or any business organization (either incorporated or not) or a bank may also have its own information assets which are to be safeguarded and protected from possible attacks and all kinds of possible threats. It is in this context that an IT Security Policy is found essential for a corporate entity.

Every organization has its own goal and its own vision in its area of operations and will strain all its nerves towards the accomplishment of such cherished objectives utilising all the resources in the process. Hence safeguarding the resources and taking care of all the elements that belong to an organization becomes its main task. Protection of its people, processes and all information especially information assets in whatever form they are, becomes the main focus of an organization if it were to become successful.

2.2 Need for a Corporate IT Security Policy

From earlier days, when IT was just an enabler most of the organizations have progressed to a stage where IT has become an inseparable part of the organization. Most of the organizations have now realized the pervasiveness of IT and especially banks are introducing their new products purely based on IT. Hence, protection of assets mainly means protection of IT assets, be it the hardware or software or network or the human elements taking care of the systems. A secure IT environment has become the basic requirement for success in any organization. Just as any organization likes to progress with more branches, more products and diverse activities, a common IT Security and protection mechanism to safeguard all its assets is not just a concern of the top management but has become its top requirement.

With the penetration of IT in almost every sphere of life and in almost every industry, the focus of IT Security has shifted from the IT Department to the entire organization, to all the departments, all the domain functional areas. Earlier, IT was one department in every organization like HR, Finance, Purchase or Sales but now that its presence is felt everywhere, IT spending, IT security, IT management has become the concern of every department in the organization. The benefits of IT spending goes not just to the IT department but to the organization as a whole. Similarly, the loser when an information asset is under threat is not the IT department but the organization in general and the asset owner in particular.

With increased access of customers, clients, vendors and third parties into the information assets of the organization, it becomes an added responsibility of the enterprise to ensure that the information is not only available to the people who should have access but also denied to those who should not. A proper and well defined IT Security Policy can only ensure documented definition of information assets, the roles and responsibilities of people associated with it and the features of processes concerned with it.

Though the need for security is static and a well-accepted one in every organization, the implementation aspects and the IT Security Policy are quite dynamic and vary from organization to organization depending upon factors like-

- dependence on IT for the key function of the organization,
- nature of data handled,
- personnel handling it and
- the statutory and legal compliance rules governing the organization.

2.3 Legal Requirements

The Information Technology Act, 2000 was the first major initiative by the Government of India to provide legal recognition to electronic records and thus paved the way for keeping records electronically. Hence, this was said to be the first significant step in the country to drive organizations realize the importance of information assets, and enforce security in the related areas and naturally, define the roles and responsibilities of service providers.

The roles and responsibilities of Internet Service Providers (ISPs) and Network Service Providers (NSPs) and other data custodians and intermediaries like banks, etc. were well defined in the IT Act, 2000. The Information Technology Act, 2000 provides legal recognition for transactions carried out by means of electronic data interchange and other means of electronic communication.

The question of due diligence to be exercised on the part of such intermediaries and the responsibilities of their employees and service providers and the question of reasonable security practices to be followed by body corporate were addressed later in detail *vide* the IT Amendment Act, 2008 in its sections 43A discussing the compensation for failure to protect data and in Section 79 providing the grounds when an intermediary can get exemption from liability.

After the above said amendment to IT Act (effective from 27 October, 2009), especially the amended Section 43A it has become a clearly documented and defined responsibility of body corporate to have proper security practices. The Act uses the phrase "reasonable security practices and procedures" meaning security practices and procedures designed to protect information from unauthorised access, damage, use, modification, disclosure or impairment.

The Amended Act also defines "sensitive personal data or information" for which the rules have since been framed by the Central Government and notified in April 2011. As a result of this it is not just an organizational necessity or a policy but also a legal requirement to have proper IT Security Policy in place and ensure its implementation. In the event of any legal dispute, involving third parties on disclosure of information or any other unauthorised access to data stored in the organization, the management has to prove that it had the IT Security Practices in place as required in the Act as otherwise it shall be liable to pay damages by way of compensation to the person affected. Non-compliance with this requirement is a serious civil liability on the part of the organization, as laid down in the section.

While organizations handle enormous amount of data of its customers, it is also their huge responsibility to ensure that such data is protected adequately. In order to claim due diligence and to claim exemption from liability, the intermediaries like Internet Service Providers (ISPs) and Network Service Providers (NSPs) and payment sites, cyber cafes, etc. have to prove the conditions set forth in Section 79 of the Act like their functions are limited to providing access to a communication system over which information made available by third parties is transmitted or temporarily stored or hosted or they do not initiate the transmission, etc. and they observe due diligence while discharging their duties.

This proviso in the Act is a huge responsibility on the part of organizations to ensure that proper IT Security Policy is not just formulated but also implemented and followed. In this context, it is worthwhile to note here that the role of Service Providers and Content Providers is becoming the subject matter of acrimonious debates with the government, the service providers and the regulators (especially TRAI), at loggerheads often discussing the techno-legal issued involved. With no exclusive legislation in India in the form of Data Communication Act or an Electronic Communication related regulations except the limited role of TRAI, it is time the judiciary interpreted the role of service provider *v.* the content provider in the area of electronic communication especially in the social networking media and the financial sector of the nation.

2.4 Essential Features of Corporate IT Security Policy

A corporate IT Security policy normally contains the following, though depending upon the nature of industry and the type of information handled by the organization, the contents may vary:

I. Preamble: a foreword, version control, document ownership, custody, etc.
II. Details of Information System Security Committee and its members
    a. Hierarchical chart of the Information System Management
III. Brief reference to various policies with objectives, responsibility areas, etc.
IV. Implementation details and responsibilities for functional managers
V. Chapters describing the various policies that are brought within the purview of the IT Security Policy
VI. Procedural Guidelines or Work Instructions on each of the above policies
VII. Description of various assets and their classification with a default classification list
VIII. Disclaimer clauses wherever necessary and applicable.

The preamble should normally contain the need for the policy, version of the document, nature of ownership of the version, reference and availability of the document (whether in electronic form or as hard-copy) with viewing access to all stakeholders, details of authority to review, add, delete or modify any part of it and such document control requirements.

Information System Security Committee: It will consist of a CISO (Chief Information Security Officer) as the topmost official in-charge of all security initiatives in the organization.

The CISO needs to report directly to the Head of Integrated Risk Management (HIRM) function and should not have a direct reporting relationship with the CIO (Chief Information Officer). The CISO's role spans across both strategic and operational dimensions and is responsible for all the administrative tasks and control related to Information Security and reports to the Owner of this function, the HIRM. *(Source: IT Governance Series, Information Security Governance for the Indian Banking Sector – IDRBT Report dated Nov. 2011).*

Reporting by CISO: Typically for a large organization, the chart will be as follows, consisting of the CISO reporting only to the CEO and different Information System Security Officers (ISSO) reporting to the CISO for their system security related activities (and of course not for their general line functions) and Information System Security Managers (ISSM) taking care of individual functional domains like HR, Operations and Development, Network, Physical Security, etc. Depending upon the nature of information handled in the respective functions in the particular area, every ISSM can have Information Security Administrators (ISAs) reporting to him, doing the job of system management and system administration in the respective functional area.

However, this can also be slightly re-drawn, as follows, with the CISO's and CIO's role properly well-defined and the CISO not reporting to the CIO and providing functional responsibilities for the Risk Management domains. *(Chart Courtesy: IDRBT – Nov. 2011, Information Security Governance for the Indian Banking Sector).*

Role of HIRM: Here, the HIRM will normally be in the rank of a Chief General Manager or a General Manager (at least a Deputy General Manager, under exceptional circumstances) and CISO will normally be headed by an official in the rank of a General Manager or a Deputy General Manager (at least an Assistant General Manager). The above is a suggestive and recommendatory architecture and depending upon the risk management structure of the organization and taking into factors like the size of the organization, corporate policy etc. certain role functions from the above may be clubbed like the Information Security Risk Management may be made in charge of the Awareness Management also.

Physical security is normally handled by a team of Security officials well versed in the particular domain like ex-officials in the Army or the Police department. There has been an interesting debate whether to bring the physical security within the overall ambit of the CISO or not, since the nature of jobs handled by physical security are entirely different from those of the software or logical security, which is more computer system oriented. Of late, it is the common practice of organisations to have a CISO who will be overall in charge of entire security environment including the physical security too and hence the physical security personnel too report to him.

The **corporate IT Security Policy** will normally consist of various policies which form part of the overall policy and will be implemented and maintained by the respective functional heads under the overall supervision, guidance and monitoring of the Information System Security set-up with the CISO at the top. The following are some of the policies that normally form part of it:

I. Physical Security Policy
II. Network Access Policy
III. Operations Control Policy
IV. Access Control Policy
V. E-Mail Policy
VI. Hardware Maintenance Policy
VII. User Management Policy
VIII. Password Policy
IX. Internet Policy
X. Business Continuity and Disaster Recovery Plan Policy

The above is only an illustrative list and not a comprehensive one. Now, let us study what each of the above policies should typically contain.

2.5 Physical Security Policy

It will consist of guidelines for movement of personnel, hardware systems within the organization right from identification of critical resources, upkeep and the nature of care required for each of them. For instance, the organization may earmark a floor for exclusive movement of top management personnel or a critical server room and provide an additional layer of physical security checks for it. Decisions like providing CCTVs, surveillance mechanism for common area in the premises or the work area or checking the entry through a smart card or a biometric checks or provision of uniforms to select personnel or providing gate passes for physical movement of all hardware equipment, allowing or prohibiting of external storage media like pen-drives or cell-phones with camera etc. are all taken care of as part of the physical security set-up. *Physical Security Policy and Controls therein, are dealt with in detail in the later chapters.*

Network Access Policy is normally framed by network administrators with sound knowledge of operations, nature of network equipment used in the organization, need to access the resources across network, criticality of information available in the network etc. Depending upon the nature of threat envisaged to the resources and the vulnerabilities in the system, the policy will decide the nature of firewalls to be used.

Firewalls may be defined as a set of hardware devices or software based systems that permit or deny access to a network resource based on a set of rules framed for the purpose. Sometimes, firewall policy will be separately handled by the organization in consultation with the IT team taking into account the nature of URL (Uniform Resource Locators) filtering to be done for the organization, permissions to be given to specific users to access common portals and web-sites like search engines or other websites in network. Such a policy will also address issues like a software based access control with features of basic routing also, ensuring that legitimate access to an external website resource is permitted.

Network Security Policy and Controls therein, are dealt with in detail in the later chapters.

Operations Control Policy is a function of the respective operations department in consultation with IT Department. Depending on the nature of organization and nature of operations handled by respective departments this policy is formulated and the related rules are framed.

Access Control Policy is a very important part of IT Security Policy. Actually, this policy has wider ramifications and far reach since it encompasses all areas of the organization, like software development, testing and implementation, network access and right upto data mining and data warehousing including physical access. Typically, in a bank, the Systems and Management Services Department will decide the nature of access to be given to a staff member depending upon the designation like clerical, sub-ordinate or supervisory or executive etc.

Therefore, a branch clerical staff will not have the powers to post the debit of a cheque when there are no funds and thereby create an overdraft, nor will he have powers to access the cash module and pay cash unless so authorised. Similarly, a junior officer in a branch will not have the powers to access the advances module and create a term loan unless so authorised in the system, as an officer of Advances Department. These rules are framed as part of the software development itself.

Access Privileges is a subset of Access Control Policy. To put it in simple words, a clerical staff member will have power to view the loan account and his privilege stops there and not to create a loan debit. This is part of Access Privilege Policy. Most of the banks in a Core Banking Solution kind of set-up give powers across different branches to view the loan accounts of all branches to facilitate loan repayment but not to create a loan account in another branch's data. This is part of the Access Privilege Policy.

E-mail Policy: Of late, most of the correspondence within the organization and quite often to a third party like customers and vendors also are handled by e-mails. Hence, e-mail policy assumes much significance. Most of the banks do provide a user id as part of the bank's e-mail server to its officers like officer@abcbank.in or a number@abcbank.com etc. In any such case, the organization has to ensure that the email is used for official purposes only and with the overall responsibility assigned to the individual user. For, a mail with an individual@mailprovider.com *i.e.* like a third party with a common e-mail service provider (like yahoo! or gmail or hotmail etc.) makes much difference compared to a mail from the organisation's email server. In the first case, the organization is also responsible for the contents of the mail, since the mail has come from the organisation's email server, though it has been sent by the individual only.

The email policy will also discuss issues like attachments that can be sent along with email, storage size for users, access possibilities from outside the intranet say from the officials' residences or a public place, etc. Depending upon the criticality of information sent through corporate emails, security initiatives like a PGP (Pretty Good Privacy, a data encryption and decryption program providing privacy and authentication for computer communication like text, files emails etc.) or a SHA512 (Secure Hash Algorithm for a cryptographic hash function, originally designed by National Security Agency in the US as part of Digital Signature Algorithm) or other types of electronic signatures can be implemented in corporate emails.

This policy will mainly address issues like allotting user id as part of the mail server in such a way that the email id is traceable to an individual so that any mail sent to or received from the email id can be attributed to the particular person. Where a group id like a troubleshooting desk or a help-desk or a call-centre kind of environment is there, where emails are addressed to an email id that is not based on an individual's name, such emails will be the responsibility of the group as clearly laid down in the policy and the procedural guidelines will stipulate the conditions and fix responsibilities for such emails clearly.

In organisations using email as part of corporate communication, security and authentication in email becomes very important. Just like any information or data, a corporate email too should conform to the standards of information security, satisfying all the basic principles of security like confidentiality, integrity, availability and non-repudiation. Hence authenticity and reliability in a corporate communication is quite significant and has to be protected at all times.

Email authentication may be broadly defined as a collection of different techniques adopted by the organization, aimed at equipping messages of the entire email communication, with verifiable information. Such authentication is usually done at Administrative Management Domain (ADMD) level, and is largely a part of the corporate policy of the organization.

Hardware Maintenance Policy

Movement of hardware and maintenance of all hardware equipment is taken care of under this policy. Corporates may choose to have proper hardware numbering or RFID (Radio Frequency Identification) by affixing tags to all hardware items to track them and monitor their movements or other means of physical verification. Such movement will be authorised by the Information System Security Managers or other functional heads of the department and the physical security department will be overall responsible for all hardware assets. Vendors visiting the organization for hardware maintenance and other upkeep will also be monitored as per the policy and will be subject to the norms laid down in it.

User Management Policy

This is one of the important policies forming part of IT Security Policy. Under this policy, the organization will decide about the roles and responsibilities of persons in charge of user management. Issues like allotment of user id will be addressed here. Normally organizations will not allot user id that is not

identifiable with any user. In other words, every user id will be identified with a particular user official of the organization only, like part of his name or a derivate of his name or his employee number, etc.

Group user ids and unidentifiable or fictitious user ids (like Guest, Anonymous, etc.) should normally be avoided and whenever given, it should be with all precautions taken like who uses that at what time with proper audit log and with traceability of the transactions tracking to the particular individual user. IT Security managers should be careful while dealing with such user ids and should closely monitor them. Deletion of users immediately after the employee leaves the organization or on a long absence or otherwise a period of inactiveness in the user, should all be closely monitored.

Setting of user rights is the most significant part in User creation and user management. Most users should have only the minimal set of privileges required for their operations, in keeping with the policy of least privilege. However, some authorization architectures may require a user with unrestricted access. It should be the conscious and policy-based decision of the management to decide and define user roles especially the complete role functions of a system manager or a system administrator.

Password Policy

There is, of late, a fairly reasonable amount of awareness on the part of organizations with regard to password policy. Most of the organizations especially banks have clearly laid down password policies in place, which stipulate that passwords should be alpha numeric preferably a combination of lower and upper characters with some special characters and be of reasonable length (normally five to eight characters and sometimes more too) with mandated periodicity of change. If the user does not change the password, the system prompts a change and forces it. Most of the banking applications enforce the password policy and implement it.

Internet Access Policy

It is common in most of the organizations to ensure that uncontrolled internet access is not provided in the systems where intranet is available, to ensure security of its applications. Hence, a proper Internet Access Policy should be in place regulating the levels of users who will have Internet Access and the nature of precautions to be taken in those systems. Wherever intranet is there, it is generally conceived to be unsafe to have an Internet access also in the same system. Or, the system should have proper firewalls and a fool-proof system of content filtering in its own internal computer systems and information to face the threat from internet.

Business Continuity and Disaster Recovery Plan Policy: In any organization, it would be the prime objective of top management to ensure whatever happens to any computer or other resources and even in the event of any disaster, the business keeps running and the organization or its customers are not affected. It is on this principle that organizations especially banks with more and more dependence on technology like Core Banking solution, etc. draft a BCDR Plan with procedures describing how to go about, in the event of a disaster or other severe business interruption. Detailed study of BCDR Plan is available under Chapter No. 18.

2.6 Methodology of Framing an IT Security Policy

Normally IT Security Policy is framed by the IT Department as part of an expert committee with members drawn from all stakeholder departments and functional heads with due approval and support from top management. The two popular approaches to framing an IT Security Policy are:

- Top-Down approach, which means that mandatory guidelines will be looked into and what the top management requires will be studied and will all be incorporated in the policy and it will be framed accordingly.
- Bottom-up approach, which means that all users especially the system managers and administrators will be enquired about the perceived threats to the system and the level of protection needed for their information assets and all related measures will be incorporated in the policy.

In practice, however, it is always a good and ideal combination of both the approaches that makes a sound and practical IT Security Policy. While the functional heads will have to be taken into confidence and their requirements studied and ease of operations ensured, it would also be mandatory to put all the legal compliance measures in place.

Before drafting a comprehensive Information Security Policy for the organisation, it is better to conduct a "people, process and technology study" *i.e.* a ppt study of the organization. Such a study conducted with all seriousness, reveals the corporate policy of the organization, the work culture of the people employed, the processes adopted in the industry and of course most significantly the technology adopted. This ppt as a study in a comprehensive manner will be very helpful to frame the corporate security policy with all the sub-policies, rules and guidelines forming part of it.

Most often business transformation involving business process re-engineering ignores the people aspect of the change initiative and in the end, the results are not satisfactory. One of the most common reasons for such failure is the lack of focus on the organisation's culture. In such a Business process re-engineering exercise, financial and other impacts like organizational, compliance, employees, HR etc. have to be studied and the corporate security policy is to be drafted.

A sound security policy should not only be useful but also be usable. The policy should not be too rigid that will ensure cent per cent protection to all information assets but will be extremely difficult to follow, nor should it be too loose and extremely simple that anyone can breach it and get away with. Hence it would be ideal to seek the opinion of all stakeholder departments like HR, Legal, Operations, Network, etc. to strike a balance between what is rigid and what is easy but still will serve the purpose. Otherwise, users will feel that adherence to policy will hamper their day to day routine and the policy will be observed more in breach. After all, it is the users who should satisfy themselves that the policy is for their protection and is there to leverage their contribution to the organization.

IT Security Policy and financial impact: While drafting IT Security Policy, the financial position of the organization as envisaged for the upkeep of information assets, should be taken into account. It would be a prudent organizational sense to involve the CFO (Chief Financial Officer) at the time of drafting the policy since he is the one who should allocate funds for procuring and implementing the various security hardware devices or software systems. It is accepted knowledge that there is no question of Return on Investment (RoI) in an investment in IT Security. In fact, investment in IT Security is like insurance and is not to be seen from the angle of financial returns.

2.7 Awareness Initiatives

However sound and practical the policy is, its success depends much on its users and how serious they take it and how much of drive and focus the top management gives to it. Hence IT Security Policy has to be given much awareness not only in the organization but also to outsiders who have a stake in the organization like vendors, Annual Maintenance Contract providers, Service Providers or typically in a bank its auditors, internet banking customers, etc. The policy should clearly define the ways to publicise and document it. HR Department should be involved in making the policy well known to all employees and the outsiders by frequently organizing training programmes and other awareness initiatives.

Committed organizations also bring out other publicity material like booklets or small Dos and Don'ts Cards on IT Security that employees are supposed to carry as part of their persona so that they realize the importance of security drives. Employees should not only be aware of all security steps taken by the organization but should also how to protect themselves, their colleagues and their organization in the event of any attack to the organization or its information assets. Security initiatives should not only be implemented but should also be taken seriously.

2.10 Reference to the Organization for Economic Co-operation and Development's (OECD) Guidelines for the Security of Information Systems is as follows.

I. Awareness of the need for security
II. Responsibility of all participants to information security
III. Response of participants to a security incident
IV. Ethics in respecting the legitimate interests of other participants
V. Democracy in ensuring compatibility with other systems
VI. Risk Assessment to identify the threats and vulnerabilities
VII. Security Design and Maintenance for effective utilization
VIII. Security Management for meaningful adoption
IX. Reassessment and review of all the principles to ensure dynamic relevance

The OECD Guidelines were developed in 1992 by a group of international experts to provide a foundation from which governments or corporate sector can construct a framework for securing IT systems. The OECD Guidelines in a broader sense continue to have their relevance globally. The guidelines emphasise greater awareness and understanding of security issues and a "culture of security" meaning security in the development of information systems and realizing the importance of security as a culture for adoption in all information systems.

2.8 Aspects of security measurement

Let us look into the various aspects of security measurement, considering different dimensions such as effectiveness, correctness, types of incidents (leading and lagging), and qualitative versus quantitative approaches, as well as differences between large and small organizations:

Effectiveness: This aspect assesses how well security measures are performing in achieving their intended objectives. Effectiveness measurement involves evaluating the impact of security controls, policies, and procedures in mitigating risks, preventing incidents, and protecting information assets. It includes analysing metrics such as incident detection rates, incident response times, and security control efficacy to determine the effectiveness of security measures.

Correctness: Correctness measurement focuses on ensuring the accuracy, integrity, and reliability of security-related data, processes, and outcomes. It involves verifying that security controls are implemented correctly, data is accurately collected and analysed, and decisions are based on reliable information. Correctness measurement helps maintain trust and confidence in security measures and supports informed decision-making.

Leading and Lagging Incidents: Leading indicators are proactive measures that predict or anticipate future security incidents or risks. Leading incident measurement involves tracking early warning signs, security trends, and predictive analytics to identify emerging threats and vulnerabilities before they escalate into significant incidents. Lagging indicators, on the other hand, are reactive measures that reflect past security incidents or events. Lagging incident measurement involves analysing historical data, incident reports, and post-incident reviews to learn from past incidents and improve future security measures.

Qualitative and Quantitative Approaches: Qualitative measurement involves assessing security aspects based on subjective judgments, opinions, or descriptive attributes. Qualitative methods include surveys, interviews, risk assessments, and expert evaluations to gather insights into security perceptions, attitudes, and behaviours. Quantitative measurement, on the other hand, involves assessing security aspects based on objective, measurable data and numerical values. Quantitative methods include metrics, key performance indicators (KPIs), statistical analysis, and modelling to quantify security risks, impacts, and effectiveness.

Large vs Small Organizations: The aspects of security measurement may vary between large and small organisations based on their scale, complexity, resources, and risk profiles. Large organizations may have more extensive security programs, complex infrastructures, and diverse stakeholders, requiring comprehensive measurement frameworks, sophisticated tools, and dedicated resources for security measurement. Small organizations, on the other hand, may have limited resources, simpler infrastructures, and fewer stakeholders, necessitating streamlined measurement approaches, cost-effective tools, and efficient processes tailored to their specific needs and priorities.

Effective Security Measurement: The security measurement involves assessing various aspects of security effectiveness, correctness, leading and lagging incidents, and qualitative versus quantitative approaches. The specific aspects and measurement methods may vary based on organizational size, complexity, and risk profile, but effective security measurement is essential for evaluating security posture, identifying areas for improvement, and making informed decisions to enhance security resilience.

Know Your Progress

Corporate IT Security Policy means an IT Security applicable to the whole organization encompassing all the functions in the organization like a bank with all its branches or even a huge multinational company with diverse products and processes spread across different geographical locations. It is needed because more and more operations are technology based and almost all organizations have realized the technology pervasiveness for their successful running and customer-centric operations. Besides, even to prove that all IT operations in the organizations are safe and secure and in tune with the legal requirements particularly after the IT Amendment Act, 2008, organizations have to put in place reasonable security practices and prove the concept of due diligence while handling customers' data.

Essentially, a sound Corporate IT Security Policy should contain various policies within it, like Network Access Policy, Physical Access Policy, Internet Banking Policy, email guidelines, IT Business Continuity and Disaster Recovery Plan, etc. All these policies individually should be drafted in consultation with the concerned user departments and in tune with the requirements of the respective data owners. There should be proper hierarchical chain in the security organization with clearly well-defined roles and responsibilities for all stakeholders. The organization should also make efforts to spread awareness about the security initiatives and related guidelines and procedures associated with the policy, to ensure that the employees are bound by it.

Key Words

ISPs	NSPs	CISO	ISOs
CIO	ISSM	Due Diligence RFID	
BCDRP	User Management		

Questions

1. Which one of the following is not a Hardware tracking initiative?
    a. RFID tag attached to the hardware item
    b. Bio-metric enabled user access system for the hardware room

c. Numbering system for all hardware equipment

d. Physical gate-pass and entry-pass for all hardware items

2. While creating user id, care should be taken to ensure that it should ______________.

a. always be alpha numeric

b. be identified to any one entity or a department and not generic

c. it should be identifiable with any one individual with his employee number distinctly

d. refer to a specific user as a derivative of his name or number and not generic

3. In a bank, if a junior clerical staff member allows a temporary overdraft without the supervising official's approval in a computerized ledger, security is lacking in _________.

a. Access Privileges Policy

b. Password Policy

c. IT Security Policy in database management

d. Network Access Policy

4. Which of the following is a major input while drafting a Corporate IT Security Policy?

a. IT Network Access Policy speaking about the network policy for departments

b. Firewalls filtering like getting the nature of websites that are to be permitted on Internet

c. Top Down approach of getting the views and requirements from top management

d. List of users as part of User Management Policy

5. Which of the following is TRUE with respect to corporate email policy?

a. All corporate emails should be digitally signed so that proper security is in place.

b. All critical mails should have proper security initiatives built into them like electronic authentication.

c. Corporates should have allowed emails to be used for critical or confidential information.

d. Only correspondence inside the organization can be by emails and all outside communication should be by normal mails only.

6. The Information Technology Act, 2000 essentially (*i*) recognizes all electronic documents with some due procedures, (*ii*) lays down rules for data protection (*iii*) fixes responsibilities for data protection on the part of body corporate (*iv*) gives 'due diligence' to data custodians and makes them responsible in certain cases only

a. All except (*i*) are correct

b. All except (*ii*) are correct

c. All except (*iii*) are correct

d. All except (*iv*) are correct

7. The IT Security Policy should insist that users should have password______________.

a. that should be changed on the first day of every month

b. that should be an identifiable to a particular individual, like part of his name but with alpha numeric characters

c. that cannot be guessed and should be alpha numeric preferably with special characters

d. with special characters and be difficult to break and should be changeable with the permission of system managers always.

8. For the success of any IT Security Programme, the awareness initiatives should always cover not only the top management but also the lowest category of staff too. (True/False)
9. In a CBS branch, all clerical staff members in banks are empowered to post all transactions covering the entire branch banking without restrictions. (True/False)
10. Return on Investment has always been a deciding factor in spending on IT Security products and related services. (True/False)

Answers

1. *b*	6. *c*
2. *d*	7. *c*
3.*a*	8. *True*
4. *c*	9. *False*
5.*b*	10. *False*

3 CHAPTER

Organisational Security and Risk Management

OBJECTIVES

After studying this chapter the readers will be able to understand the concept of Organisation level Security, Enterprise-wide Security for different kinds of industries like banking, medicine, software, etc. All aspects of Risk Management right from definition of risk as a component of threat, vulnerability and impact and up to complete risk control are also discussed in this chapter.

3.1 Organisational Security

In the previous chapter we have already explored that IT Security is not only the concern of top management but the responsibility of the entire organisation cutting across different cadres. Now, let us see what an organisational security is and the different aspects to it. While corporate security is normally for a corporate business undertaking, organisational security may be used to denote the security perspectives for even a small organisation, whether incorporated or not, proprietary or partnership or any other form of ownership. Therefore, by and large, most of what has been said of corporate security will hold good for organisational security as well. Points to be observed before drafting the Security Policy, constituents of the policy and all other related features are all the same. Depending on the nature of industry the security focus will shift and the procedures and guidelines will vary accordingly.

There is no *"one size fits all"* solution to information security. The security measures that are appropriate for an organisation will depend on its circumstances, the harm that might result from its disclosure or accidental or deliberate loss or destruction or just an improper use or misuse of its assets, etc. The RBI's Gopalakrishna Working Group Report on Information Security, Electronic Banking, Technology Risk Management and Cyber Frauds published in April 2011 says that "The guidelines are not 'one-size-fits-all' and the implementation of these recommendations need to be risk based and commensurate with the nature and scope of activities engaged by banks and the technology environment prevalent in the bank and the support rendered by technology to the business processes".

Therefore, a proper risk-based approach to deciding what level of security the organisation needs or the information needs, is of paramount importance before drafting the security policy for the organisation. Though the broader understanding of security will remain the same, the thrust areas and the operational guidelines will all change depending on the nature of the data handled, its criticality, confidentiality, volatility, etc.

3.2 Public Sector Organisation

There is sometimes a marked difference between the way data is handled in a public sector organisation and a private sector organisation. In addition to the normal procedural guidelines in a private organisation, the data handled in a public sector organisation assumes much more significance and needs to be treated with utmost confidence. The situation will be much more complex if the organisation is itself a mission-critical organisation like an atomic energy plant, a defense department, an investigation agency or the likes of it. In all such cases, while drafting the IT Security Policy, in addition to the normal precautions, additional care has to be taken on "Need to Know" basis even within the organisation. There should be layers of filtering and control and one wing of the organisation should not expose the data to other wings.

Public data and classified information

In any public sector organisation or a department of the government, there have always been interesting debate on *what* is public information. Most of the public sector organisations and government departments have always found it difficult to draw a line between public information and private or classified information. The problem is much more evident and more complex if all or most of the information is kept in electronic form. In this context, the Information System Security Department and the System related personnel in the organisation have a crucial role to play in identifying and classifying the huge information in the organisation and the related data, reports, etc. and dealing with them on the basis of such classification.

3.3 Right to Information Act, 2005

In this context, the much-publicized Right to Information Act is of great assistance in classifying the information in public sector organisations. Though the Act was not passed with the purpose of Asset Classification in the system security environment of government organisations in mind, the Act serves the purpose of identification of information criticality, confidentiality and the resultant classification. This Act was passed in India mainly with a view to ensure transparency in government functions. Quite often, there have been debates on how the RTT Act clashes with the Official Secrets Act, the Public Records Act and the Public Records Rules, with the government defending on how the information is classified by it.

Now with more and more records being maintained electronically and the entire state administration moving forward in e-governance, the question of classification of files (*i.e.* information, records, etc.) assumes enormous amount of significance. The Act gives some exemptions from the disclosure of information which can be denied to the public (*i.e.* treated as private information) like

I. information whose disclosure will affect the security and integrity of India

II. such disclosure would be a breach of privileges of the Parliament/Assembly

III. a commercial secret is available to a person due to a special relationship of trust

IV. a confidential information obtained from foreign governments, etc.

Needless to say, it is the asset classification stage (as already discussed in the earlier chapter) that has to be handled very carefully. Like it was said earlier, the onus of classification of information and facing the consequences of inadequate or improper classification lies on the part of the owner be it the government official or otherwise.

Hence these Acts do not technically come under the purview of Information System Security (ISS) Policy, but still its drafting or implementation in an organisation, it does provide a reasonable ground for asset classification which is an essential part of the ISS Policy. A proper study of the Act and the interpretation of the Act so far as seen in the judgments in the past by various High Courts and the Supreme Court, will make the job of Information classification easier for the asset owners in the organisation to categorise the information asset.

Therefore, it can be said that the CISO or the ISO of the functional department in public sector organisations and public sector undertakings, where the Act is applicable, can work in tandem with the Central Public Information Officers of the public authority for interpretation of judgments on the legislation and an unambiguous classification of information asset within the organisation.

3.4 As it is now clear that organisation security and the related policy will depend much on the nature of the organisation, the nature of products and services, the criticality of information dealt with etc., let us now look at the unique features of some select popular industries and their information assets.

IT industry including software

In an organisation mainly dealing with IT products or services like hardware manufacturing or service delivery or software design, development including Business Process Outsourcing (BPOs), Knowledge Process Outsourcing (KPOs) etc. wherein predominantly all critical information is stored in electronic form, the IT Security Policy assumes enormous significance and every department will work closely in liaison with the IS Security Department for asset classification and other security related activities.

In software development, the Intellectual Property Rights (IPRs) of the software, coding standards etc. have to be looked into. Rules regarding usage of licensed software, permission to access the software, source code, etc. are all to be addressed carefully (even for testing like a White Box Testing involving testing of the programs reading the source code and understanding the logic and testing it). Wherever possible, the hardware patenting is to be done and such information should be treated as confidential and classified with restricted access. The Information System Security Managers or other designated functional In-charge officials have to be additionally careful since all users will be tech-savvy and enforcement of security disciplines like use of firewalls, access restrictions through proxy servers, usage of pen-drives, email access including sending attachment through emails etc. have to be done cautiously with a fool-proof system with deterrent action in the event of breach.

Telecom Sector

ISS Policy in the case of a telecom sector or a communication company will have to look at details of public information, private data, where they handle the customers' data and where they are owners of the data and where they are just custodians. It would be worthy to note that as per the concept of 'due diligence' enshrined in the IT Amendment Act, 2008 under section 79 "Exemption from liability of intermediary in certain cases", is available to intermediaries such as telecom service providers only under specific circumstances like when the transmission was not initiated by them or their function was limited to the extent of providing access and they have observed due diligence, etc.

Therefore, such organisations should necessarily have a sound ISS Policy in place with well-defined procedures and guidelines including Asset Classification, Access Control measures and all 'reasonable security practices and procedures'. Not only such policy should be in place but should also be practiced and properly implemented.

To a considerable extent, TRAI (Telecom Regulatory Authority of India) also regulates maintenance of records and other governance issues in the telecom sector.

According to a KPMG Report on "Information Security in the Telecom Sector" published in 2011, "The Indian Mobile subscribers are looking for more than voice services from the telecom operator. The most recent initiative aims at convergence of voice and data received from multiple sources, both web based and real time video streams, in mobile handheld devices. Services such as m-Commerce,

enables users to perform commercial transaction as well as official communication wherever they go. However, these technological advancements pose a challenge to overall information security landscape within a telecom operator. While users download and install Mobile Apps on their devices, the basic security measures such as firewall & encryption needs to be ensured. At the same time, sharing of subscriber's financial and personal information through these applications on the mobile devices demands a high level of security that will increase customer trust and reduction in possibilities of fraud & leakage".

Much more than any other industry, in the Telecom Sector, it is extremely important to make the employees accountable for information security since third party data are always been handled by the firm. Hence employees must be made aware of security and responsibility in handing data by having security as part of their employment contract or job description. Digital Rights Management (DRM) *i.e.* copyright or an anti-piracy technology *i.e.* the right over an information asset to prevent piracy and unauthorised access or copy or downloading or otherwise copying of the information file more commonly a music file should be taken very seriously and employees should be adequately trained on DRM issues including the consequences of a breach of the laws of the land relating to DRM. Similarly, Information Leakage Prevention should be enabled at the end user level too.

Banking Sector

With the advent of technology in the banking sector and with all banks completely relying on technology for most of their products, a proper and well-documented IT Security Policy is an absolute necessity in the Banking Sector. The Central Bank of the nation, Reserve Bank of India, constituted a working group under the chairmanship of RBI Executive Director Shri G. Gopalakrishna. The group examined various issues arising out of the use of IT in banks and made its recommendations in nine broad areas as follows:

I. IT Governance
II. Information Security
III. IS Audit
IV. IT Operations
V. IT Services Outsourcing
VI. Cyber Fraud
VII. Business Continuity Planning
VIII. Customer Awareness programmes
IX. Legal aspects

The report was uploaded on the RBI website on January 21, 2011. Besides recommending banks to beef up security measures in banks to properly strategise IT controls to make them more effective, banks have been told to designate an officer of the rank of GM/DGM/AGM as the Chief Information Security Officer for the bank, to take up responsibility for making and implementing policies to protect information, who will report to the risk management function only. He will not report to the Chief Information Officer who will play a role in executive decision to own the IT functions in banks for leveraging alignment of business and technology. In its detailed report, circulated to all banks in April 2011, the committee has set out the critical components of an ISS Policy in banks like scope, information strategy, roles and responsibilities of all stakeholders, periodic review of the policy and exception handling guidelines focusing on how to handle non-compliance etc.

More information on the Gopalakrishna Committee reports and recommendations are provided in the later chapters under relevant heads.

Medicine and Hospital Industry

With more and more hospitals entering the Indian corporate arena, it is natural that hospitals and medicare organisations also look for proper information system mechanism in place. Much confidential health related data are handled in such organisations requiring utmost care. Loss of misplacement or mishandling of any health data or manipulation at some level may affect the lives of individual and may cause huge business, ethical and legal damage to the institution.

Though cybercrimes involving manipulation of hospital data or medicare information are extremely rare in India and not much has been reported so far, it is generally feared that the day is not far off and hospitals have to be prepared for any such attacks. Especially, when the organisations have presence in the US or deal with US clients, the medical information is to be handled with much more care and attention. In the US, corporates have to comply with the norms of Health Insurance Portability and Accountability Act (HIPAA) that is applicable to any application that deals even remotely with health care providers, health insurance carriers, personal student information, or human resources. The Act stipulates extensive liability for defaulters. Though India does not have such legislations, health care related data are still to be dealt with utmost care with proper security initiatives in place.

Manufacturing and other industries

In those organisations, where IT is mainly an enabler and the core function of the organisation is say manufacturing or dealing in automobile or other consumer goods, the IT Security will focus on the nature of information stored in the system as well as in physical form. Of late, even in such industries, though the core function is non-IT, every activity in the organisation is still IT-based and correspondence and records are mostly in electronic form.

Hence, treatment of information asset, asset classification, definition of roles and responsibilities of all stakeholders, etc. will all be the same. In these days of increasing cyber-crimes as a result of data espionage, corporate spying, etc. the design, plan documents and other top management information of such organisations have to be protected with utmost care. It has been quite common that purely a manufacturing industry like cement industry too sometimes go in for an Information Security Management System (ISMS) certification like ISO 27001, just to make it their unique selling points among its rivals, giving a message that all data and electronic communication are treated with utmost care and confidentiality there.

In short, in almost every industry in general and in banking and other service industries in particular, information security is always a balance between customer service or ease of use on the one hand and regulatory guidelines and organisation policy on the other. If the product or service is too liberal and very easy to use, then there is bound to be some compromise on the security front. If the practices and uses are very complicated involving much restrictions, then perhaps the customer data and money are safe but the operational strictness and delay in systems arising therefrom will itself drive the customer away and the organization is bound to lose business.

Hence the organization has to always strike a reasonable balance between ease of use and other parameters like cost, operational policy on one hand and the security of data on the other. Perhaps information security is the converging point where all the factors like ease of use, customer service, operational guidelines, compliance initiatives etc. all converge.

Info Security in banking

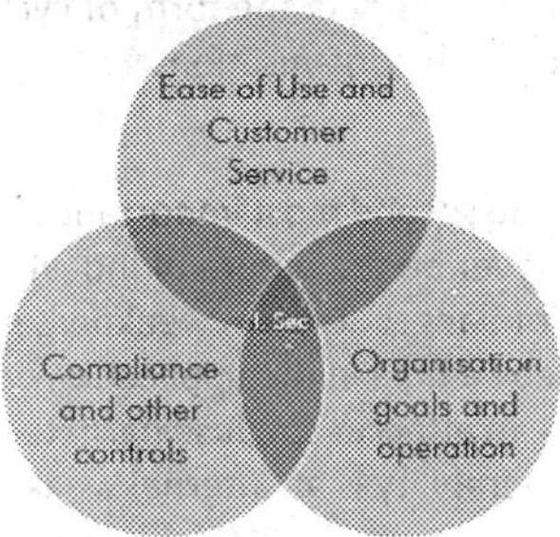

After Exploring the structure and unique requirements of different categories of organisations in the previous sections, let us now look at the underlying governing principles how a system security policy is drafted. In the first chapter we studied *what* is an information asset which is to be protected, *why* to protect it (because of the criticality of the asset or confidentiality etc.) and subsequently the manner *how* to protect it (by drafting a well-documented ISS Policy). Let us now look at the dangers to an information asset or areas *against* which an information asset is to be protected. Information Asset faces threats and attacks from many quarters known and unknown, anticipated and unanticipated, man-made and Acts of God. A proper protection mechanism will take into account all the threats that an information system may have and analyse them effectively to ensure the ISS policy is well drafted.

3.5 Risk Management is a systematic process of identifying, assessing, prioritizing, and mitigating potential risks or uncertainties that could impact the achievement of objectives within an organisation. It involves analyzing potential events or situations that may pose a threat to the organisation's assets, operations, or goals, and then taking proactive measures to manage or mitigate these risks. The goal of risk management is to enhance decision-making processes, minimize the negative impacts of uncertainties, and optimize the overall performance and resilience of an organization.

Threats and Attacks

Before going into the aspect of Risk Management or Risk Assessment we have to define 'risk'. The definition of 'risk' takes us a step lower since risk is a derivative of other factors like 'threat', 'vulnerability' and 'impact'. Though all these three words are quite common in every day usage, in risk analysis, these words have specific connotations. Let us define 'threat' first.

Threat can be defined as an 'act of coercion proposed to elicit a negative response, a statement of an intention or an act to inflict pain, injury, damage or loss to another person or an asset and is often criminal in nature'. The essential part of 'threat' is the act or an external event. This understanding of threat as an external event or an act from an external source with potential to cause harm is absolutely necessary in a study of risk analysis. Threat is often perceived, anticipated if not expected, but feared and prepared for, as part of risk analysis and risk management. It should be understood clearly that threats always existed and shall exist and can never be eliminated be it in an information system scenario or in other walks of life.

Threats can be man-made, natural or a result of any human action or a systemic activity too. While most of the threats can be anticipated or expected, some may never be anticipated like Acts of God and natural disasters normally called '*force majeure*' which are purely unforeseeable circumstances but which anyway and compulsorily, have to be planned for in Risk Management. Threats can be man-made, human error, technical failure, system failure, hard-disk crashes, floods, cyclone, power surge, UPS failure, loss or theft of system, etc.

Threat analysis and threat modeling is the description of security issues and all security aspects taking into account the nature of information asset like software, a computer application or a hardware, etc. and then deciding about the attacker's motive, the impact it can create, etc. Such a study is essential

in order to identify the nature of threats like what can be detected and prevented and those over which man has no control (like nature's fury in the form of cyclone or floods etc.) so that the next step of risk analysis can be started for the organisation.

Vulnerability

After 'threat' in the study of risks, the second most important concept is 'vulnerability'. Every system be it in computerized or not, whatever be the nature of industry, has some weaknesses in it, which when exposed becomes a source of danger. It is this weakness in the system which is often referred to as 'vulnerability' meaning thereby a hole in the application which can be a flaw or a bug or other form of susceptibility which allows an attacker to cause harm to the system or the information asset. From this, it is quite clear that vulnerability is an internal weakness in the system whereas threat is an external event.

Bugs in the system, untested software, weak hardware, weak controls in the system, mal-functioning hardware, allowing very weak passwords, lack of anti-virus software are all vulnerabilities in the system. Since vulnerabilities are mostly man-made or at least can be detected, they require immediate action. In some systems, the top management or the security managers may consciously allow certain vulnerabilities to exist since the cost of removal of such vulnerabilities may be huge and the impact of such vulnerabilities may be quite low causing minimal or almost nil damage to the system. It should be the security managers' main concern to plug all the vulnerabilities and be aware of the unplugged ones and to ensure that those are not exploited by any threat.

When such vulnerabilities are thus consciously left to remain in the system, they constitute the unmitigated or residual risk as part of the Risk Management exercise. There should be periodical and constant study of effectiveness of controls in such a situation, to monitor how such vulnerabilities cause a concern.

Impact is the effect when a threat meets a vulnerability. When the weakness gets exposed and if an external event occurs in the form of an attack which results in some effect on the system or an information asset, then the effect is called 'impact'. Business Impact Analysis (BIA) measures the effect of resource loss and escalating losses over time, in order to provide senior management with reliable data to enable the management in decision making on risk mitigation and continuity planning. It is a formal analysis of the effect on the business if a specific set of Information System services are not available. It identifies the minimum set of services that an organisation will require to continue operations.

Risk is said to materialize when a threat meets a vulnerability and there is an impact. Risk always refers to a potential or an anticipated loss or damage to the system and is said to occur when there is an attack or a threat to the system causing an impact to it. Hence Risk = Threat + Vulnerability + Impact. From this formula, it is clear that more threat means more risk and more threat but with nil vulnerability it means no risk. Since vulnerabilities are certainly bound to exist and threats are always external factors, risk will be there, so long as there are unattended threats and attacks which will exploit the vulnerabilities.

A practical definition of risk can be 'risk is the potential of damage to a system or associated assets that exist as a result of the combination of security threat and vulnerability.' Risk is a probability of unfavourable condition and in financial sector it is the probability of actual return being less than expected return. It is a source of danger to the organisation and a possibility of incurring loss or misfortune or the effect of uncertainty on objectives, whether positive or negative. Risk ratio would be defined as the ratio of the probability of an issue occurring as against to an issue not occurring.

There are different scientific formulae available for calculating risk for an organisation. One of the popular formulae is:

Risk = Probability × Damage Potential.

Based upon this, on a scale of 1 to 10 rating assigned to probability and damage potential, overall risk rating can be done.

For example, if Probability =10 and Damage Potential = 1 then Risk = 10 × 1 = 10.

If Probability =1 and Damage Potential =10, then Risk = 1 × 10 = 10.

Risk Management

Risk management is the identification, assessment, and prioritisation of risks followed by coordinated and economical application of resources to minimize, monitor, and control the probability and/or impact of unfortunate events or to maximize the realisation of opportunities. Risk Management is the overall study of all vulnerabilities in the system, possibility of all attacks and threats and the gravity of impact when a threat meets a vulnerability. Hence risk management involves within it, steps to identify threats, identify vulnerabilities, eliminate vulnerabilities, classify impact, arrive at the gaps, plug the weaknesses wherever possible and at last manage the residual risks arising out of unattended and unforeseen threats and unmitigated vulnerabilities.

Typically, under the popular Plan-Do-Check-Act method, Risk Management will appear as follows:

Risk Analysis is the study of the various threats, vulnerabilities and impact and the resultant risks. It is a process of identification of what can be prevented and what should be prevented and analysis of various vulnerabilities and identification of what can be eliminated (and at what cost). It involves analysis of various threats and security incidents and the impact such incidents will have on the system and the feasibility of elimination of risk and at least mitigation of the adverse impact of such incidents.

Risk Mitigation is the task of mitigating risk and reducing the potentiality of threats or attacks to happen or eliminating the weaknesses so that risk does not materialize. Risk Mitigation is part of Risk Management since it would be endeavour to eliminate every risk possible and prevent the attack from happening.

Risk Elimination is a concept that is much spoken about and generally accepted to be more idealistic. Security analysts are aware that cent percent elimination of risk cannot happen. Whatever the measures like ensuring dependable complete back-up, fool-proof controls and effective review mechanism as a result of proper corrective and preventive be in place, it cannot be guaranteed that all risks have been completely eliminated.

Risk Appetite

It is often said that more risks more is the business potential. However, in the area of security, it cannot be said that more risk will ensure more business. On the other hand, more risk will only mean more exposure and more concern and less concentration on business and resultant loss in business too. Some business organisations, after a study of risks and a proper risk assessment, still make a conscious decision of putting up with the risk, rather than spend on the software and hardware to eliminate the risks. Such organisations are said to have a large risk appetite. However, in such cases too, it would be the security managers' responsibility to make the top management especially at the CIO and CISO level, aware that such exposure to risk is left open. In such cases the top management may like to exhibit its risk appetite and put up with such risks and do business for strategic reasons.

Residual risks

Sometimes, after a thorough risk analysis, the security managers still feel that some risks still do exist and have to be taken care of in the days to come or after the risk mitigation systems (like procurement of software or hardware like a fire-wall or an updated anti-virus or an anti-malware and spyware etc.) are in place and until such time, the systems have to be monitored with extra care with careful incident management system and very prompt and effective follow-up for every security incident. In

such cases, when the top management is aware that after proper risk management too, some risks still exist, they are called the residual risks, which are yet to be attended.

3.6 Risk Metrics

To understand the concept of risk management and to ensure that proper risk analysis has been made in the organisation, modern day risk specialists resort to a process what is called Risk Measurement and Risk Metrics. A measure is a process of assigning a number to an entity and here it is the risk as a combination of threat and vulnerability. Metrics is the process of interpreting or quantifying the assigned number in a properly formulated and rated system. Application of metrics to risk as a part of Risk Management is often resorted to in large organisations especially while going for an ISO (ISMS) certification (about which we will be discussing in the Chapter on Standards and Frameworks). This gives a better and intelligible with an empirical value to the risk treatment that the organisation wants to give to the particular threat (or vulnerability).

Risk Management in Indian Banking especially from the view point of Basel accords have been categorized as

I. Credit Risk

II. Market Risk

III. Operational Risk

Many non-financial risks especially the political risks, technology risks are all normally classified under operational risks in banking in India.

On the question of risk management in Indian banks, it is worthwhile to note the contribution of the successive Basel accords. Now, Basel III being introduced, in a phased manner lays much more emphasis on risk management including mainly risk disclosures thereby giving a comfortable feeling to the stake holders.

Basel III Implications for Indian Banking. One of the main significant challenges posed by Basel III apart from the increased capital standards is that of creating a new risk management culture with a great vigor and accountability. In effect, Basel III is changing the way banks look at their risk management functions and might imply them to go for a robust risk management framework to ensure a true enterprise risk management. (Source: http://www.iibf.org.in/documents/reseach-report/Report-25.pdf -- Page 292 Para 8.6.)

Basel III is an evolutionary step with a significant improvement over the earlier Basel I and II. Technology risk is adequately covered with focused approach towards the treatment of risk comparable to international standards and in tune with the enhanced penetration of technology in Indian banking.

Basel III framework implementation would lead to reduced risk of systemic banking crises as the enhanced capital and liquidity buffers together lead to better management of probable risks emanating due to counterparty defaults and/or liquidity stress circumstances.

3.7 Downstream Liability

It is a risk that organisations should certainly take into account as part of their Risk Analysis. Downstream liability refers to the third party liability of organisations *i.e.* liabilities of organisations to third parties to whom they may not have any direct contractual obligations but still legally (or technologically) the likelihood of making them liable cannot be ruled out. For instance, if an organisation is a victim of a DDoS attack and its network is compromised and is used as a zombie to further generate a DDoS Attack or at least to spread virus, there is a downstream liability of such organisation towards the actual victims of such attacks, though the organisation would not have intended any such attack. We

have to concede that the legal position of downstream liability is always being disputed and there is room for ambiguity and interpretation. Hence, the question of liability to pay compensation in such cases is always debated.

3.8 Risk Management In Banking

In the banking industry, Risk Management is of very great significance. In the past two decades, after the introduction of Basel-I and Basel-II norms and the recently introduced Basel-III with new global regulatory standard on capital adequacy and liquidity, Risk Management has been given utmost importance in banks in India. With the advent of technology and its complete penetration in the banking industry, Technology Risks are being analysed and have been made part of Operational Risks in banking. IT Business Continuity and Disaster Recovery Planning is a separate document in most of the banks and is being systematically drafted with top management approval and implemented.

3.9 Classifications of security attacks in IT security

Security attacks in IT security can be classified into various categories based on different criteria, including the target, the method of attack, the goal of the attacker, and the impact on the system or network. Let us see some common classifications of security attacks in IT security.

By Targeted Component:

Network Attacks: Target the network infrastructure, including devices such as routers, switches, and firewalls, to disrupt communication, intercept data, or gain unauthorized access.

Host Attacks: Target individual computer systems or devices, exploiting vulnerabilities in operating systems, applications, or services to compromise confidentiality, integrity, or availability.

Application Attacks: Target web applications, mobile applications, or other software systems, exploiting vulnerabilities such as input validation flaws, injection attacks, or authentication bypass to gain unauthorized access or perform malicious actions.

Physical Attacks: Target physical assets, facilities, or hardware components, such as servers, workstations, or storage devices, through theft, vandalism, or tampering to gain unauthorized access or cause disruption.

By Method of Attack:

Malware Attacks: Include various types of malicious software, such as viruses, worms, Trojans, ransomware, and spyware, designed to infect systems, steal data, or disrupt operations.

Social Engineering Attacks: Manipulate human behaviour through deception, persuasion, or coercion to trick individuals into disclosing sensitive information, providing access credentials, or performing unauthorized actions.

Denial-of-Service (DoS) and Distributed Denial-of-Service (DDoS) Attacks: Overwhelm systems, networks, or services with excessive traffic or requests, causing them to become unavailable or unresponsive to legitimate users.

Man-in-the-Middle (MitM) Attacks: Intercept and modify communication between two parties, allowing the attacker to eavesdrop on sensitive information, tamper with data, or impersonate one of the parties.

SQL Injection Attacks: Exploit vulnerabilities in web applications or databases by injecting malicious SQL queries to retrieve or manipulate data, bypass authentication, or gain unauthorized access.

Phishing and Spear Phishing Attacks: Use deceptive emails, messages, or websites to trick users into revealing sensitive information, such as login credentials, financial details, or personal information.

Brute Force Attacks: Attempt to guess passwords or encryption keys through repeated trial-and-error, exploiting weak or default credentials to gain unauthorized access to systems or accounts.

By Goal of the Attacker:

Data Breaches: Aim to steal sensitive information, such as personal data, financial records, intellectual property, or trade secrets, for financial gain, espionage, or sabotage.

Financial Fraud: Target financial systems, transactions, or accounts to steal money, credit card information, or other valuable assets through fraudulent activities such as unauthorized transfers, identity theft, or payment card skimming.

Espionage and Intelligence Gathering: Target government agencies, organizations, or individuals to gather intelligence, trade secrets, or classified information for political, military, or economic espionage purposes.

Disruption and Sabotage: Aim to disrupt or disable systems, networks, or critical infrastructure, causing financial loss, operational disruption, or reputational damage to organizations or governments.

Ransomware Attacks: Encrypt data or block access to systems and demand ransom payments from victims in exchange for decryption keys or restored access.

By Impact on the System or Network:

Confidentiality Attacks: Compromise the confidentiality of data by unauthorized disclosure or exposure to unauthorized individuals or entities.

Integrity Attacks: Compromise the integrity of data by unauthorized modification, alteration, or deletion, leading to data corruption or loss of trustworthiness.

Availability Attacks: Disrupt the availability of systems, networks, or services, rendering them inaccessible or unusable to legitimate users.

Non-repudiation Attacks: Undermine the ability to prove the authenticity or origin of data or transactions, allowing attackers to deny their actions or disown responsibility.

Understanding the nature of threats: The organizations can better understand the nature of threats they face and develop appropriate countermeasures to mitigate risks and protect their information assets.

3.10 The information security attacks

Information security attacks encompass a wide range of malicious activities aimed at compromising the confidentiality, integrity, and availability of information assets. These attacks can target various components of IT infrastructure, including networks, systems, applications, and data. Here are some common types of information security attacks:

Malware Attacks:

Viruses: Malicious software that infects systems by attaching itself to legitimate programs or files and replicating when executed.

Worms: Self-replicating malware that spreads across networks and systems, exploiting vulnerabilities to infect other computers.

Trojans: Malware disguised as legitimate software to trick users into downloading and executing malicious code, often leading to unauthorized access or data theft.

Ransomware: Malware that encrypts data or blocks access to systems, demanding ransom payments from victims in exchange for decryption keys or restored access.

Spyware: Malware designed to secretly collect sensitive information, such as keystrokes, passwords, and browsing habits, from infected systems.

Phishing and Social Engineering Attacks:

Phishing: Deceptive emails, messages, or websites designed to trick users into revealing sensitive information, such as login credentials, financial details, or personal information.

Spear Phishing: Targeted phishing attacks that personalize messages and use social engineering tactics to increase their effectiveness, often targeting specific individuals or organizations.

Whaling: Phishing attacks that target high-profile individuals, such as executives or celebrities, to steal sensitive information or conduct financial fraud.

Baiting: Social engineering attacks that lure victims into downloading malware or disclosing sensitive information by offering fake incentives or rewards, such as free software or prizes.

Denial-of-Service (DoS) and Distributed Denial-of-Service (DDoS) Attacks:

DoS Attacks: Overwhelm systems, networks, or services with excessive traffic or requests, causing them to become unavailable or unresponsive to legitimate users.

DDoS Attacks: Coordinate large-scale attacks using multiple compromised devices (botnets) to flood target systems with traffic, amplifying the impact and making mitigation more challenging.

SQL Injection and Code Injection Attacks:

SQL Injection: Exploit vulnerabilities in web applications or databases by injecting malicious SQL queries to retrieve or manipulate data, bypass authentication, or gain unauthorized access.

Code Injection: Inject malicious code (e.g., JavaScript, PHP) into web applications or server-side scripts to execute arbitrary commands, steal data, or compromise the integrity of systems.

Man-in-the-Middle (MitM) Attacks:

Eavesdropping: Intercept and monitor communication between two parties to steal sensitive information, such as login credentials, financial data, or confidential documents.

Session Hijacking: Take control of an ongoing communication session between two parties by intercepting and manipulating data packets, allowing the attacker to impersonate one of the parties and perform unauthorized actions.

Insider Threats:

Insider Attacks: Malicious activities carried out by individuals with authorized access to systems, networks, or data, often motivated by financial gain, revenge, or ideology.

Insider Data Theft: Unauthorized access or exfiltration of sensitive information by employees, contractors, or trusted insiders for personal or malicious purposes.

Insider Sabotage: Intentional destruction, modification, or disruption of systems, networks, or data by insiders to cause financial or reputational harm to organizations.

Advanced Persistent Threats (APTs):

Targeted Attacks: Sophisticated and stealthy attacks conducted by well-funded adversaries, such as nation-state actors or organized cybercriminal groups, to infiltrate and compromise specific targets over an extended period.

Data Exfiltration: Covert extraction of sensitive information from compromised systems or networks by APT actors, often using advanced techniques to evade detection and maintain persistence.

Zero-Day Exploits:

Zero-Day Attacks: Target vulnerabilities in software or hardware that are previously unknown or unpatched, allowing attackers to exploit them before vendors release security patches or updates.

Zero-Day Exploits: Malicious code or techniques used to exploit zero-day vulnerabilities, enabling attackers to gain unauthorized access, execute arbitrary commands, or compromise systems without detection.

Comprehensive Security Measures: These are just a few examples of the many information security attacks that organizations may face in today's digital landscape. To mitigate the risk of these attacks, organizations should implement comprehensive security measures, including regular patching, employee training, access controls, and threat detection mechanisms.

Know Your Progress

Organisational Security is the study of Information Security with particular reference to the specific organisation depending upon the nature of products and services handled, the types of customers and other factors. Information dealt with in a public sector organisation say a government department may be entirely different from that dealt with by a consumer goods retail showroom. Within the broader principles of information security and all policies associated with it, organisations may have specific focus on certain areas of security in tune with the type of goods and services dealt with by them. Organisational Security will largely depend upon the nature of assets, risks associated with it and the risk management criteria. Risk is said to be a factor of threats, vulnerability and impact. Threat or an attack is an external event that may cause harm to a resource. Vulnerability is an inherent weakness or a hold in the system that will be exploited and when faced by a threat, it will have a serious impact, called risk. Vulnerability is part of the system whereas threat is always an external event. Organisations should take care to analyse the different threats to the computer resource, vulnerabilities in the system and the impact they may have and then only draft the ISS Policy for the organisation. Risk Management is the overall study of all risks associated with the industry like the possibility of different threats attacking it, vulnerabilities and the gravity of impact when a threat strikes. Though risk can never be completely eliminated, it can always be controlled by proper risk analysis.

Key Words

Right to Information	IT Governance	HIPAA	Risk Management
Risk Analysis	Threat	Vulnerability	Impact
Risk Appetite	Residual Risks	Risk Control	

Questions

1. Which of the following is not a threat?
   a. UPS failure in a critical server.
   b. Absence of a firewall in the system.
   c. Sudden hard-disk crash in a non-critical application.
   d. Employee Unrest and absenteeism of system managers.
2. Which of the following is not one of the areas of recommendations in Gopalakrishna Committee Working Group of RBI?
   a. IS Audit.
   b. Business Continuity Planning.

   c. Customer Awareness Programmes.
   d. Core Banking Solution.

3. Which of the following statement is TRUE in a Public Sector Organisation?
   a. All information dealt with is confidential and protected from public view or access.
   b. The Right to Information Act permits all information to be made available when required.
   c. The Right to Information Act permits classification of information but does not speak about the classification based on Information System Security and Risk Management.
   d. The central and the state governments and other owners alone own all information assets and only they have the powers to change the classification based only on public interest.

4. In a computerized environment, the inherent and existing situation which may become a risk is normally known as:
   a. Threat and potentialities
   b. Weakness and bugs
   c. Vulnerabilities
   d. Inherent risks

5. White Box Testing is normally referred to the type of testing involving________________.
   a. reading the entire source code by the testers and understanding the logic and testing
   b. usage of a testing tool called 'White Box' to read the source code and perform the testing
   c. testing based on the input and output from the programme which is common in IT industry so that the security of program source code and their access is ensured
   d. complete system testing based on all banking applications without hiding anything from the testers and in a transparent manner so that proper test results come out

6. Ideally in a bank, it is recommended that the Information Security structure will have________________.
   a. the Chief Information Officer (CIO) in the rank of General Manager, handling all information related architecture, their safety, security and maintenance
   b. the Chief Information Security Officer (CISO) in executive cadre (AGM or above) and will always report to the CIO directly.
   c. CISO and CIO will both report to the Risk Management Department and will be responsible for the information assets and their security in the bank
   d. CIO will be a top executive aligning business and technology and CISO will not report to him

7. As part of Risk Management, full form of B.I.A. is ________________.
   a. Business Impact Analysis
   b. Banks Impact Analysis
   c. Business Impression Analytics
   d. Bank's Inherent Analysis

8. Right to Information Act with a view ensures public sector banks keep all electronic data in proper upkeep ensuring easy retrieval. (True/False)

9. ISO 27001 is a ISO certification for compliance of standards on Information Security Management System. (True/False)

10. Basel III is the new global regulatory standard on capital adequacy and liquidity giving importance to Risk Management. (True/False)

Answers

1. *b*	6. *d*
2. *d*	7. *a*
3. *c*	8. False
4. *c*	9. True
5. *a*	10. True

4

CHAPTER

Security Governance

OBJECTIVES

After reading this chapter, the readers should be able to understand:

I. The meaning and significance of IT Security Governance.

II. How it is closely aligned with IT Security Management.

III. IS Security Policy and how all these are mainly aligned with the business strategy of the organization.

IV. Related concepts like corporate governance, IT governance and certain industry-specific IS Security Governance issues.

4.1 Security Governance is the act of conducting the policy and affairs of a state or organisation by constituting, wherever necessary, a set of rules and standards in the process, for effectiveness. Governance includes assignment of decisions on issues like policy, framework, standards including effective monitoring. Security governance needs to provide a framework in which the decisions made about security issues are aligned with the overall business strategy and the culture of the organization. Security governance is concerned with setting directions, establishing standards and principles and wherever necessary and called for, prioritizing investments in the process.

4.2 Security governance is different from management. Security governance is about decision making *per se*, whereas management is about making and implementing specific decisions. Security Governance therefore, involves the top management by setting responsibilities and putting in place practices, with the goal of providing strategic direction, ensuring that objectives are achieved, risks are managed and resources are used optimally. Security governance involves the main task of evolving rules, interpreting it and transforming it into meaningful and practical functions.

4.3 Security Governance mainly involves the steps right from people and processes at the top, how the data and information are handled in the organisation, how the application handles security, the network and other layers handling the data and information and related assets and the physical infrastructure which takes care of physical access to information assets. The entire gamut of dealing with these, setting standards, monitoring and effective supervision comes under the overall architecture of Security Governance. (See Diagram below)

SECURITY GOVERNANCE

People and Processes

Data and Information - Access

Application

Network Architecture

Physical Infrastructure

4.4 Policies

Just as we saw in the earlier chapter No.2 the Security Policy of any corporate consists of different policies, security governance in any organisation also contains various policies that are to be effectively monitored and efficiently governed. Policies like Email Policy, Internet Access Policy, Password Policy etc. have much impact on Security Governance in any organisation and its success or effectiveness depends much on the implementation and effective monitoring of all these policies.

4.5 Framework

Detailed study of framework and standards is provided in the Chapter on IS Audit and Regulatory Compliance. However, a brief insight into Framework is furnished here. In the absence of a proper and well defined framework focussing on roles and responsibilities, the main responsibility is too often delegated to the Chief Information Officer who also acts as the Chief Security Officer. In the absence of job segregation, he suffers conflicting demands with regard to IT functionality and the related cost decisions and may not be in a position to leverage the resources and authority necessary to address the problem across multiple business lines or divisions. Sometimes scant regard is given to this issue at the CEO or board level and information security efforts are frequently under-funded in proportion to the risk and magnitude of the harm that incidents may cause to the organisation.

4.6 Key Responsibility Areas

Typically every organisation will be having a Work Manual or a Job Card associated with all designations which will describe the nature of job assigned to that designation and the responsibility associated with it. It is this Key Responsibility Area (KRA) that is of great significance in security governance because based on this, the security initiatives will be framed and focus areas defined. For the successful implementation of security and effective security governance, organisations should endeavour to designate all employees based on the task assigned to them and make their responsibilities clear and unambiguous. Right from the CIO or CISO, up to the lowest level of subordinate members of staff who are just users of the system, every entity in the organisation should have proper designation with well-defined KRA.

To have well defined KRA, organisations normally go in for Job Cards or other types of Work Manuals or Work Instructions. If due to contingencies, any employee is assigned a dual responsibility, he would be bound by the KRA of both the designation and be aware of the responsibilities and job functions of both the tasks taken up by him.

4.7 Information security is often treated solely as a technology issue, when it should be mainly treated as a governance issue. Well defined KRA will remove this ambiguity of focus that the information security deserves at every level of the organisation. Otherwise, information security will be seen as a technology issue, handled by the technology department only and not as a governance issue. Information Security is industry-neutral and not specific to any industry. The level of computerisation and the level of criticality of data handled in the organisation may decide how penetrative information security is in the organisation but nevertheless, it encompasses the entire organisation and hence governing it should be a major concern right from the apex level.

4.8 Security Governance in Public Sector Undertakings

Though security governance *per se* is common to all undertakings public or private, small or big, the significance of governance varies according to the nature of industry, the type of data handled, the criticality of information dealt with etc. In the case of incorporated companies in India, wherein even filing of application for creation of charge over the company's assets, in favour of the lending institutions, is done electronically and many government levies are paid electronically, security governance assumes very huge importance. Similarly, records as mandated by SEBI (Securities and Exchange Board of India) may also be kept electronically. In all such cases, it becomes a huge responsibility on the part of the corporate organisations to ensure that security governance initiatives are in place and adequate security is provided to records stored electronically.

4.9 Security Governance In Banks

As more and more banking transactions are becoming paperless and technology oriented, with only electronic records as evidences, it has become increasingly essential on the part of banks to have proper security governance initiatives in place. In this context, it would be worthwhile to mention that the Reserve Bank of India (RBI) in its various reports has recorded its attention and awareness on the technological need of the nation towards making banking paperless, chequeless and cashless,". As the regulator, the RBI is aware that the answers to these questions are not easy and nobody has a readymade answer. Such an amount of complete e-governance may take time to achieve, but it is not impossible as it is already happening globally and we as a nation cannot lag behind.

With Core Banking completely redefining the banking practice in India and with the increasing thrust on e-governance, no wonder that the Government of India has launched its Digital India initiative on July 1, 2015. The digital India is an initiative with a vision to make all citizens digitally literate and bring internet and e-governance to all sections of the society focusing on inclusive growth in areas of electronic services, products, manufacturing and job opportunities etc. E-governance is going to change into m-governance or mobile governance, which is going to be a reality soon.

Launching the initiative, the Prime Minister said that digital India ensures high speed digital highways to unite the nation with an open and transparent government. Such transparent administration is the basis of e-governance.

With so much of thrust on e-governance and m-governance, and the already existing Core Banking Solution, the Indian banking system is now witnessing a paradigm shift towards the way banking was practised in India. The very concept of banking in India is getting re-defined with the convenience

of "anytime, anywhere banking" to Indian customers, with a paperless banking, 'bank customer' leaving the way for 'branch customer' and the branch concept and branch records on the decline. There is now a movement towards integration of core banking solutions of various banks, which is expected to bring in operational efficiency and reduce the time and effort involved in handling and settling transactions, thereby improving customer service and facilitating regulatory compliance.

Technology is changing the cultural and business landscapes beyond recognition and the world over, organisations are using transformative power of technology to create business value for today to enhance the growth for tomorrow. And major Public Sector Undertaking in India, especially the banking sector cannot be any exception. To be on a par with the peers, all banks have to put in place security governance architecture in place, as part of their Information Systems Security Policy.

Irrespective of whether the bank is on an in-house software development or an outsourced software, e-governance has to be taken seriously, from a regulatory perspective, from a competitive edge point of view and also to ensure better organisational controls including MIS generation etc.

Security Governance in banks also depends to a great extent on the level of computerisation, level of technology penetration in banks. For instance, private sector players like ICICI Bank and Citi Bank with a large volume of technology products and heavy dependence on technology, have put in many security initiatives in place. Some private sector banks have introduced a grid information at the back of the card, which the customer should provide when prompted. This ensures that the card is physically with him when he does an internet banking transaction. Some banks have introduced the system of session generated PINs and have issued the devices (small pen-drive like gadgets) to their account holders, that would display the PIN which is valid for the session, which the customer will enter, to authenticate his transaction.

More on the practices of banks in dealing with the security issues in electronic delivery channels like ATMs, Internet Banking, etc. will be discussed in the chapters on Software Controls.

It should be the constant endeavour of banks to strike a perfect balance between what is very strict and secure and what is too loose and liberal. If the bank is weak in security governance, some customers may prefer the bank, on the (superficial) relief and happiness that the bank asks fewer questions and gives less hassles for an e-transaction but on the other hand, when the customer loses money, as a result of any vulnerability in the bank's systems, the same customer will, naturally, accuse the bank of being too liberal with highly insecure practices.

4.10 Compliance to Policies is a Must in Any Organization

Detailed study of all compliance issues, banks' responsibilities to comply, the regulatory guidelines that are to be mandatorily complied with are provided in Module D under the Chapter on "IS Audit and Compliance". A brief insight into the compliance issues is given here.

Organisations especially banks have to comply with not only their regulatory guidelines (like RBI, TRAI, SEBI, etc.) but also their own policies and guidelines internally defined and accepted and approved. Consequences of non-compliance has serious ramifications and repercussions ranging from a simple payment of penalty to cancellation of the business license and ultimate closure of the organization itself.

Training on essentials of information security is a major area coming under security governance in any organization. Organisations conduct many training and awareness programs for their staff members. In fact, the Gopalakrishna Working Group 2011, of RBI has suggested training and awareness programs to not only all levels of staff members but also to customers by sensitizing them on subjects like frauds, protection of PIN and other cyber crime related areas. Security impacts every cadre of employees. Awareness initiatives should cover all the categories of employees and the seriousness of awareness should percolate from the top management to the lower categories of employees.

4.11 Monitoring

Success of security governance lies on the level of monitoring which the organization can ensure on implementation, adequacy of policies, compliance of policies, etc. Such monitoring initiative should include:

I. the reasons for non-compliance if any.

II. treatment of non-compliance.

III. corrective action wherever necessary and,

IV. feasible and preventive action wherever possible,

This is done to prevent recurrence of non-compliance. Security Incident Management, classification of incidents and their follow-up activities come under monitoring and are an integral part of security governance.

4.12 Before we conclude this chapter it is worthwhile to have a look at security governance from the psychological aspects of crime. From times immemorial, man has always been lured by lust, desires or greed. Analysis of fraud has always proved that there are three constituent factors to a fraud or a crime. Sometimes also known as Fraud Triangle, the three sides to a fraud are as follows:

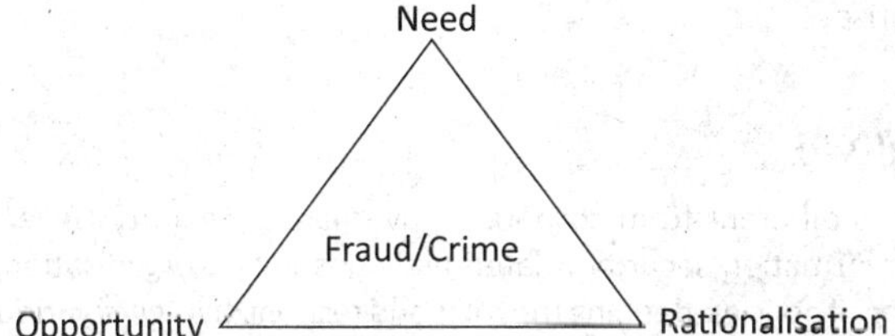

4.13 The picture above shows that behind every act of crime or fraud there are always the three factors in greater or lesser degree. First the need for the asset or money or property or a desire or greed. Second is the opportunity left behind by the owner of the property or asset or what is called the unmitigated risk or the vulnerability in the system. The third (and of course relevant for a study of psychology and not for a discussion in Information Security) is 'Rationalisation' meaning thereby the attitude of the fraudster to rationalise his fraudulent activity and justify himself stating 'every one commits a mistake so what if I do add one?'

4.14 It is this side of 'Opportunities' that Risk Analysis is all about. A proper study of risks will ensure that all vulnerabilities are taken care of and the system is well protected. Security is always considered to be only as strong as the weakest link. We have already seen that security is not a product but a process - a series of many activities ever dynamic and changing. Human element is generally considered to be the weakest link in security. Security is not a hundred per cent automated process and it is the human factor that implement security. Opportunities which sometimes tempt human beings, make the human factor the weakest link in security.

4.15 Before we conclude, it would be worthwhile to note that the best part of security governance lies in comparing the governance initiatives of the organisation with the Best Practices followed in the peer level industries and the Standards that may be adopted. *We have covered these areas (like ISO and ISMS Standards, COBIT and other practices etc.) in detail under Chapter 8.*

4.16 Though security governance is not a one-size-fits-all model that all organisations will have to follow a uniformly laid down policy and follow the guidelines evolved from it, there are many broader procedures and guidelines that may be uniformly applied across different industries and organisations. It is in this context that a study of best practices assumes importance. For instance, in the case of IT and IT enabled services, a study of IT Service Management and the relevance of all agreements and contracts incidental to it, is to be made. In the case of banks and other data critical industries wherein

security takes front stage, going in for compliance with ISMS and probably certification under the relevant standards of ISO 27001 will be useful.

4.17 Security Strategy is the high-level vision and direction for the security governance framework. It aligns with the organization's mission, values, and goals, and defines the scope, roles, and responsibilities of security governance. A security strategy also identifies the key security risks, threats, and opportunities that the organization faces, and sets the priorities and objectives for addressing them.

4.18 Security Policies are the formal rules and guidelines that specify how the organization should manage and protect its information assets. They establish the baseline requirements and expectations for security performance, compliance, and accountability. Security policies cover topics such as access control, data classification, encryption, incident response, backup, disaster recovery, and more.

4.19 Cloud Security Governance: Enterprises are increasingly pursuing the business advantages of migrating technology platforms and services into the cloud environment, leveraging one or more of the three main cloud service areas – Infrastructure as a Service (IaaS), Platform as a Service (PaaS), and Software as a Service (SaaS). These advantages include but are not limited to rapid information system deployment, significantly reduced operating costs, massive economies of scale, processing speed, and agility. However, subscription to these services often imply security and compliance challenges for enterprises.

Know Your Progress

Security Governance is different from corporate governance. Security Governance is the overall management of all information security related activities in the organisation, right from the top management's framing of policies, defining the roles and responsibilities of various users of the system and right upto the monitoring of effective implementation of all security initiatives.

Security Governance is an integral part of the organisation's information security structure and encompasses the information security policy, guidelines and procedures, framework and standards if any applicable.

Awareness and training are very much essential parts of security governance. Awareness programmes should be conducted not only for the employees but also for customers especially in banks. Banks should take steps to sensitize the customers on bank frauds, security of their user id, their passwords and PINs.

Effective monitoring is an essential part of security governance since only at this stage, the organisation will decide about the follow-up action on security incidents, corrective and preventive action and governance will be complete on a review and effectiveness of such follow-up action.

Key Words

Security Governance	Framework	Standards	Compliance
Regulatory	SEBI	KRA	TRAI

Questions

1. Information Security should normally be treated as____________________.
   a. governance issue that also includes technology, management and related areas
   b. technology issue that also includes governance and other organisational areas

c. management issue that is the concern of top management mainly but which may impact the lower rungs of management

d. serious issue of the system administrations and system managers since they are the ones who should be aware of security and be responsible for creating awareness too.

2. In Human Resource Management as part of security governance, KRA means_________.

a. Key Resource Areas that identifies the human resource potential and gets the best out of employees in security governance

b. Key Responsibility Assignments since it deals with responsibilities of top management which get delegated to lower levels in security governance

c. Key Responsibility Areas because it identifies persons with their roles and responsibilities which is essential in security governance

d. Key Resource Analysis since it analyses the key resources in HR and then security initiatives are assigned to individual employees based on their capability

3. The major task facing banks in India is the path towards a paperless, chequeless and cashless banking and it is_________________________.

a. impossible in today's scenario, although RBI has mandated it as per policy guidelines

b. quite an easy task provided the regulators namely the RBI evolves all the procedures and guidelines for the banks to follow and makes it mandatory

c. it is extremely difficult in today's conditions and may take decades for banks in India to follow and put in place

d. not easy and will take some time, but still has been happening globally and hence the nation has to proceed towards the goal

4. Security Governance essentially follows which of the below given steps ?

a. Handling people and processes at the top and right down up to the physical infrastructure governance including setting standards, monitoring etc.

b. Taking care of all security architecture in the top management level right from planning upto execution as per Plan Do Check Act model.

c. Ensuring proper awareness is spread on organisation security among all cadres of employees in the organisation with top management commitment.

d. Evolving proper standards for security, implementing them benchmarking them with the best in the industry.

5. "Customers normally prefer a bank which does not have strict security procedures implemented in it." Which one of the following justifies this ?

a. True, because such banks involve less procedures and Internet Banking with such banks is quite easy.

b. We cannot say because security governance basically ensures security of not only the bank's systems but essentially customers' balances with the bank.

c. False, customers do not prefer such a bank, but only those banks which enforces many procedures and insists on strict compliance.

d. True, because such banks spread a positive message to customers that their money is safe even without much hassles of security governance.

6. Electronic records maintained by a corporate undertaking are not valid as per the guidelines of SEBI. (True/False)

7. Compliance, monitoring and training are essential constituents of security governance in any organisation. (True/False)

Answers

1. *a*	5. *b*
2. *c*	6. True
3. *d*	7. True
4. *a*	

5 CHAPTER

Physical and Environmental Security

OBJECTIVES

After reading this chapter, the reader should be able to appreciate the various physical security issues and the devices and electronic gadgets used in implementing physical security. Environmental security issues, their areas of concern and related controls that should be in place.

Knowledge has always been considered to be power. The noted Chinese thinker and military strategist Sun Tzui in his famous book "The Art of War" reportedly written around 400 BC states that the defender of a village or a kingdom needed to anticipate enemy forces and develop specific defenses against them. Probably it is one of the earliest strategies to face a threat and ensure physical security.

5.1 Physical security is as old as history. We often read that in most of the ancient civilizations, the rulers did not place critical or confidential information in any permanent or physically easily accessible form. Confidentiality and maintenance of critical physical assets was always the prerogative of the ruler probably with the closest and choicest few of disciples and ministerial staff.

Physical Security is probably the simplest and the most fundamental form of security. It is the most fundamental, because its planning and implementation is quite easy to understand and does not require any technical know-how. Physical Security has been implemented right from mythological times in India. Interestingly, the earliest reference to physical security for an administrator or a kingdom dates back to the days of Kautilya (also known as Chanakya) who discusses the nuances of securing the physical barriers of a kingdom in his famous administrative treatise "Arthashastra" written around 300 B.C. Physical security of the rulers, the critical areas of the kingdom, the key personnel and of course valuable assets, has always engaged the attention of policy framers. Hence it can be said that physical security has been spoken about, right from the earliest days.

Physical movement of hardware equipment forms an essential part of physical security. Organisations have systems like hardware numbering, RFID (Radio Frequency Identification) based tracking etc. as part of Inventory Control and Management Systems. There are many customized software available for inventory tracking and inventory management. Putting in place proper inventory management including the hardware consumables will go a long way in not only physical monitoring but also in asset classification because identification of costly and critical equipment can easily be made with the help of such software. RFID token based monitoring will also help restricting movement of costly equipment out of the bin or the premises itself, as may be required. Using RFID is an effective preventive measure in physical security of hardware equipment as well as personnel who carry an RFID tag as part of their person.

Physical Security includes all the security initiatives to physically protect the information asset, the information asset owner, hardware and software associated with the physical asset. Basically it involves all those critical steps right from identifying the physical assets, its protection techniques, controls to be put in place and monitoring the effectiveness of measures taken to protect it. The main steps, therefore, can be summarized as follows:

I. Identifying the assets to be protected
II. Identifying the threats to such assets
III. Understanding the vulnerabilities of those assets
IV. Prioritisation of vulnerabilities
V. Amount and criticality of impact of risks to those assets
VI. Taking steps to protect such assets
VII. Implementing protection mechanism
VIII. Analysing the gap and studying the uncovered risks (residual risks)
IX. Review and effective monitoring the security measures taken

5.2 Let us now study the above steps of physical security in detail. All assets especially in information system, have a physical form to it. Hence, identifying the physical asset to be protected is the basic and a simple step. We have already seen in the earlier chapters that any asset may be classified depending on its monetary value, criticality, confidentiality, uniqueness and other factors. Hence depending upon such factors, the security initiatives are to be put in place. For instance, a costly high-end router may have to be protected in a secure area and its movement to be carefully documented. Nowadays smaller devices are hardly a few centimeters in size and have the capacity to store huge gigabytes of data. Hence physical security of such devices pose enormous responsibility to the security managers in any organisation.

A data centre room and the main entrance to an organisation or a car parking area in a company cannot be treated on the same level of criticality in physical security, though it is true that all these areas are anyway to be protected. The organisation has to identify what level of security the main entrance should have, probably called the first level and the next level say entry to the banking hall or visitors' hall or discussion room can have the second level.

The first level can have just an entry pass or a visitors' pass that would entitle the visitor to visit the building or probably the visitors' hall only. Then for entry into critical areas like data centre or a server room or the Network Operating Centre an additional level of security (say the third level or third layer of security) can be introduced. Entry to such area should be normally restricted unless accompanied by an employee of that department or that room and with a bio-metric entry or an entry in the Visitors' Book.

Issue of Vehicles Pass and Visitors Pass may be done at the first level at the main entrance. In the second level, permission to carry pen drive or a computer or an i-Pad, a tab or any mobile or any other electronic gadget with camera etc. may be handled and decisions may be taken accordingly. Similarly, for taking out any physical asset from the organisation too, strict rules should be in place. Organisations should have proper procedures to record movement of assets from out of the premises with a Pass sometimes with a remark "Returnable" or "Non-Returnable" so that the further follow up on such assets may be taken based on such classification.

Perimeter Security

Quite often organisations may like to guard their physical assets from any attacks right at the fence before entry in to the premises itself. Such perimeter security includes steps like barbed fencing, lubricated fencing, electronic walls, perimeter surveillance, CCTV surveillance at the main entrance or

even a few metres before the main entrance. Of late, use of electric fencing is also being experimented, though it is quite risky and involves legal issues. Electric fencing is a barrier that uses electric shocks normally to prevent animals (and sometimes human being too) from crossing a boundary which gives electric shocks to persons or animals coming into contact with. The shocks may be strong enough to deter them but mild enough not to cause a lethal injury. Premises housing critical infrastructure or highly mission critical systems, confidential equipment etc. may have sophisticated intrusion prevention devices or intrusion detection devices and movement in those areas may have to be meticulously monitored.

After identifying the information assets that are to be physically protected, the next major task will be to identify the threats to such assets. We have already seen that 'threat' is an external event or an attack which, if materialized, may cause an injury or a harm to the asset. Threats to a parking area may be different from the threat to a critical area like a data centre. Hence the physical security protection initiatives have to be designed accordingly. For the main entry, vehicles check, personal check would suffice, whereas for a data centre or a network centre, some employee to accompany the visitor will be desirable and may be essential too, as per the Information Systems Security Policy.

The next major task will be to understand the vulnerabilities to those assets. Since threat become risks, only when they meet some vulnerabilities in the system, risk actually materializes and therefore, organisation has to identify the vulnerability in any system. Improper check at the door, absence of visitors' book at critical areas, absence of CCTVs in main areas, inadequate guards are all vulnerabilities and it is these vulnerabilities that an unsuspecting fraudster will capitalize on and create a risk to systems.

After understanding the vulnerabilities, the organisation has to prioritise the vulnerabilities as to what is most critical and needs immediate attention. For instance, absence of security guard in an off-site ATM even for an hour or two, in a secluded area may be a source of great danger and may pose a major risk whereas in an on-site ATM it is not. The following are some of the commonly known vulnerabilities in physical security:

I. Frequent movement of hardware assets from and to the service centre
II. Improper records for movement of hardware items
III. Lack of procedure to format hard disk or other storage devices before they are given for servicing or surrendered in a buy-back arrangement
IV. Absence of security guards in critical areas during duty change-over timings
V. Inadequate procedure for vehicle check
VI. Inadequate procedure to check service personnel
VII. Letting the service personnel attend to problems in critical areas, unaccompanied

Analysing the vulnerabilities in information assets will lead us to the next step in study of criticality of impact of risks to those assets. If such vulnerabilities are a major risk to the organisation, then they should be attended to immediately involving the top management wherever necessary.

This should be followed by taking steps to protect such assets by plugging the vulnerabilities, spending on such infrastructure or enhancing the physical security measures in place or introducing any new area and additional step in physical protection like posting of an additional security guard, implementing a new procedure etc.

Implementing protection mechanism has to be done with utmost care and only when so felt necessary, can be conducted on an *ad hoc* basis. If the vulnerabilities will recur and the threat is likely to surface again, protection initiatives should be permanent and should be well documented.

Wherever the steps taken are not effective or what is planned could not be implemented, a proper analysis of the gap is to be made and the uncovered risks (residual risks) are to be addressed. It should

be the conscious decision of the top management to put up with such residual risk perhaps knowing well that mitigation of such risks may prove too costly and incurring such huge expenditure for such a small risk may not be a financially prudent decision.

In the end, a proper and balanced review of entire physical architecture, the threats faced, risks managed including those faced should be made. Based on such review, decisions like enhancing the preventive controls or detective controls, financial aspects of such preventive steps etc. are taken.

5.3 Physical Security Equipment

In physical security, it is the hardware that matters most. Having seen the features that influence the decision on physical security, let us now discuss some of the most popular physical security enablers like human resources, equipment and devices.

Human Resources in the form of security guards, armed guards, watchmen and other related personnel constitute physical security staff. While selecting recruits for such assignments, care must be taken to verify their antecedents. Much more than the value of goods in their custody, it is their integrity and their commitment that greatly influences the success of physical security in any organisation. Normally organisations prefer retired army officials or police officials since the main task involved would be managing the security personnel like security guards etc. Taking care of perimeter security, movement of hardware items in and out of the premises, movement of personnel in and out of the premises, protecting the vital resources, giving an additional layer of security for key areas like server room, CEO's cabins, etc. will be the main task involved at this stage.

After the HR component, it is the physical hardware gadgets and devices that play a vital role in physical security. Organisations have to decide the kind of weapons that are to be used and take care of license issues involved. For instance, banks do have the procedure of accompaniment of gun-trotting armed guards whenever cash in excess of a specific amount is to be transported between branches or to and from the currency chest. Similarly, outsourced ATM vendors do have the procedure of armed guard personnel accompanying cash in the van for loading in ATMs. It should be the duty of the Chief Security Officer to ensure proper personnel with licenses to handle the weapons are posted in such jobs.

Nowadays metal detectors are put to use at the main entrance in most of the organisations, which scan even the vehicles entering the premises. Though there are different types of metal detectors that can be deployed, the three most common metal detectors are as follows:

Very Low Frequency (VLF) detectors are the most versatile metal detector types, based on the range of metallic objects that can be found with them. Pulse Induction (PI) metal detectors send repeated pulses of electrical current to the search coil, producing a magnetic field and the coil transmits a pulse toward the ground, generating an answering pulse from the target object. They are used to detect objects buried deep underground, but they cannot discriminate against different types of metals. This flaw makes their use on inland sites extremely difficult. The Beat Frequency Oscillator (BFO) is the simplest (and oldest) type of metal detector technology and is a good starting point for learning how metal detectors work. The basic beat-frequency metal detector employs two radio frequency oscillators which are tuned near the same frequency.

In practice, however, it is commonly observed that even the security personnel who view the vehicles and personnel entering the premises, are neither aware of the features of the metal detector nor conversant with their capabilities to detect.

Video Surveillance

The next most popular physical security system is the CCTV and Video Surveillance mechanism. It is common in most of the organisations to install a camera at not only critical areas but also in common areas in the premises with a centralized monitoring computer that keeps displaying the images for viewing by the designated system security official. Nowadays reliable 24-hour CCTV surveillance is required for the ATMs in any bank. Especially in ATMs, a professional, fast-reacting system is required and hence cameras come well equipped with instant reactions to be of use in times of robbery and other kinds of attacks and other accidental damages like system failures etc. Besides reliable recording, the system should also enable real time transmission, clarity of recording, long-time video recording, simultaneous multi-site monitoring, enormous amount of storage and quick retrieval in times of need.

Among CCTVs, there are many variants and it should be a policy decision based upon factors like

I. Purpose of monitoring

II. Clarity required in the pictures

III. Evidentiary value of pictures

IV. Volume of picture to be captured

V. Criticality of the place

VI. Light availability in the place and the necessity to capture in darkness

VII. Movement of personnel anticipated in the area

Based on all these parameters, the CSO in charge of physical security will take the conscious decision about the nature of cameras to be deployed, the bandwidth of line to be procured and the type of storage to be preserved for it. With the ever increasing rise in cyber-crimes especially card skimming and fraudulent withdrawals from ATMs and PoS purchases, the CCTV footages in ATMs are a great boon to investigators and it is not just a favour from banks but a duty on their part to provide the necessary evidences in the form of CCTV clippings whenever required by the investigating agencies.

Of late CCTV surveillance is often being debated as an invasion into privacy. It has been a matter of very interesting debates whether such surveillance is necessary and If really felt so, whether organisations are justified in installing such cameras at all places in the work area. In many employees circles, such video monitoring of the work places is not well received by the employees. Quite naturally so, most of the employees find such monitoring itself an intrusion into their privacy and they do not want to be watched while at work.

It is becoming quite common to see CCTVs installed in most of the bank branches monitoring and recording a few places in the banking hall, cashier's cabin area and other select cabins in the branch. Organisations whether bank or others, a customer-centric institution or otherwise, should take care to see that installation of such CCTVs in very well within the overall Information Security - Physical Security monitoring and well documented with the consent of top management.

Alarms are the next major physical security gadget used in organisations. Even in rural bank branches, it is quite common for banks to install burglary alarm system, which is sometimes connected to the nearest police station, where the alarm sound will be heard. Besides, the volume of alarm is normally pitched very high and it automatically goes off, even when the main power is off, the moment the cash vault door or other designated door is sought to be opened by an intruder.

As an additional layer of security, critical rooms and highly secure part of the premises may be equipped with bio-metric enabled security check. Identified users already registered with their bio-metric information alone can access the secure area. Any new comer who has joined may have to first get his bio-metric (thumb impression, palm or retina) registered with the organisation and with such authorization only, he can enter the premises.

Fire extinguishers too come in different variants. There are different types of fire extinguishers like water extinguishers (used for paper, cardboard etc.) dry chemical extinguishers (filled with foam or powder like potassium bicarbonate or sodium bicarbonate pressured with nitrogen), carbon dioxide extinguishers (used for electrical or computer fire, etc). Of late, many organisations also go in for fire

sprinkler system used in factories and even in basement parking lots which when triggered, provides adequate pressure and flow-rate to water distribution to sprinkle water in specified areas.

By and large, physical protection to an information asset can be in any of the ways as shown in the diagram:

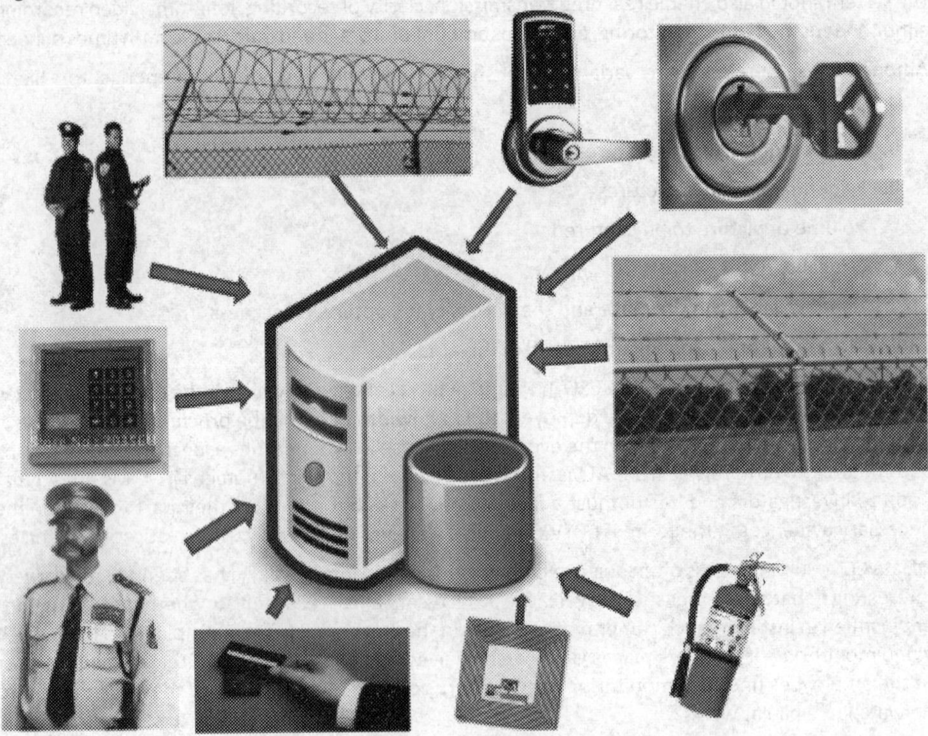

Physical Access Control mechanisms for Information Assets

5.4 Intrusion Prevention Systems (IPSs)

IPS are those that prevent an intruder from physically entering the system. In the physical security types as discussed above, fencing, posting of security guards, compound walls, barricades, bio-metric enabled door locking systems, smart card enabled door locking systems, manual door locking systems, etc. come under the category of Intrusion Prevention Systems. Devices such as monitoring through CCTVs, Video Surveillance, entries in the register etc. are mostly of Intrusion Detection types wherein they help in detecting which intruder would have done what and the type of corrective and remedial measures to be taken.

5.5 Decisions of the type of Physical Security is more an enterprise decision and not a technological decision, since the top management in consultation with the CISO and the CIO and if necessary with the assistance of external professional consultants will decide on the nature of device to be deployed, depending on factors like criticality of equipment, cost of replacement, amount of maintenance and service required, technicalities of maintenance and of course a proper Risk Analysis. Return of Investments in such investments should not be a criterion, since such investments are in the nature of insurance only.

5.6 Physical Security involves the co-ordination with the local fire service personnel of the city. Officials of Fire Service departments of the state inspect business establishments and certify them on their fire safety norms. Compliance with fire safety norms like availability of fire extinguishers, availability of emergency fire exit, conducting mock fire drills and evacuation tests etc. form part of such exercise. Periodic inspection is also conducted by fire service departments.

5.7 Environmental Security

The terms physical security and environmental security of information collectively refer to measures taken to protect systems, building and related supporting infrastructure including all information assets against threats associated with their physical environment. In the earlier part of this chapter, we discussed issues concerned with physical upkeep and protection of assets and in this part, let us focus on environmental issues.

Environmental security plays a vital role especially in those areas that are terrorists afflicted, prone to theft and larceny like an off-site ATM in a remote location, a rural branch of a bank in a village not accessible easily by road or with an access only through a river bridge that is prone to get submerged in times of floods etc. In all such cases, physical security assumes the greater role of environmental security also, since the information assets have to be protected from the environment as well.

Environmental security of information normally refers to protection of information assets against threats emanating from the environment. Some areas are prone to cyclones, floods, power surges, extreme temperatures etc. wherein the information assets have to be protected and guarded against such threats. Protection in such cases could be in the form of reliable UPS, generators, heaters, Air-conditioners, false-ceiling, false-roofing, vinyl flooring, raised flooring, etc.

Environmental security basically involves the study of threats posed by environmental events and threats to individuals, communities or nations and all kinds of environmental problems, mainly from an international perspective. Though it involves steps on prevention of or management of environmental risks and conflicts, from a study of information security we have to confine ourselves with the threats to the physical care of information assets or its maintenance and disposal causes to environment.

Physical protection of an information asset and human activity impacts carbon dioxide emission, functioning of servers and the heat generated by it impacting regional and global climatic and environmental changes. Study of green servers and energy conservation in this context is of greater relevance in physical security of information asset.

Organizations may also include within the scope of environmental security the threats that information assets may pose, such as those posted by e-waste and other electronic garbage. It is the responsibility of organizations to ensure that the disposal of e-waste does not harm the environment.

E-waste refers to discarded electronic or electrical devices such as old scraps of computer peripherals, wiring equipment, and electrical devices. There is a lack of consensus even among technical experts on how to dispose of such e-waste and how to protect the environment from it. Legally, it is now a compliance requirement for organizations to establish proper procedures for dealing with and disposing of old scrap hard disks, monitors, and all other computer devices and peripherals. In addition to environmental hazards, handling such e-waste poses a threat to human beings involved in reuse, recycling, or disposal. The disposal of e-waste is increasingly becoming a global concern, with various disposal methods being discussed in conferences and seminars, yet there is no globally accepted practice.

Pollution control guidelines are to be followed. Such guidelines differ on the basis of the nature of industries like chemicals, hardware manufacturing, engineering, computer chip making and designing and programming etc. For a software industry or a bank, the environmental security will normally focus on the following:

i. AC equipment

ii. Power generators and the fumes generated by it

iii. Data cabling and electrical cabling

iv. E-wastage and threats due to scavenging

v. Disposal of old unusable electronic gadgets etc.

Know Your Progress

Physical Security is the study of physically securing the information assets, the threats and attacks to it, the vulnerabilities in the system and the risks that it is exposed to. There are different types of physical threats to an information asset like man-made attacks in the form of theft, larceny, burglary etc. natural disasters like floods, cyclone, etc. and environmental attacks like extreme temperature.

Depending upon the type of physical threat feared and the nature of vulnerabilities, the remedial and protective steps to ensure physical security are taken. Intrusion prevention steps at the perimeter level includes steps like fencing, posting of armed guards, barricades, etc. and intrusion detection steps include monitoring equipment like CCTVs and video surveillance. Ensuring optimum physical security involves steps like posting of personnel, deploying adequate security gadgets, utilizing proper equipment like appropriate fire extinguishers and other devices.

It should be the constant endeavour of CISO to ensure that the assets are guarded against not only all physical threats but also environmental attacks of that locality. Besides protecting their assets from environmental threats, organizations should also take steps to ensure that the environment is safeguarded from threats posed by the organization itself through the disposal of e-waste.

Key Words

E-waste	Intrusion Prevention	Intrusion Detection	Surveillance
CCTV	Perimeter Security	Metal Detector	RFID
Bio-metric	Barricades	Fire Extinguisher	Electric Fence

Questions

1. Electric fencing is used by organisations to prevent ....from entering the premises or the compound by ....

a. people, giving them mild shock when they try to trespass

b. people and livestock, giving them mild shock to deter them from trespassing

c. animals, giving them shock enough to cripple them for the time being

d. unauthorised entry, passing high voltage shocks through the wires

2. .... is normally considered to be the most versatile metal detector based on the range of objects that can be detected.

a. High Detector Objects

b. Pulse Induction (PI) type

c. Beat Frequency Oscillator (BFO)

d. Very Low Frequency (VLF)

3. For successful tracing of hardware equipment, through RFID________________.
   a. hardware equipment is to be numbered properly and well maintained by personnel with RFID devices with them
   b. hardware and personnel to be tracked should have the radio frequency tags attached to them
   c. persons who are monitoring the hardware equipment should have the RFID devices with them
   d. it would be very difficult since all hardware equipment cannot be monitored through it, technologically
4. For protecting computer and electrical devices against fire the type of fire extinguishers used is____________________.
   a. dry chemical extinguishers
   b. power based extinguishers
   c. carbon dioxide based extinguishers
   d. sprinklers based extinguishers to forcibly put out fire
5. Which of the following statement is true in the case of CCTV Video Surveillance ?
   a. Video Surveillance is required only for critical hardware equipment since it is very costly to implement and lay the cables for the same.
   b. Video Surveillance is not possible in the case of off-site ATMs because a 24 x 7 recording will consume enormous amount of disk space.
   c. CCTV cannot be installed in public places like car parks, lobby, etc. in organisations especially public sector banks, because it amounts of violation or privacy rights.
   d. Video Surveillance is required not only to watch the movement of hardware equipment but also to monitor movement of human beings too.
6. As part of physical security, Bio-metric checking is a____________________.
   a. powerful Intrusion Prevention System
   b. useful Intrusion Detection System
   c. dependable monitoring system to check the movement of unauthorised personnel
   d. reliable authorization process for hardware equipment and personnel
7. In the IT industry, pollution control guidelines and environmental pollution procedures____________.
   a. do not apply since nothing on chemical treatment is dealt with here
   b. are normally applicable, since disposal of e-waste etc. do form part of environmental control
   c. cannot be applicable since there is no pollution from IT industry and there must be separate guidelines for IT industry
   d. can be optionally made applicable if the IT industry is also engaged in hardware manufacturing or servicing or other kinds of polluting activities.
8. Perimeter security refers to protecting the compound wall of the industry. (True/False)
9. Sprinkler extinguishers are normally used to put out fire in closed areas other than the computer rooms. (True/False)

10. CCTV and Video Surveillance footages are normally recorded and preserved for the specified period as per the policies of the bank. (True/False)

Answers

1. *b*	6. *a*
2. *d*	7. *b*
3. *b*	8. False
4. *c*	9. False
5. *d*	10. True

6

CHAPTER

Hardware Security

OBJECTIVES

After reading this Chapter, the readers will be able to understand the nuances of hardware security, different hardware and peripherals to a computer and types of equipment to protect those devices. Different types of network devices commonly used in banks and protection mechanism for all such devices are also discussed.

6.1 Hardware

We have already seen that hardware is the body of any IT organisation. If hardware is the body, then software is the soul or life that makes the body function. Hence, there can be no debate on which is - hardware or software - more crucial and more critical for the success of an organisation. We have also seen how physical security is very important in protecting the hardware assets in any organisation. In this chapter, we will discuss the various hardware equipments used in IT, especially in banks, and how security is to be enforced for all this hardware.

Basically hardware used in banks can be classified into the following categories:

I. PCs, Laptops, Nodes or Workstations used as desktop or as front-end
II. Servers that are connected to a number of PCs or nodes or workstations
III. Network related devices like routers, switches, hubs
IV. Peripherals like printers, fax machines
V. Customer centric delivery channel equipment like ATMs, PoS Devices
VI. Other devices like Mobile phones

In this section, we will focus on the security concerns of all these hardware equipment.

Days are gone when the officials in the organisation had some physical files in their desktop, stacked one above the other or in a huge filing cabinet at the side. Now-a-days, most officials keep just a laptop or a desktop PC at their working places. The PC is used as a standalone system to store the individual records of the official and when connected, acts as a workstation accessing the intranet resources or internet resources as may be required and does computing as a front-end processor accessing a remote server of the organisation.

In this scenario, it would be the responsibility of the individual official to physically take care of the hardware along with the attachments like mouse, keyboard or monitor as the case may be. The

Information Systems Security Policy of any organisation also makes this ownership and responsibility clear on the part of individual owners and custodians of the respective hardware equipment.

Work from home

Of late, it has become quite common for people to work from home in many IT corporations and MNCs. In such cases, the laptop systems provided to an official is sometimes kept at the office and sometimes brought to home where the official works. In these cases too, the ISS Policy of the organisation has to provide for this scenario so that the physical security of the laptop while at home or during transit and while at office is properly taken care of with due procedural precautions in place.

Similarly, there are occasions when some designated officials of the organisations are entitled to carry pen-drives or portable hard-disks with them, wherever they go, carrying enormous amount of confidential and classified information about the organisation, considering the sensitive and responsible cadre that the employee occupies. In these cases too, it will be with proper procedures laid down in this regard with adequate precautions classifying the nature of information and the type of hardware the employee takes.

On the other side of Work From Home is the concept of Bring Your Own Device (BYOD) a practice of allowing the employees to bring their own PCs --- or in the modern days, their own tabs, mobile phones, etc. — to the office and work on them. A physical use of their own PC is BYOD and sometimes when the employees bring their own technology that gets integrated into the organisation's data or otherwise, access to the data is permitted with it, it is BYOT (Bring Your Own Technology).

The concept of BYOD is gaining in importance with more and more employees using their own PCs or mobile devices and freely accessing the critical data of the organisation from such devices. Though quite common and very useful from the employees and the management perspective too, this practice of BYOD is a cause for growing concern for the security managers. Security in a BYOD environment mainly addresses the following issues:

I. Device Management:
    - Ensuring that all devices connected to the network comply with security policies.
    - Implementing measures for remote device tracking, monitoring, and management.

II. Data Protection:
    - Encryption of data on devices to prevent unauthorized access in case of device loss or theft.
    - Establishing protocols for secure data storage and transmission to mitigate the risk of data breaches.

III. Authentication and Access Control:
    - Implementing strong authentication mechanisms such as multi-factor authentication to enhance access security.
    - Defining and enforcing access controls to restrict unauthorized users from accessing sensitive information.

IV. Network Security:
    - Securing the network infrastructure to protect against unauthorized access and potential attacks.
    - Implementing Virtual Private Network (VPN) solutions for secure data transmission over public networks.

V. Application Security:

- Ensuring that applications on BYOD devices are regularly updated and patched to address security vulnerabilities.
- Monitoring and managing permissions for applications to prevent malicious activities.

VI. User Education and Awareness:

- Providing comprehensive training to users about security best practices and the potential risks associated with BYOD.
- Encouraging users to report any security incidents promptly.

VII. Policy Development and Enforcement:

- Developing clear and comprehensive BYOD security policies that align with organisational objectives.
- Enforcing adherence to policies through regular audits and assessments.

VIII. Endpoint Security:

- Installing and updating antivirus, anti-malware, and endpoint protection software on devices.
- Implementing measures to detect and respond to security threats on individual devices.

IX. Incident Response and Monitoring:

- Establishing an incident response plan for timely detection, containment, and resolution of security incidents.
- Implementing continuous monitoring systems to identify unusual or suspicious activities.

Addressing these issues comprehensively helps organisations create a secure BYOD environment that balances the flexibility and productivity gains associated with BYOD while mitigating the associated security risks.

After the PCs, laptops, net books and notebooks, the next common hardware used in banks is what is commonly known as 'servers'. A server platform refers basically to a software program but is quite often referred to the hardware in which the software runs, used essentially to provide 'service' to many client systems (PCs or nodes) connected to the server in a network. The client-server is the most common architecture in banks, be it a branch in a LAN (Local Area Network) or a WAN (Wide Area Network) spread over a vast geographical area across the globe. Servers normally have a high processing capacity, higher storage capacity and other hardware resources depending upon factors like

I. Operating System and the Database to be deployed

II. Number of client PCs they serve

III. Amount of processing speed required

IV. Volume of data to be stored

V. Availability required like 24 x 7 basis

VI. Requirement of redundancy, backup and reliability.

Servers are used for multifarious purposes like database servers e.g. Oracle, Sybase, SQL Server, Windows Cloud Servers 2012 for cloud computing, Windows Server 2008, Linux Server and Unix servers from IBM, HP, Sun in their respective Unix flavours. Besides these Operating System based servers, there are also servers used for specific utilities like Print Server, Network Server, Mail Server, Web Server, WAP Server, etc. all of which cater to the individual uses.

Just like PCs have designated uses and ownership, the servers too should have specific ownership, custody, use and access. Assignment of individual ownership and responsibility as well as custody of commonly accessed servers across a huge network, has always engaged the attention of top management.

Organisations often lack proper water tight arrangement in fixing the responsibilities for maintenance of servers. This has been one of the grey areas in ISS Policy implementation in most of the undertakings especially in those banks and undertakings wherein hardware maintenance and server system related jobs are outsourced.

In the event of even a small incident especially when there is no proper Incident Management System in place (*Incident Management is dealt with in detail in Chapter 17*) such undertakings find it difficult to fix responsibility and ultimately somehow tide over the crisis more on an *ad hoc* basis.

The other commonly used servers are:

a. ***Web Server:*** Stores files related to websites and serves them through Internet to client users in web browser. Apache is regarded to be the most popular web server program.

b. ***Mail Server:*** Basically a program responsible for receiving, routing, and delivering e-mail messages. It is the computerized equivalent of post office enabling sending mails through a series of mail servers along the way to its intended recipient.

c. ***File Server:*** Normally software or dedicated hardware with the program for storing files and making them accessible for reading and writing to clients (*i.e.*, users) across a network.

d. ***Print Server:*** A software or a dedicated hardware that manages one or more printers in a network, sometimes with capability to block some printers and permit some printers enabled by switches or VLAN (Virtual LAN) switches.

e. ***Network Server:*** A dedicated server which manages network traffic. Sometimes it runs some special network management software like HP's Open View or CA's Network Monitoring Software (NMS) or other such tools

f. ***Database Server:*** It allows clients to interact with a database like an Oracle Server or a Sybase or SQL Server allowing different client users to access the database running in this dedicated server.

Technically, however, it is possible for a computer to be both a client and server simultaneously, by connecting itself and accessing its own resources. A single computer can have multiple server software applications running on it. It is the program and the hardware resources in the system that distinguishes itself from a PC and makes it a server. Many large enterprises employ numerous dedicated server machines.

A collection of servers in one location is commonly referred to as a ***server farm***. If very heavy traffic is expected in any server, of late it is a common practice to deploy ***load balancing*** essentially a software that is usually employed to distribute the requests among the various servers so that no single machine is over strained.

Due to the continual demand for more powerful servers in ever decreasing spaces, higher density configurations have been developed. Typically, in banks with pressure to process large volume of data and store enormous amount of data in systems like data warehouse etc., there is always an ever increasing need for huge storage occupying less space. A ***blade server*** is a stripped down server computer or to be precise, a design optimized to minimize the use of physical space and energy. In other words, blade server incorporates a number of sets of server hardware, each housed inside a high-density module known as a blade enclosure, within the space normally occupied by a single computer server.

6.2 Network Related Devices Like Routers, Switches, Hubs

In these days of networking, with almost nothing happening with a standalone computer, the importance of network equipment needs no specific emphasis. Without network and some sort of connectivity, no computing will be complete and literally nothing happens in a computerized world. Computer Network devices are sometimes known as communication devices as they mainly transmit or enable transmission of communication across network. Based on the functionality and the need, the most appropriate of these devices is to be selected. Modems, Routers, Switches, Bridges, Gateways, Firewalls, LAN Cards, CSU/DSU, ISDN Terminals, trans-receivers are some of the well-known network devices. Let us briefly discuss the features of these and the security concerns associated with each.

MODEM is the abbreviated form for Modulator and DEModulator. It is a device that transforms digital signals into analog signals (*i.e.* sound which only can traverse through telecommunication lines) and put them in the telecom network and then at the other end of communication, from the telecom network converts the analog data back to digital data and puts them in computers. Modems are also used in ISDN (Integrated Services Digital Network) to ensure faster reliable transmission of data along with voice and other data formats also.

Repeater is used to connect two segments of network with retimings and which regenerates the signals to proper amplitudes and sends them to other segments. Normally the number of repeaters in a row is limited by network architecture to ensure fast transmission of data.

Router is among the most commonly used network equipment in banking and all network-centric organisations. Router is an intelligent device that reads the information in each data packet and is used to route data packets between two networks. Depending upon the particular type of router, its capability to rewrite the routing pattern, to route the packet through the shortest path, to store the routing information, to readdress the packet etc. can all be properly exploited.

Router is an important device to be protected and securely handled from security point of view. A fraudster getting access to routing design and architecture can create *havoc* in the organisation, which can be detected only by people with requisite expertise in the field. Since routers can do some switching functions and some firewall functions. So, it is essential that access to router should be well protected. Physical access to router should be restricted and any configuration changes to routers should be meticulously documented and with proper authority.

Gateway It translates information between different network data formats or network architectures. Normally it operates at the application layer of OSI (Open Systems Interconnection) Model but sometimes it can operate at the network or session layer of OSI model also, doing essentially the activities of protocol translation and signal translation.

Switch In a telecommunications network, a switch is an intelligent device that channels incoming data from any of multiple input ports to the specific output port that will take the data to the proper address of the packet. By proper configuration of switches, it can be ensured that one segment of LAN is not accessible to another or a VLAN is created within a group of PCs in a LAN segment. Thus management can ensure one PC or a group of PCs in a LAN is not accessible to the other PCs. Hence it is all the more essential that switch configuration and the necessary documentation should be kept highly confidential. There are many security issues concerning switches and maintenance of switch configuration. Unauthorised access to switching devices in a network or the switch configuration falling into wrong hands can cause irreparable damage to the network.

There are many vendors and brands for this networking equipment. Some of the popular ones are: Cisco, D-Link, Intel, Nortel, Juniper, etc. A well designed IT infrastructure with the proper placement of the routers, servers, gateway and switches can reduce the operational cost and enhance the overall performance dramatically. A well protected configuration of all these devices will go a long way in enhancing the security architecture of the organisation.

Network Interface Card (NIC): It is a computer circuit inside the computer (which was a separate card in the earlier computer systems, a few years ago) which connects the computer in a network. While the IP Address is basically a network address of 4 sets of digits delimited by dots allotted by a software and dynamically identifying the computer system in a network, the NIC is the corresponding hardware address also known as the MAC (Media Access Control) given to the network adaptor when it is manufactured, by the original manufacturer and is always permanently embedded and unique to the system.

From a study of IT Security point of view, the MAC address and the IP address are of vital significance especially for cyber forensics purposes for identifying and tracing a data packet in a network and is a very important digital evidence in the cybercrime scenario. The MAC address with the IP Address is of absolute importance in crime detection and evidentiary value. Unlike the IP address, the MAC address in the hardware is often a set of six pairs of two characters each (alpha numeric) out of which the first three octets most often represent the manufacturer of the card (like Dell, Cisco, Nortel, etc.) and is allotted and embedded at the manufacturing stage.

Besides the above network appliances, nowadays many devices and gadgets are available across the shelf to study, monitor and analyze the network, some with its own embedded software and operating system and some with the standard operational system like Windows.

Network Meter is one such gadget app for Windows Vista and Windows 7, developed by Keat, providing an IP monitoring tool for the desktop sidebar, with features like display of signal quality, IP address, External IP address, IP lookup with Google maps, Speed test, upload and download speed and amount of usage. It effectively monitors the network irrespective of whether the connection is secured or not.

Study of network devices will not be complete without understanding the latest in the series *viz* gizmo devices. Simply called 'gizmos', it is a term often referring to a mechanical or any other device whose name is not known or is forgotten or a device which cannot be named. Especially in these days of increasing spyware (*i.e.* a software which does spying in the computer system tracing the addresses, email ids, user names, passwords or other vital information), these digital gadgets act as hardware spies.

For a study of IT Security, there are many factors associated with a spying device like a spy camera affixed in a pen or in a button in shirt, or in a wrist watch or in a sunglass etc. A spyware device has to be looked at from the angle of legal permission to use the same, digital forensic significance, the social threat, invasion of privacy etc. Of late, it has become fashionable to plant a spy camera in a shirt button or a wrist watch and to video record the conversation and use the same (or misuse it, if so required too). Such a strategy is often adopted not just for cyber espionage or other forms of spying but even by the Press as a sting operation to trap a person performing an illegal activity like receiving a bribe etc. to make good news story perhaps as investigative journalism.

From a network security and hardware security point of view, it is worthwhile to note that spy camera and recordings are of various types. Spy cameras (very small button sized devices) have been installed by cyber criminals near the numeric pad of the ATM or near the card swiping or dipping slot in an ATM and the finger movement of the hand is recorded when the PIN is typed. Enabled with a GSM communication, the information is passed on to the nearest receiving station around 100 meters away. Such a technology is adopted in many hotel rooms and many unseemly places too to spy the movement of people or to videograph their activities. Though the technology adopted and the communication strategy followed may be different, from an IT security perspective, it is absolutely illegal from a legal point of view (not just unethical from a social angle) and certainly punishable.

Besides the network related equipment, there are many peripherals like printers, fax machines etc. that are normally used in organisations. There are many types of printers and some of the popular ones are as follows:

I. Dot Matrix Printers working on the pixel.

II. Toner Based Liquid Inkjet Printers.

III. Solid Ink Printers.

IV. Dye Sublimation Printers.

V. Inkless Printers.

VI. Fast Line Printers connected to Servers.

Nowadays printers with IP addresses *i.e.* IP based printers have become quite common. In a huge office set up, when a IP printer is used, it becomes easier for the system administrator to control the use of printer, print the relevant and important documents only and to ensure that proper network security is built around the printer. In all these it is the printer enabled with IP addresses that should engage the attention of security managers and be of interest in our study. Security Managers should decide on issues like giving access to such printers or restricting it configuring the network accordingly or enabling access only from some systems in the network etc. Besides, even the print-outs in such devices have to be maintained, depending upon the nature of information getting printed.

Care has to be exercised about the printer buffer in such printer and any buffer as a result of incomplete printing or discarded printing jobs has to be cleared and such print-outs have to be destroyed immediately. It is such IP based printers that cause a great deal of concern to security managers since some do not know the criticality of such printers and the fraudsters will be looking for such vulnerabilities in the system for information stealing or unauthorised access to information.

The latest in printing technology is 3D printing also known as additive manufacturing, is a process of making three dimensional solid objects from a digital file. This is an additive process, since it involves laying down successive layers of material until the entire object is created. Due to the increased usage, the cost of 3D printing is coming down and is becoming more common especially in medical usage, engineering and manufacturing sectors. From security point of view, the enhanced clarity of 3D printing is by itself a threat if the security of the design of the product is an issue.

ATMs and other Customer centric delivery channel equipment: Of late, ATMs are becoming the most sought after delivery channel for customers. Banks these days display notice boards discouraging customers from entering the premises for normal cash withdrawals when there is an ATM in the premises. Hence ATMs as a hardware device play a vital role and have to be carefully guarded against threats and attacks. Though ATMs maintenance are normally outsourced by most of the banks, it is still imperative that bank officials should be reasonably aware of ATMs, their hardware components, the criticality in each of these and the security initiatives that should be in place to protect them.

There are many other hardware devices and gadgets like Mobile phones that are used in organisations especially in banks which are critical hardware devices. Criticality of such devices, instructions on maintenance of such devices and Operating Manual on those devices should be made available to persons who operate them and the related service engineers. Such documents should be well protected against unauthorised use.

Having studied the security issues in hardware devices and equipment and before we go into software security, let us discuss the security concerns in some networking designs and architecture. These are not hardware boxes but are sometimes dedicated hardware equipment or have dedicated computer systems used exclusively. Only some of the popular networking systems and methodologies are discussed here.

Very Small Aperture Terminals (VSATs) are hardware devices used in data communication especially in WAN network. VSAT comes with an ODU *i.e.* an Out Door Unit consisting of a dish shaped antenna for receiving and transmitting data, voice and other signals and an IDU *i.e.* an In Door Unit which is a small device used for transferring data, voice and video from the computer to the ODU.

Maintenance of VSAT equipment is quite crucial for organisation, though in practice, VSATs require very less maintenance and are quite rugged. Since VSATs are normally placed on roof-tops of high rise buildings, sometime on rental basis, access to them is a cause for concern. Physical protection of VSATs should be given importance.

Cabling used in communication, especially those involving very huge cost like Fiber Optic cables should be well protected and guarded against physical loss or theft or sabotage.

Other communication equipment like Radio and Wireless Communication and related devices should be well protected. There should be proper documentation on physical maintenance of these, like a well drafted Service Level Agreement with conditions for physical access and restricted access and responsibilities for failures, etc.

Network equipment like Firewalls and dedicated Firewall Servers: Access to Firewall Servers should be strictly restricted and physical access to such systems should be strictly monitored. While firewalls should be in place for restricting and monitoring access to outside world, access to such firewalls itself should be restricted to ensure that security features are not compromised at the administrator level.

Network equipment and communication devices where MPLS (Multi-Protocol Label Switching) devices should be properly configured and well protected. Similarly, organisations which have opted for MLLN (Managed Leased Line Network) from providers like MTNL or BSNL or others should have proper dedicated systems for the purpose and they should be well protected from physical attacks.

We will be studying more on network threats in the later chapters.

Hence it would suffice to note here that there is nothing like a hundred per cent secure network, though it should be a constant and persistent endeavour for the security managers to aim for it. In a network, any computer is always prone to an attack or has been part of some attack at some point of time.

A standalone computer is certainly the safest and most secure. But these days, it would be almost impossible to visualize any computer worthwhile and to be of some use, if it is not connected. In network parlance, an air-gapped computer is one that is neither connected to the internet nor connected to other systems that are connected to the internet. If any computer system requires utmost security and in depth security because of the data kept in the system, 'air gaps' are implemented. For example, in a computer which has stored and which processes credit and debit card transactions or those which contain some critical data. In most of the organisations, critical systems like payment and industrial control systems are on internal networks and are not connected to the company's business network, so that intruders cannot enter the corporate network through the internet of the organisation.

Hardware Attacks:

Manufacturing backdoors: Manufacturing backdoors can allow unauthorized users to circumvent normal security measures and also gain root access to the hardware. Likewise, backdoors can then install malware or other malicious code.

Eavesdropping: The malicious actors gain access to protected memory without opening other hardware devices.

Inducing faults: Such kinds of attacks disrupt the normal behaviour of a device. It can have knock-on effects as other hardware and software relying on the normal operation of the infected hardware then fail to function.

Hardware modification: In this, the modifications are aimed at tampering with a device's normal functioning and overriding restrictions on its operation.

Backdoor creation: These are the hidden methods for bypassing normal computer authentication systems.

Counterfeiting product assets: These attacks can produce extraordinary operations and allow malicious access to systems.

Know Your Progress

If hardware is the body of IT, software is the soul. Together they constitute the complete IT infrastructure. Right from PCs and Servers different types of hardware are used in IT organisations especially in banks. Many network equipment items are also used in banks, such as modems, routers, and switches, each with specific functions and features tailored to individual needs. It would be the security managers' responsibility to understand the delicacy of hardware equipment and ensure that security is not compromised on the use of such devices.

Like general purpose hardware devices, there are also network equipment and other dedicated hardware boxes specifically used for a particular software or a particular technology. Network equipment quite often are used as spying devices by cyber criminals. In such a case, the job of security managers become more complex rendering the security initiatives a techno-legal issue. Especially when a hardware is owned by the employee and is being used in the organisation, as a Bring Your Own Device, it becomes all the more difficult to ensure security for the organisation data as well as for the personal data of the user and owner of such devices.

Key Words

PoS Devices	Web Server	Load Balancing	Mail Server
Blade Server	Router	Switch	VSATs
BYOD	Air gaps computer		

Questions

1. In BYOD kind of environment, the security concerns are mainly with regard to ________.
   a. the safety of the data in the device and the security of the organisation data that is being accessed from anywhere
   b. the application of RBI guidelines on the use of BYOD as per RBI BOD circulars issued from time to time in this regard
   c. applicability of security initiatives for the devices as may be prescribed by the owner of the device
   d. application of the security policy of the organisation when it is in conflict with the security guidelines for the device as may be prescribed by the owner of the device being used for the organisation
2. Printers enabled with IP addresses are preferred by organisations because________
   (*i*) IP address can be traced and such printers can be accessed from anywhere
   (*ii*) access to such printers can be restricted and allowed as per policy in force
   (*iii*) such printers give absolute clarity in printing and cannot be stolen easily
   (*iv*) they can be installed in a remote location over a network access also
      a. All except (*i*) are correct
      b. All except (*ii*) are correct
      c. All except (*iii*) are correct
      d. All except (*iv*) are correct

3. Which one of the following can be called an air gap in computers?
   a. A computer that is well protected by a Firewall.
   b. PC that is not connected in a network and not used in the connectivity.
   c. A network protocol that permits the authorized user to access the network resource.
   d. A network IOS permitting the data access through specific authorization only.
4. Blade Servers can best be described as ________________.
   a. servers that occupy only rack space and are environment friendly
   b. servers capable of blade like sharp processing under the latest Core technology in processing that will enable huge CBS data processing
   c. enabled with high-end sharp processors and introduced by HP specifically for use in Big Data operations
   d. stripped down version of servers optimizing the server space incorporating a number of hardware sets
5. In software access control, the process of confirming that a user is what he claims to be is____________.
   a. Both IP Address and MAC address serve as cyber forensic evidences that can be captured from a computer system
   b. IP Address is generally dynamic and can be changed whereas a MAC address is permanently embedded into the system
   c. Both IP Address and MAC address can be changed dynamically in a network, depending upon the network protocol
   d. IP Address is protocol independent whereas a MAC address is assigned by the manufacturer himself
6. What is the other name for additive manufacturing technology?
   a. Bar Code printing
   b. 3D printing
   c. IP Sec manufacturing
   d. Print Server manufacturing
7. A load balancing server is put to use mainly for the purpose of________________.
   a. reducing the work load of a common print server to distribute the printing jobs among various printers
   b. balance the work of front end processes accessing the CBS server so that the network traffic is not unnecessarily overburdened at one point and free at other points
   c. distribute the network traffic or queries from various servers into a common database server and thus reduce the strain on its processor
   d. evenly distribute the queries and mails from various servers among a server farm and ensure every query or mail is processed immediately
8. A VLAN cannot be configured without the use of a Gateway to serve as a router. (True/False)
9. Like BYOD, the other technology used these days is BYOT. (True/False)
10. VSATs are communication equipment used for transmission of digital data only. (True/False)

Answers

1. *a*	6. *b*
2. *c*	7. *c*
3. *b*	8. False
4. *d*	9. True
5. *c*	10. False

7

CHAPTER

Software and Operational Security

OBJECTIVES

In this chapter, need for security in software and the different types of security initiatives in it and those in software applications especially in banking industry are presented. After reading this chapter, you would have understood, the meaning and significance of Operational Security a broader concept that encompasses the entire process of asset classification and identification leading to Risk management and ultimately ending with taking measures for security. A brief insight into operational security aspects of various industries is also provided.

7.1 Software Security is a major critical area in any undertaking especially in those organisations that deal with software or is highly software dependent. Let us discuss the different types of software used in organisations especially in banks and the issues concerning their access, maintenance and security.

Software can be broadly classified as:

a. **System Software:** Normally the operating systems that are essential to run the computer like the age-old MS-DOS, Windows in all its versions and releases, Unix (with all its variants and brands). Linux (different flavours) etc. Of late, routers come with their own Operating Systems like the popular routers of Cisco coming with their Operating System called IOS (Internetwork Operating System) used on the vast majority of Cisco routers. For mobile phones, operating systems like Android considered to be the most popular of Mobile Operating Systems, or Windows Phone 7 for Windows based mobile phones are also available.

b. **Application Software:** This software is developed to handle a specific task or a series of tasks to cater to the particular requirements of users, such as Core Banking Solutions. BaNCS developed by TCS, Flexcube from iFlex and Finacle from Infosys are all classic examples of Banking Application Software (CBS products) in the banking industry. Besides, customized applications for Foreign Exchange modules, Funds and Treasury Management, Inventory Management, Internet Banking, RTGS (Real Time Gross Settlement) and related e-payments are also available that can integrate into the existing CBS application and database in banks.

c. In the context, a study of 'apps' would be quite relevant here. Perhaps in the present world of computerization and a mobile becoming almost part of a body, everyone uses the word "apps" which commonly denotes a self-contained program or piece of software designed to fulfil a particular purpose. Hence an app is basically an application software normally a small, specific purpose one, downloaded by a user to a mobile device. Though the word 'app' is an abbreviation for 'application', which may be downloaded in a computer system and used in Internet as an independent software program. In today's parlance, the word is used to refer to an application downloaded and used in mobile and normally refers to a mobile application only.

Security concerns in a mobile and mobile app will be later dealt with in the Chapter on Software Security Controls while discussing the various types of mobile applications.

d. **Off-the-shelf software:** Software that generally provides standard functions applicable across a variety of users in different industries is called off-the-shelf software. If developed exclusively for users, such software would otherwise prove very costly and be unaffordable. Software like MS Office and utility programs such as Adobe Photoshop are examples of such software that can be procured and used.

e. Now-a-days, Open Source Software are also available, which can be downloaded or procured almost free of cost and can be customized since the source code for such software will also be available along the executable programs. Such software is gaining in popularity in modern days, since users have the liberty to access the source code and amend wherever required and have a customized and appropriate solution almost free of cost, with no stringent licensing regulations.

Besides, there are also other kinds of software sometimes referred to as **'rogue software'** which security managers should be aware of and be prepared to manage in times of need. Malware (short form for malicious software) is a software that is written and designed to cause damage or other loss to computer resource or systems. It is these kinds of software that are unauthorised and unintended that the security managers should be concerned about much more than the first four kinds of software discussed above.

Adware is an advertising supported software package which automatically plays, displays or downloads advertisements when the user is just browsing. Often considered to be an irritation, still they are sometimes viewed too.

There are many other specific-purpose software applications sometimes packaged with particular hardware, such as data backup and recovery software useful for certain operating systems. Security managers should address issues relating to all such software applications that are running in the organisation and ensure that the ISS Policy especially in areas of Access Control, Authorization and Authentication provides for proper security in such software too.

We have already seen the meaning and significance of Access Privileges and Access Rights. Now, let us discuss two terms that are closely associated with it namely Authorization and Authentication.

Authorization is the process of giving permission to someone to access or do or have something. In physical access, we have already seen that only authorised personnel can be permitted to enter a protected premises or to enter a particular room like server room. The process of granting permission for such entry is called authorization.

Authentication is the process of determining whether someone or something is, in fact, who or what it is declared to be. When a user id is entered, the process of asking for password is the verification that the user is actually the person who he or she claims to be and this is authentication. We normally authorise a user and authenticate the transaction (of verification of password, or access right or posting of an entry in the database etc.). Though in such cases, authentication of entry precedes the authorization of user to post a transaction or access the database, in practice, both are normally done concurrently.

Authentication and Authorization work together to prevent a multitude of application security attacks. Both are security initiatives working on different technologies. Especially for authentication there are different technologies and software utilities.

Work from home

As seen earlier under hardware security, officials have to work from home or while in travel or otherwise outside the intranet of the organisation, quite often. In all such cases, much more than anything else, it is the logical security that is to be monitored and security managers should ensure that it is never compromised. Proper authentication mechanism should be in place. While working from home or from outside the premises and outside the intranet, is a facility provided by IT firms, the security department concerned would always do well in implementing fool-proof security mechanism in place.

Logical Access to the central corporate resources is anyway to be permitted and hence should be meticulously monitored through a well-documented access control mechanism in place. Proper Information Security Policy should be in place providing for proper safeguards and controls in the form of ring fencing the sensitive data and segregating the same. The problem gets confounded especially the data owner *i.e.* the organisation may not know from which device or what type of device (a mobile or a notebook, a PC etc.) the user may be accessing the data and the exact browser and Operating system features that go with the hardware, while working from home.

No study in Software Security will be complete without a reference to testing methodologies and techniques and how they impact security in software applications. Therefore, let us now discuss some of the testing methodologies with special reference to the impact such testing will have on IT security and software security:

I. Unit Testing

II. White Box Testing

III. Black Box Testing

IV. Integration Testing

V. Volume and Stress Testing

VI. System Testing

VII. Installation/Uninstallation Testing

VIII. Security Testing

IX. User Acceptance Testing

X. Alpha Testing

XI. Beta Testing

The above is not a comprehensive list, but a typical list of testing that is normally performed in software. In practice, however, some or more of these will be combined as one process and individually identifiable processes of all these tests may not exist.

Proper testing of software is a precursor to secure software. Every functionality in the software is to be tested. ***Unit Testing*** is done by the program developers or a team within the development group itself and requires complete knowledge of program, source code, functionality, design, all functionalities and user requirements.

White Box **Testing** refers to checking the internal logic, reading the entire program source code to verify its conformance to user requirements and hence needs a thorough knowledge of programming language and the entire design. Reading the pseudo code, design documents like High Level Design and Low Level Design and use of coding standards, reusable codes, naming conventions etc. are form part of this process.

Without reading the source code, looking at the program inputs and verifying the outputs and testing every functionality with respect to user requirements and standards is called ***Black Box Testing***. It is sometimes called Verification and Validation Testing also. It does not require any deep knowledge of programming language in which the software is written.

Integration Testing is the process of testing every module *i.e.* independent functionality in the program, for its compatibility and integration with the other modules in the software, as part of a network, or a client server process etc.

System Testing is the combination of many aspects of system as per user requirements. Install/Uninstall Testing refers to how the program performs when installed and when installed in different simulated environments like operating systems, processors, networks etc. ***Volume Testing*** and ***Stress Testing*** is also done under simulated conditions to verify whether the program handles the volume of data or the network data that it will be subject to, on a live run on implementation. Many software utilities are available to undertake tests by simulating volume, traffic and stress.

Security Testing needs special mention for our study. Testing the software for its compliance to the security policy of the organisation, its adherence to the norms, licensing policy etc. are all covered here. Besides, Access Privileges, Access Rights and user requirements on security issues are taken care of and verified at this stage. It is pertinent to note that certain security issues may not be known to users and it would be the responsibility to bring to light those issues and provide for the same and verify conformance.

For instance, typically in a bank, the user level functionaries may not know the security implications of accessing the database from across a network, implications of DoS(Denial of Service) attack or a DDoS (Distributed Denial of Service) Attack, or a Phishing attack and it would be the responsibility of the technology department to take care that proper security initiatives are in place to face such threats.

Similarly, firewall configurations may not be known to the users and it would be the duty of the designers and system managers to decide where to place the firewall and what to classify as the Demilitarized Zone (DMZ). In a networked environment, DMZ is a firewall configuration for securing the LAN when organisations place a firewall in between the local systems and the outside Internet traffic.

While discussing Security Testing, some of the well-known cyber-crimes which are a result of improper or inadequate testing deserve special mention here.

a. ***Trapdoors:*** Sometimes computer programmers insert a code or overlook a process in the program during the repeated process of testing or debugging the programs, so that it does not become a block or slow the testing process. In the final editing or alpha testing phase, this is eliminated. This is called trapdoors. But sometimes some misguided programmers deliberately leave this which then facilitates them to insert a Trojan horse or a Malicious code. From security point of view, Trapdoors are quite critical and have to be carefully eliminated by proper testing methodologies.

b. ***Salami Technique:*** Little drops make an ocean. Salami Technique or Salami Slicing is an interesting technique based on the principle that sometimes a series of many small actions, often performed by clandestine means, together results in a larger action which would by itself be difficult to perform. To give a banking example, suppose a programmer writes a small program which rounds off all the paise or one rupee or two upto the nearest five rupees in all the interest bearing accounts at the time of account closure and credits the difference to a particular account during the end of day operations. The daily balancing will agree showing no errors and even a prudent customer when he verifies the interest payments too will assume that the amount has been rounded off to the nearest rupee or the nearest five, as per the policy of the bank and may not prefer to lodge a complaint. This is a very serious computer programming deliberate act which can be detected only by a code walk through as a result of White Box Testing or by a circumspect, discerning and prudent auditor on noticing one particular account getting some credits almost on a daily basis.

User Acceptance Testing popularly abbreviated as UAT is the most common among all tests that is transparent to the user. In this phase, program output is shown to the user and his acceptance is obtained, often as part of the deliverables and as part of the Software Development Life Cycle itself. This may be a repetitive and reiterative process and may have to be done a number of times, with more versions of the software.

Alpha Testing is the near final phase in which a virtual user environment is created and complete testing is done. Of course, some minor design changes and debugging are yet undertaken.

Next stage *is* ***Beta Testing*** a process in which testing is done by end-users or others and is the last stage before the product is released for commercial use in the market. From security this is the most important stage since if something escapes attention at this stage or if a security vulnerability is left unplugged, it may create *havoc* later resulting in loss of contact, loss of renewal and loss of reputation.

Alpha /Beta Testing is a testing model which is of late gaining in importance and is very commonly spoken about. It is sometimes also known as Split Testing. A/B Testing is the task of comparing two versions of a software or a web page or a program and use it under two different circumstances with similar system resources. When two versions are compared from a user perspective or two versions of a web page are shown to two different visitors, the one with a better review and better performance is considered. Since it is based on experiment of two different versions or variants which may be called A and B under controlled experiment looking for the better review and result, it is called A/B testing.

7.2 Cloud Computing

Cloud Computing is a system whereby resources, software and information are available as commonly accessible over the Internet and are provided to user computers on demand or as per resource requirements as a service and not the entire product. Instead of owning and maintaining physical servers or infrastructure, users can access and use computing resources on a pay-as-you-go basis from a cloud service provider. Cloud Computing provides a flexible and scalable way to meet the demands of various applications and workloads. It is like paying for the actual consumed electricity or water that is available over a common reservoir. Typically, we do not pay for the water purification plant or the voltage requirement of electricity etc. but pay for the actual consumption of water conforming to our norms and electricity as per our requirement. Cloud Computing is exactly this system of paying not for the product but for the actual service made available to us over the Internet.

Cloud Computing services are increasing in popularity with many reputed vendors including Microsoft offering cloud services making specific resources available to users as a service. Since information, database etc. are all maintained as a commonly accessible resource, many serious security concerns have been expressed in this. Security technology in Cloud Computing is evolving day by day and cloud providers are vying with one another to offer secure cloud services with enhanced features of user authentication, reliability and availability. Cloud Computing is considered to be among the fastest growing IT segment and therefore, the security issues in providing private clouds are also being addressed and the technology is fast evolving.

7.3 Some of the main attributes to ensure before building a secure network are:

I. Hardware security and Reliability and their adaptability to changes
II. Adoption of standard protocols and open interfaces
III. Ability to alter throughputs, latency and connectivity to protect high speeds
IV. Maximum adoption of a single operating system across the network
V. Automation of optimization of network resources
VI. Automation of security architecture and report generation

VII. Scalability and ability to seamless integration while adding new modules

VIII. Review and Scalability of security capacity and its effectiveness.

7.4 Operational Security

Every industry, every organisation has some basic operations as their essence. For instance, in a banking industry, the journey of a voucher, the trail of a transaction, the back-end operations of General Ledger related activities are all the operational activity. In a software development company, the entire Software Development Life Cycle (SDLC) constitutes the operational activity and in a hardware manufacturing industry, the entire process of manufacturing right up to the point of sales and recovery of sale proceeds. In addition to the main activity, the other support services like HR related activities of recruitment, training, payroll and infrastructure like premises etc. also do form a crucial part of the organisation's activity.

Hence, operational security is that part of security or to be precise, the entire gamut of security measures that encompasses the security initiatives of the organisations as a combination of various processes at different stages from the overall identification and planning right upto the execution with preventive and detective activities. Broadly, operational security involves the following steps:

I. Identification of critical information of the organisation

II. Treatment of such information *i.e.,* classification

III. Identification of threats and vulnerabilities

IV. Risk Analysis and Risk Management

V. Planning for Risk Mitigation and Risk Controls

VI. Application of measures for Security in all those identified areas

VII. Monitoring the effectiveness of steps taken; corrective and preventive action

Though the above are the generic steps applicable for any class of industry or organisation, the emphasis on a particular step or the focus area in a particular stage may vary depending upon the particular type of organisation and the nature of product or process dealt with. We will identify some of the most popular industries and study the process of operational security individually.

7.5 Banking

Typically in a Banking Industry, the customer centric activity is the principal activity and IT in a bank has always been an enabler to leverage customer service and profitability. Though in modern times, banks introduce a product or a service mainly based on IT and communication. IT still continues to be a means to achieve the ultimate end of customer service, profitability, competitiveness, etc. Hence operational security in a bank should focus on branch banking leading on to the back-end operations at branches, MIS operations at the administrative offices and Funds or Treasury Forex operations etc. at the corporate level.

Operational Security in banks starts with the time a customer enters the bank and the journey of a voucher starts, either as physical voucher or an automatically generated voucher or an e-voucher. A proper operational security in banking is a co-ordinated effort of the following functions:

I. Systems and Procedures

II. Technology: Software and hardware and their capabilities

III. Work-force: Their capability, willingness, etc.

IV. Human Resources Management: Job Card and Key Responsibility Areas

V. Top Management: Need and criticality of various procedures

VI. Compliance: Internal procedures and external like regulatory.

Drafting the Operational Security in banks involves the above critical steps since it has to be a multi-pronged approach involving all these. First the system and procedures department has to be clear about the critical areas of information handled in the bank, followed by the involvement of technology department to decide the ways to protect them. This decision should take into account the capabilities of work-force in different layers of authority, their individual key responsibility areas, the job allocation if any and lastly the criticality assigned to the individual procedures and compliance issues.

While ensuring that there is proper demarcation of duties, it should also be noted that there is no overlap of functions and no job is done by two persons nor is the same person responsible for doing it and checking it. Maker-Checker principle should be duly enforced and ensuring security in one layer of authority should be an independent function or embedded into the system itself such that the data entry stage takes care of it simultaneously when the data is being entered.

Operational Security in the Banking Industry for the CBS, other delivery channels like ATMs, Internet Banking, Cards etc. is being handled in different chapters of this book under specific areas like Threats, Security Controls, Regulations, etc.

7.6 Telecom Industry

Broadly operational security will be industry-neutral but there will be some finer aspects to be taken care of which are industry-specific. Hence there may be certain issues that are specific to telecom industry. The important among them are the call logs, event logs and all other forms of trail. E-records are accepted legally as records, thanks to Information Technology Act, 2000. It is now the responsibility of telecom providers to preserve call logs called Calls Detail Record (CDR) which normally consists of details of calling number, called number, duration of call, type of call, phone number called, communication success or failure flag, etc. Especially in times of a dispute, telecom companies should have proper system of preserving and producing the CDRs in the event of a necessity to produce as evidences for investigators. This should be part of operational security issues addressed by the top management.

Since Network Service Providers (NSPs) providing telecom service are custodians of customer data to a very large extent, they are also bound by 'Due Diligence' as provided for in the I.T. Act and should satisfy the 'reasonable security practices'. Operational Security in the NSPs should be strong enough to take care of reasonable security practices in the organisation not only to protect the company from any external threat but also to protect the top management in the event of any employee frauds and internal threats.

VoIP Eavesdropping

VoIP is a technology that allows telephone calls to be made over computer networks like the Internet. This technology converts analog voice signals into digital data packets and supports real-time, two-way transmission of conversations using the popular protocol Internet Protocol (IP). A major threat that faces telecom industry is VoIP Eavesdropping. Technically, it is possible to eaves drop a conversation in a telecom network using VoIP. Now-a-days VoIP devices are commonly available and are being widely used. By usage of some specific software tools and gaining access to the medium carrying the voice calls, a VoIP telephone instrument or a communication channel can be compromised. Some open software tools are also available which the attackers will freely use and capture the data packets that traverse through a network. Unfortunately, tools are available for converting the data packets back into voice conversation (analog data) too. Hence operational security in telecom industry has to be built on these taking into account such threats.

7.7 IT Industry

IT industry normally handles software and hardware manufacturing, servicing and maintenance related activities. Sometimes it also handles customer information and acts as custodian of information. Software and hardware issues need separate controls for enhancing security.

7.8 BPO and KPO Industries

Generally, in the case of all IT industries especially in the case of BPO (Business Process Outsourcing) and KPO (Knowledge Process Outsourcing) industries when data relating to customers are extensively handled, it is much more important that proper operational security initiatives are in place. Some of the major security concerns in a BPO industry that should be addressed are:

I. Threats posed by employees

II. Unrestricted use of external devices or communication by email etc.

III. Inadequate or lack of security audit

IV. Ambiguously fixing of responsibility

V. Unrestricted or poorly monitored third party access

In the famous case relating to the arrest of the CEO of auction site "baazee.com" Shri Avneesh Bajaj in 2004, the security initiatives and responsibility of corporate entities (*i.e.* such companies) were debated. Security analysts, techno-legal professionals in the country became aware of the responsibilities of such companies *vis-à-vis* the obligations of employees.

7.9 The other industries wherein operations are to be studied with particular reference to the nature of job handled include insurance, health and hospital, HR, government and defence related industries. In all these cases, though the broader aspects of operations security remain the same, data classification and data criticality do make some difference and hence are to be handled accordingly.

7.10 Service Level Agreements (SLAs) and third party contracts are to be drafted with much care to provide for operations security to restrict access to third parties. Besides restricting access to critical areas, SLAs or other forms of contracts should also provide for penalty or other means of redress like arbitration etc. in the event of any breach of security to the operations handled in the organisation.

Having discussed in detail about the operations security of different industries, let us now discuss some of the measures and the steps involved.

The first step involved is an assessment of security initiatives taken by the organisation involving experts from different fields. At this stage, review of operational security measures taken so far, effectiveness, adequacy of steps taken, inadvertent disclosure of information noted if any, breaches already observed and corrective or preventive action to be taken etc. are all put in place.

We have already seen that human resources constitute the weakest link in security. This statement is of particular significance in Operational Security. Insider threat issues are to be adequately addressed at this stage. Deliberate misconfigurations in the systems and non-observance of procedures or intentional or inadvertent identification of criticality of information or ignoring clearly warning signals etc. are to be handled and operational security enhanced based on the study, as part of corrective and preventive action.

7.11 User Level Controls

In any industry, more so in banking, though IT department is the enabler, the actual transactions take place at the operational level by the actual users of the systems. Hence, transactions are initiated, carried out and verified (sometimes referred to as 'posted' and 'passed' and 'authorised') by the field officials or the operational staff members who handle the systems. It is at this level, that some critical controls do exist.

Such controls include generation of daily reports, proper upkeep of records, maintenance of reports in the system (electronically) and wherever needed in physical printed formats, their checking and signing and follow up and preservation ensuring integrity of data and enabling proper retrieval wherever necessary.

Reference to what is popularly known as *'exception reports'* in banks will be quite appropriate in this context. Any transaction that is not routine comes under this category and it is very well part of the operational control in organisation to observe and record such *abnormal transactions* or *critical transactions* on a routine basis. Some of the common abnormal transactions or exception report transactions or those that require the personal attention of the branch head are:

I. Payment of a cheque issued, which is not recorded against the account holder

II. A temporary overdraft in current account

III. Excess drawing over the drawing power in CC(Cash Credit) account

IV. Accounts opened without proper introduction etc.

It is the user or the functional officers or branch managers who are responsible for such transactions and the reporting in such transactions should form part of operational control in the bank.

Care should be taken to follow up all such reports, preserve them and take immediate corrective action based on such reports. Reporting such transactions to the top management and bringing it to their knowledge is always part of operational control and may be done manually or preferably automated, the software should provide for it.

Definition of such user level controls is often left to the individual bank or organisation's Manual and Work Instructions as per the key responsibility areas assigned to different areas of authority in the organisation. Based upon such reporting and adherence to such controls, constant and periodic review of the effectiveness and efficiency of operational controls will be made, taking into account the feedback from the users and operational staff.

7.12 Software Security Techniques

Software Security is like protecting a bank vault. You're fully aware that there are people out there that want to exploit your software, and your goal is to prevent them from doing so.

To do this, security teams must leverage common security best practices and mitigation tactics like the below:

- **Patching your Software:** This is the process of fixing software vulnerabilities as they are discovered.
- **Using a Firewall:** Firewall is software or hardware that sits between your computer and the internet and helps protect your computer from unauthorized access.
- **Restricting Administrative Privileges:** Limiting the privileges of users who can access sensitive data can help with reducing attack surface, minimizing the risk of a data breach.
- **Encrypting your data:** Data Encryption is a common cybersecurity practice that involves transforming readable data into an unreadable format. Decryption reverses this transformation.
- **Two-factor authentication:** Two-factor authentication requires you to provide two pieces of information, such as a password and a code generated by a mobile app, in order to log in to your account.

- **Employee training:** Employee training is essential for software security. Employees need to be aware of the risks associated with using software and how to protect themselves and their company's data.

Know Your Progress

Operational Security refers to security in the operations which is the core activity of the organisation. Though broadly all industries have common goals of ensuring Operational Security adequately, certain finer issues unique to the industry may have to be addressed with special care and attention. For instance, in banking it is the criticality of security of accounting information, the banking transaction, in a telecom industry it is the confidentiality of information relating to communication and upkeep of records etc. Similarly, in a BPO kind of industry it is the data that is handled that constitutes the key activity of the industry, which is to be protected with all security initiatives in place.

Key Words

SDLC	Cloud Computing	VoIP	Eavesdropping
BPO , KPO	Diligence	SLA, DoS, DDoS, Salami Attack	

Questions

1. Operational Security in a bank is normally a co-ordinated activity involving __________.
    a. Systems Department, Labour Union, Top Management and the expenditure involved
    b. HR factors including work-force, Systems Department, Expenditures Department, Top Management for sanction of funds
    c. Systems Department, HR functions, Work-force with well-defined responsibilities, top management commitment
    d. HR Department, Top Management, Funds Department, Employees Welfare Associations
2. In a telecom industry, some of the important areas for concern in Operational Security are____________.
    a. Service Level Agreements with consumers, Applicability of IT Act, volume of data, working hours like late night working
    b. Confidentiality of data handled, telecom channels used, vulnerabilities in communication, preservation of electronic records
    c. Integrity of data handled, Availability of data, threats from outsiders to the data, physical access to data handled
    d. Availability of data handled, threats from insiders, physical access restrictions, volume of data handled
3. VoIP Eavesdropping is the technique of________________.
    a. Wiretapping a communication with the help of telecom lines interception
    b. Intercepting a telecom channel with a TCP/IP protocol used in voice communication like Internet
    c. Wiretapping a communication and recording the voices and using it in internet with an IP address for the purpose

   d. Using IP based devices to eaves drop a communication and converting it into digital data and then back into a voice conversation to hear the same

4. Which of the following is not a threat faced by a BPO/KPO?

   a. Funds constraint to implement security initiatives

   b. Human factor and employees working in the business processes

   c. Lack of or inadequate information security audit

   d. Sometimes third party access without much restriction

5. Human element is considered to be strongest link in information security. (True/False)

6. In networking and communication, MPLS means________________.

   a. Multi Point Linear Switching

   b. Multi-Protocol Label Switching

   c. Multi Point LAN System

   d. Multi-Protocol Label System

7. In Cloud Computing, the computer and software resources are____________.

   a. not easily made available to users but only with a process of strict authentication

   b. easily available to users and the data is like Wikipedia and easily accessible

   c. available to users with proper authentication more as paid service and not as a product

   d. restricted among the private owners of cloud and made available to registered users of the private cloud

8. Cisco is popularly known for its brand of hard-disks. (True/False)

9. Black Box Testing is done by people who need not know the programming language. (True/False)

10. Operations Security in a bank involves all types of vouchers - system generated or manually prepared. (True/False)

Answers

1. *c*	6. *b*
2. *b*	7. c
3. *d*	8. False
4. *a*	9. True
5. False	10. True

8
CHAPTER

Security Standards and Best Practices

OBJECTIVES

At the end of this chapter, the readers will know the meaning and significance of Standards like ISO in general, their relevance particularly in the field of Information Security like the ISO 27001 standards, how they enhance security environment in I.T. and why banks and financial organisations are increasingly moving towards such certification. Besides, the chapter also focuses on other best practices in Information Security accepted globally and certain specific standards and legal compliance requirements as per some specific laws applicable in other countries as well.

8.1 Introduction

We have seen earlier that Information System Security is the commonly accepted and dynamic concept applicable for any industry that deals with information. Though the system is common in any type of industry, there was a need felt globally, for evolving a generally accepted standard that may be referred and used in all industries so that whatever is applicable from those widely accepted norms may be adopted in a particular organisation or bank.

Organisations felt the need for commonly accepted standards which would be dynamic so that whatever is applicable and relevant to the particular organisation be adopted and those that are not relevant may be expressly declared as not applicable.

Hence, the standards should be dynamic enough to provide for such a broader framework, a generic format of standards and yet be specific enough so that an analysis of the existing scenario be made and gap analysis be done, to ascertain how best the system can be improved.

As already seen in the earlier chapters, Information Security mainly rests on the pillars *viz.* Confidentiality, Integrity, Availability, Non-Repudiation and Authentication and hence in any organisation wherein if any of these pillars are weak that will deteriorate the Information Security structure. To ensure formal assurance to customers that data in the organisation is secure enough, which is a must especially in a finance critical industry like banking and insurance, of late, ISO standards of Information Security is normally referred to.

International Organisation for Standardisation, popularly known as ISO in short is the world's largest developer and publisher of international standards. It is a network of the national standards institutes of over 160 countries, one member per country. It is an independent, non-governmental international organization with central secretariat in Geneva, Switzerland that develops and publishes standards to ensure the quality, safety, efficiency, and interoperability of products, services, and systems.

ISO standards cover a wide range of industries and sectors, providing guidelines, specifications, and requirements for various processes. Structurally, its members are mostly representatives of the respective governments of member nations with a good mix of private sector and business representation. Because of this organisational structure, ISO ensures the dynamism of private sector with the power and commitment of public sector with deep inroads into the business needs.

ISO is an organisation which has over the years evolved standards. The ISO 9000 family of quality management is among the most popular standards internationally. This is mainly on quality management standards as the features of a product or service which are required by a customer. Quality Management System (QMS) is what an organisation does to ensure that its products or services satisfy the customers' requirements satisfying with the requisite quality ensuring compliance with all legal regulations.

The focus of this chapter will be mainly on ISO 27000 standards, though there are other ISO/IEC standards and methods relating to Information Security, Risk Management and related areas, Occupational Health & Safety Advisory Services (OHSAS) ISO 18000 series standards, ISO 14000 series for the Environmental Management etc.

Before going into the details of these Information Security Management System (ISMS), let us have a look at some of the most relevant standards and methods in quality management principles applied specifically to Software Development Life Cycle (SDLC).

ISO/IEC 12207:2008 establishes a common framework for software life cycle processes, with well-defined terminology, applicable for software industry. It contains processes, activities, and tasks that are to be applied in a typical software environment, whether acquisition of a software product or service or its supply, or development, operation, maintenance and disposal of software products. This is specifically for the process associated with defining, controlling and enhancing software life cycle processes.

ISO/IEC 15288:2008 is for systems and software engineering related to the processes for the same and related terminology. In other words, it establishes a common framework for describing the life cycle of systems created by humans and defines a set of processes and is applied in the hierarchy of a system's structure. These standards may be configured with one or more of the constituent elements *viz.* hardware, software, data, humans, processes, procedures, facilities, etc.

ISO/IEC 90003:2004 is another standard that is relevant in this context. This is a standard exclusive for the software industry and provides guidance for organizations in the application of ISO 9001:2000 to the acquisition, supply, development, operation and maintenance of computer software and related support services. ISO/IEC 90003:2004 does not add to or otherwise change the requirements of ISO 9001:2000 and the guidelines provided herein are not intended to be used for certification. The application of ISO/IEC 90003:2004 is appropriate to software that is part of a commercial contract with another organization.

8.2 ISO 27000 Standards

This popular standard from ISO, has been prepared to provide a model for establishing, implementing, operating, monitoring, reviewing, maintaining and improving an Information Security Management System (ISMS). Popularly referred to as ISMS, these standards are adopted by organisations as a result of security requirements and often influenced by the needs for security and the objectives and its implementation largely depends on factors like the nature of business, size, scale of activity, criticality of data handled, etc.

This International Standard promotes the adoption of a process approach for establishing, implementing, operating, monitoring, reviewing, maintaining and improving an organization's ISMS. An organization needs to identify and manage many activities in order to function effectively. Any

activity using resources are managed in order to enable the transformation of inputs into outputs can be considered to be a process. Often the output from one process directly forms the input to the following process. The application of a system of processes within an organization, together with the identification and interactions of these processes, and their management, can be referred to as a "process approach".

The process approach for information security management presented in this International Standard encourages its users to emphasize the importance of:

(*a*) Understanding an organization's Information Security requirements and the need to establish policy and objectives for Information Security;

(*b*) Implementing and operating controls to manage an organization's Information Security risks in the context of the organization's overall business risks;

(*c*) Monitoring and reviewing the performance and effectiveness of the ISMS; and

(*d*) Continual improvement based on objective measurement.

8.3 ISO – ISMS

Broadly, these standards (ISMS) consists of the following chapters :

I. Scope and General

II. Application and Normative Reference

III. Terms and Definitions

IV. Establishing and Managing the ISMS, Records and Documents

V. Management Responsibility including Resource Management, Training etc.

VI. Internal Audits (ISMS Audits)

VII. Review of ISMS (Management Review including review input, review output)

VIII. ISMS Improvement (Corrective and Preventive Action)

BS 7799 was very popular, guidelines later adopted as ISO 27001 made as a structured set of guidelines and specifications for assisting organisations in developing their own information security framework. Totally ISO 27001 has 11 domain areas, 39 control objectives and 133 controls in all which are discussed in brief, and not enumerated, in the following paragraphs in this chapter. The security controls represent information security best practices and the standard suggests that these controls should be applied depending on the business requirements.

ISO 27001 suggests development and implementation of a structured Information Security Management Systems (ISMS), which governs the security implementation and monitoring in an enterprise. The standard is designed to serve as a single reference point for identifying the range of controls needed. All such controls are applicable to most situations where information systems are used.

The importance of the ISO 27001 standards can be easily gauged from the fact that the Working Group of G Gopalakrishna (RBI) on Information Security, Electronic Banking, Technology Risk Management, Cyber Frauds has emphasized the significance of adoption of these standards, their conformance and certification of banks in India.

8.4 What are the Benefits of ISO 27001?

Some of the main advantages are:

I. Minimises risks and ensures better risk management practices

II. Enhances the vendor status and exhibits your commitment to vendors

III. Brings the organisation to compliance with legal and statutory requirements

IV. Reduces information security violations and ensures better data security

V. Ensures better business continuity and disaster recovery practices in place

VI. Gives market leverage because the global recognitions of ISO 27001 certification

It would be pertinent to note that savings in cost of manufacture or straight Return on Investment is not part of ISO 27001 standards nor a direct result of the certification. However, conformance to the standards and compliance to the certification procedures will minimise the business risks, ensure business continuity, increase business efficiency all of which do pave the way for better operational efficiency and enhanced profits.

One of the reasons for worldwide acceptance of ISO 27001 standards or the ISMS is the applicability of Plan Do Check Act (PDCA) Model in its approach, which makes it formal, easy to understand and procedural.

Now let us have a brief look at the chapters mentioned earlier and the salient features of some of the important clauses mentioned in the standards.

While the first two chapters deal with scope and general introduction of ISMS and the need for the same, the chapter on terms and definitions lays down the definition of some of the most important and significant words used in the document/usage of the words in the security scenario and the contextual meaning of such words is properly documented in this chapter.

The chapter on records and documents defines the policy, statement of applicability, steps involved in formulating a risk treatment plan, process involved in implementing and operating the ISMS, monitoring, reviewing and identifying the documentation requirements and all other measures relating to control of documentation and control of records, etc.

The next chapter is on Management Responsibility including procedures for management's role in ISMS, utilization of and availability of resources for proper implementation of ISMS including factors like training, awareness and competence of all human resources and maintaining proper records for all these.

Audit programmes, procedures for conducting regular audits to monitor implementation of ISMS in the organisation, maintenance of records thereof, conformance of such audit functions to security requirements are all discussed in this chapter. Audit criteria, scope and methods for conducting the audit and all other relevant procedures relating to audit are also addressed in this chapter.

The steps related to improvement of ISMS procedures are discussed here. Continual improvement of the procedures and effectiveness and efficiency of the system through audit programs, monitoring and review are mandatory as per this chapter. Commonly referred to as CAPA(Corrective Action and Preventive Action).

Corrective actions mentioned in the process include identifying the Non-Conformities with ISMS requirements, defining the cause for such non-conformities, evaluating the need for actions to ensure that such non-conformities do not recur and implementing those actions are all part for corrective action. Similarly, preventive action mainly involves identification of potential non-conformities and taking action to prevent such non-conformities. CAPA should be constantly reviewed for their effectiveness and efficiency and be discussed at the management review meetings as well.

The importance of ISMS can be gauged from the fact that the recent Gopalakrishna Working Group on Information Security, Electronic Banking, Technology Risk Management and Cyber Frauds has made elaborate mention about the ISMS and has stated that Commercial banks should implement Information Security Management. The committee reports:

The best known ISMS is described in ISO/IEC 27001 and ISO/IEC 27002 and related standards published jointly by ISO and IEC. ISO 27001 is concerned with how to implement, monitor, maintain and continually improve an Information Security Management System while ISO 27002 provides detailed steps or a list of security measures which can be used when building an ISMS.

The ISO has come out with its latest standards called the ISO/IEC 27001:2013 which is being gradually adopted by organisations. ISO, in its official introduction of these standards states that "The information security management system preserves the confidentiality, integrity and availability of information by applying a risk management process and gives confidence to interested parties that risks are adequately managed. It is important that the information security management system is integrated with the organization's processes and overall management structure and that information security is considered in the design of processes, information systems, and controls. It is expected that an information security management system implementation will be scaled in accordance with the needs of the organization".

8.5 Cobit-Control Objectives in IT

Another popular framework being spoken about is the COBIT from ISACA (formerly known as the IS Audit and Control Association), a worldwide renowned professional body representing IT auditors. This framework has matured from quite modest beginnings as a guide for computer auditors on best practices in IT management controls into a comprehensive model or tool to guide the implementation of sound IT governance processes/systems.

The current incarnation, COBIT v4, is described by ISACA as "an IT governance framework and supporting toolset that allows managers to bridge the gap between control requirements, technical issues and business risks". COBIT enables clear policy development and good practice for IT control throughout organizations, emphasizes regulatory compliance, helps organizations to increase the value attained from IT, enables alignment and simplifies implementation of the COBIT framework. The latest in COBIT is COBIT 5 which provides a comprehensive framework that assists enterprises to achieve their goals and deliver value through effective governance and management of enterprise IT.

COBIT 5 is the only business framework for the governance and management of enterprise IT. This evolutionary version incorporates the latest thinking in enterprise governance and management techniques, and provides globally accepted principles, practices, analytical tools and models to help increase the trust in, and value of, information systems. COBIT 5 builds and expands on COBIT 4.1 by integrating other major frameworks, standards and resources, including ISACA's Val IT, Risk IT and BMIS. We have also aligned COBIT 5 with significant guidance and standards, including ITIL and ISO.

Though not a certification standard like ISO, COBIT is often referred to as a model, as a framework with best practices discussing the toolset serving as a guide to IT managers to study the IT and IS Security environments in their organisations, assess the requirements, benchmark them with the best ones in the industry and study the gap with the overall view to enhance the security initiatives.

GAISP (Generally Accepted Information Security Practices) was once developed from many international works and activities on Information Security and later modified and amended to be presented as a bigger worldwide standard. However, thanks to the popularity and global acceptance of ISO/IEC 27002 and the certificate under ISO 27001, this project did not gain popularity.

GAIT (Guide to the Assessment of IT risk) is the Institute of Internal Auditors guidance to identify key IT risks such as SOX Compliance and HIPAA in the US and gained some reasonable popularity in the US that has an impact especially in the financial sector like banks, payment card industry, insurance, health and related sectors.

Study on Security Standards will not be complete without reference to some popular scenario in the US and those nations or organisations having business associations with the corporate in the US.

The Sarbanes-Oxley Act (SOX) was signed into law in 2002 and named after its authors: Senator Paul Sarbanes (D-MD) and Representative Paul Oxley (R-Ohio). This Act mandated a number of reforms to enhance corporate responsibility, enhance financial disclosures, and combat corporate and accounting fraud. As per the Act, the CEO and CFO must personally certify that their organization has the proper internal controls, that their financial reports are accurate and complete and that the data they use for financial reporting is accurate and secure. The report also includes a clause on the effectiveness of internal controls around financial reporting. The necessary infrastructure should be designed to protect and preserve records.

Popularly known as HIPAA (Health Insurance Portability and Accountability Act) this Act protects health insurance coverage for workers and their families when they change or lose their jobs. Establishing national standards for electronic health care transactions and national identifiers for providers, health plans, and employers. The Act mandates security and confidentiality of electronic health care information, with a potential need to associate signature capability with information being electronically stored or transmitted.

Gramm-Leach-Bliley-Act (GLBA) was signed into law in 1999 and resulted in the most sweeping overhaul of financial services regulation in the United States by eliminating the long-standing barriers between banking, investment banking, and insurance. The information security program must include assigning a designated program manager for the security related activities, conducting periodic risk and vulnerability assessments, defining procedures for making changes in lieu of test results or changes in circumstances etc.

PCI DSS Payment Card Industry Data Security Standard is a very popular standard that nations like India should seriously consider and adapt. The standard imposes specific card holder data security control requirements on merchants and banks handling cards or the data concerned, the standard enforces structure compliance activities, including routine independent security assessments by accredited PCI (Payment Card Industry) professionals, with an overall mission to protect the credit card industry. The standards are gradually getting evolved with the latest version (v2) having been introduced in January 2011 with a time-bound provision for revisions every 3 years.

SAS 70 Statement on Auditing Standards 70, is another standard though on auditing and attestation, that has relevance to information security. It discusses a method for auditors to check and to attest the control status of the financial services. Though audit and security are generally closely related to each other, adherence to this standard is a formal acceptance that security controls are in place. Often, SAS 70 reduces the need for interdependent financial services companies to audit each other's security arrangements continually since receiving a positive SAS 70 report from a trustworthy auditor is generally taken as due diligence.

ETSI – TC Cyber

ETSI (European Telecommunication Standards Institute) is an independent, non-profit organisation with worldwide presence evolving globally applicable standards for Information and Communication Technology covering mobile, Internet, broadcast and all communication technologies. It is officially recognized by the European Union as a European Standards Organisation. With a significant presence in the ICT Security standardization areas, ETSI opened a new Technical Committee popularly known as TC CYBER in March 2014. TC Cyber focuses mainly on the following areas:

I. Cyber-Security
II. Security of infrastructures, devices, services and protocols
III. Security advice, guidance and operational security requirements to users, manufacturers and network and infrastructure operators

IV. Security tools and techniques to ensure security

V. Creation of security specifications and alignment with work done in other ETSI committees.

8.6 CIA triad - Confidentiality, Integrity, Availability

Confidentiality, Integrity, and Availability (CIA) are three key principles in information security. Here's how they apply to maintaining the confidentiality of information:

Confidentiality: This principle ensures that information is only accessible to authorized individuals or entities. Measures to enforce confidentiality include encryption, access controls, and policies governing the handling of sensitive information. It's crucial to protect data from unauthorized access, disclosure, or theft.

Integrity: Integrity ensures that information is accurate, reliable, and trustworthy. It involves protecting data from unauthorized modification, deletion, or alteration. Measures to maintain integrity include data validation checks, digital signatures, and access controls to prevent unauthorized changes to data.

Availability: Availability ensures that information and resources are accessible to authorized users when needed. This involves preventing disruptions to services, systems, or data. Measures to ensure availability include redundancy, backups, disaster recovery plans, and monitoring systems for potential threats or failures.

Confidentiality is about keeping information private and accessible only to those with the proper authorization, while integrity ensures that the information remains accurate and reliable, and availability ensures that it remains accessible when needed. These three principles form the foundation of information security and are essential for protecting sensitive data from unauthorized access, manipulation, or loss.

8.7 Importance of Confidentiality

Confidentiality in the context of IT security refers to the protection of sensitive information from unauthorized access or disclosure. It ensures that only authorized individuals or systems can access certain data or resources, maintaining privacy and preventing unauthorized parties from viewing or obtaining valuable or sensitive information.

Confidentiality is typically achieved through encryption, access controls, and secure communication protocols. Encryption techniques scramble data so that it can only be understood by authorized users who possess the appropriate decryption key. Access controls involve mechanisms such as passwords, biometrics, and role-based access control (RBAC) to limit access to sensitive data based on the user's identity and permissions. Secure communication protocols like HTTPS and VPNs ensure that data transmitted over networks remains confidential by encrypting it during transmission.

Confidentiality is a fundamental aspect of information security and is often accompanied by other security principles such as integrity (ensuring data remains unaltered) and availability (ensuring data is accessible when needed) to form the CIA triad (Confidentiality, Integrity, Availability).

8.8 Components of Confidentiality

Confidentiality is a fundamental aspect of information security that ensures that sensitive data is only accessible to authorized individuals or entities. It involves protecting information from unauthorized access, disclosure, or theft. Here are some key features of confidentiality:

Access Control: Confidentiality relies on implementing robust access control mechanisms to restrict access to sensitive information. This includes user authentication, authorization, and encryption techniques to ensure that only authorized users can access confidential data.

Encryption: Encryption is a key technique used to maintain confidentiality by converting plaintext data into cipher text, which can only be deciphered with the appropriate decryption key. This helps to protect data while it's stored, transmitted, or processed.

Data Classification: Confidentiality often involves classifying data based on its sensitivity and implementing appropriate security measures based on the classification level. This helps organizations prioritize their security efforts and allocate resources effectively.

Policies and Procedures: Establishing clear policies and procedures related to the handling of sensitive information is essential for maintaining confidentiality. This includes defining who has access to what data, how data should be handled, and consequences for violating confidentiality policies.

Physical Security: Physical security measures, such as access controls, surveillance systems, and secure storage facilities, are essential for protecting confidential information from unauthorized physical access.

Training and Awareness: Educating employees about the importance of confidentiality and providing training on security best practices help reinforce the significance of safeguarding sensitive information and reduce the risk of human error or negligence.

Monitoring and Auditing: Continuous monitoring and auditing of systems and networks help detect and prevent unauthorized access or breaches of confidentiality. This includes logging and reviewing access logs, conducting regular security assessments, and implementing intrusion detection systems.

Protection of Confidential Data: Confidentiality is critical for preserving the privacy and integrity of sensitive information, and organizations must implement a comprehensive set of security measures to effectively protect confidential data from unauthorized access or disclosure.

8.9 Different types of Confidentialities

Security Service Confidentiality: This refers to the confidentiality provided by security services such as encryption, access controls, and data masking. It ensures that sensitive information is protected from unauthorized access or disclosure by encrypting data in transit or at rest, enforcing access controls to restrict access to authorized users, and masking or obfuscating sensitive information to prevent unauthorized exposure.

Data Integrity: Data integrity ensures that data remains accurate, consistent, and trustworthy throughout its lifecycle. It prevents unauthorized modification, alteration, or tampering of data by ensuring that only authorized users can make changes and that any changes are logged, monitored, and verified to maintain data integrity.

Connection Confidentiality: Connection confidentiality ensures that communication between two parties is protected from eavesdropping or interception by unauthorized entities. It is achieved through the use of encryption protocols such as SSL/TLS to encrypt data transmitted over a network, ensuring that only the intended recipients can decrypt and access the information.

Connectionless Confidentiality: Connectionless confidentiality refers to the protection of data transmitted in a connectionless communication environment, such as UDP (User Datagram Protocol) or IP (Internet Protocol). It ensures that data packets are encrypted and protected from interception or tampering, even in the absence of a continuous connection between the sender and receiver.

Traffic Flow Confidentiality: Traffic flow confidentiality protects information about the communication patterns, volume, and timing of data transmissions from unauthorized disclosure or analysis. It prevents attackers from monitoring or analysing network traffic to gain insights into user behaviour, communication patterns, or sensitive information.

Access Confidentiality: Access confidentiality ensures that access to sensitive information or resources is restricted to authorized users or entities. It involves implementing access controls, authentication mechanisms, and authorization policies to verify the identity of users and enforce least privilege access, preventing unauthorized users from accessing or modifying sensitive data.

Authentication Confidentiality: Authentication confidentiality protects the confidentiality of authentication credentials, such as usernames, passwords, or cryptographic keys, during the authentication process. It ensures that authentication credentials are securely transmitted and protected from interception or disclosure, preventing unauthorized access to user accounts or systems.

Comprehensive Confidentiality: These different types of confidentiality measures are essential components of information security, working together to protect sensitive data, ensure data integrity, and maintain the privacy and confidentiality of communication channels and user credentials. By implementing comprehensive confidentiality measures, organizations can mitigate the risk of unauthorized access, data breaches, and privacy violations, safeguarding their information assets and maintaining the trust and confidence of stakeholders.

Know Your Progress

Information Security normally consists of Confidentiality, Integrity, Availability and Non-repudiation with Authentication added to it as another important pillar Adapting the earlier BS 7799 standards on information security, ISO has come out with ISO 27001 and 27002 standards evolved mainly for security. The standards address risks associated with the security architecture, controls for containing the same and puts in place the procedures to address the whole issue by virtue of its global acceptability, comprehensiveness and wider reach, almost all security conscious organisations have recognized the importance of these standards. Gopalakrishna Working Group of RBI on Internet Banking in its report in 2011 has also underlined the significance of Information Security Management System as enshrined in ISO 27000 series standards. Besides, these standards there are also frameworks like the one evolved by ISACA called COBIT etc. that can be referred to ensure a robust information security architecture is in place in US, however, there are some more regulations and legal enactments like SOX, HIPAA, PCI-DSS etc. that are all applicable in the banking and related areas.

Key Words

ISO	ISMS	PDCA	SDLC	PCIDSS	OHSAS	SOX
SAS 70	HIPAA	COBIT	ISACA	GLBA	GAISP	

Questions

1. Which of the following is not an objective of ISO 27001 standard?
    a. Enhancing profitability in operations by leveraging technology.
    b. Increasing customer confidence by increasing information security initiatives.
    c. Leveraging technology and information security with an overall objective for better customer orientation.
    d. Ensuring better business continuity and disaster recovery management.

2. Which of the following is correct?
   a. ISACA is the Information Security and Control Association certification standard for Control Objectives popularly called COBIT.
   b. COBIT is not a standard for adoption but only a framework from ISACA.
   c. ISACA is the certifying body for following the framework given in COBIT.
   d. COBIT is the control objectives from ISACA as per the ISO 27001 standards.
3. Which of the following is true in the case of PCI?
   a. Conformance to this standard has been mandated for all banks by RBI.
   b. Credit Card Industry in the US should conform to these standards.
   c. ATM Cards in the US and Canada adhere to these standards for global recognition.
   d. Credit Card Industry in the US conforms to these standards.
4. ISO 27001 standards are basically________________.
   a. an extension of ISO 9001 standards certification but more on security
   b. a certification standards based on the earlier BS 7799 standards
   c. further improvement over ISO 27000 standard with more focus on security
   d. conformance to BS 7799 standards with additional clauses on security.
5. In the US, the popular Sarbanes Oxley Act (SOX) compliance________________.
   a. is applicable for all banking and finance related industry including credit cards
   b. is for adoption by all banks and financial institutions like the British standards BS 7799
   c. includes a certificate from the CEO/CFO that security controls are in place
   d. is basically a certificate of compliance to all legal, statutory and regulatory rules
6. Gopalakrishna Working Group of RBI mentioning about security in electronic banking __________.
   a. advises banks to go in for ISMS and the related procedures as per ISO 27001/27002
   b. instructs banks to go in for ISO 9001 certification along with security as per 27001 standards
   c. recommends banks to ensure all security practices are completely in place and to produce the ISO 27001 certification for review periodically
   d. mandates banks to take ISO 27001 certification and ensure compliance with all ISO standards
7. ISMS procedures involves monitoring and reviewing the effectiveness of all security initiatives by a process of________________.
   a. continuous improvement and corrective and preventive action
   b. continuous improvement ensured by constant audits, routine inspection and review
   c. continual improvement and procedures relating to Corrective and Preventive Action
   d. continual improvement of all security initiatives by constant review meetings

8. Which of the following is not a step as part of ISO 27001?

(*i*) defining the policy, (ii) defining the statement of applicability, (iii) formulating a risk treatment plan, (iv) implementation and operating the ISMS (v) cost assessment of ISMS

a. (*i*)

b. (*ii*)

c. (*iii*)

d. (*v*)

9. ISO 90003 is a standard formulated for____________________.

a. banks and financial institutions

b. certification by the banks in their IT environment

c. use by the IT industry for software and hardware in general

d. adoption by the software but not for certification

10. ISO 9001 certification is a must for certification under ISO 27001 standards. (True/False)

11. Plan Do Check Act model has been used very well in ISO 27001 standards. (True/False)

12. SAS 70 is a statement on Accounting and Standards. (True/False)

Answers

1. *a*	7. *c*
2. *b*	8. *c*
3. d	9. *d*
4. *b*	10. False
5. *c*	11. True
6. *a*	12. False

B

MODULE

IT SECURITY CONTROLS

9 CHAPTER

Asset Classification and Controls

OBJECTIVES

At the end of the chapter, readers will know the meaning and significance of Information Asset Classification, the different criteria for classification, different types of hardware assets and the security controls applicable to them and types of software assets and their security controls. The nature and effectiveness of various types of controls for software and hardware assets and the ways to monitor them periodically to review their effectiveness is also discussed in this chapter.

9.1 Asset Classification and Control

We have already seen earlier in Chapter 1, what exactly constitutes an Information Asset. To give a quick recap, Information Asset refers to any data or information that is stored in any medium physical or in logical (like in a database) format or is in transit, which has some value for the parties associated with it. We have also seen that there are three parties to an Information Asset namely Owner, Custodian and User.

9.2 We have also seen in the same chapter that we have to secure only such information that is needed to be kept and preserved. As already seen, information can be classified on the following parameters:

I. Criticality
II. Confidentiality
III. Availability and
IV. Purpose.

9.3 Based on criticality, information may be classified as Most Critical, Critical and Least Critical or Insignificant. What is available in the public domain, what can be recreated easily and what is quite easy to get may be called least critical and that which is more difficult, on these parameters, may be called Critical and then Most Critical.

Based on Confidentiality, information may be classified as Most Confidential or Private, Confidential and Least or simply as High, Medium and Low. What is confidential to one group of users may not be confidential to the other group. For instance, the HR data of an organisation's employees may be treated as confidential to all employees but not within the HR department who need the data for their routine processing like salary, leave etc. Some information may be private to one individual and confidential to that particular employee alone and never to be revealed to anyone else. Confidentiality itself may again be classified as High, Medium and Low depending upon the nature of secrecy involved

in it. Some information may be confidential based on time. For instance, exam results or any such information are classified as confidential upto the point of time, the data is officially released and not after that.

9.4 Protection of Information Assets

Depending upon the value, the information assets have to be classified, treated and protected. In other words, the security initiatives and measures to protect a particular information asset depends mainly on the nature of information asset. Protection mechanism includes the policies and practices that are in place or that should ideally be in place to protect them. Therefore, depending upon the nature of information, the nature of criticality and classification, the protection mechanism evolves.

Controls are essentially the initiatives that are taken by top management to protect an information asset. As we have already noted that security is not a product but a process and is not static but a dynamic process, controls to be put in place are also dynamic in nature and keep varying from asset to asset and may for the same asset from time to time.

Risk Materialisation is a concept when a threat meets its matching vulnerability. Taking the study of risk further and in the same context, the word 'control' can be easily understood and appreciated. Control is the countermeasure or the administrative safeguards and steps taken to meet the risk and eliminate or at least minimize the impact of risks in the information assets. Hence, to understand IT Security and to make the Information Asset safe and secure, proper controls must be in place. An efficient and effective security control and organisational awareness about the same will ensure security of IT assets in the organisation.

Hence, ideally the control objectives and control policies in any organisation especially in banks do not normally specify the type and extent of steps initiated but contain the nature of initiatives and the broader protection mechanism. For instance, in the earlier days of bank computerisation, the control measures spoke about protection of branch data maintained in branches in standalone systems called ALPMs (Advanced Ledger Posting Machines) or in later stages in Total Branch Automation or Computerisation (TBA or TBC branches) in a distributed database environment which may no longer hold good in these days of Core Banking environment when bank branches do not maintain any data (except the overnight balance file along with the account numbers maintained in one of the PCs in the case of some banks to serve as an emergency information).

9.5 Control of Hardware Equipment

Hardware is an essential component of information asset. Control of hardware equipment Involves essentially the following steps:

I. Identifying the hardware information asset
II. Recording the hardware right from procurement stage
III. Classifying the hardware on the basis of factors like criticality, monetary value
IV. Keeping an inventory control
V. Monitoring the movement of hardware, inter-department, intra-department etc.
VI. Constantly reviewing the controls initiated for their adequacy and effectiveness

The first step in hardware asset control lies in identification of hardware which is to be monitored and controlled. This itself is crucial, because due to lack of knowledge and exposure in technology, organisation especially banks often fail to identify critical and costly hardware equipment and unnecessarily spend time on protecting some minor equipment, which may appear huge in size.

Technology is ever changing and constantly striving towards reduction in the size of hardware equipment and increase in the capacity to store or process.

Now-a-days we get very small equipment weighing around 50 to 100 grams and hardly one or two cubic centimeters in volume but with a capacity to store TB of data. Such equipment (like pen-drives, chips etc.) are to be handled with utmost caution and care with proper identification procedures, upkeep, traceability during the entire life-span of the equipment until the stage of ultimate destruction. Hence hardware asset control assumes enormous significance. Policies and procedures to identify every hardware equipment should take into account not just the financial value of the equipment but also their use, their area of availability, rules on their movement from one department to another, intra organisation movement and also movement outside the organisation.

Recording the hardware equipment

The hardware details should be recorded with distinct number right from the point it enters the organisation throughout its life span. For recording such number and later inventory control, **Bar Coding** is considered to be an effective tool. Bar Coding should be done at the first point of entry into the organisation and recorded. Such a system will ensure fool-proof maintenance of not just the physical entry of hardware equipment but will also be helpful for the financial and accounting purposes. Bar code scanners should be made available in every department in the organisation and should be used even for the smallest item recorded.

Bar Code

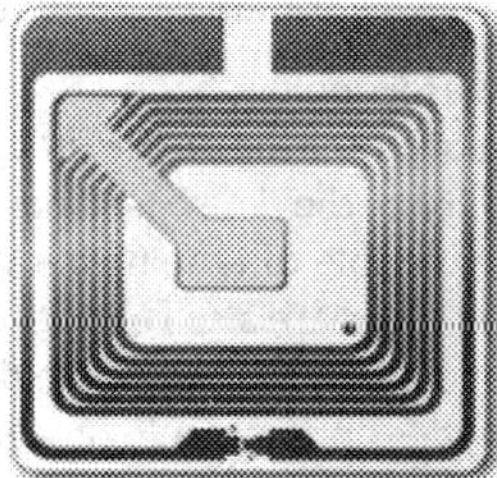

RFID Circuit

QR (Quick Response) Code

2D Bar (Data Matrix) Code

As against plain linear bar coding, shown above, the picture at the side shows a 2D Bar Coding (also known as matrix code), which is increasing in popularity these days. These 2D bar codes are capable of recording more information about the product namely price, quality or description etc. or perhaps the security number etc. (as against the linear bar code which can carry the product number only) and hence are quite useful as part of physical security control too.

Another kind of 2D code is a QR code, which is made up of black modules placed on a white background in the shape of squares. Any kind of data, including binary and alphanumeric data, can

be included in the encoded information. QR Codes were first created by the automotive industry to track cars during the manufacturing process. More recently, however, they have gained popularity for more commercial applications, including marketing campaigns that target mobile phone users and entertainment. Web address storage QR Codes can be found in periodicals, on signs, etc. When a user scans an image of a QR Code using a bar code scanner application on their phone, text, contact details or a web page opens in the phone's browser.

Bar Coding has become such a dependable, advanced and useful technology these days, that it is being increasingly used as an effective hardware movement control too. There are mobile phones that can read and scan bar codes. There are Asset Tracking apps available for use in the mobile phones which can easily tell us what assets we have, where they are at this time etc. By virtue of these features, these apps serving as asset management tracking devices, are a blessing for security managers to locate the assets especially while in transit.

Bar code reading is of different types popular being:

I. Pen type reader
II. Laser based reader
III. Camera reader
IV. CCD (Charge Coupled Device) or LED reader
V. Other types including multi-directional reader

Bar Coding as a technology has quite a few standards and sometimes, coded in one particular standard may not be read in another, since they are specific to the particular proprietary standard only. Of late, compared to the earlier line based bar coding, 2D Bar Coding is being increasingly used. Many mobile handsets are capable of reading bar codes and bar codes can be stored and sent through mobiles too. However, these are also subject to standards and the proprietary formats. Mobile handsets like Blackberry and most of the modern day mobile gadgets in the form of iPhones have the capability to read bar codes and transmit bar code images.

Inventory Control

Just like BarCoding technology used for identification of hardware equipment and control, the other dependable and affordable technology widely prevalent is RFID (Radio Frequency Identification). RFID is growing in popularity not just for hardware tracing and monitoring but also for tracking employees' movement inside a huge office complex.

RFID tags are affixed to the equipment or as part of the employee's person and the employee is supposed to carry it like a smart card or other cards. From cost point of view, RFID tags are costlier and may cost around Rs.10 to Rs.20 per piece since it works on antenna circuit design with the RF signals getting radiated, while bar coding is much less than one rupee per equipment. Even if the bar has got erased due to wear and tear, the organisation can bar code it again, in view of the cost factor.

From security point of view, both the systems bar coding as well as RFID are vulnerable and have their own shortcomings. In both, there is no camera involved and the Bar code reader has to be shown to the object or RFID reader is to be placed at strategic points in the hall to ensure that when the employee walks or when the material is getting shifted to another place, the RFID reader identifies the object from a range of 3 or 4 metres depending upon the capacity and capability of the bar-code reader or RFID reader. If the RFID reader should catch the image from a distance (say more than 1 metres), then the reader should be of a higher capacity and capability with additional features like ultra-violet reading.

Again from information security point of view, in both the above technologies, the connectivity is done through cables with RJ45 jack and in practice it is normally an externally visible cable. Hence if any fraudsters want to bypass the RFID or Bar Coding Surveillance, they would disable (*i.e.* physically remove) the cable temporarily, shift the equipment and then replace the connectivity. Hence from security point of view, factors like connectivity for such monitoring, nature and type of cables, whether they are part of any VLANs etc. are to be looked into. A prudent IS Auditor will look into these aspects while conducting the IS audit in such organisations.

From security point of view, there are other limitations as well. RFID tags or bar-code attachments should not be easily removable and swappable from one device to another, since any fraudster will be induced to make such easy swap movement from one item to another and bypass the security surveillance. Spoofing of data in such equipment is also possible in both these technologies.

In short, Access Control to an information asset must be from physical angle and from software angle (*i.e.* logical, virtual or remote access). Any software asset will be accessed from any of these and hence the control should cover all these, as depicted below:

9.6 Traditional Methods to Control Hardware Assets

As stated above, the traditional method of physical control of information assets to ensure security, involves one or more of the following steps:

Access to hardware assets can easily be controlled by traditional methods some of which are listed below:

I. Physical check of persons before entry into the hardware area
II. Posting a security guard at critical areas restricting entry
III. Installation of CCTV in critical areas
IV. Monitoring through CCTV surveillance
V. RFID and other electronic controls
VI. Swipe cards or bio-metric enabled cards permitting entry for authorized persons
VII. Entry restriction mechanism to server room or the place
VIII. Installation of camera at critical entry points taking photos at that point

After a proper classification and inventory control through an accepted system, it would be next step to constantly review the adequacy and effectiveness of the system followed. If found inadequate or ineffective, organisations should switch to a better system.

9.7 Control of Software Assets

Software Assets in any organisation can be broadly grouped as:

I. Data and information
II. In-house developed software applications
III. Procured or outsourced software and related applications.

Any control measures for the three stated above will have to ensure that the Software Assets are preserved intact and conform to and rest firmly on all the three pillars of security namely, Confidentiality, Integrity and Availability and of course the fourth one that is, Non-Repudiation too.

In short, controls should

I. be part of the systems and not a standalone.
II. be preferably integrated into the system and not a standalone and removable.

III. not handicap or slow the system but effectively enhance the functioning.
IV. be easy to implement.
V. ensure capability of measuring its effectiveness.
VI. be dynamically upgradable.
VII. be dynamically customizable.

IT Asset Management

Of late, IT Asset Management(ITAM) is being increasingly spoken about in software and allied industry circles. IT Asset Management (ITAM) is a comprehensive approach to managing an organization's IT assets throughout their lifecycle, from procurement to disposal. ITAM is the overall broad-based activities taken by the organisation for proper control and management of all the IT assets of the organisation. In the case of hardware IT assets, ITAM involves activities like tracking the hardware their location, their uses, book value, status of usability, etc. Effective IT Asset Management helps organizations optimize their IT resources, enhance decision-making, ensure compliance, and reduce overall costs. It also helps organisation to track those assets that are lying underutilized or unutilized (which would be a drain on the amount spent), verify whether employees are using the right equipment, right tools and at the right places, check whether hardware assets are properly serviced and the third party maintenance vendor provides service efficiently and effectively etc.

In the case of Software Assets, a properly well documented ITAM which is automated will ensure that

I. all software assets are taken care of,
II. only licensed software is used,
III. all databases are properly protected,
IV. upgrades and updates wherever applicable are always available,
V. all software procured are being effectively utilized,
VI. proper deliverables are obtained from third party maintenance vendors,
VII. anti-virus vendors are delivering their upgrades and updates in time,
VIII. Annual Maintenance Contracts are available and renewed in time.

There is software available to check version control and other features of all the software running, to monitor the use of any software utility, to verify whether any unlicensed software is running, to check where any software is installed and how it is used, and to manage all such related factors with regard to software and database usage.

Any IT Asset control especially Software Asset control should certainly check the use of unlicensed software or free downloaded software running in critical systems. Free downloads including test versions or demo versions of utilities or other unlicensed or uncontrolled usage of software in critical computer systems even PCs that contain valuable or sensitive data pose a great threat to the system and is a great risk to the organisation. Hence, Software Asset control should always monitor the use of free utilities and freely downloaded software running in the systems. Even if one PC in the organisation runs such free untested downloaded utility it is a great risk to the organisation since unknowingly the organisation exposes itself to Trojans and Malwares through that one system.

Besides the IT Asset Control for the software and utilities running in the organisation, any critical organisation especially banks have to ensure that their databases are safe and secure and are maintained always. The layer above the database is the actual application developed for the organisation.

Different layers in Information Security

Application Controls

In addition to the controls at operating system level, database level, organisation should also have in place controls at application level.

Meaning and significance of Access Control and Privileges has already been discussed in the earlier introductory chapters.

Access Privileges are normally unique for hardware and software information assets. It is easier to have a proper access privilege for hardware equipment or a critical server in a physical set up, since it can be done with a simple door access control mechanism or an id card with bar coding or perhaps even on a still simple mechanism of having the entries made in a register before entering the critical area.

Access Privileges in the case of software information assets is a little trickier and complicated. It should be defined and properly placed at different levels right from the operating system, the database, the applications or the customized programs running on top of it, upto the front-end user interfaces running on top of everything. In such a design, the access privileges typically can be set up right at any point or level, right from the operating system level as part of, for instance, the Active Directory, Settings and Tools.

The responsibility of the Windows Systems Managers or anyone assigned with the powers and role of Systems Administrator is immense. After studying the corporate information security policy, they have to finalise the privileges in tune with the Policy and ensure compliance and implementation.

For instance, the banking application software running at branches will have proper controls like clerical staff member posting an entry, the supervisory official passing or authorizing the entry and if necessary the branch chief authorizing or verifying or approving the entry in exceptional cases or in cases above a particular amount, etc.

Top executives from the corporate offices of the organisation like the Head Offices or Registered Offices of banks may have access to certain important or major current accounts of specific branches for a limited purpose of viewing the account so that they can be aware of the current and updated balance in those critical accounts dynamically, but they will not have powers to post any transaction or do any data entry from their systems. All such requirements are taken care of at the application level.

9.8 OSI Model

Looking at the OSI Model, it's evident that more than a few security protocols are required to be fully protected. All potential access points and sites where hackers could obtain access to your network, data, and organization must be carefully considered.

The Human Layer: Humans are the weakest link in any Cyber Security strategy, and they are alone responsible for 90% of data breaches. Mission-critical assets are protected from a variety of human threats, such as cybercriminals, malevolent insiders, and careless users, by human security controls including phishing simulations and access management rules.

Security Strategy: Education and Training, which include instructions on how to recognize and deal with phishing attacks, strong password strategies, system hardening, and cyber security awareness, are the best ways to keep the human layer secure. Access controls are a smart notion for protecting the human layer since they can reduce the amount of harm that could result from a successful attack.

Perimeter Security: The physical and digital security techniques that safeguard the entire company are included in Perimeter Security controls. Here, we must first define our perimeter before determining the sort of data being transmitted across this layer, and then we must secure both the data and the device.

Security Strategy: This includes firewalls, data encryption, antivirus software, device management (which is crucial if your company has a bring-your-own-device policy), and setting up a secure demilitarized zone for further security.

Network Security: Network Security measures to safeguard a company's network and guard against unwanted access. The key worry of the Network Layer is what users and devices can access once they are within your system.

Security Strategy: If no one person has access to everything, then any successful cyberattack only results in a small portion of the network being breached. The best practice for security at this layer is to only give employees and devices access to the parts of the network that are 100% necessary for them to do their jobs.

Endpoint Security: Endpoint security measures safeguard the network connection between devices.

Security Strategy: Endpoint encryption is required to make sure that the devices are operating in secure environments.

Application Security: Controls for Application Security guard against access to an application, access to your mission-critical assets by an application, and internal application security.

Security Strategy: The most basic thing you can do here is to keep your programs up to date. This guarantees that the application is as secure as possible and that any known security vulnerabilities are addressed.

Data Security: Data Security measures protect the storage and movement of data, which is the target of cybercrime. The most care must be taken with this layer because it is the foundation of your company.

Security Strategy: At this level, keeping things secure entails file and disc encryption, frequent backups of all crucial data and procedures, two-factor authentication, enterprise rights management, and rules that make sure data is erased from devices that are no longer in use or that are being given to another employee.

Know Your Progress

Information Asset refers to any data or information that is stored in any medium physical or in logical (like in a database) format or is in transit. Information Asset is to be protected against all kinds of threats and exposure to risks should be mitigated. Asset should be classified according to the value attached to it like monetary value, confidentiality value, etc. Depending upon the value of criticality and importance, the security around the asset will be built. Security Control is the management's initiative to protect the asset from all types of attacks.

Control of hardware equipment can be done by manual monitoring, supervision or by a system of barcoding of all the assets so that the movement of any asset beyond the physical barriers of the store room and the overall monitoring and movement of assets can be recorded and managed. There are different types of barcoding the most appropriate ones would be chosen, depending upon the factors such as the data to be stored etc. Similarly, RFID is also a technology used for supervision and control of hardware equipment including the physical movement of equipment.

On the software side, which also constitutes an important information asset, the value of software, database, criticality and confidentiality of data constitute the significance of the software asset and the asset should accordingly be protected and controlled. Software asset control involves steps on different layers of software like the operating system lying at the bottom of the pyramid, the database lying just above it, application developed for the organisation lying one step above and the user access just above it. Setting proper access privileges is also part of software access control, which is normally done depending upon the nature of activities and the role functions of the user.

Key Words

Barcoding	RFID	2-D Barcoding	Surveillance
Application Layer	ITAM	Inventory	

Questions

1. RFID is a technology to monitor physical movement of assets and to____________.
   a. guard it against theft, pilferage and misuse
   b. secure it against all kinds of unauthorised access and to record any access to it
   c. restrict the movement of assets by radio frequency and to provide information to server
   d. monitor the movement of assets to any place inside or outside the complex and to alert the server
2. Control of Information Asset essentially involves steps in____________________.
   a. Controlling and curtailing access to the information asset
   b. Monitoring mechanism of top management to control the information from other layers
   c. Initiatives taken by management to protect the information from unauthorised access
   d. Initiatives taken by top management to protect the information from other layers
3. Bar Coding is an internationally accepted technology which can be used to protect ________________
   a. any kind of information asset in whichever form it is maintained
   b. any hardware asset of the organisation from any kind of unauthorised use
   c. any software asset by proper bar coding the label in the media like DVD, CD etc.
   d. any physical asset and to keep proper record of any movement of such asset
4. The different layers in software will normally be the following one above the other are___________.
   a. Operating System, Database, Application, User Interface
   b. Operating System, Application, User, Database

c. Operating System, User, Database, Application

d. Database, Operating System, Application, User Interface

5. Access Privilege for the users in an application normally refers to__________________.

a. Privileges or rights given to users to accept any application and process it

b. Rights given to users to access the database as per the role assigned to him/her

c. Rights given to users to supervise the data and functioning of the database

d. Rights of access given to users to access the database other than through a front-end process and through an Application Interface at the back end

6. Which of the following cannot be done through an automated process of IT Asset Management?

a. IT Asset procurement and calculation of Return on Investment.

b. IT Asset Monitoring including its physical movement, use and over-use or misuse.

c. Control of all IT Assets right from the stage they are procured upto their destruction.

d. Assessment of the usage of IT asset right from the point of its procurement.

7. Proper inventory control of all physical information assets can be ensured by___________.

a. keeping all inventory under lock and key of top management and recording movement.

b. keeping all assets under dual custody and maintaining fool-proof documentation.

c. putting an automated IT Asset Management to cover all valuable inventory items and monitoring them effectively.

d. judicious use of RFID or Bar Coding or other suitable technology and thus ensuring monitoring irrespective of the size and value of the inventory.

8. Which one of the following is not part of Access Privileges in Physical Access Control mechanism for a server room?

a. Having a register at the door, instructing the staff to make an entry and sign the register before entering the centre.

b. Installing an access mechanism at the entrance, in which the staff members swipe their card before entering.

c. Installing a front end computer system for the users to login with password and get their entry authenticated, before entering.

d. Installing a bio metric device at the entrance to the room, in which the officials can mark their thumb impression and get it authenticated before entering.

9. Is hardware access control through RFID considered to be costlier than Barcoding? (True/False)

10. Use of unlicensed software is not an Information Security issue but only a legal issue. (True/False)

Answers

1. *b*	6.*a*
2. *c*	7. *d*
3. *d*	8. *c*
4. *a*	9. True
5. *b*	10. False

10 CHAPTER

Physical and Environmental Security Controls

OBJECTIVES

After reading this chapter, readers will be able to know the meaning and significance of physical control of information assets, the environmental controls that are required and essential in any organisation, the impact and effectiveness of or lack of any such controls and steps to be taken to enhance such controls in the organisation.

10.1 Introduction

Physical security layer is the most tangible layer in a security set up. It is often said that what you see is what you should secure. Not to undermine the importance of software security and logical security, physical security certainly is of very key significance in any organisation.

Defense in Depth

This is a term often used to denote the coordination of all controls that should be in place - Physical, Logical, Network, Software and Environmental. No control should be isolated from the other, though every control should be distinctly verifiable and manageable at the same time. It is the coordinated use of multiple security counter measures to protect the integrity of the information assets, based on the principle that it would be difficult for an attacker or an intruder to defeat a complex and multi-layered controlled system than to penetrate a single barrier.

Minimising the probability of an attacker to strike, a well-designed strategy of this kind helps system administrators and security personnel identify people who attempt to compromise a computer, server, proprietary network or ISP (Internet Service Provider) and all the vulnerabilities therein. Defense in Depth normally consists of all network controls like Intrusion Detection Systems, Intrusion Prevention Systems etc. software controls like firewall, anti-spyware, anti-malware (*about which we will be studying in the later chapters).* We will be studying the physical and environmental controls here.

Broadly, physical and environmental security controls include physical security measures such as personnel involved in security, premises security, and hardware upkeep. Similarly, environmental controls in an IT organization or a bank typically refer to measures taken to monitor, control, and review steps ensuring a clean environment, especially in IT-related areas. This includes maintenance of AC units in proper repair, servers at appropriate temperatures, ensuring an environmentally friendly atmosphere, and proper disposal of e-waste and unusable electronic equipment like disks.

Much more than any other control, physical control is always considered to be a layered approach. Every organisation will have a perimeter security for the premises like frisking the visitors, entry pass for the visitors etc. at the main gate (probably with the principle of permit all with some caution and checks), a second layer for the operations department or the business units and wherever necessary a third layer for the most critical areas like data centre, network operation centre, data storage centre etc. (wherein the principle will be to deny all and permit those with specific authority only).

10.2 Earlier in Chapter 5 we discussed physical security measures for an Information Asset. In this chapter, the focus will be on such physical security controls more from a management angle, like categorization of high risk areas, personnel security, high critical areas, categorization of controls, need for controls, adequacy and effectiveness of existing controls, review of such controls, etc.

10.3 Physical controls are essentially concerned with hardware equipment and the people who are associated with it. Peopleware is a term that is commonly used in the context of physical information asset. The terms can refer to anything that has to do with the role of people in the development or use of computer software and hardware systems, including such issues as developer productivity, teamwork, group dynamics, etc. Despite the level of automation and computerisation, there is always the involvement of people in any information asset, right from the stage the information asset is created, Peopleware assumes significance. The psychology of programming, project management, organizational factors, human interface design, and human-machine-interaction are all important components of physical asset that needs to be brought as part of physical control initiatives.

10.4 There are many electronic devices used to exercise control on physical security like CCTV, Video Surveillance, posting of armed guards, etc. Detailed analysis of all these has already been made under Chapter 5. In this chapter we will be discussing only the controls that can be exercised with the help of these physical control devices.

In the case of CCTVs, banks and organisations should take care to study the volume of data created by the CCTVs, since the question of storage and retrieval is a big issue. There are instances and incidents getting widely reported when a criminal or even a terrorist is nabbed with the help of a CCTV footage in the next few hours of sabotage, before he boarded the flight to flee the nation from the city or otherwise leaves the city where the incident took place. In banks in India too, many ATM fraudulent withdrawal cases have been solved with the help of CCTV footage recorded by the banks. But still, issues on storage, retrieval of images, periodicity of preservation of images are yet to be solved.

Especially in banks, when a customer notices fraudulent ATM withdrawals from his account, a few days after the incident, and by the time he lodges a complaint with the bank, approaches the investigating agencies and the police actually files the report, it would be already a delay of a few months and by that time the bank says the ATM footages are not preserved or are overwritten.

In the case of video surveillance especially in banks, the position is much more complex. Though it is one of the most effective physical access control, video surveillance has many practical issues such as choice of place where the camera is to be kept, lighting the area, recording and preservation of various pictures, vulnerabilities in the physical location of the camera etc. There are instances of bank robbery where the robbers immediately after entering the banking hall, cover the camera eye or disable the camera recording completely and then start their criminal operations.

In order to make the physical access controls through CCTV quite successful, and to serve as truly useful controls, organisations have to put many initiatives in place. It is not just enough if CCTVs are installed in lots of places in departments, functional areas including parking spaces, entry points into the premises right up to the protected area like server room or the Board room etc. The entire exercise of such surveillance and controls will be effective only when such images are stored, analysed and acted upon.

Video Surveillance normally involves these four stages;

I. Capture through Camera and proper positioning.

II. Sensors, Analytics and Data Management Engines with proper software.

III. A common control centre to store the data enabling quick retrieval and use.

IV. Responders and Actuators with steps like metadata tagging and behavioural analytics, etc .

The vulnerabilities in the usage of armed guards in banks is already well known and is often widely reported in the press. Banks normally outsource the physical security management to an agency who takes care of posting of personnel at the bank's premises including ATMs and other critical areas. Banks should exercise control over the manner of posting, verification of persons who get posted including their antecedents, their physical fitness to undertake the job, the hours of duty assigned to them etc. In the case of an outsourced security management, it is the Service Level Agreement that should be taken care of as an effective security control measure.

Especially in the case of ATMs, it is often reported that many bank robberies and ATM thefts could have been prevented if only the security guards posted at the premises were healthier, younger and smarter. In most of the Indian cities, especially the metropolitan centres, the police department often organizes meetings with bank executives whenever there is an ATM theft or an attempted one involving either loss of huge money or loss of human life, and advices the bank management to ensure deploying physically fit security guards at the premises.

Unattended ATMs will continue to be among fraudsters' favourite targets. The best way to guard against ATM attacks is to regularly inspect devices for skimming and shimming devices and frequently test ATM software.

Banking institutions also should regularly review transaction logs for suspicious activity. Banks should routinely undertake inspection of logs at the ATMs application server and at the other levels of ATM applications too, so that even some jackpotting attacks could be detected and controls put in place in time.

10.5 Environment Controls

This is one of the latest issues concerning the IT industry, that is engaging the attention of modern day technologists.

Green Servers

The previous generation of servers were all designed and built to meet the organisations seemingly ever increasing demand for more processing power at the least time possible occupying the least space. These days the cost of power is going up globally, power consumption is also becoming a constraint and emission related features are also being spoken about, a new range of dedicated servers with a high performance with least power consumption and least space are now being introduced. Considering how crowded many metropolitan cities are especially in countries like Japan or even most parts of India where data centre spaces are becoming scarce and proving to be very costlier, it is but natural that green servers which essentially mean servers with least power consumption and least space occupying, are being increasingly considered by these organisations.

Deployment of green servers is considered to be one of the ways to save the plant making more business sense and exhibit a commitment towards eco-consciousness. In these days of fierce competition to bring out more and more eco-friendly servers complying with environmental control norms, manufacturers are coming out with servers that consume less than 10-20 watts of power that can run Linux or the RISC based processors (Reduced Instruction Set Computer) that are in use for almost three decades now.

From environmental security point of view, green servers are very important because they ensure compliance with all emission control norms, especially from internationally accepted standards like ISO also. They consume less power with less emissions and hence are more eco-friendly. At the stage of procurement itself, organisations now-a-days stipulate emission, power consumption and other environment-related conditions as part of the technical specifications in addition to the conventional processing capacity, High Availability and backup and fault-tolerant related specifications. In this drive to be more and more eco-friendly, companies have introduced servers with no power cord and taking power through Ethernet with no moving parts without even a fan inside that was traditionally used to cool the system inside.

Blade Servers are generally considered to be "green" servers and are often used by organisations. Blade Server is a stripped down server with a modular design, using minimum physical space and with minimum power consumption. As against a standard rack-mounted server with a power cord, network cable etc., a blade server is mounted on an enclosure together called a blade system that has within it cooling, networking capabilities with the least consumption of power. The blade system offers the same server capabilities with just half the server density and space occupation. Many leading server manufactures like HP, IBM have their variants of blade systems often deployed in many critical data centres that are conscious about power consumption and space consumption.

Blade Server

Blade Servers offer power saving and space saving ensuring no compromise on the quality of processing nor the processing speed. Hence, from the environmental security point of view the security policy of organisations should take care to provide for power consumption, space saving etc. as factors for consideration at the stage of procurement. Besides, control measures should also include periodic inspection of functioning of such servers, monitoring their usage and maintenance.

10.6 Lighting

Lighting controls now-a-days increasingly engage the attention of builders and they include factors like power saving, solar energy utilization at the time of construction of premises itself. In most of the nations, organisations are rewarded for utilizing solar energy and putting in place power-saving initiatives. Buildings are awarded "Green" Certificates and are motivated by reward schemes by governments and NGOs. Therefore, it is proper that environment security controls include lighting as a main factor with its proper upkeep and maintenance.

In the discussion of lighting, it is pertinent to note that environment control and power savings initiatives also include sensor based lighting that is often deployed in many buildings. Sensor based lighting also called Motion Sensor lighting turns the lights on when there is some motion in the area under sensor and turns it off when the motion stops. When a person enters a hall or a premises, as they are in motion, the light will turn on, just moments before they are entering the area and will go off, the moment they leave the area. Besides being a power saving measure, such lighting system is a dependable physical security control too, since movement of persons and equipment can be easily monitored and if necessary recorded.

Besides just sensor based lighting, there are many other devices that are sensor based which can be deployed in any organisation that is conscious about environment. In all such cases, the control measures should include maintenance of such devices, the security concerns in such devices and the technology involved in such gadgets it impacts the security environment of the organisation.

10.7 e-Waste

We have seen in earlier chapters, especially Chapter 5, that e-waste and its disposal are capturing the attention of organizations with increasing concern. There seems to be no globally accepted practice for disposing of e-waste. From a security standpoint and when exercising security controls, especially from an environmental perspective, organizations must ensure that e-waste is disposed of judiciously. By e-waste, we mean old and unusable electronic gadgets such as hard disks, old and discarded external storage media like floppies, CDs, DVDs, DAT drives, and all such electronic equipment like routers, switches, and circuit boards.

Information Security Policy should have clauses to ensure that old and discarded hard-disks are not only formatted, but also physically destroyed or degaussed so that any tools running in them would not be able to retrieve data from it. It should be the responsibility of data owner to ensure that unused storage devices are disposed off under proper authority and with due procedure being followed with proper records maintained to prove that no data was there at the time of disposal and nothing is recoverable too.

Especially in the case of old mobile handsets, there must be clearly laid down policies that such devices should be physically destroyed, since data from cell-phone handsets can be recovered with software tools, even after they are deleted. From the security and data theft point of view, old discarded Xerox machines pose a very great threat. With the increasing use of modern day photocopiers with memory and storage capabilities, when more copies can be taken from the memory of the machine itself, this capability of photocopier itself is a major threat for the security managers in dealing with such machines.

Data critical establishments using such machines should take care to ensure that the data stored on the disk or in memory is properly protected whenever such machines are given for servicing, or taken out and to destroy the data completely or remove the hard-disks whenever they are surrendered under buy-back or discarded to the dustbin.

Compared to disposal or destruction of a software asset, the disposal of a hardware asset is easier. Disposal of the hardware may be in stages when we destroy or remove one part of it and make the other part reusable in the same organization or otherwise put it into some use elsewhere also. Sometimes a hardware asset may get a premature 'death' or 'end-of-life' because of some inherent defect in manufacturing and not because of use, may be sent back to the user and then the defect rectified. The process of rectifying the defect normally present in manufacturing or otherwise rendered unfit for the immediate use of the intended user, after testing and certifying the same as fit for use is called 'refurbishment'.

Refurbished products are the ones that were sent to the user but found to be defective or otherwise unusable whereas the 'used' products have normally lived their full lives. The main difference between "refurbished" and "used" products is that refurbished products have been tested (again) and verified now to function properly, and are thus free of defects, while "used" products may or may not be defective.

Here, the study of 'buyback' seems relevant especially as the most popular, commercially remunerative and legally permissible way for disposal of an information asset. Most of the vendors offer 'buyback' of old hardware assets as an option when selling a new product of the same brand or of same type. From IT Security point of view, it is this aspect that deserves special mention. Even a small carelessness on the part of the user in not deleting or completely destroying the data will expose the user or the organisation to a very great extent of data theft or misuse. The normal or perhaps the routine act of taking out something useful from anything that is treated as rubbish or thrown into the dustbin, called 'scavenging' may sometimes put the organisation into a messy situation.

In the computer world, dumpster diving refers to the methods adopted for getting information by searching through waste or trash discarded by the owner or the user. Though the words 'dumpster diving' means the act of looking through the trash literally, in the context of IT and cyber-crimes, it is most often used to refer to the deliberate act of taking out data and misusing them or using them for a fraudulent purpose with a criminal intention of what is called in legal terminology *'mens rea'*. Scavenging and Dumpster Diving are sheer technologies which though *per se* are not crimes, but often become a criminal offence when used with a specific criminal intention of putting the data so retrieved, for unlawful purposes. To guard against scavenging and dumpster diving, organisations normally resort to shredding the documents before discarding them.

Scavenging is another area of concern that security managers should be engaged in. Scavenging is the task of taking out data often with malicious intention, from storage devices that are discarded as unfit for use. This is becoming a major activity often resulting in cyber-crimes inducing the fraudsters to take such devices and recover the data from them and use them for malicious purposes like cyber stalking, data piracy or sometimes selling of such data to rival companies. It is these acts of cyber-crimes that are a breach in cyber security which can be prevented by proper environment friendly security controls in place.

Environment security controls also include upkeep of devices other than chips, processors and computers but which are enablers for the proper functioning of IT systems, like AC equipment, power generators, etc.

From the age old box type window AC equipment, to the days of split air-conditioners in which the equipment is kept open and the cooling vent is alone kept inside the room and the central air conditioning system of ducts passing the air conditioning and blowing cool air, we have these days many modern variants. Present day systems include Precision Air conditioning which are so called because they are specifically designed for computer rooms and server rooms controlling the temperature to a particular level set. Many energy efficient systems, no-noise and eco-friendly systems have also been introduced. Systems Security Policy should address the issues involved in exercising proper controls in maintaining such equipment, complying with environmental norms.

Power Generators are another area of concern from the physical security as well as environmental security control point of view. From the point of view of noise created by them, space occupied and the emission of fumes from them, they are certainly a great hazard to the environment. However, modern day IT industries and banks often use noiseless, least pollutant systems that serve as power inverters and not just generators. Control measures for organizations should include proper Annual Maintenance Contracts (AMCs) and Service Level Agreements (SLAs) for this equipment, ensuring reliability and functionality even during power outages.

10.8 Fire Extinguishers are a useful control for physical security and fire hazards for computer rooms and all other physical assets. There are different types of fire extinguishers that are to be deployed for different physical environments like what is applicable for an open area fire or fire in parking area is certainly not applicable for an office room where electrical cabling would be there. Especially in the case of computer rooms and spaces where such electronic gadgets are located the fire extinguishers to be used should be gas based and water sprinklers. Every organisation has its own Security Department with trained professionals to deal with different kinds of fire hazards including the redeployment of personnel, moving of personnel, head-count of staff members, drills etc. Of late, most of the orgnisations do conduct mock drills periodically to make staff members aware of the fire risks and to train them on how to react in the event of fire without panicking.

Depending upon the nature of industry, the security controls measures do vary. For instance, in the case of banks, the emphasis will be more on the data stored in the system and the AC equipment and related peripherals to keep the servers and other system running. In the case of data centres, the focus will be on the minutest detail of power requirement, ensuring High Availability of data, redundancy and backup at every point and at every time etc. In the case of other communication industries, the emphasis will be on the communication equipment running and the redundancy and backup will be built around to ensure that network and connectivity never fails.

Hence, environmental system control measures deployed should be constantly reviewed periodically to ensure that proper protection is available to all information assets. Just as the environment itself keeps changing and technology is ever evolving, security controls in environment should also be dynamic and be always ready to cope with the changing demands of the industry.

Know Your Progress

Physical and environmental security controls include physical controls of security like personnel involved in security, premises security, hardware upkeep, etc. Similarly, environmental controls in an IT organisation or a bank, normally refers to the measures taken to monitor and control and review the steps taken to ensure a clean environment especially in IT related areas like maintenance of AC in proper repair, maintenance of servers in proper temperature. Physical security control measures include proper use of CCTV, posting of armed guards, deployment of video surveillance camera, etc.

Physical security control measures also include steps taken in the area of peopleware *i.e.* managing the people who take care of information assets. Environment security controls include measures taken in the area of maintaining the systems in an eco-friendly manner, going in for less power consuming equipment like blade servers, green servers, etc. procuring less noise polluting equipment etc. While disposing of old and unusable assets like discarded hard-disks or other storage devices care should be taken to destroy the data contained there and ensure no data is recoverable from such systems and that no information falls into the wrong hands.

Sometimes when a physical information asset it may not need to be disposed off but it may be put to use after some minor repair work. Such a process is called refurbishment and refurbished assets may be used subject to their conformance to standards and use. Disposal of assets involves many significant steps like a decision on whether to sell them under buyback, ensuring that no data is recoverable from it or otherwise they are not hazardous to the environment etc.

Key Words

Peopleware	Green Servers	Blade Servers	Scavenging
Buyback	Refurbishment	Dumpster Diving	Sensor based lighting
e-Waste			

Questions

1. Peopleware is a term normally used to denote____________.

a. people working in computer programming

b. people working in computers involved in activities related to it like software

c. software used by people used in computers and mechanization

d. hardware deployed by people for running human resource related packages

2. Scavenging is often considered to be a crime when it involves ______________.
   a. taking out data from a network equipment when data travels to another point
   b. reading the data in a discarded disk and blackmailing the data owner
   c. maliciously altering the data from a computer when it is received for servicing
   d taking out data from a discarded disk and then reusing it for malicious purpose

3. A server that is least power consuming and very eco-friendly is often referred to as_______.
   a. White server
   b. Power saver server
   c. Green server
   d. Blade system

4. Precision air conditioning is a kind of air conditioning system that is deployed to______.
   a. control the temperature to a particular level set, especially for computer rooms
   b. precisely gives cooling air always with no failures
   c. precisely measures the power consumption for the AC system and to ensure economy
   d. maintain the precise level of AC for particular time of the day like evening, night etc.

5. While surrendering any old hard-disk under buyback arrangement, care should be taken to?
   a. Physically destroy the disk and burn it ensuring no data is recoverable from it.
   b. Degaussing it and thus ensuring that no data can be recovered from it.
   c. Formatting it and defragmenting it and removing the sector allocation tables from it.
   d. Formatting it so that all data in it is lost and the disk shows zero bytes.

6. The technology by which servers are stacked occupying the least space physically in a data centre room is________.
   a. part of blade server system
   b. server mounts in server room
   c. Green server in data centre
   d. Server array in data centre

7. Refurbishment is a process in handling physical assets it involves ___________.
   a. the discarding of the old asset ensuring it is not used by other third parties
   b. a stage before disposal of old asset when all data from the asset is recovered
   c. the taking of all the data from an old hardware and transferring them to a new hardware after repairing it
   d. attending to the problem in a hardware asset and keeping it in good repair for use

8. The Treatment of old print-outs from computers is not included in the category of e-waste. (True/False)

9. Deleted data from a mobile handset cannot be recovered. (True/False)

10. CCTV footages are a major tool in crime prevention. (True/False)

11. Sensor lighting are a major step towards physical security control as well as environment control. (True/False)

Answers

1. *b*	7. *d*
2. *d*	8. True
3. *c*	9. False
4. *a*	10. False
5. *b*	11. True
6. *a*	

11
CHAPTER
Software Security Controls

OBJECTIVES

After reading this chapter the readers will be able to know the various controls that are to be put in place for a safe and secure software development, the different types of software applications in use, the various security initiatives that are to be implemented to make them secure, security controls in databases, security controls in operating systems that have a bearing on software development, etc.

General controls affecting software security are given in this chapter. Controls that are specific to software development right from the stage of coding, issues concerning software upkeep and testing, implementation and maintenance are however, dealt with in detail under Chapter 13. Intricacies related to testing, controls to be effected at the stage of testing and the various testing methodologies are also dealt with in Chapter 13.

11.1 As we have already seen, security is not a product but a process. It should be in place in the software right from the stage of identification of software, its design, (like a High Level Design), Planning (Low Level Design), development (coding, pseudo codes etc.), testing, implementation (deployment, use), maintenance (scope for refinement, improvement, identifying the need for future version releases) etc.

There are many schools of thought with regard to the stages in software development. Some analysts talk about 4 D's *viz.* Discover, Design, Develop and Deliver while others say it must be Define, Design, Deploy, Evaluate and Refine. Broadly, it can be conveniently said that the following significant stages exist:

I. Planning: identifying the need for a software, its applicability, user requirements, etc.

II. Design: Freeze user requirements, decide the Operating System, language, RDBMS

III. Develop: Pseudo code, coding, coding standards, use of library, unit testing, etc.

IV. Testing: Different types involving the user wherever necessary

V. Implementation: At the user site after completing documentation, version control

VI. Maintenance: With constant review, monitor, identifying the need for later versions

Needless to say security should be taken care of in all these stages. Though typically there will be a Quality Analysis team or a Quality Control or a Testing Division which will give quality certification to the product before release, including adherence to security standards wherever necessary, it would still be prudent to build security as an integral part in all these stages right from planning stage itself.

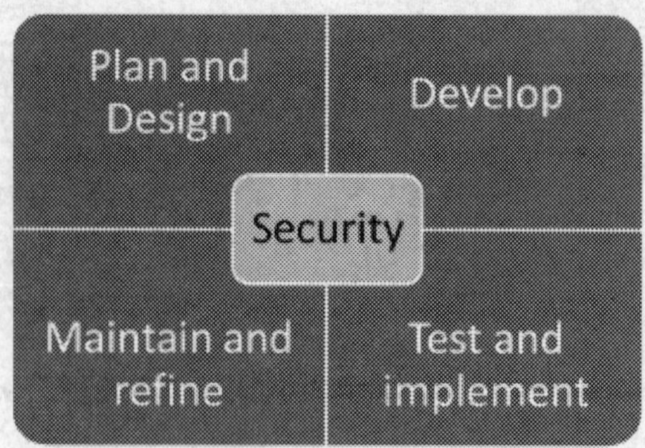

Security in Software Development Life Cycle

In planning stage, the user sometimes may not know the security implications of a particular output or a specific feature. It should be the responsibility of the software development team to impress upon the user the security implications of the feature and sometimes it may be proper and prudent not to include the feature or to continue manual work for that aspect, without computerisation at all. It should be a call that security managers should take involving the user preferably at the top management level.

At the development stage, many organisations deploy an Information Security professional or a developer with expertise in Quality Analysis (QA) and/or security as part of the development team itself to ensure that security is not ignored. Software developers would normally be concerned with compilation, its running successfully and the look and feel for the user. Presence of a security professional at the stage of development team will ensure that access to the coding library is available to the right developers at the right time. Reuse of codes should be followed and procedures or functions should be called wherever necessary without the need to write the code and strain the processor every time the process is adopted. Unnecessary routines, unnecessary procedures should be avoided. Besides, software library, procedures and functions being called in the programs should be accessed at the right place and with a proper access control only.

Pseudo code is writing of the programs in natural language (independent of actual coding syntax and principles of the software language) with compact mathematical notation wherever required. It is easier for people to understand than conventional programming language. It normally forms part of the design stage of development. Developers should get the security clearance at the time of pseudo code itself, so that the hassle of an insecure software getting ready and finally not getting passed at the QA stage is avoided. All access privileges at the application stage and wherever necessary at the operating system stage should be taken care of. Privilege rights and levels of access as per the design of the software as accepted by the user that should be provided for.

At the stage of testing, due consideration is given to the security considerations in different types of testing to be done, as detailed later in Chapter 13.

Security has to be looked into at various layers right at the Operating System (OS) to the Input and Output Processes, Network, Database Settings, the Application Code, Application Server Layer and Front-End Application Settings. Hence, one has to accept that even experts in one field, say the RDBMS, Oracle may not have the requisite expertise in other areas like the OS or Network. Management should strive to co-ordinate the efforts of all the players and put the best security measures in place in line with the Information Security Policy.

IT Security Mechanisms

IT security encompasses a wide range of mechanisms and practices aimed at protecting information and systems from unauthorized access, use, disclosure, disruption, modification, or destruction. Here are some key security mechanisms commonly employed in IT security:

Access Control: Access control mechanisms ensure that only authorized users can access resources or perform certain actions within a system. This includes authentication (verifying the identity of users), authorization (determining what actions users are allowed to perform), and accountability (tracking and auditing user actions).

Encryption: Encryption involves converting data into a format that is unreadable without the correct decryption key. It helps protect data confidentiality, ensuring that even if unauthorized users gain access to the data, they cannot understand it without the appropriate key.

Firewalls: Firewalls are network security devices that monitor and control incoming and outgoing network traffic based on predetermined security rules. They act as a barrier between trusted internal networks and untrusted external networks (such as the internet), helping to prevent unauthorized access and protect against various network-based attacks.

Intrusion Detection Systems (IDS) and Intrusion Prevention Systems (IPS): IDS and IPS are security mechanisms designed to detect and respond to unauthorized access or malicious activities on a network or host system. IDS passively monitor network traffic or system activity and generate alerts when suspicious behaviour is detected, while IPS can take automated actions to block or mitigate threats in real-time.

Vulnerability Assessment and Penetration Testing: These mechanisms involve assessing and identifying security vulnerabilities in systems, networks, and applications. Vulnerability assessment typically involves automated scanning tools to identify known vulnerabilities, while penetration testing (or ethical hacking) involves simulated attacks by security professionals to identify potential weaknesses and exploit them to assess the effectiveness of security controls.

Security Information and Event Management (SIEM): SIEM systems collect, aggregate, and analyse log data from various sources within an IT environment to identify security incidents, detect anomalies, and facilitate incident response and forensic analysis.

Security Policies and Procedures: Establishing and enforcing security policies and procedures is essential for ensuring consistent and effective security practices across an organization. This includes defining acceptable use policies, data handling procedures, incident response plans, and other guidelines to govern the behaviour of users and administrators.

Multi-factor Authentication (MFA): MFA requires users to provide multiple forms of identification (such as passwords, biometric data, or security tokens) to verify their identity before granting access to systems or data. This adds an extra layer of security beyond traditional password-based authentication.

Security Patch Management: Regularly updating and patching software and systems is crucial for addressing known security vulnerabilities and reducing the risk of exploitation by attackers.

Backup and Disaster Recovery: Implementing robust backup and disaster recovery mechanisms helps ensure that critical data and systems can be restored in the event of a security breach, natural disaster, or other catastrophic event.

Multi-layered Approach: These are just a few examples of the many security mechanisms and practices employed in IT security. Effective security requires a multi-layered approach that combines technical controls, policies, procedures, and user education to mitigate risks and protect against evolving threats.

Types of security mechanisms in IT security

In IT security, various types of security mechanisms are employed to protect information assets, systems, networks, and applications from unauthorized access, data breaches, and cyber threats. These security mechanisms encompass a range of technologies, tools, and practices designed to enforce security policies, mitigate risks, and maintain the confidentiality, integrity, and availability of data and resources. Some common types of security mechanisms in IT security, are:

Access Control Mechanisms: Access control mechanisms regulate who can access systems, networks, applications, and data, and what actions they can perform once authenticated. Types of access control mechanisms include:

Authentication: Verifies the identity of users or entities seeking access through methods such as passwords, biometrics, smart cards, and multi-factor authentication.

Authorization: Determines the permissions and privileges granted to authenticated users based on their roles, groups, or attributes, ensuring they have appropriate access rights.

Accounting: Records and tracks user activities, access attempts, and resource usage to create an audit trail for monitoring and compliance purposes.

Encryption Mechanisms: Encryption mechanisms transform data into an unreadable format using cryptographic algorithms to protect it from unauthorized access or interception. Types of encryption mechanisms include:

Symmetric Encryption: Uses a single key to encrypt and decrypt data, suitable for encrypting large volumes of data efficiently.

Asymmetric Encryption (Public-Key Encryption): Uses a pair of keys (public and private) for encryption and decryption, enabling secure communication and key exchange between parties.

Hashing: Converts data into a fixed-length hash value, ensuring data integrity and providing a unique identifier (hash) for verification.

Firewall Mechanisms: Firewall mechanisms monitor and control incoming and outgoing network traffic based on predetermined security rules, protecting networks from unauthorized access and malicious activities. Types of firewall mechanisms include:

Network Firewalls: Inspect and filter traffic at the network layer (e.g., TCP/IP packets) based on source and destination addresses, ports, and protocols.

Application Firewalls: Analyse and filter traffic at the application layer (e.g., HTTP, FTP) to detect and block malicious or unauthorized activities.

Next-Generation Firewalls (NGFW): Combine traditional firewall capabilities with advanced features such as intrusion prevention, application awareness, and deep packet inspection for enhanced security.

Intrusion Detection and Prevention Systems (IDPS): IDPS mechanisms monitor network and system activities for signs of unauthorized access, misuse, or security breaches and take preventive or corrective actions. Types of IDPS mechanisms include:

Network-Based IDPS (NIDPS): Analyses network traffic to detect and respond to suspicious activities, such as network scans, malware outbreaks, and intrusion attempts.

Host-Based IDPS (HIDPS): Monitors activities on individual hosts (e.g., servers, endpoints) for signs of malicious behaviour, such as unauthorized access, file modifications, or privilege escalation.

Vulnerability Assessment and Management: Vulnerability assessment and management mechanisms identify, prioritize, and remediate security vulnerabilities in systems, applications, and infrastructure to reduce the risk of exploitation. Types of vulnerability assessment and management mechanisms include:

Vulnerability Scanners: Automated tools that scan networks, systems, and applications to identify known vulnerabilities, misconfigurations, and security weaknesses.

Patch Management Systems: Tools and processes for deploying security patches and updates to remediate identified vulnerabilities and ensure systems are up-to-date with the latest security fixes.

Identity and Access Management (IAM): IAM mechanisms manage user identities, roles, and access rights across systems and applications to enforce least privilege access and ensure only authorized users can access resources. Types of IAM mechanisms include:

Identity Provisioning: Automates the process of creating, managing, and deprovisioning user accounts and access rights across multiple systems and applications.

Single Sign-On (SSO): Enables users to authenticate once and access multiple applications or systems without needing to re-enter credentials, enhancing convenience and security.

Privileged Access Management (PAM): Manages and monitors privileged accounts and access to critical systems and resources to prevent misuse or abuse by unauthorized users.

Security Information and Event Management (SIEM): SIEM mechanisms collect, correlate, and analyse security event data from various sources (e.g., logs, network traffic) to detect and respond to security incidents in real-time. Types of SIEM mechanisms include:

Log Management: Collects and stores logs generated by systems, applications, and devices for analysis, monitoring, and forensic investigations.

Security Analytics: Applies advanced analytics techniques, such as machine learning and behavioural analysis, to identify patterns, anomalies, and indicators of compromise in security event data.

Incident Response Orchestration: Automates the process of responding to security incidents by coordinating actions, workflows, and responses across security tools and systems.

Combination of Mechanisms: These are just some examples of the types of security mechanisms employed in IT security to protect organizations' assets and infrastructure from a wide range of cyber threats and vulnerabilities. Organizations often deploy a combination of these mechanisms to create layered defenses and enhance overall security posture.

11.2 Operating Systems (OS)

Security as part of the OS is perhaps what lies underneath all security initiatives in software. If OS level security is not in place all security whatever the application has built will fail exposing the software to unauthorised access.

Application
Device Drivers and I/O
Memory Management
CPU Management
Hardware

The critical servers in most of the banks are on Unix platforms, in some flavours of Unix depending upon the hardware boxes like HP-UX or the IBM-AIX or the Sun Solaris versions. Hence organisations especially banks will do well to have trained Unix Systems Managers and Unix Security experts in their HR force to take care that all Operating system level security initiatives are in place with the necessary configuration.

Unix as an operating system has its own security features built into it and probably is the finest among operating systems when configured properly and implemented. That is why, most of the critical

databases in the country especially in the financial sector run on Unix operating system. Some of the most significant security features in Unix are:

I. *User accounts* with the concepts of *super user*, *group* and user accounts
II. Access Control *objects* like inode, UID, default permissions, etc.
III. General Security Principles
IV. Organisation of files and directories
V. Configuration files
VI. Management Issues
VII. Mounting file systems and Protection of files
VIII. Audit logs and User Accounts trails

When properly configured, access by any user can be easily traced, proper monitoring of server access can be done and access to database can be managed. However, it would be the primary responsibility of the system managers to co-ordinate with the hardware suppliers and set all the default settings with proper documentation and top management approval and in line with the Information Systems Security Policy. Since Database Layer is located on the top of the Operating System, if the basics of O/S level security is compromised it may cause a major disaster.

Once installed, and configured the O/S it would then be the responsibility of system administrators to go as per the policy and guidelines to put all User Management principles in place and to ensure proper implementation of Access Control.

11.3 Windows Security

Though all operating systems will have the broader functionalities of user management, memory management, system registry, etc. there are some finer differences in the manner system files are maintained by the O/S. In Windows the *Registry* is the central database for all configuration related files. Modification in the *Registry* can be done through *Registry Editor* called the *regedit.*

Active Directory in Windows is a useful feature for managing the user accounts, identifying the credentials, information protection, system and application settings and serves as the central location for configuration information. Using this efficiently and with proper settings, system managers can enforce many security features like user management, computer management and management of hardware peripherals like printers and other objects, from his central location itself.

Access Control, Access Restriction, Loading of RDBMS and other software in the Operating System, configuring a printer in a network, addition of peripherals in the network for access by other users etc. can all be managed by a properly well designed Windows Systems Management and efficient system manager.

Linux OS

Linux is a classic and popular example of free and open source software and has been originated from its predecessor, UNIX, which was known for its security related features. Linux comes in different flavours and versions and has almost the same security foundation as UNIX, and in some cases, with several enhanced security features. Linux firewall is often reported to be having many more secure features, and affordable in terms of usage than Windows firewall. One can comfortably rely on the default levels of Internet security to work on Linux. However, configuring the powerful Linux firewall can be a complicated task for a novice home user. Linux and all the UNIX-based OS's have a file structure that keeps the similar files, such as data, program files, configuration files etc. This allows a better placement of security policies to protect sensitive areas of the file system. A super user in Windows can run several system-level or application-level services whereas in Linux, any user can only run the daemons meant to be run by that user. This prevents the possibility of an attack to compromise the entire computer at a time.

11.4 Databases

A few decades ago, many banks in India were on flat file system and the earlier databases with the programming languages like COBOL, dBase, FoxPro, Novell Netware and other similar software packages. With the advent of huge computerisation and networked environment and the need for very high processing power and massive volume of data to be handled, banks moved on to RDBMS (Relational Database Management Systems). Many RDBMS are now available like Oracle, Sybase, Informix, MS SQL Server, etc., with Oracle database being the most popular and in use in most of the banks in India.

Before choosing a particular RDBMS, quite often banks discuss the system security requirements and their conformance with standards and their own security policy. The decision on choice of a particular RDBMS will be a conscious one, depending upon the system requirements, system affordability based on the financial strength, user friendliness, nature and type of data to be handled. Above all, these days, since most of the banks entrust the job of major ERP solution or a CBS to an IT major who performs the role of system integrator. It is the system integrator who performs the task of putting in place all the critical servers (*i.e.* hardware), the compatible software (*i.e.* RBDBS along with the application) and the connectivity (network). Depending upon the nature of Service Level Agreement and the nature of order given to the system integrator, the banks are involved in the process of such selection.

Schema

The structure of the database system described in a formal language stating how the database is organised in various tables and other objects, the set of formulas ensuring compatibility between different parts of the structure etc. is called database schema. It defines the objects in the database. Security should be considered right from this stage of drafting of schema itself since it is at this stage that all tables, views, relationships, procedures, etc. are all defined in detail.

Every RDBMS be it Sybase or Oracle or SQL Server has its own security features and it would be the responsibility of the application developers to make the best use of such features. For instance, though the strength of password in Oracle and how it is stored has often been debated. Oracle provides many security features and products like Identity Management, Integrity, Authentication and Access Control, Roles, Data Encryption, High Availability and User Authentication to ensure that the identity of a user, host or client is correctly known.

To access a database, a user must supply a valid username and associated password of the database. These prevent unauthorized use. Oracle also provides authorization, to ensure that a user, program, or process receives the appropriate privileges to access an object. In the later versions of Oracle, stored program units can add an additional level of security restricting to the user, access to a predetermined set of rows and columns of a table.

Database security (in IT security)

Database security involves implementing various techniques and strategies to protect the confidentiality, integrity, and availability of data stored in databases. These techniques aim to prevent unauthorized access, ensure data accuracy, and mitigate the risk of data breaches or loss. Here are some common techniques of database security:

Access Control: Access control is a fundamental technique that regulates who can access the database and what actions they can perform. It involves implementing user authentication mechanisms such as usernames and passwords, role-based access control (RBAC), and attribute-based access control (ABAC) to enforce least privilege access and restrict unauthorized access to sensitive data.

Encryption: Encryption is used to protect data at rest and in transit by converting it into an unreadable format that can only be decrypted with the appropriate cryptographic key. Techniques such as Transparent Data Encryption (TDE) encrypt entire databases or specific columns within databases, while Secure Socket Layer (SSL) or Transport Layer Security (TLS) encrypt data transmitted between clients and servers.

Database Auditing and Logging: Auditing and logging mechanisms capture and record database activities, such as user logins, queries, modifications, and access attempts, to create an audit trail for forensic analysis and compliance purposes. Database administrators can use audit logs to monitor and analyse user activities, detect suspicious behaviour, and investigate security incidents.

Data Masking and Redaction: Data masking and redaction techniques protect sensitive data by replacing or obscuring sensitive information with anonymized or pseudonymised values in non-production environments or when sharing data with third parties. Techniques such as masking, tokenization, and redaction help organizations protect sensitive data while maintaining its usability for testing, development, or sharing purposes.

Database Firewall: A database firewall acts as a protective barrier between the database and external networks, filtering incoming and outgoing traffic to prevent unauthorized access and malicious attacks. Database firewalls monitor and analyse SQL queries, database commands, and network traffic to enforce security policies and detect and block suspicious activities.

Database Activity Monitoring (DAM): DAM solutions monitor database activities in real-time to identify and respond to security threats and compliance violations. These solutions analyse user interactions with the database, detect anomalous behaviour, and generate alerts or notifications to alert administrators of potential security incidents or policy violations.

Database Patch Management: Regularly applying patches and updates to the database management system (DBMS) and associated software components is essential to address known vulnerabilities and security weaknesses. Database administrators should implement a robust patch management process to ensure that the database environment remains secure and up-to-date with the latest security patches and updates.

Backup and Recovery: Backup and recovery strategies are essential for ensuring the availability and integrity of data in the event of data loss, corruption, or system failures. Organizations should regularly backup database data and implement reliable recovery procedures to restore data to a consistent state in case of emergencies or disasters.

Database Hardening: Database hardening involves configuring the database environment according to security best practices and industry standards to minimize security risks and vulnerabilities. Database administrators should disable unnecessary services, remove default accounts and passwords, apply access controls, and configure security settings to harden the database against potential attacks.

Database Security Training and Awareness: Educating database administrators, developers, and users about security best practices, policies, and procedures is crucial for maintaining a secure database environment. Training programs and awareness initiatives help raise awareness about security threats, promote good security hygiene, and empower individuals to recognize and respond to security risks effectively.

Protecting sensitive information: The organizations can strengthen the security of their databases and protect sensitive information from unauthorized access, data breaches, and other security threats, by implementing these techniques and strategies.

11.5 Application Level Security

Front end is a term used to refer to the user interface (most often a Graphical User Interface mode) collecting inputs in different screens and processing it to conform to a specific format that the database at the back end can use. The front end is an interface between the user and the back end which is the data.

Most of the RDBMS come with their front-end. Query Languages are command line interfaces and the experts can send queries as per the syntax of the RDBMS and get responses. But from users' perspective, they have to enter the data in a particular format, often in the screen which as part of the front-end application collects the input and transmits it to the database and gets the output response and displays it.

Typically in banking, Oracle has front end application software called Oracle Developer Suite. Similarly, there are other front-end applications like Visual Basic,.net (Dot Net), Java, PowerBuilder etc. some of which are easy to develop and user friendly with individual characteristics of security, resource utilization like memory, etc.

Earlier, quite a few banks were using a native character based front-end software which was extremely easy to understand occupying very minimum network bandwidth with the least front end processing resources. Some co-operative banks still use such a banking application with character based front end. However, all the major banks and most of the small banks including a substantial number of co-operative banks too have migrated to a Graphic User Interface front-end.

MS Access database offers a variety of front-end development tools. Though the RDBMS and the front-end are two different entities by themselves, it is always prudent to go with the particular front-end that will have better sync with the RDBMS and will ensure better access ensuring ease of use, security, faster retrieval etc. Choice of front-end application has many security considerations, besides other factors like network, ease of use, dependability etc. Security should never be compromised for ease of use and ease of implementation.

Many security features can be built as part of the front-end itself. For instance, user authorization and authentication, setting privilege rights for users can be enabled programmatically in the front-end application also. Developers have to clearly design the program and decide whether the checks and controls are to be done as RDBMS user or as the front-end application user. Having more validations done at the back-end will also be a constraint on the bandwidth from the front-end system to the back-end. To arrive at such a design level decision, factors to be taken into account are the capabilities of the front-end processors, nature of front-end client (like a thin client or a dumb terminal), capacity of the front-end hardware used, etc.

It is also common to have a separate set of application servers at the back end which act as the interface between the user and the actual back end database server. In such a scenario, the application server capacity to process, to validate and to store the application level controls are all to be seen. In larger volumes of data and greater necessities to handle enormous traffic, such a set up (of a user interface, application server and then database server) may be necessary. Security should be initiated in all the three layers.

Restrict back-end access

In any case, the important point to be noted emphatically, access to the database should always be through the front-end and a menu driven, application driven access only and never through a back-end access like a query mode updating, inputting etc. RDBMS log should always be enabled to ensure that any attempt to update any table or alter any value in any object (column, table, etc.) through a back-end access is always logged and the security policy should ensure that such an access is always with proper authority, with the actual query and command getting approved and recorded with username and other details.

Notwithstanding the resource overheads and other constraints, there must be proper database level controls to ensure that row level locking or a column level locking is always enabled whenever possible and wherever feasible, to ensure proper security is built. With the upswing in technological upgradation and the emerging scenario of positioning third party access to the bank's critical database mostly in the form of system integrators or the CBS software providers help-desk officials, it would be highly risky and a grave exposure if back-end access to a database, especially an update command (and not just a select command to view), is not properly monitored or controlled.

Though many cases of such wrong updates without a valid and proper 'where' condition in the command in the SQL and of course immediate rectifications, were unofficially reported, it is still the banks' information security policy and the Chief Information Security Officer (CISO) of the bank who would be held accountable for any adverse update or data manipulation or unauthorised data diddling.

Care must be taken to properly log all back-end accesses and to resort to such an access, only with all precautions in place like

I. The presence of system officials in the data centre.

II. Ensuring the number of rows or columns to be updated and checking the output.

III. Doing roll-back without committing to the database, if the result is not the desired one.

IV. Get such action properly ratified by the top management.

V. Have a proper review mechanism to learn from such accesses and ensure non-repetition.

In short, such occasions to access through back-end SQL must be extremely rare like sometimes as part of some maintenance which may not be possible as part of the front-end application. Such cases should be extremely rare and exceptional. It would be a wrong design of the programme or result of ineffective or inadequate testing if the application software warrants frequent updates through a query language only, not provided for in the front-end menu.

There are also controls like which can be exclusively handed at the software side like input data validation and output data validation controls, error handling and error reporting controls, audit logs maintenance and controls on its upkeep etc. Controls which are built in, as part of the configuration of operation systems like user management, registry editor, network user level access and their rights, system administration's roles and responsibilities and monitoring of system users and system managers' rights and privileges and user management etc. are to be looked into and properly monitored.

Database sub-system should be well designed to define, create, modify, delete and read data in a computer system with proper logs and trail with no room for modification of such trails and logs. Any database trail should be read only and should not be deleted or modified. Like the server level logs at the OS, application too should have the logs enabled that are only viewable and readable only. Some RDBMS will have their own logs, which if enabled takes up enormous space and processing resources. At the time of designing and installing the RDBMS, the management may take a conscious decision not to enable the RDBMS log and to have their own application logs. In such a case such a decision should be a balanced one taking into account all the systemic risks and user level vulnerabilities involved in it.

Some of the most common Database Controls are:

I. Access Controls.

II. Application Software Controls (updating or deleting a record, maintenance of records, etc.)

III. File Handling Control like file maintenance, file retrieval, etc.

IV. Concurrency Controls including integrity verification.

V. Cryptographic Controls.

VI. Audit Trail Controls.

VII. Output Controls.

Output Controls deserve a special mention, because, effective Output Controls ensure that proper data in the right format is presented to the authorised users with due authentication. Here querying of the database, fetching records from production servers, output formats are all quite important. Wherever enabled, row level security or column level security may be ensured so that all the data from a particular table (*i.e.* a file) are not always available to all. For instance, though the details like names, employee numbers, date of joining, etc. of even top management may not be a classified information, details such as salary and allowances, disciplinary action history and confidential reports are certainly classified information and should not be available in any manner be it on the screen or as part of any print-outs. However, it is common practice to have such information as a separate table with restricted view access only.

Especially in banks, control of print-outs is a very critical area. Issue of duplicate draft to replace a draft or a gift cheque that is wrongly printed or has got jammed in the printer due to some printer hardware error are all very sensitive areas and should be properly addressed. Upkeep of print-outs is another area of concern. Since banks do deal with the financial status and sometimes the confidential information of customers also, any print-out with secret information lying unattended on the desk or at the printer is a serious cause for concern. As we have already seen in the earlier Chapter 5 briefly and in Chapter 10 in detail, cyber crimes arising out of scavenging are on the rise. Hence, Care should be taken to use the shredder wherever available or otherwise completely destroy those confidential or critical, security papers or print-outs that are incompletely printed or are aborted by the printer halfway or are no longer required.

11.6 Now let us have a look at some of the software related security controls in electronic delivery channels like ATMs, Cards, Mobile Banking, e-Banking etc.

ATMs

ATMs and Debit Cards transactions are increasing day by day. With the RBI encouraging electronic banking and all the banks moving forward to the electronic era, the volume of ATM transactions compared to personal cash transactions in branches is always increasing. As on 31 May 2015, all banks in India had totally deployed 1,83,887 ATMs in the nation (91,299 as on site ATMs and 92,588 offsite) and total volume of ATM transactions was Rs. 726 million, and the amount involved was Rs.20,90,730.62 million rupees and through PoS terminals it was Rs.1,23,253 million. (Source:: https://rbidocs.rbi.org.in/rdocs/ATM/PDFs/ATM11C999C9044E4DA5B57B8F01809A839D.PDF)

To be added to the present number of ATMs in India are another 7000 ATMs called "White Label ATM" in which the hardware and lease is under the ownership of a private non-banking company acting as the service provider, with special permission obtained for the purpose by RBI (in vogue since 2012). These ATMs are owned by the companies and get their commission amount transaction-wise from the account holder's bank (and not from the ATM user directly). In reality, however it is reported that these ATMs do not get the increased usage as was projected, at the time of introduction, probably because of the sentimental value attached to banks in India by customers when customers feel comfortable dealing with specific banks and also maybe because the cost of maintenance is not worth its efforts as felt by the ATM companies.

Such widespread usage of electronic channels is a source of increased security concern. In the case of ATMs, physical security of ATMs, their upkeep, door mechanism, access control at the door, authentication of the PIN have all been discussed earlier. On the software security side, the first point of consideration is the PIN travelling to the server. ATM vendors have their own mechanism and system of processing the PIN (when they are entered at the ATM) from the ATM to the server and

getting it authenticated. How the PIN travels whether in an encrypted manner or otherwise guards against a sniffing attack or a Man in the Middle Attack are all areas of concern to be sorted out at the stage of design and implementation of the ATM software.

According to EAST (European ATM Security Team), a non-profit organisation founded for dissemination of ATM related information, fraudsters are using techniques that will prove effective at self-service channels even after the EMV rollout for these devices is complete. EAST has reported that "Card-trapping attacks were up 18 percent from the first six months of 2014 to the first six months of 2015. This type of fraud involves "trapping" a card in the ATM's card reader, so that a user thinks the ATM has malfunctioned and has "eaten" his card. In reality, a fraudster has manipulated the card reader to trap the card so they can retrieve it later. EMV cards are not immune to this type of attack, especially if the PIN also is compromised by a well-placed camera".

Since there is more money in ATMs and ATMs are gradually replacing the cash transactions in bank branches, fraudsters are targeting ATMs and the cash kept inside. ATM malwares are on the increase and there are organized gangs researching on ways to exploit the vulnerabilities in ATMs.

Commonly known as "jackpotting" attacks, some malware attacks command ATMs to dispense cash without the need for a card. The earliest instances of this type of attack impacting ATMs were reported in Eastern Europe. Jackpotting has since been identified in the U.S. and other parts of the world also. Another recently reported ATM malware is what has been named as "Greendispenser", publicized towards the end of 2015, which reportedly infects the target machines through a boot-enabled CD-ROM drive. This malware is basically a small software normally reportedly installed by the fraudulent ATM vendors. With just a few commands, the thief can empty an entire machine. After the heist, the malware deletes itself, seemingly in order to evade detection.

Other software concerns in an ATM transaction include transmission of transaction data from the Visa or Master Switch to the CBS centre (or the bank's own database) and then back to the ATM with an approved flag to enable the ATM hardware to dispense the cash. As we have already seen, an ATM withdrawal though it is one single transaction to the customer is actually a series of transactions, involving many hops and more so if it involves withdrawal from the ATM of another bank. In all these cases, interface at the Payment Gateway is involved and encryption at such level should be carefully ensured. Aborting transaction or incomplete transaction or failure of connectivity leaving the session giving room for a sniffer attack or a Man in the Middle attack should never happen.

All transaction failures, all exceptions should be carefully handled at the application interface level and the customer should be advised suitably. In many banks it is common to throw the system's message in the print-out available to the customer like "Unable to process" or "Transaction failure". It will be a better practice to capture the system's message or the failure flag with the error code displayed and then make a user friendly message available to the customer instead of a systemic message involving technological jargon. From security perspective, instead of giving the customer a routine message 'Unable to process' or some such stereotyped text, the customer should be presented a user-friendly message like "Network failure in this ATM" or "Dispenser failure in this ATM" or "Entered amount is in excess of the limit" or "Contact another ATM".

With the central switch level monitoring of all ATMs in place including the availability of cash, functioning of printer at the ATM etc. it would be easier to capture the exact position and display/print the correct user-friendly intelligible reason for failure. Such a clear message will not only guide the customer better but also not compromise on the security front by not revealing much to the fraudster accessing the ATM on the amount of cash kept there etc.

Security in ATMs can be enhanced by installing bio-metric enabled ATMs (an experiment which has already been tried in some areas in banks in India with reasonable success) which will ensure that the user physically comes to the ATM and their bio-metric features (thumb or palm) is validated and authenticated.

On the question of Security in ATMs, Card Cloning and Spying Devices in the ATMs to capture the ATM PIN at the time of data entry continue to be the biggest menace. The *modus operandi* is cloning of cards with a skimmer and an encoder after getting them from fraudulent means or from courier before delivery by opening of such envelopes and then even by stealing the ATM PINs with the help of a small hidden camera placed in the ATM machine itself. In all such cases the biggest evidence has been the CCTV surveillance placed by the banks. Hence physical security, software security, network security in ATMs should all be enhanced.

Many banks have started immediate steps to overcome the card cloning and skimming frauds, by replacement of the magnetic strip based cards to a chip-enabled cards, which reportedly cannot be cloned by skimmer devices. In all such cases, security controls should be dynamic enough under constant review and monitoring of their effectiveness.

Some banks have introduced good features in enhancing the security features of cards, by introduction of features like jitter technology in their ATMs by which the card while going inside the swiping device shakes and moves in with a jitter. Thus, the possibility of any skimmer device capturing the magnetic strip information when the card travels in, is avoided. Another feature being followed that new ATM cards have to be first used in ATMs only and cannot be straightaway used in PoS Merchant establishment. Thus it is ensured that skimmed cards or cloned cards are not used in the shops before it reaches the customer (since ATM usage involves a second factor authentication of PIN).

11.7 Mobile Banking

It does not need a seer to say what is going to be the future of mobile banking in India. With more and more mobile apps freely available and people resorting to a mobile for all their domestic information and even requirements including their banking needs, no wonder that financial transactions have a huge upswing through mobile phones, cutting across user profile. With a high penetration and such enormous increase in volume, mobile banking is going to rule the banking industry in the years to come. With Bluetooth technology (a short range, wireless low-cost technology and standard in place and with General Packet Radio Service (GPRS) - a method of sending and receiving data faster with the phone always on with data and voice transmission both being done simultaneously) and other related features in built, the mobile phone is going to be a one point convergence for the user.

With the mobile, one will operate a bank account, give instructions to the electronic oven to switch on, to the car gate to open, to the stock broker to trade stocks, to the lights to switch on and the list goes on.

Payment Banks

Perhaps banking itself may have to be redefined (worldwide and particularly in India). There is a paradigm shift from personal banking and dependence on banks-visits to Mobile banking, when people are using mobile and still access their bank accounts and operate them. From a personal banking era, the Indian banking is gradually moving to an electronic era ('impersonal banking' to use an uncharitable phrase), in which the personal rapport between the banker and customer is getting blurred and will go towards almost nil.

The start of this trend was perhaps with the advent of digital wallets or banking wallets or what was popularly known as Pre-Paid Instruments (PPI) considered to be the precursors of Payment banks in India.

Digital wallets are mobile wallets that enable users to make one click payments *via* mobile phone, with the card information already entered as a one-time step in the database of the wallet provider. Mobile wallets are basically apps that have payment functionalities. Prepaid payment instruments are normally issued in the form of smart cards or magnetic stripe cards or just an internet account facilitating access to the account, enabling purchase of goods and services against the value stored

on such instruments. This value can be stored and enhanced by cash, by debit to a bank account or a credit card. Started initially as a mechanism for payment for cabs and utility bills, these PPIs have now come to stay with their increasing popularity and post a very great competitive threat to the conventional, traditional banks in India, mainly from the volume of transactions perspective.

Payment Banks meaning thereby "Digital Wallet or Mobile Currency", used to book movie tickets, pay utility bills, do shopping, etc. is the result of an innovation-friendly regulatory policy of RBI. It is a part of financial inclusion to reach out to the masses with more than 90 crores cell phones in a nation of around a billion population, through the 1.5 lakh post offices (when bank customers figure is itself around 60 crores only). The number of transactions through wallets and other PPIs have more than doubled in a year by August 2015, which is phenomenally more than the growth rate of credit cards or debit cards.

India's premier payment bank Paytm launched its Paytm Wallet in 2014, which is now the country's largest mobile payment service platform with over 40 million wallets, becoming a preferred mode of payment for many utility services like cab booking.

The Reserve Bank of India (RBI) in April 2015 allowed 11 business houses, including Reliance Industries, the Aditya Birla group and leading telecom companies Airtel and Vodafone to start payments banks. Bharti Airtel and Reliance Industries had earlier tied up with Kotak Mahindra Bank and State Bank of India, respectively, for payment bank services.

On the security side, many security features are enabled in Mobile Banking like fraud detection and secure application development like looking at peoples' behaviour to spot out-of-pattern transactions and to record how far from normal they are for that particular customer. Other lines of controls include simply not storing sensitive financial and account information on devices, and encrypting transactions and any data that is on the device.

There are more operating systems for mobile handsets (unlike the standardized OS Windows, Unix and Linux for computers) like the popular ones Microsoft's Windows 7, Apple's iOS and Google's Android and Blackberry's OS besides other less popular ones. This lack of standardization and diverse OS, data storage mechanism in the handsets, communication protocols in mobile, capabilities in a mobile communication are all major serious constraints that are faced while introducing security practices or standardized controls in mobile banking.

Bank of America has a security control "SiteKey" in its mobile banking accounts. SiteKey is an extra layer of security used by the bank as two-factor authentication as an additional layer of identity verification for signing to Online Banking. It prompts the user to enter the password after the user sees the SiteKey image and the image title that the customer has already selected. The bank's website recognizes the device the customer is logging in from. If the customer does not log in from the device already registered, the site asks a challenging question.

Mobile Security essentially consists of features provided by the Service Providers, App Providers and, what the User has customized and set for themselves .

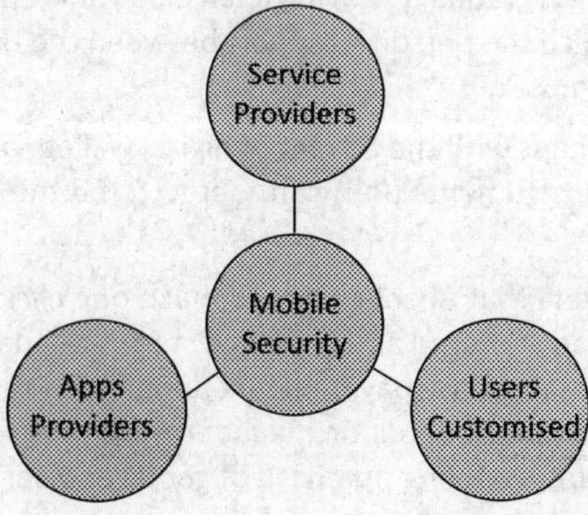

11.8 Internet Banking

Internet Banking is another major area of concern that is engaging the attention of banks these days, with the ever growing usage of e-banking or Internet Banking. With banks becoming more and more competitive and trying to showcase their technological strength introducing more and more electronic products, Internet Banking is probably going to be the future and will gradually replace personal banking slowly and steadily.

Banks have introduced many security features in Internet Banking like a Two Factor Authentication (TFA) asking for the customer's PIN at the time of actual debit or other transaction in addition to the login user id and password. This additional requirement is an RBI initiative insisted upon banks recently. In the case of an online payment, in addition to what the customer *has* physically, *i.e.* the card with details thereon like the 3-digit CVV or CVC number (Card Verification Value or Card Verification Code) printed in the card, the customer has to enter something what he knows, *i.e.* a PIN or a password that he only knows. This additional factor of what he knows besides what he has, is an added security feature.

Besides, some banks have also introduced features like One Time Password (OTP) which is a session generated password normally a number that is communicated to the customer in their mobile which the customer will enter as an additional authentication mechanism. Sometimes instead of a mobile, the customer is given a hardware token (like a pen drive) which displays the PIN and is available for a few seconds called a session which the customer has to enter. This technology of possession of the hardware token (*what the customer has)* and the knowledge of PIN (*what the customer knows)* is a two-factor authentication and a good security feature.

Since security in Internet Banking is a serious issue, RBI was gradually and cautiously encouraging banks to introduce Internet banking issuing guidelines and closely watching the industry response and the customer acceptance to the same. In fact, the cooperative banks in India were permitted to introduce Internet Banking with transactional facility (*i.e.* facility of funds transfer as against the earlier facility of viewing only) very recently only, *vide* RBI Circular dated 5 November, 2015. This permission to introduce Internet Banking was given to State Co-op banks and District Central Co-Op Banks under certain conditions only like stipulations on Capital to Risk (Weighted) Assets Ratio (CRAR), Net Worth, Gross NPA, Net Profit etc.

11.9 Credit Cards

Payment by credit cards is another popular electronic delivery channel. e-commerce payments are growing in usage these days, with banks competing with one another in offering various schemes and 'offers' to bring more and more customers into the credit card fold, like take-over facility, cash-back facility, discounting facility in select merchant outlets, permitting only credit card payments to avail discount in some air travels, etc.

Some cards also do have grid information with numbers printed in the various grids (alphabets) at the back of the card and the on-line e-commerce session will prompt you to enter the number in a particular grid. Thus it is ensured that the card is physically with the user at the time the transaction takes place. However, a better feature that has been introduced by some banks is the PIN enabled cards, which prompt the customer to enter a PIN number at the PoS (Point of Sales) counters so that the card if stolen cannot be used by the criminals. Since such cards also do have the customer's photo on them, the PoS merchant establishment can ensure that the customer actually comes to the shop and the card is swiped in his/her presence only and the PIN is entered by him/her.

Total number of credit card transactions in all credit cards in India during May 2015 was 6,01,33,308 and the amount of transactions was Rs.1,88,656.20 million. (Source: https://rbidocs.rbi.org.in/rdocs/ATM/PDFs/ATM11C999C9044E4DA5B57B8F01809A839D.PDF)

While there is no doubt about the increasing popularity of credit cards. It is with caution that India and RBI as a regulatory body allowed credit cards without going in for aggressive marketing.

On the security front, through credit card frauds are comparatively less compared to debit cards or ATM cards, the card transactions or disputed transactions normally are those reported from foreign PoS terminals in respect of credit cards. In the event of such disputes, normally the customer gets a routine and stereotyped reply from the bank that all security initiatives are in place and the bank is not liable. It is time that the grievance mechanism in banks is geared up or offices like the banking ombudsman are well equipped to handle technology frauds in banks.

More and more initiatives are being taken by the regulator Reserve Bank of India and the efforts are endless. Verified by Visa and Mastercard are all some common initiatives. India has launched its own indigenous debit card payment network called "RuPay" to compete with the multinational Visa and Mastercard helping banks reduce cost of debit card transactions and extending payment network in rural areas. Though contemplated in 2005, the idea has recently been implemented and many banks have since started using it. More and more public sector banks in India are offering RuPay cards in India, besides select private sector banks and co-operative banks. Usage of these cards is bound to increase in the days to come, especially with around 10,000 e-commerce websites in addition to ATMs and PoS in the nation.

This will pave the way for enhancing the security features in card transactions, keeping the data nationally in our own servers within the overall control of our own regulators RBI as against the necessity to store the data in the servers of other multinational corporations. National Payments Corp. of India Ltd. (NPCI), jointly owned by banks, is the nodal agency to manage and promote RuPay, to control the electronic payments in the country.

With such enhanced usage, card usage in India may too become a grey area for security concerns for the banks, especially in view of the fact that most of the card users are not tech-savvy and may not be aware of the techno-legal nuances in a card transaction. Credit card insurance *i.e.* indemnifying against the losses arising out of a card transaction is at a very early stages in India, and only few insurance companies offer this to their users. The PoS establishments and the banks are already parties to such insurance schemes, as per international best practices.

Know Your Progress

Software Security control mainly rests on the software and encompasses all the phases of Software Development Life Cycle. Security is not an attachment to the software after development but should be imbibed in it all through, right from the design, code writing, development, testing and implementation. The users should be made aware of security implications in different stages of software.

Security in software should be in all the layers *i.e.* from the bottom most layer of Operating Systems running in the hardware taking care of memory management, CPU utilisation, user management and upto the topmost stage of users' applications running on them. Every OS such as Unix, Windows or Linux has its own security controls and the developers should take care to exploit and use those security features, customise them as may be necessary and build their applications. It should be a conscious decision of the top management in case any of the security features in the OS is not used. Users should be involved in utilising the security features to ensure it not only conforms to their requirements but also ensures legal compliance and ease of use.

After the OS, it is the database security that is of importance. Oracle, MS SQL Server or Sybase being the popular databases have their own security features in their various versions like Access Control and Privileges, User Management, File Management, etc. All features available in the RDBMS should be studied and used and well defined in schema. Next, application level security is of utmost importance. Here, the various controls include front-end validation, back-end database validation, user management. Access to the database should always be through the front-end and menu-driven application only and never through an SQL query in the back-end unless the situation actually warrants so, in exceptional circumstances and that too under very rigorous security controls like ensuring logs, trails etc.

After all the application level controls, security initiatives at the electronic delivery channels like ATM, Cards, e-Banking and Mobile Banking should be enhanced. With the ever increasing use of these alternate channels in banking, security should never be compromised for ease of use in these channels. RuPay is an Indian initiative, a card payment gateway launched by National Payment Corporation of India. More and more banks in India are issuing the RuPay cards as against the Visa and Mastercards issued earlier. From security perspective, data is stored and processed in Indian servers ensuring better regulatory compliance besides cost savings.

Key Words

Software Development Life Cycle	High Level Design	pseudo code	Payments Bank
Schema	Application server	Front-end application	PPI
Back-end access	Output control	Audit Control	Digital Wallet
Active Directory	Windows Security	Linux Security	jackpotting
RuPay	Credit Card grid data	Mobile Security	PoS

Questions

1. Windows feature for managing the user accounts, identifying the credentials, information protection, system and application settings serving as the central location for configuration information is called ________________.
    a. Windows Registry
    b. Windows Security
    c. Active Directory
    d. WinSet up.
2. Which of the following is popular as Open Source software?
    a. Linux
    b. MS Office
    c. Windows Active Directory
    d. Unix OS
3. For modifying the settings of registry entries in ________ OS, the regedit is used.
    a. Windows
    b. Unix
    c. MS SQL Server
    d. Oracle
4. Which of the following is not an RDBMS?
    a. Sybase

b. Oracle
c. Unix
d. MS SQL Server

5. Writing the program in natural language independent of programming software for others to know the flow is called_________________.
   a. Coding Development
   b. Pseudo code
   c. Schema management
   d. Low Level Design of Software
6. In ATMs, security is enhanced by which of the following technologies?
   a. Skimmer technology
   b. Jitter technology
   c. Encoder technology
   d. GPRS
7. Which of the following is considered to be a fore-runner of Payment Banks?
   a. NBFCs
   b. RuPay
   c. Financial Inclusion
   d. Digital Wallets
8. Which of the following is not a software security control?
   a. User Authentication
   b. User Access Privileges
   c. Biometric Authentication
   d. Data and input validation
9. Which of the following types of access to the database should be avoided as far as possible?
   a. Menu-driven and user level access
   b. Front-end access through keyboard
   c. Character based access as against a GUI based
   d. Back-end access through SQL
10. Rupay is an Indian Payment Gateway launched by __________________.
    a. National Bank Card Corporation of India
    b. National Payment Corporation of India
    c. National Payment Gateway of India
    d. National Payment Coordination Company of India Ltd.
11. Oracle is the most popular RDBMS used in most of the banks in India. (True/False)
12. In brown label ATMs, the connectivity and cash handling alone (and not the ATM machine) is the responsibility of the sponsor bank. (True/False)
13. ATM Banking involves the use of GPRS technology in communication. (True/False)

Answers:

1. *c*	8. *c*
2. *a*	9. *d*
3. *a*	10. *b*
4. *c*	11. True
5. *b*	12. True
6. *b*	13. False
7. *d*	

12 CHAPTER

Network Controls

OBJECTIVES

This chapter briefly describes of various network devices used in an organisation their uses in data communication, the security features available in the devices and the controls to be exercised for ensuring proper security governance. The chapter also deals with the communication gadgets, communication channels and media and the normal security controls that can be put in place and ways to enhance them not only in the hardware devices but also in those communication channels, protocols and methodologies.

12.1 Network security is a complicated subject, which is always handled by well-trained and experienced professionals. It consists of the policies and their implementation to ensure proper and effective utilization of network gadget to prevent misuse, modification, or denial of a computer network and resources. Before delving into various computer networks, devices, and security issues, let us briefly examine some of the most commonly deployed network equipment used in various organizations and banks:

I. Hubs

II. Modems

III. Routers

IV. Switches

V. Bridges

VI. Multiplexers

Though the list above enumerates the hardware gadgets, it does not comprehensively cover all the network gadgets used in modern days. This is only an illustrative list. Furthermore, some network equipment or gadgets may have features similar to one or more other pieces of equipment.

Hubs

A hub is a device that serves as common termination point for multiple nodes that can relay signals along the appropriate paths. It is a physical connectivity for a number of computer systems. It provides an easy way to handle shifting of the machines and reconnections. There are also some intelligent hubs that contain the built-in intelligence to communicate network management information to a software package.

Modems

Modems modulate the digital signal that a computer system handles, into an analog signal that a telecommunication line handles, at the sending end so that the data can be transmitted, and perform the reverse function at the receiving end by demodulating the signal from analog to digital while the data enters the computer.

Routers

Routers are intelligent network devices connecting different networks together, which use the software-configured network address to make decisions on forwarding the data packets to a specific destination. Routers normally operate at the network layers and are among the most used network gadgets in any organisation, typically in most banks. Router configuration has a major security significance. Some routers come with the capability to use session encryption between specified routers. Such a capability prevents the unauthorised snooping by men in the middle and ensures connectivity between two sites with secure routes.

Routing tables (information on routing the data across network) are always confidential information and routing mechanism and the connected design should be kept as a classified information for use within the network management department strictly on a need to know basis only.

With such great dependence on network almost all banking products including the indispensable CBS, the ubiquitous ATMs and the omnipresent internet banking, routers configuration and backup for routers, redundancy for router availability have all assumed enormous significance and banks should ensure proper network access controls to protect router information.

A feature that is being built into some routers is the ability to use session encryption between specified routers. Because traffic travelling across the Internet can be seen by people in the middle who have the resources (and time) to snoop around, these are advantageous for providing connectivity between two sites, such that there can be secure routes.

Switches

Switches are basically hubs but with intelligence, providing dedicated transmission channels for each user. With such capability, it is easier for a switch to forward data to its destination by using the hardware MAC (Media Access Control) address in the data packets. Thus we can block data transmission to one segment or one PC in a LAN or make one segment or one PC restrict itself from access by any other user.

Configuration of switches is very important from a security perspective. In a LAN environment, if the security management wants to restrict access to one PC the switch can be configured accordingly and hence it should be the duty of security administrators to ensure switch configuration in line with the security policy and to protect all systems in line with the classification of criticality accorded to it.

Bridges

Bridge is a network device which divides networks to reduce overall network traffic. It allows or prevents data from passing through it by reading the MAC address. Bridge is normally selective about the traffic it allows through, since it does the filtering by station address.

Multiplexers

A multiplexer is a device that accepts lower-speed data streams from terminals and combines them into one high-speed data stream for transmission to the other end. At the other end, it converts the combined data stream into the original multiple lower-speed terminal data streams. Physical security of such 'mux' equipment, as is normally called, is very important since inadequate control on such devices will cause the network to fail completely.

12.2 Controls In a Layered Network

The seven layer model of the ISO/OSI (International Organization for Standardization/Open Systems Interconnection model) is a familiar framework for layering network protocols. For the purpose of this course, it would be sufficing that we have a very brief idea of the seven layers especially from the view of how security is built in these and how every layer protects or safeguards the traffic of data from security perspective. Typically, security services at the bottom protects traffic from the higher layers.

In a layered approach, when data gets passed to the lower layers, messages in the protocol are called N - Protocol Data Units (PDU). Data gets transmitted by invoking facilities at the lower layer and adding it headers and trailers and reassembling the PDU at every stage. The headers in the PDU stores the security relevant data.

Application
Presentation
Session
Transport
Network
Data – Link
Physical

Seven Layers of OSI Model

Security in all these seven layers are built as per the features of the layer. For instance, in physical layer, it is the physical security of the equipment, the cables, type of cabling used and upkeep and maintenance of cables and connectivity that matters. In the data-link layer, the security will be physical and one step above it. In networks and transport layers, it is the routers and switches that sits on these layers which should be configured to ensure security. In the presentation and then in the application layers, it is the software program (and off-the-shelf applications like MS Office or customized ones developed for the organisations) that should take care of security like ensuring access control, access privileges, implementation of various policies like password policy, Interact Access policy and conformance to standards etc.

As against the seven layered approach discussed above, the TCP/IP (Transmission Control Protocol/ Internet Protocol) has only four layers as below:

Application
Transport
IP/Internet
Data Link

Typically in a TCP/IP transmission, security in communication is taken care of in these above layers. Though the OSI approach of seven layer model has been under use for a number of years, of late it is the TCP/IP protocol that has become very popular and being referred often.

Security (IP Sec)

IP is a connectionless and stateless protocol that transmits IP packets and hence each datagram, which is essentially a basic transfer unit associated with a packet switched network, is treated as an independent entity. Earlier there was no security protection and there was no order of packets in the earlier version of IP version 4 published in 1981. IP-V6 was subsequently introduced and IP Security architecture has since been in place.

IP Sec is basically an Internet Protocol suite - a group of protocols - for securing IP based communication and ensuring security controls by authenticating and encrypting each IP packet in a communication session. IP Sec is an end-to-end security scheme operating at the internet layer of the IP suite or stack illustrated above. It can be used in protecting data flows between a pair of hosts (*host-to-host*), between a pair of security gateways (*network-to-network*), or between a security gateway and a host (*network-to-host*). Some other Internet security systems in widespread use, such as Secure Socket Layers (SSL), Transport Layer Security (TLS), and Secure Shell (SSH) operate in the upper layers of the TCP/IP mode stated above. IP Sec protects any application traffic across an IP network. Proper use of the features enhances the network security in any organisation.

Though IP Sec provides host-to-host security, it does not provide user-to-user security nor application-to-application security. It increases protocol processing overheads and time and latency, as sender and the receiver both perform cryptographic operations.

12.3 VLANs

VLAN

In all cases of LAN security (and in WAN environment too), security should be in-built in the hardware infrastructure and provided for in software too. In this context, it would be relevant to study briefly about VLANs. Virtual Local Area Network (VLAN) is a group of hosts with a common set of requirements, which communicate as if they were attached to the same broadcast domain regardless of their physical location. Though a VLAN has the same attributes as a normal and physical LAN it allows for end station to be grouped together even if not located on the same network switch physically. A VLAN membership can be configured through software instead of physically relocating devices or connections.

By using VLANs, one can control traffic patterns and react quickly to relocations. VLANs provide the flexibility to adapt to changes in network requirements and allow for simplified administration. VLANs are created to provide the segmentation services traditionally provided by routers in LAN configurations by taking care of scalability, security, and network management. Hence from security point of view, VLAN architecture is very significant and it would be the main concern of security managers in any organisation to take care of the VLAN architecture, to physically protect the VLAN cabling and to secure the VLAN design ensuring it does not fall into the wrong hands. VLANs are essentially private communications over a public network.

Tunneling is another concept that should be read in the context of VLAN and security through VLAN switches. By tunneling, a single VLAN can be configured to support customers who have multiple VLANs, while preserving customer VLAN ids and keeping the traffic in different VLANs properly segregated. Besides better security, tunneling also enables flexibility in topology and protocol with enhanced compatibility and interoperability bypassing the local network that may be in place.

Of late, many banks and organisations using a public telecom network, go in for Multiprotocol Label Switching (MPLS) network. MPLS is a highly scalable data-carrying mechanism not depending upon any specific protocol and works independent of it in an MPLS network, data packets are assigned with labels. Packet-forwarding decisions are made solely on the contents of this label, without the need to examine the packet itself. Since it operates at a layer that is generally considered to lie between traditional definitions of layer 2 (data link layer) and layer 3 (network layer) it is often referred to as a "layer 2.5" protocol.

MPLS is a mechanism in high-performance telecom networks that directs data from one network node to the next, based on short path labels rather than long network addresses, avoiding complex lookups in a routing table. MPLS itself is not a security protocol, it can be used in conjunction with other security measures to enhance network security. While MPLS itself doesn't provide encryption,

additional security measures such as IP sec or MPLS over encrypted tunnels can be implemented to ensure the confidentiality of data transmitted over MPLS networks. MPLS traffic is just as open across a carrier's network as regular IP. However, it does provide VPN capabilities and from that angle it is secure enough. Hence it can be said that the security of an MPLS VPN is as good or as bad as that of a dedicated circuit.

In an MPLS connectivity, all units in remote locations say bank branches, administrative offices like regional office etc., ATM centres or other sites are all connected to the headquarters or the data centre through MPLS cloud. The Data Centre may itself be connected to either the MPLS cloud or typically to the Internet.

Quite often there have been discussions on the relative merits and demerits of the kinds of lines *viz* leased lines, VPNs and MPLS. While cost wise, leased lines are costlier compared to VPNs, MPLS depends upon the service provider and their technological architecture. On the security front, since leased lines are dedicated to a specific customer's traffic, they are more secure compared to VPNs which function over the public Internet that are less secure. MPLS has no inherent encryption since its security depends heavily on the network and the configuration therein.

Communication Channels

Telephone systems offer us the connection services for use in organisations especially in banks to establish connectivity across different parts of the country. Such services can be terrestrial lines with cables drawn as dial up lines or as leased lines. From security perspective, there is a basic difference between these two lines. In the former, data goes as part of the public system whereas in the latter there is a possibility for, which we can opt for, what is called a VLAN IP Sec. Even otherwise the line and connectivity is 'leased' to us. In essence, this term 'leased' does not mean solely dedicated with security. To overcome this, it would be prudent to opt for IP Sec enabled lines with VLAN from the telecom providers, so that it serves as an additional security for the connectivity part and for the time the data is in transit, besides the application level security that software will anyway have.

For long distance, typically in a WAN set up, satellite channels established through VSAT (Very Small Aperture Terminal) are taken. In a VSAT connectivity too, in addition to the physical security for the Out Door Unit (ODU) and the In Door Unit (IDU) for the VSAT equipment, there must be software based security initiatives in place like cryptography etc. so that the data in transmit is adequately secure.

Voice over Internet Protocol (VoIP) is the transmission of voice over packet-switched IP networks and is one of the most important emerging trends in telecommunications. As against the traditional circuit-based telephony, VoIP transmits voice in digitized format as data packets and comes at a lower cost and greater flexibility. However, from security perspective it needs careful study of the security problems involved in it and VoIP components should not be simply plugged into the already secured network hoping it is also part of the security network.

Many security measures implemented in traditional data networks are not applicable to VoIP, like firewalls, Intrusions Detection Systems etc. which must be customized for the VoIP component. Besides, implementation of various security measures can cause a marked deterioration in the quality of transmission or sometimes may cause delay because of firewalls or blocking of traffic and related features. The introduction of firewalls to the VoIP network may also complicate certain aspects of VoIP like dynamic port trafficking and call setup procedures etc.

VoIP leverages the internet as an infrastructure for voice communication carrying data packets like general internet traffic. It uses a shared broadband circuit for many kinds of data packets be it data, voice, or video, perhaps reducing the cost of transmission some time. Since the traffic is internet bound, offering Unified Communication (UC) as an integration of computer and network, it is more prone to the inherent threats of internet like eavesdropping, session hijacking etc. To make a VoIP communication safe and secure, many security initiatives should be in place like the study of all the open ports, analyzing the traffic, vulnerability to a DoS or a DDoS attack etc. From the traceability

point of view, even if a simple voice telephone handset is attached to a VoIP using it for just a voice communication, tracing the same is much more technologically complicated than a simple cell phone communication which are traceable with details recorded as part of the cell phone tower communication.

Network Address Translation (NAT) is a powerful tool that can be used to hide internal network addresses and enable several endpoints within a LAN to use the same (external) IP address. Basic NATs of translation of one to one IP address is normally used when there is a requirement to interconnect two IP networks with incompatible addressing. Sometimes, it may be necessary to hide an entire IP address space behind a single IP address (or in some cases a small group of IP addresses) in another (usually public) address space. In all such instances, NAT is used. To avoid ambiguity in the handling of returned packets, a one-to-many NAT must provide higher level information in outgoing communications and must maintain a translation table so that return packets can be correctly translated back.

It has been often debated whether NAT is itself a security feature or not. Though introduced as an enabler of translating the IP addresses, NAT has of late been deployed to deliver some security features too. Although NAT routers are not purchased for their security benefits, NAT routers inherently function as effective hardware firewalls also, since they prevent unsolicited, unexpected and unwanted traffic from the public internet cloud entering the user's private LAN network. Since all incoming data packets have the same IP address or the single IP address of the router, the router identifies the computer that should receive the incoming packet by the one which actually sent a packet first out to the source of the returning packet.

Cryptography

Cryptography is the practice and study of hiding information. Modern cryptography intersects the disciplines of mathematics, computer science and engineering. To ensure security in transmission of data or information, a popular method is to encrypt the message with a specific algorithm so that the intended recipient alone will be able to decrypt the message and no other intruder can do that. Cryptography has been extensively used while communicating among banks, especially financial remittances and related communications like ATM cards, e-payments etc. Even historically, there is a record of several early Hebrew ciphers and in old Indian books too cryptography finds a place like Kautilya's Arthashastra.

From a security angle, quite often we hear that the cell phones have their own patented cryptographic technologies giving their subscribers a confidence that their communication cannot be attacked by network threats like packet sniffers etc. In this context, there have been frequent debates on whether the state has the power to ask for decryption tools or otherwise revelation of the details of communication and whether the provider is bound to keep the confidentiality in view of the contractual obligations with the subscriber. It is now a confirmed legal position that any communication is always subject to the provisions of the law of the land and within the broad parameters of freedom of communication, data privacy and due diligence as provided for in the laws. Therefore, the details of any communication have to be revealed if so sought by the state or as part of judicial proceedings, as provided by the law.

Steganography is the art and the science of writing hidden messages in such a way that no one apart from the sender and the intended recipient suspects the existence of the message. It is considered to be a form of securing the message in an obscure manner. Visible messages may appear to be some common often innocuous text and the hidden text or message may be in some invisible ink and the receiver will know how to take it out for reading.

Steganography is advantageous over cryptography because in a cryptography the message goes encrypted and will not be opened or readable to any one. Sometimes, in a communication territory or a nation or a channel, encryption itself may be banned for security reasons. In steganography it

could be a normal mail or a picture or an audio file or any other communication outwardly but only the receiver will be able to read the hidden text or message contained in it.

In computers especially in data communications, steganography is a useful and interesting technology for researchers. From security perspective, it is at the same time a dreaded tool in the hands of criminals especially terrorists. It has been used in quite a few terrorist attacks in the recent past. Detection of steganographically encoded packages is called steganalysis. The simplest method to detect modified files, however, is to compare them to known originals. Often, in a communication, no one will normally know the original version of the file or the picture and hence detection of steganography used in a picture or an audio file sent over an email involves the use of specific software tools and may be a little difficult, if not impossible.

Quite often, there have been clashes between law and technology. Something done for technological gain may be unlawful or illegal and therefore punishable, when done with an intention of criminal purpose. For instance, steganography is a technology but when done with a purpose of sending some communication in some terrorist outfit or in a criminal gang, the same becomes an evidence in prosecution and the activity will be called illegal.

Password Technology And Password Cracking Technology

Password is a string of characters used to verify the identity of a user during the authentication process. Passwords are typically used in tandem with a username; they are designed to be known only to the user and allow that user to gain access to a device, application or website. Passwords can vary in length and can contain letters, numbers and special characters.

Password is sometimes called a passphrase, when the password uses more than one word, or a passcode or passkey, when the password uses only numbers, such as a personal identification number (PIN).

A password is a simple application of challenge-response authentication, using a verbal, written or typed code to satisfy the challenge request. The order and variety of characters are often what determines the difficulty, or security strength, of a given password. That is why security systems often require users to create passwords that use at least one capital letter, number and symbol.

For a password to be an effective security mechanism, its details must be kept secret. Otherwise, unauthorized users could gain access to the files and securities one is trying to protect.

How to create a secure password

Passwords, when carefully created and protected, increase safe and secure interactions online and in the workplace and can prevent password cracking. To maximize the strength and efficacy of passwords, organizations often establish password policies. These policies are designed to help users create strong passwords and adopt best practices for managing login credentials. Below are a few examples of the practices that contribute to effective password management and creation:

- A minimum length of eight characters and a maximum between 16 to 64 characters. While there is no limit to the length of a password, it does reach a point of diminishing returns.
- Include both uppercase and lowercase letters with case sensitivity. This increases the number of variables at play and, therefore, its difficulty.
- Use at least one number.
- Use at least one special character.
- Avoid using easily guessed elements such as names of children, pet names and birthdays.
- Consider using a password management tool.

The most important components of strong passwords include sufficient length and a mix of character types. Security experts recommend using passphrases that combine several words and interchange numbers and symbols but are still fairly easy to remember.

Strong passwords don't just depend on the code or the individual; they also depend on the expiration date. Corporate password policies often place an expiration date on their users' passcodes, forcing users to replace old passwords with new ones. Password time periods commonly span 90 to 180 days. Sophisticated password creation systems may also force users to create new passwords that don't share major similarities to their previous iterations.

Password cracking is the act of uncovering a user's password. Websites use encryption to save your passwords so that third parties can't figure out your real passwords. Malevolent hackers and cybercriminals use password cracking methods to get around encryption safeguards, uncover your passwords, and access to your personal information.

Types of Password Attack

Dictionary Attack: In this type of attack, a dictionary file is loaded into a cracking application that runs against user accounts. This dictionary is a text file that contains several dictionary words commonly used as passwords. The program uses every word present in the dictionary to find the password.

Brute-Force Attack: In a brute-force attack, attackers try every combination of characters until the password is broken.

Rule-based Attack: Attackers use this type of attack when they obtain some information about the password. This is a more powerful attack than dictionary and brute-force attacks because the cracker knows the password type. For example, if the attacker knows that the password contains a two- or three-digit number, he/she can use some specific techniques to extract the password quickly.

12.4 Protocols used in Network

Though we will not be discussing in detail the characteristics of all the protocols used in a network - public or private - and the security features associated with each, it would certainly be relevant to study the security features of some of the most commonly used protocols used in network like http, ftp, TCP/IP.

HTTP

It stands for Hyper Text Transfer (or sometimes Transport) Protocol and is the standard used in world wide web for web accessing port 80, to communicate especially for hyper text documents in the web. HTTPS is HTTP Secure or often referred to as HTTP over Secure Socket Layer or Transport Layer Security (TLS) and is considered to be the secure version of HTTP protocol. It is a combination of HTTP with SSL/TLS providing for encrypted communication securing identification of a network web server. HTTPS connections are often used for payment transactions on the internet especially for financially critical transactions.

Especially in banks, the use of HTTPS is quite significant, since it creates a secure channel over an insecure network ensuring reasonable protection from attacks like eavesdropping etc. and signaling confidence to the user that the server certificate is verified and trusted.

Using HTTPS is compulsory for any website involving financial or critical transmission of data when the user trusts the certificate authority to vouch only for legitimate website. All banks now-a-days also display User Awareness material in their websites telling the user-customers to ensure that the address bar in their internet banking page displays a "https" and that a lock symbol is displayed on the page is always displayed clicking which gives the server certificate details.

FTP

File Transfer Protocol is a standard network protocol used to transfer files from one computer to another over a TCP network, often the Internet. SFTP is Secure File Transfer Protocol, a network protocol that provides a secure and encrypted method for transferring files over a secure data stream and is considered to be the secure version of FTP protocol. SFTP is an extension of the SSH (Secure

Shell) protocol and is designed to provide secure file transfer capabilities. People are normally used to upload web pages and documents to a web server that hosts the web content. It permits users to enter through an authentication mechanism of username and password. File Transfer Protocol is used for accessing port 21, when we want to upload or download any file or document from or to an internet site or a remote web server with the IP address of the server and with the server's permission as a registered user of its resources.

Though FTP is ideal for transferring files to a remote location, it is not known for its security, because it transmits data over a network in plain text only. FTP is prone to attacks by hackers and interceptions. If a fraudster attempts to login with incorrect User Id and password repeatedly, it locks the user disabling the profile which may sometimes be made use of by the attacker to launch his attacks. SSL (Secure Socket Layer) which we have already discussed, is considered to be a secure usage of FTP access. It ensures that communication is encrypted and hence the exposure to interceptions etc. would not be there.

Though the use of anonymous FTP is sometimes recommended for transferring non-confidential data, this is also fraught with risk with anonymous FTP, anyone can upload to the server without a username or password and could be transferring pirated software or malicious programs, virus etc. Hence FTP is essential in a networked environment and how best to make it secure depends on the need and the resultant configuration. From security perspective, FTP deserves utmost consideration, since FTP entry or uploading or downloading with FTP access should be permitted strictly on the basis of authenticated entry only. It should be a conscious decision of developers to permit or deny FTP access in any application and be based purely on the application needs alone.

Simple Mail Transfer Protocol (SMTP) is an Internet standard and a widely used protocol for email transmission in IP networks used for outgoing mail transport in port No.25. Mail servers use SMTP for sending and receiving messages but user-level client applications use SMTP for sending messages to a mail server only and for receiving messages, client applications usually use either the Post Office Protocol (POP) or the Internet Message Access Protocol (IMAP).

Since, SMTP uses relay *i.e.* sending mails to another mail server on another domain, this feature is best misused by spamsters to send bulk mails and spams since STMP would not check to verify that the sender was actually he, who claims to be. There are some ways to check this and one way to do this, is to verify whether the sender-computer is in the ISP's local network. Security can also be enhanced by using the SMTP AUTH mechanism by which authentication is enabled. Mail relay options can also be used to prevent unauthorized mailings, such as promotional mails or bulk and spams and the relay options in the mail server should be configured accordingly.

Telnet

The word 'Telnet' is itself quite interesting. Telnet is both the name of the protocol, as well as the application that uses the protocol. Telnet is part of the TCP/IP protocol suite and by default uses TCP port 23. Telnet servers are usually Unix-based, though the protocol is also used for accessing network devices. Telnet can be said to refer to a protocol used on the Internet or a LAN to provide an interactive text-oriented communication facility using a virtual terminal connection to a remote server.

Since Telnet is a network protocol and often used in accessing remote servers, its study assumed significance. Earlier Telnet was in Unix based systems on a command-line interfaces. Because of security issues while accessing a remote server especially on configuration issues in systems running Windows NT etc., telnet access sometimes is not a preferred communication and secure shell (SSH) started to be used.

The term Telnet sometimes also refers to the client side since it can run on almost on any computer system. Loosely, Telnet also means establishing a connection with the Telnet protocol, either with command line client or with a programmatic interface with a remote server, when text books use the phrase 'telnet to the server' etc.

In all these cases, it would be pertinent to note that security is to be built into the application whenever a Telnet access is provided. Most developers do not permit Telnet access other than a front-end menu and screen interface. From security perspective, Telnet access is rarely given and is highly restricted by system managers.

While accessing a server through the various protocols as mentioned above, sometimes applications allocate logical ports for data transmission, in which case the developers should be trained to ensure proper and secure usage of such logical ports assigning other numbers for the services. An efficient white box testing team should be able to detect any improper or deliberately misleading assignment of port numbers, which will serve as a serious security lacuna paving the way for unauthorized access to the database.

TCP/IP is a suite of protocols and perhaps the most widely used in communications these days. It is the backbone of the internet today, comprised of two protocols, TCP and IP. The Internet Protocol (IP), is the network layer of the Internet which routes the data packets to its destination, though providing no guarantee for delivery. Transmission Control Protocol (TCP) runs on top of IP, providing a connection oriented service between the sender and the receiver, guaranteeing the delivery ensuring that the packets are delivered in sequence using mechanisms like sequence numbers, acknowledgements, 3-way handshakes and timers.

TCP/IP was not built originally for security, (for that matter, even Internet itself was not built for secure communication when it was originally used by the US army, more for intra-defence department communication). In the years to come and with Internet almost being built on TCP/IP protocols it has now become more of a problem. The widespread use and availability of the TCP/IP protocol suite has exposed its weaknesses. There are quite a few well-known vulnerabilities of both TCP/IP itself, and of some protocols commonly used along with TCP/IP (such as DNS) as detailed below:

TCP "SYN" attacks

Also called SYN flooding, it takes advantage of three-way handshake in TCP with sequence numbers when a computer receives the SYN request from a sender, it must keep track of the earlier partially opened connection and if it doesn't, there is no 'sync' which breaches security.

IP Spoofing is an attack where an attacker pretends to be sending data from an IP address other than its own. The IP layer assumes that the source address on any IP packet it receives is the same IP address as the system that actually sent the packet — it does no authentication. Many higher level protocols and applications also make this assumption, so it seems that anyone able to forge the source address of an IP packet (called "spoofing" an address) could get unauthorized privileges.

Sequence guessing

A TCP Sequence guessing is an attack in the form of an attempt to predict the sequence number used to identify the packets in a TCP connection. The attacker correctly guesses the sequence number so that he can send counterfeit data packets in that place from another host controlled by him. He can do this by monitoring the traffic and using the same IP address and attempt even a DoS attack.

Similarly, connection hijacking is another vulnerability. When two hosts are desynchronized, discarding packets from each other, an attacker if he is in the same communication path, can eaves-drop and can replicate packets and then inject forged packets with the correct sequence numbers (and potentially modify or add commands to the communication). This is often done in a desynchronized state or in the middle of an established connection.

DNS Attacks: DNS is primarily used to map hostnames to IP addresses (e.g. 192.38.11.1), but it can also be used to do the reverse; mapping IP addresses to hostnames. An attacker can use this feature to fool the name-based authentication.

It would be pertinent to note that despite all the security vulnerabilities, TCP/IP is still the widest used protocol and efforts are continuing to combat all the weaknesses as stated above.

12.5 Intrusion Detection System (IDS)

Intrusion detection and prevention systems (IDPS), are network security appliances that monitor network and/or system activities for malicious activity. The main functions of intrusion prevention systems are to identify malicious activity, log information about said activity, attempt to block/stop activity, and report activity. When cyber criminals prowl and keep hanging around looking for resources in the vulnerable systems and start the attack, it is the well configured IDS that should play a vital role and send an alert to the systems or the persons manning them.

Trojan infected systems, open ports, unmonitored entry points, unpatched systems etc. are the most vulnerable which will be capitalized upon by cyber criminals. The IDS immediately alerts that a breach has taken place and serves as a warning system, so that real time responses can be initiated.

An Intrusion Detection System (IDS) is an active process or device that analyzes system and network activity for unauthorized entry and/or malicious activity. There are different ways an IDS detects anomalies which depends upon the nature of features built into it, the configurations and the settings. However, basically the main function of IDS is to catch perpetrators in the act before they do real damage to resources.

IDS often comes as a dedicate device or software application that monitors network and/or system activities for malicious activities or policy violations and produces the necessary reports. It is primarily focused on identifying possible incidents, logging information about them, and reporting attempts.

Intrusion Prevention Systems (IPS) are basically network service devices used to monitor network and system activities for malicious activities and attempt to or stop intrusion *i.e.* thwart the attacks. While the IDS are used only to detect the activity, log them or give a report or a warning or alerts, the IPS actually takes the next and important step of preventing the attack from impacting the information asset.

Some important terminologies associated with IDS and IPS are false positive and false negative. Sometimes the system will be ill-configured or some rules inappropriately framed by which the system incorrectly identifies a benign activity (*i.e.* one which is not harmful) as being malicious. This is called false positive.

On the other hand, sometimes a malign or harmful activity will be left unidentified as such and will pass as benign and harmless, which is called false negative. Both these are equally dangerous and should be corrected immediately. Technologically, if the systems are configured to decrease the false negatives, it may result of increasing the false positives too. Hence it needs a deeper knowledge of **'tuning'** the system and adequate analysis of the system behaviour and the system requirements.

In addition, organizations use IDS (and also Intrusion Prevention System IPS) for other purposes, such as identifying problems with security policies, documenting existing threats, and deterring individuals from violating security policies. IDPSs have become a necessary addition to the security infrastructure of nearly every organization. The two popular methods of IDS are NIDS (*i.e.* Network based Intrusion Detection System and HIDS (Host-based Intrusion Detection System).

Intrusion detection and prevention systems (IDPS), are network security appliances that monitor network and/or system activities for malicious activity. The main functions of intrusion prevention systems are to identify malicious activity, log information about said activity, attempt to block/stop activity, and report activity.

Intrusion prevention systems are considered extensions of intrusion detection systems because they both monitor network traffic and/or system activities for malicious activity. The main differences are, unlike intrusion detection systems, intrusion prevention systems are placed in-line and are able to actively prevent/block intrusions that are detected. More specifically, IPS can take such actions as sending an alarm, dropping the malicious packets, resetting the connection and/or blocking the

traffic from the offending IP address. An IPS can also correct Cyclic Redundancy Check (CRC) errors, unfragment packet streams, prevent TCP sequencing issues, and clean up unwanted transport and network layer options.

12.6 Firewalls

Firewalls are access control devices for the network and can assist in protecting an organisation's internal network from external attacks. Therefore, they are border security products existing between the internal network and the external network. Wherever the server is allowed to be accessed from outside, such connection will be allowed by firewalls. Hence firewalls may not protect the web server software, which should permit all web traffic. Similarly, firewalls may not protect any insider attacker, since all internal users are already in the internal network.

There are two types of firewalls: application layer firewalls and packet filtering firewalls. Each is used depending upon the security policy of the organisation and the specific requirement based on factors like confidentiality, criticality, etc. Application layer firewalls also called proxy firewalls which are positioned above the Operating System like Windows NT or Unix. Firewalls rules *i.e.* the configurations done as per the related policy defines how traffic from one network is sent to another. In the absence of specific permission to allow the traffic, firewall drops the packets or denies the traffic. Here, the firewall itself should be well protected from attack and should not have any vulnerabilities. Typical function of a firewall is depicted in the diagram below:

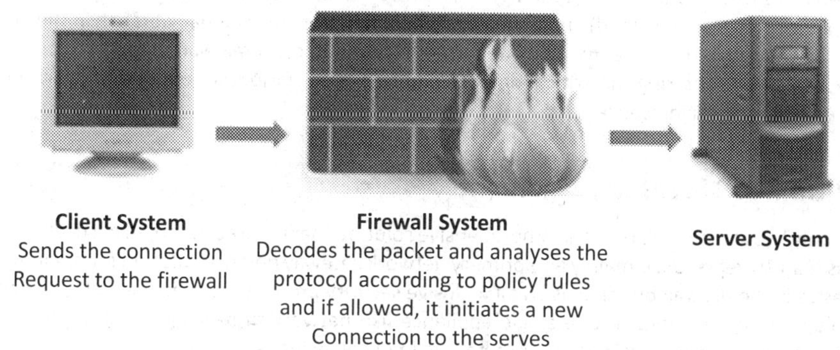

Client System
Sends the connection
Request to the firewall

Firewall System
Decodes the packet and analyses the
protocol according to policy rules
and if allowed, it initiates a new
Connection to the serves

Server System

As against the application layer firewalls, providing mechanisms to route traffic that is destined for certain ports specifically to a system behind the firewall, the second type of firewalls namely Packet Filtering firewalls enforce the policy rules through the use of packet inspection filters. The filters undertake stateful inspection *i.e.* a process of examining the packets and determining whether the traffic is allowed based on the policy rules and the state of the protocol. In other words, when the protocol is in a certain state, only certain packets are expected and permitted. Since these types of firewalls do not have the overload of extra connection setups (on behalf of the client, as stated in the diagram above), they have the capability of handling a greater amount of traffic.

Next Generation Firewall is increasingly being spoken about these days. Technologically, it is an advanced feature firewall, with an integrated network platform combining a traditional firewall with other network functionalities like application firewall, IPS and Deep packet inspection and sometimes also including SSL interception. By virtue of these abundant features like NAT, stateful inspection, VPN support, etc. these are called Nextgen Firewalls. Because of these features, these firewalls help the decision making process of a firewall as per the configuration set, while dealing with network traffic.

Normally, port analysis can be done with the help of the command line as part of the operating system, real time traffic and network analyser. Port Mirroring, sometimes also called SPAN (Switched

Port Analyzer), is a method of monitoring network traffic, with the features of port analyzer. It is used on a network switch to send a copy of network packets seen on one switch port to another network switch port monitoring it.

DMZ

A study of firewalls will never be complete without understanding the technicalities in a demilitarized zone commonly called DMZ. It is essentially a computer host or small network inserted as a "neutral zone" between the organisation's private network and the outside public network. It prevents outside users from getting direct access to a server that has the organisation's data. A DMZ is an optional and more secure approach to a firewall and effectively acts as a proxy server as well.

In a DMZ configuration, a separate computer receives requests from users within the private network for access to Web sites or other companies accessible on the public network. The DMZ host then initiates sessions for these requests on the public network. Users of the public network outside the company can access only the DMZ host. The DMZ may typically also have the company's Web pages so these could be served to the outside world. However, the DMZ provides access to no other company data. In the event that an outside user penetrated the DMZ host's security, the Web pages might be corrupted but no other company information would be exposed.

Typically in a bank, especially a Core Banking Data Centre contains the main data centre running the prime database (often oracle database), there are a number of application servers which provide the connectivity from a user-level system (like a bank branch, an ATM, Internet in the case of e-banking, mail server or other functional servers). In this environment, a data packet coming from Internet Banking user (*i.e.* Internet cloud) and a data packet coming from its own bank branch in the intranet cannot be treated in the same manner. The former is prone to carry malware and has to be 'frisked' or checked before entering the critical database. In such a scenario, the role of demilitarized zone assumes enormous significance.

12.7 Unified Threat Management

Commonly known as UTM, this is a comprehensive solution that is of recent origin particularly in use for less than 10 years. Used mainly as a primary network gateway defence solution for organizations, it is basically the firewall bundled as an all-inclusive security product that has the ability to perform multiple security functions in one single appliance like network firewalling, Intrusion Prevention System, gateway antivirus, VPN, Content filtering, load balancing, etc.

A single UTM appliance simplifies management of a company's security strategy, with just one device taking the place of multiple layers of hardware and software. With UTMs, from one single centralized console, all the security solutions can be monitored and configured. The UTM has a customized OS holding all the security features at one place, which can lead to better integration and effective functioning rather than deploying a collection of disparate devices.

Let us conclude with the threat of system generated logins. Some computers when prompting the user to register or to log in want to ensure that the person logging in is actually a living person and not a system automatically creating user id, logging in and thus flooding the communication. To ensure that robots or systems generated access are denied entry, of late, a new technique called CAPTCHA is used, which is an acronym for "Completely Automated Public Turing test to tell Computers and Humans Apart". This is a type of challenge-response test used to ensure that the response is generated by a person. The process usually involves one computer (a server) asking a user to complete a simple test *i.e.* type the picture like alpha numeric characters in the screen which the computer has generated. The following are some of the examples, which the user will look at and enter in the screen. These are normally case sensitive and the user has to carefully note whether the character is upper case or lower.

In the examples given above, the words are:

I. IIBFSeCuriTy

II. MGUs5Rgod

There are many improvements in CAPTCHA, being adopted these days. Since repeated data entry and multiple, thousands of access through ROBOTs is becoming a bigger attack to network for a remote access and data entry, improved CATCHAs are being deployed these days. One such common improvement is a CATPCHA with Maths *i.e.* a captcha which will give you a very simple mathematical question like "2 + 3 =" and you have to type the answer as 5 in the space provided, so that the system will understand that a human being is accessing the application and not a machine.

In short, CAPTCHA is a software control built on the premise that, it would be impossible for a computer to read the images and do data entry. Thus the user authentication is confirmed that it is a human being who is accessing and not a computer system or other mechanical device.

SIEM

As part of network security and network controls, a concept that is increasingly becoming popular is Security Information and Event Management (SIEM). This is a term for software products and services and gets its name since it is a combination of SIM *i.e.* Security Information Management and SEM *i.e.* Security Event Management. The features of SIEM mainly include gathering data mainly on the network, analyzing and presenting such information from network, identity and access management, vulnerability management, policy compliance tools, etc.

Typically SIEM products have the capabilities of alerting and notifications, retaining the historical data and assisting in such data retrieval and log management. There are many SIEM products including a few from global companies like HP, IBM etc.

According to a lecture on 28 Feb, 2015 delivered by Shri G Padmanabhan, Executive Director, RBI "Today, tools like Security Incident and Event Management (SIEM), Network Behaviour Anomaly Detection (NBAD), Data Leakage Prevention (DLP), etc. are available which provides deep visibility into operations and quickly detect a security breach. Besides, one approach being increasingly adopted by banks – apart from procuring tools and having rules – is following the age-old and time tested method of using analytics. We have all read about the advantages of Big Data and Big Data Analytics. While this is more often used for business development and customer behaviour analysis and customer preferences, there is scope of using this for mapping general customer behaviour patterns and whenever there is an exception or an outlier, the computer system could trigger a warning."

(Source: https://rbi.org.in/scripts/BS_SpeechesView.aspx?Id=945, retrieved on 17 Nov. 15)

Net neutrality

Net neutrality is based on the principle that Internet Service Providers (ISP) should treat all data on the Internet without discrimination based on the content, site, platform, application etc. Though net neutrality is not directly related to the security administration in a network, it has a direct bearing on the security features of the network. There have been considerable amount of debates on why the Internet should be open and why all data should be treated equally.

Some service providers object to the concept of net neutrality since they feel that they should have the right to ensure free traffic of that content only which has been provided by the particular content providers (or service providers) with whom they have a contractual obligation and they should have the right to block or prioritize the contents in a network.

From security perspective, with net neutrality in place, security features in the content, will become the responsibility of the service providers who would have the right to block or permit or enhance the speed in, any network depending upon the content. With the contents of traffic being made widely known or forming part of the contractual obligation between the parties, information security

concerns too get shared between the two and any laxity on the part of one will adversely affect the other, impacting grossly the data owner ultimately.

SOAR

SOAR stands for Security Orchestration, Automation, and Response. It is a comprehensive approach to cybersecurity that combines three key elements: orchestration, automation, and response. SOAR platforms are designed to streamline and enhance an organisation's ability to respond to and manage security incidents efficiently.

SOAR plays a crucial role in strengthening the cybersecurity posture of the organisations by providing a unified and automated approach to incident response. It enables faster and more effective response to security incidents while promoting consistency, collaboration, and compliance with regulatory requirements.

SOAR enables integration and orchestration of various security technologies and tools to work together seamlessly. SOAR platforms automate routine and time-consuming tasks associated with incident response, allowing security teams to respond faster and more efficiently to security incidents.

Honeypot

A honeypot is a security mechanism designed to detect, deflect, or study attempts at unauthorized use of information systems. It acts as a decoy system or network, luring potential attackers away from critical systems to gather information about their tactics, techniques, and procedures.

Honeypots are deployed to attract and identify attackers attempting to exploit vulnerabilities. By analyzing the activities on the honeypot, security professionals can detect and understand emerging threats. Honeypots are valuable tools for security researchers and analysts to study the behaviour of attackers, malware, and various types of cyber threats. Researchers can gain insights into the latest attack methods and vulnerabilities.

Honeypots can serve as an early warning system by detecting and alerting security teams to potential threats before they can affect production systems. Information gathered from honeypots helps organisations build threat intelligence. This intelligence can include details about attack vectors, attacker tools, and tactics, aiding in the development of more effective security measures.

By observing the attacks directed at honey pots, organisations can identify potential vulnerabilities in their systems and take proactive measures to address them before real systems are targeted.

12.8 The Information Management Security

Information management security refers to the set of practices, policies, and technologies implemented to protect the confidentiality, integrity, and availability of organizational information assets. It involves safeguarding sensitive data from unauthorized access, disclosure, alteration, or destruction while ensuring that authorized users have appropriate access to the information they need.

12.9 Advantages of Information Management Security

Protection of Confidentiality: Information management security measures such as encryption, access controls, and data classification ensure that sensitive information remains confidential and is accessible only to authorized individuals or entities. This helps prevent unauthorized access, data breaches, and the exposure of confidential data to unauthorized parties.

Preservation of Integrity: Information management security mechanisms safeguard the integrity of data by preventing unauthorized modifications, alterations, or tampering. Techniques such as data validation, checksums, and digital signatures help ensure that data remains accurate, consistent, and trustworthy throughout its lifecycle.

Maintenance of Availability: Information management security measures help ensure the availability of information assets by protecting them from disruptions, outages, or denial-of-service attacks. Redundancy, fault tolerance, disaster recovery planning, and backup systems help minimize downtime and ensure that critical information remains accessible when needed.

Compliance with Regulations: Implementing information management security controls helps organizations comply with regulatory requirements, industry standards, and contractual obligations related to data protection and privacy. Compliance with regulations such as GDPR, HIPAA, PCI DSS, and others helps mitigate legal and regulatory risks and build trust with customers, partners, and stakeholders.

Risk Management: Information management security enables organizations to identify, assess, and mitigate security risks associated with their information assets. By implementing risk management practices such as risk assessments, vulnerability management, and security controls, organizations can reduce the likelihood and impact of security incidents and breaches.

Protection against Cyber Threats: Information management security helps organizations defend against a wide range of cyber threats, including malware, phishing, ransomware, and insider threats. By deploying security technologies such as firewalls, intrusion detection/prevention systems, end-point security solutions, and security awareness training, organizations can detect and respond to security threats more effectively.

Enhanced Business Continuity: Effective information management security measures contribute to business continuity by minimizing the impact of security incidents, disasters, or disruptions on organizational operations. Disaster recovery planning, incident response preparedness, and backup/recovery solutions help organizations recover quickly from security incidents and maintain business continuity.

Protection of Reputation and Trust: Information management security helps protect an organization's reputation and build trust with customers, partners, and stakeholders by demonstrating a commitment to protecting sensitive information and ensuring data privacy and security. A strong security posture can enhance brand reputation, increase customer loyalty, and differentiate the organization from competitors.

Implementing Robust Security Measures: The information management security is essential for organizations to protect their valuable information assets, comply with regulatory requirements, mitigate security risks, and maintain the trust and confidence of stakeholders. By implementing robust security measures and practices, organizations can effectively safeguard their information assets and achieve their business objectives securely.

Know Your Progress

Network and connectivity is the essence of modern day computing. Hence if proper security controls are not in place to check network access, the result would be disastrous. Many network gadgets are used in organisations, with each device having its own specific features like hubs, routers, switches, bridges, etc. All these are to be properly configured with all security features built in.

Network configuration is of utmost importance be it the OSI Model of seven layers or the TCP/IP model of 4 layer approach. There are security concerns in the network impacting the network and the data that flows through it. IP Sec is an Internet Protocol suite for securing IP based communication and ensuring security controls by authenticating and encrypting each IP packet in a communication session. VLAN is a security feature allowing for computers in a LAN to be grouped together even if not located on the same network switch physically.

Multi Protocol Label Switching (MPLS) is a highly scalable data-carrying mechanism not depending upon any specific protocol and works independent of it. Voice over IP is the transmission of voice over packet-switched IP networks and is one of the most important emerging trends in telecommunications. As against the traditional circuit-based telephony, VoIP transmits voice in a digitized format. Network

Address Translation (NAT) is a powerful tool that can be used to hide internal network addresses and enable several endpoints within a LAN to use the same (external) IP address. Basic NATs of translation of one to one IP address is normally used when there is a requirement to interconnect two IP networks with incompatible addressing.

There are many protocols used in communication like ftp, http, https, tcp/ip, telnet etc. all of which have some security features and are useful for certain kinds of transmission. Firewalls are access control devices for the network and can assist in protecting an organisation's internal network from external attacks. UTM (Unified Threat Management) is a comprehensive security solution which serves as firewall, Intrusion Prevention and Detection and content filtering also. The security feature which is used to confirm that the person at the other end doing the data entry is a human being and not a computer system is called 'captcha'. These days, captchas come in different formats including giving some mathematical questions and prompting the user to give answers to these as a form of authentication. There are also Security Incident and Event Management products available that monitor the security and give detailed reports on various ports and traffic in the network.

Key Words

DMZ	Captcha	Firewall	IP Spoofing
DNS Attack	IPS	IDS	Protocol
Telnet	http	NAT	Steganography
VoIP	VLAN	IP Sec	Tunnelling
SSL	Router Tables	OSI Model	TCP/IP
MPLS	Cryptography	Net neutrality	SIEM
False positive	False negative	SOAR	Honeypot

Questions

1. Which of the following devices reads MAC address of a computer system?
   a. Modem
   b. Multiplexer
   c. Hub
   d. Bridge
2. Information on routing the data across a network is called the ________.
   a. Routing table
   b. Routing IP Sec configuration
   c. Routing the firewall
   d. Switching the data throughput
3. Devices that accept lower speed data streams from terminals and combine them into one high speed data stream are called ________.
   a. High-end Switches
   b. Multiplexers

   c. VLAN Switches

   d. Cisco Routers

4. As against the 7-layered OSI Model, a typical TCP/IP has only four layers, which are _____.

   a. Application Physical, IP/Internet, Data Link

   b. Application Transport, IP/Internet, Physical

   c. Application, Transport, IP/Internet, Data Link

   d. Network, Transport, IP/Internet, Physical

5. .... is a group of hosts with a common set of requirements, which communicate as if they were attached to the same broadcast domain regardless of their physical location.

   a. LAN Switch

   b. IP Sec LAN

   c. IP Sec WAN

   d. VLAN

6. The process of configuring a single VLAN to support customers who have multiple VLANs, while preserving customer VLAN ids and keeping the traffic in different VLANs properly segregated is called __________.

   a. Tunnelling

   b. VLAN routing

   c. VLAN IP Sec

   d. VoIP

7. A widely used protocol in the internet to transfer files from one system to another is—

   a. HTTP

   b. SFTP

   c. FTP

   d. TCP

8. Access control devices used in networks which can assist in protecting an organisation's internal network from external attacks are called—

   a. VLAN Switches

   b. IP Sec routers

   c. Firewalls

   d. Cisco

9. UTM functioning as a firewall with many other security features like IDS, IPS etc., refers to _________.

   a. United Threat Monitoring

   b. Unified Threat Monitoring

   c. Unified Threat Management

   d. United Threat Management

10. The technology used to confirm that the user is a human being and not a computer is________.

   a. captcha

b. catcha

c. catcher

d. hatcher

11. MPLS stands for _________.

a. Multi Point Linear Switching

b. Monitoring Protocol and Linear Switching

c. Management of Protocol Label Switching

d. Multi Protocol Label Switching

12. The standards used in world wide web for accessing the internet is_________.

a. https

b. http

c. tcp/ip

d. ftp

13. Net Neutrality is the concept of _____________.

a. ensuring that all service providers charge equal tariff to subscribers as network service providers

b. treating all network traffic irrespective of who is viewing it

c. treating all networking traffic without discriminating about the content or the data being transmitted

d. discriminating between the network and treating all service providers neutrally

14. In the case of VoIP transmission, the voice travels as analog data and gets converted as digital with the help of modem. True/False

15. IP Spoofing is an attack where an attacker pretends to be sending data from an IP address other than its own. True/False

16. Telnet Access is not a preferred communication because of security considerations. True/False

Answers

1. *d*	9. *c*
2. *a*	10. *a*
3. *b*	11. *d*
4. *c*	12. *b*
5. *d*	13. *b*
6. *a*	14. False
7. *c*	15. True
8. *c*	16. True

13

CHAPTER

Controls in Software Development and Maintenance

OBJECTIVES

In this chapter, we will discuss the security issues concerning software development and maintenance in an organisation. We will also learn about software development in different environments like in-house model, where software is developed by a team of the organisation's own employees and an outsourced or procured one wherein software is purchased from a third party vendor and customized to specific requirements. Security issues in both the scenarios are studied in the chapter. The various security initiatives that are to be in place in software, right from the stage of development to that of testing and then maintenance and the final stage of destruction.

13.1 Introduction

Software Security is a generalized expression used for describing any software which provides security to the software program including the operating system and all data stored within the software or the computer and network in general. Broadly speaking, antivirus software, firewall, anti spyware etc. are all software security initiatives only. While some software programs are specifically written as security software (like firewall) and can be separately procured, many operating systems and RDBMS also come preloaded with security software and tools:

1. A decision on the deployment of software security is to be taken after considering factors like the operating system and its variant, version etc. the nature and type of data, its criticality, importance, etc, the type of users *i.e.* proneness to attack, nature of system in network and its weaknesses, vulnerabilities in the entire system and above all the corporate systems security policy and compliance regulations.

2. Application security involves the entire process of software development, deployment and implementation commencing from the stage of development. Basically, it is trust that the organisation will have in its software and hence sometimes becomes a complicate process to understand and assure.

3. Weakness in software can be discovered in many ways, and the most appropriate time would be to find it out, at the time of testing and before implementation or release. Software testing and review normally involves various steps like–

I. Vulnerability scanning,

II. Code review,

III. Penetration testing and

IV. Static Analysis

4. The **Open Web Application Security Project (OWASP)** is a worldwide not-for-profit charitable organization focused on improving the security of software. It does not recommend any particular product or software security service and is open to all. It helps taking conscious decisions on software security and to know the strength and vulnerabilities in software.

5. A design flaw in software is a serious mistake and is often passed off as a software bug. Though software bug and design flaw are closely associated with each other, a design flaw is much more serious because a flaw in the design of the software (*i.e.* a stage much before the actual coding and development) will be too costly in rectification starting from redesigning, rewriting the code, review at every stage, rework in integration and system testing and naturally consuming enormous amount of human, system and other resources.

6. A software bug may be a small error in software which has resulted in an unexpected result or a faulty output, that went undetected (sometimes in the form of a trapdoor *i.e.* a feature undetected or unplugged which allows unauthorized access to the system resources and data) which can be rectified easily by rewriting the particular unit code. However, at times, software bug could be serious enough that rewriting the particular software unit code, may have repercussions in the other units of the software (affecting some other data entry screens from a user perspective) and involving touching many other parts of the program. Such effects, also referred to as 'ripple effects' in software metrics have to be studied in detail so that the root cause for the bug is found out.

7. The faulty output will have much varying ramifications, depending upon whether it is a result of software bug in the application software, or in the database itself or somewhere else *i.e.* network traffic speed issues or an operating system issue. Hence bug fixing is often an exercise entrusted to the experts in testing well versed in the security features of the operating system, nuances of coding and preferably the language, network configurations and other areas associated with development. A bug report naturally should carry all details of the bug and sometimes becomes part of a security incident necessitating a formal follow-up action.

(Incident Management has been dealt with in detail in chapter No.16)

8. Some of the most common software bugs and design flaws are:

- Writing unnecessary code (avoidable use of system resources)
- Writing it too hard-coded (*i.e.* with less parameterization leaving no scope for changes in design or data validations or in data entry screen)
- Writing codes that are too generic leaving too much for customization or asking too many input data, frustrating the data entry operators
- Not using the authentication as per the corporate policy
- Not adhering to the standard practices and regulatory practices

9. A good software and design is one which—

I. Ensures proper authentication

II. Takes into the requirements from compliance angle even without the user demanding it and guiding the user on the same

III. Ensures security in software and guiding the user on what is secure

IV. Authenticating the user first and authorizing the transaction later

V. Separating the data and control instructions and not processing any control instructions from untrusted sources

VI. taking in data through an EDI or an API only with proper validations

VII. use cryptography optimally

VIII. taking the user into confidence in all stages of development and discussing the vulnerabilities, compliance, resources, etc

10. Typically in a CBS environment, the data centre and related architecture in a bank will be roughly as follows: The operating system being at the bottom layer with a high-end server (normally a Unix OS Server) running with a huge processor and the RBDMS *i.e.* the Oracle database which consists of the entire bank data (All deposits, advances *i.e.* assets, funds, treasury, HR and all data being accessed and used by the employees and customers). This data is accessed through the various application servers like CBS, ATM Application server, Internet Banking server (or servers), Mail Server etc. depending upon the nature of transaction from the customers or branches. Being at the top is the customer or the user or the employees who access the relevant application and through that the actual database, depending upon whether he is an ATM user or a branch user or an Internet banking user.

11. From security perspective, understanding of this architecture is essential since this gives a clearer picture how a customer or a user accesses the bank data from a branch or a cloud in the form of Internet and where all application servers are placed, where a firewall functions and how actually the data is secured by banks.

13.2 Software Development

Various models of software development are available. Developer and the user discuss and finalise the operating system, the RDBMS to be used and all related factors including the choice of a particular model with the type of testing to be done. For the purpose of this chapter, our focus of discussion will be on the security scenario in different models of software development, different operating systems, different RDBMS that are deployed and licensed. Though an in-depth study of different models of software development are not to be provided here, we will have a bird's eye-view so far as it concerns Information System Security.

Software Development Life Cycle Model or SDLC as is popularly called, is a set of activities related to the various steps involved in software development. In SDLC, there is a relationship between activities in a particular order, which if performed in a manner that satisfies the steps in the same order, will produce desired product. SDLC is essentially the sequence of activities in software production right up to the point of delivery to the user.

SDLC tells us how the various activities are actually broken into and organised. SDLC model specifies how these activities are organized in the entire software development effort. We give below some of the popular SDLC models. This is only an illustrative list and not an exhaustive one:

1. Waterfall Software Development Model
2. Prototyping
3. Iterative Enhancement
4. The Spiral Model
5. Object Oriented Methodology
6. Dynamic System Development Method

A detailed study and analysis of all these models may not be necessary for the scope of this chapter. However, the relevance of security, significance of security initiatives in all these models is certainly necessary at this stage.

For instance, in waterfall software development model, it is split into various phases like analysis, design, coding, testing and maintenance. In all these steps irrespective of phases, security has its

implications. Users have to identify the security requirements at the design stage driving home the security needs to the developers so that the level of user access, criticality of information handled can be incorporated in the software at this stage. Similarly at the point of maintenance, information security has to be addressed adequately. Developers have to deploy various FAQs (Frequently Asked Questions) so that the need to seek frequent clarifications from the developers or the help-desk does not arise. Any good software should be self-maintaining, with sufficient online help material and maximum menu driven options with minimum need to call the help-desk thereby necessitating the least access to the maintenance team. Developers should bear this in mind and ensure that minimum access is necessitated to the database or other information resources in the system.

Prototyping, involves development of software with overall functionality and showing it to the customer and then refining it slightly to suit the individual needs of the customer. Here, since security requirements may be different for various customers, the design changes and refinement stages assumes significance. For instance, though a prototype developed for one organisation should normally suit the other, it may not be completely so, as user level security requirements may vary and hence some customization may certainly be necessary. The developers cannot have a "one-size-fits-all" security scenario for all organisations. In the same industry, another user organisation may have many more security controls and hence may not require enormous controls in software development.

In iterative software development model, software will be developed iteratively, like the design stage itself getting iterative and completed. It may involve redesigning also. However from security perspective, it will be a one-time requirement of understanding the security implication in every stage and providing for the same.

Spiral model is a recent model wherein the activities are organized like a spiral with many cycles. Each cycle in the spiral begins with the identification of objectives for that cycle and the different alternatives are possible for achieving the objectives and the imposed constraints. Here too, security requirements for every particular stage, every cycle in the spiral are understood and addressed and then the development moves over to the next cycle.

In sum, irrespective of the particular model of software development adopted, it is the security requirements of software as envisaged that must be properly understood for implementation.

Software Security Assurance is a process that helps in designing the software implementing it and ultimately protects the data and other resources used by the software. Besides the resources like hardware, network related utilities, human resources, etc. software or the application so developed is itself a resource and hence must be afforded appropriate level of security it deserves.

The software security assurance process begins with the first step of identifying and categorizing the information which is used by the software. The information should be categorized according to its nature as already discussed in earlier chapters. Security considerations are to be taken into account depending upon the nature of impact of a security violation in the software or in the data, as envisaged by the owner of the software or owner of data. Sometimes, in a worst case scenario, security violation may even entail loss of human life besides loss of other resources that are measurable or quantifiable.

Software development plays a vital role in the security scenario of any organisation especially in an information system-based organisation or in a computerised environment like banks and other financial institutions. Whatever be the amount and effect of controls other areas may have, if software development is not taken care of properly, all other controls will be in vain. Security is always as strong as its weakest link.

While studying security controls in software it should always be borne in mind that security is an integral part of software, an inseparable ingredient and not an attachment or an addendum to it. Though security is always considered a module forming part of software development, when once completed and integrated, it should be an inseparable module without which the entire application should fail.

Following is an illustrative list of factors influencing the level of security in software:

I. Expected use of the software: critical, non-critical, confidential, etc.

II. Capability of the software: Operating system, RDBMS, front-end applications, etc.

III. Level of user awareness and requirement

IV. Discussion with the users and their expectations

V. Cost and technological considerations

VI. Expected life time of the software

VII. Expected periodicity of upgrades and updates in the software

Security requirements in software are normally finalized as part of the design document taking into account the needs of the owner of the software, ease of use by the users, reach of the software and criticality. However, in most cases the users or the owners may not be fully aware of the security implications of a particular utility or a feature of the software. It becomes the onus of the developers to make the software owners (or the top management) to make them aware of the security ramifications of any particular requirement they may put forth.

Typically in a Core Banking environment, it is easy for any branch staff member to view the accounts of any customer of any other branch, in any part of the nation. This is a facility and a feature of CBS. However, if any staff member keeps viewing the account or the specimen signature of the customer of any other branch regularly with no transactional necessity, then it becomes a security issue and such access should be monitored and logged (*i.e.* recorded).

There are areas in which the software developers can play a major role in even educating the users and top management on the features of any particular application. Factors influencing the security environment in software development should be taken into account before deciding the rules and procedures as part of the security policy for the organisation. Often, the top management or the security managers have to strike a balance between what is too simple to use or ultimate ease of use with security constraints on one hand and what is too strict and too secure conforming to all norms making even normal transactions difficult, driving the users or customers away, on the other.

In-House Software Development

In India, except the Indian Overseas Bank, no other bank ventured into this huge task of in-house software development for the entire bank. Almost all banks have their own IT team with qualified and talented human resources in software development and some small utility programs and report generation programs are developed in–house. Hence a brief study into the areas of security in an in-house developed environment will still be relevant. The small utility programs quite often run on standalone systems or in a distributed database or a LAN type of set up and sometimes get uploaded into the main database like ERP data or the whole enterprise data like CBS. It is in such cases, that development of software is to be viewed with all the seriousness it deserves. Though such a utility is developed and used in standalone systems sometime in simple MS Excel format, when they get integrated and uploaded into the main data of the enterprise, there comes the point of security seriousness.

The point when such data gets integrated into the main database through API (Application Programming Interface) or through a simple ODBC (Open Database Connectivity) or through an FTP (File Transfer Protocol) - based uploads, care should be taken in ensuring that all the security considerations in the main database are still adhered to. In many cases data gets uploaded by an EDI (Electronic Data Interface) with the help of a front-end menu option that runs an FTP program inside and uploads. In all such cases, security for the utility or the front-end application should be in tune with the security standards set for the main database and the software application.

Of late in many organizations, their own ERP data and outputs from such data is given or sent to banks, based on which banks do their processing of the corporate customer's request such as NEFT transactions, ECS remittances, credit advice generations, etc. In all such cases, the EDI (Electronic Data Interchange) process should take into account the type of data received, its compatibility with the bank's own application software. Such data should go through the DMZ studied earlier, the firewall, the application software of the bank and ultimately the bank's own database.

Taking data from an external source and an outside database is itself a concern for serious software bugs and update failures. Data cleaning must be proper and the entire data should be studied well for its accuracy, compatibility and appropriateness before letting it inside the bank's database.

The problem is much more complex if such a utility or software is an outsourced or a locally procured one. Sometimes it is a COTS (Commercially off the Shelf Software) that are easily available for specific purposes. Care should be taken at the stage of procuring such software and the decision to go in for such software should be a conscious one taking into account the need for the same and the software and data security constraints if any.

In-house development also has its own software security risks. Though most of the issues, as detailed below are common to an external and outsourced software also, the problem is more pronounced in the case of an in-house software only. For instance, in an outsourced software, user requirements will normally be frozen and the software design will be finalized at an early stage and every subsequent requirement will be taken as an addition on billing only. In the case of in-house, user requirements will be an ongoing occurrence since the user and the developer being in the same organisation may not take the issue of user requirements and software development seriously as two distinct functions. The chart below elucidates some of the issues and problems faced and the causes for the same.

Problem	Causes	Corrective action
Software inadequacy	Improper understanding of requirements	User requirements documentation
Insider threats to security	Lack of proper Key Responsibility Area and Role function Absence of proper job allocation and responsibility areas	Sound HR Policy and verification of antecedents Clear HR documentation and role functions
Software vulnerabilities	Improper testing and lack of seriousness in testing	External testing or proper testing methodology
Frequent failures in software	Improper testing or lack of independent testing	Testing documentation and preferably external testing
Need for frequent revisions in software	Inadequate user interaction and inadequate understanding	Proper preparation of User Manual and Systems Manual
Absence of or unsatisfactory maintenance support	Lack of proper documentation like user or system manual and absence of trained personnel at helpdesk	Enhanced version control documentation and better HR Policy and training

In addition, there are some unique problems associated with an in-house software development like dependence on one particular team of officials for the entire software development, making one team as indispensable, lack of proper documentation at the system level, absence of well documented Business Continuity and Disaster Recovery at the HR level and at the technology level, etc.

If the software development is made in-house, the users and the developers being in the same organisation or in the same institution, renders them closer to one another rendering the requirements less formal and lack documentation. Frequent requirements for software enhancement, hardware improvement, additional resource mobilization, etc. will be made and the developer has to cope with such issues, which in an outsourced environment will be more formal and be part of the agreement and be billed accordingly.

Whether in-house or outsourced, there are some basic software development issues that are to be addressed carefully to ensure security and to put the security controls in place. Optimum utilization of resources, secure usage of software library, secure access to reusable codes, secure coding standards, secure naming patterns etc. are some of the features that software developers should take care to follow. Controls on these issues have already been dealt with in detail under Chapter 11.

Frequently used functions and procedures in software are normally kept as routines and made use of in the software, stored from general software resources often referred to as a library. Maintenance of such library and the source code is to be kept secure. Especially reusable software source code should be kept with limited access to the software developers and with proper access control only.

Another major area of concern in software security is Version Control. Especially in in-house development, it should be the responsibility of the Quality Assurance Department or any other related department vested with the function of software testing and final release for usage, to ensure that only one version and the latest one is released to the user and the earlier versions are stored with proper documentation for archival purposes and for reference for future development.

Version Control and version documentation are closely related. User Manual and System Manual should be closely associated with the version the manual refers to. Whenever any patch is released it should be clearly identified with the version number. There should be clear documented policy to define a patch, a version, a release and upgrade. Software development department should take care to ensure all these terminologies are well defined and documented. For instance, change of one small word or one minute aspect in a front-end screen need not be called a version but be called a patch and be released accordingly. Such patches will go with the particular version number, normally shown in every screen in some top corner of the front-end application and will not entail any amendment to user manual or system manual. In the case of major changes, that may come with version release number and revision if necessary in the manuals too.

As part of the documentation in software development, different types of manuals are very important. Developers should take care to record the functionality and significance of every procedure or function they use in the code. Sometimes *inline comments* in the source code itself, may be used that facilitate any future reader of the source to understand why that particular procedure was introduced or the routine was called at that time.

Documentation mainly includes Systems Manual and User Manual. The System Manual intended to be used by the programmers or the help desk officers and other maintenance team, system related details will be available like database design, schema, validations done etc. This could be a restricted document for use on Need to Know basis only. In User Manual, it will be less technical and more user friendly wherein different screens of the package will be displayed guiding the user what to enter as data in every screen and the functionalities of every screen. This will be an open document with not much security controls.

Upkeep of source code and Escrow arrangement: Whenever software development is outsourced, organisations utilizing the third party developed software would be under constant fear about the continuous availability of the developers' support. Sometimes some critical resources (often human resources) may cease to be available at the developers' end or some times the developer firm itself may close its operations, thereby jeopardizing the support to the user organisation.

To overcome the risks of such an eventuality, organisations enter into an arrangement as a contractual provision with the software developer organisation, whereby an independent trusted third party receives the software source code from the developer organisation and keeps it in sealed conditions, on a contractual stipulation that the same would be opened only in the event of the developer

organisation winding-up and on specific request for the same from the user organisation. Such an agreement is referred to as **Escrow Arrangement or Software Escrow**.

From security point of view, keeping an Escrow Arrangement is always considered to be a proper software security control, which no organisation can afford to ignore. The Security Policy should provide for such an agreement stipulating the terms and conditions and the circumstances under which the agreement is to be signed, with whom and the timings when it should be utilized.

Risks involved in an outsourced environment: Outsourced software development carries with it certain inherent risks. In addition to the risks of insider threats at the developer organisation, lack of BCP-DR at the developers' site, excess dependence on one individual or two, with no other resource to fall back upon, are all the risks associated with the outsourced software development scenario. Service Level Agreement (SLA) should be drafted very carefully taking into account all the factors like security in the software, availability of resources, conformance to the set standards of the user organisation, compliance with legal and other regulatory guidelines, etc. Frequent job rotation, improper understanding of user requirements, lack of post-implementation support, lack of technological know-how etc. are all major impediments in an outsourced environment.

Hence controls for security in an outsourced environment include factors like ensuring proper (SLAs), timely support, valid NDAs (Non-Disclosure Agreements) with the third party, proximity of vendor-third party either physically or logically with proper access control mechanism and security features built in.

13.3 Cloud Computing

In cloud computing, local PCs need not have all the computing resources or storing of software or applications. The network of computers that are in the cloud (normally meaning the Internet) handles them. User PCs need not have the huge hardware or software and related infrastructure. It is enough to have an interface browser. Already yahoo mail and gmail are used by millions. The users do not have an email program in their systems nor are they storing the mails in their systems. These are taken care of by the respective service providers. This is a simplified version to serve as an example of cloud computing.

In cloud computing, the responsibility of procuring software licenses, providing for all applications in every PC or to every new entrant in the organisation etc. no longer exists. All PCs will have only a web-based service which hosts all the programs the user would need for his job. Remote machines owned by others will take care of all services like providing an email application, a word processing application, a spread-sheet or perhaps a database access too. It is like using the water or electricity as much as we want and paying for our consumption from a channel, without bothering about how they are stored or processed or treated or provided to us. There are many cloud service providers like Microsoft, IBM, Amazon, AT&T etc. who offer all cloud services including storage, application, interfaces, etc.

In the picture above, though PCs are shown as users, it could be any user says a PC user or a Mobile user, an iPad user, tablet user, etc. The point of emphasis is that the local users of PC or laptops, etc. do not store any application nor any data but only keep a web-based utility to utilize all these that are kept in the Internet cloud by the cloud provider. The Cloud Service Providers normally offer three types of services: Infrastructure as a Service (IaaS), Platform as a Service (PaaS) and the more popular ones Software as a Service (SaaS), meaning thereby that all these are available with the cloud provider and the user utilizes these services. For instance, the cloud client or the user does not store the application software but only operates the same which is installed and maintained at the cloud provider's systems only.

There are many distinct advantages of cloud computing which makes it grow in popularity and usage day by day. Many leading IT firms offer cloud services and conduct road shows and product demos to show case their products to exhibit their capability in offering cloud computing and related services. Some of the main advantages include:

- Low cost of ownership
- Adoption of high level computing
- Convenience of scalability and sustainability
- Locational independence
- 24 x 7 support (as offered by the cloud provider)
- Pay as per usage

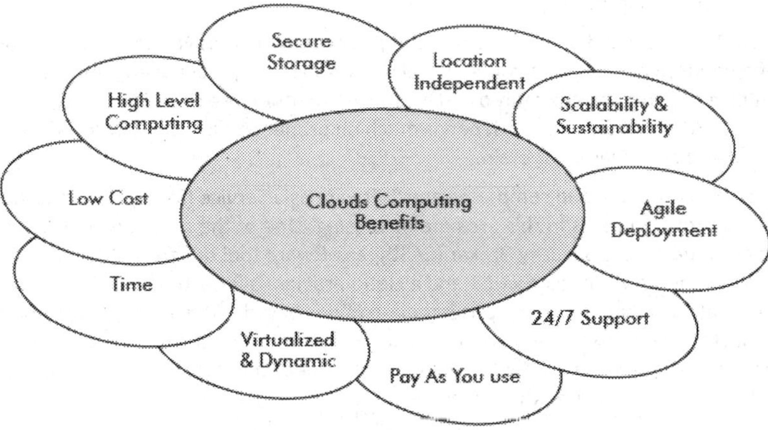

Advantages of Cloud Computing

For a study of software security control, cloud computing is really critical. Ever since cloud computing increased in popularity and private cloud service providers entered the market security concerns have been on the rise. Organisations feared, not without reason, how there could be security when the application, the database, operating system and many connected utilities are not stored locally and are all available in someone else's platform and are only used 'as a service'.

Sometimes the cloud providers *i.e.* organisations providing software, platform and infrastructure face security issues and sometimes the customers utilizing such services to face the issues. Customers have to ensure that the provider has taken proper security measures (as part of the contractual obligations) since their data and many confidential information lies in the cloud which does not belong to them. They are basically the tenants of a public cloud service. Cloud Security is an emerging subject and many private cloud providers are coming out with more and more cloud security products. However it would be in the best interest of both the parties especially the customer availing the cloud services to have proper contracts in place ensuring all security initiatives are taken.

In view of such wide-spread use of cloud computing, cloud security too is growing in importance and has become an evolving inseparable sub-domain of computer security. There are broadly three types of cloud services:

I. Private cloud

II. Public cloud and

III. Community cloud.

From security perspective, essentially there are two main stake holders and only two types of concerns:

(*i*) security issues of the cloud provider

(*ii*) security concerns of the cloud user *i.e.* the customer.

Just like other security concerns, in cloud computing, insider threats is often considered to be a major threat. Access to the data from across the cloud or physical access to the data centre and access privileges to employees, access management are all growing concerns. Sometimes, the cloud providers store the data of more than one customer on the same server. In such a case, unless the server is properly configured and unless there is fail proof access control, there is always the apprehension faced by any customer whether his data is exposed to another and every customer living under the fear of data spying by another.

Another security concern in the case of cloud computing is the extensive use of virtualization in the server configuration. Since virtualization is normally an additional layer between the OS and underlying hardware it must be properly configured and well secured, otherwise it will lead to exposure of data to third parties. Hence cloud security depends much on proper configuration of the servers and the access control and privileges set therein.

With the increasing use of cloud computing and Software as a Service (SaaS), and BYOD (bring your own device) security concerns in this area are increasing. One of the security initiatives is the use of Bit glass or Cloud Access Security Broker (CASB), a software tool or service that sits between an organization's or the user's infrastructure and a cloud provider's infrastructure. This is essentially a cloud security gateway that helps enterprises move to cloud based and mobile deployments securely, at the network level, access level and on the device. Depending upon the nature and functionality of the cloud service, organisations prefer to deploy security mechanisms like Data encryption, tracking, Access Control mechanisms and other types.

There is no specific cloud security program or cloud security standards that can be uniformly adopted to showcase that the particular cloud provider or the user is quite secure. However there are some initiatives like the Cloud Security Alliance's Open Certification with some certification courses and attestation programs that are reportedly complemented to other standard certifications like ISO 27001 etc., not forming part but just assisting in such security areas.

In short, an effective security system in a cloud scenario will have to be in the form of preventive control by reducing vulnerabilities and strong authentication, detective control in the form of proper IDS and corrective controls in the form of immediate follow-up action like restoration and rebuild. Of course, the routine pillars of information security like confidentiality, integrity and availability have all to be ensured with proper additional initiatives like authentication, application security, data privacy and other regulatory compliance based initiatives.

13.4 Big Data

A study of software security in banks and financial sectors will not be complete without knowing about the nuances of Big Data, its usage and its security implication

The phrase "Big Data" is gaining in usage of late. Big Data may be broadly defined as a collection of data sets which is essentially very huge and naturally so complex that it is considered to be difficult to work on, deploying traditional database management and analysis tools. Big Data is not a separate software or a special kind of RDBMS that has suddenly come into use, but could be any data, any RDBMS wherein the data itself is so huge and complex that its analysis, study and perhaps storage and retrieval need some extra knowledge and technology.

Especially banks dealing with an enormous data related to customers and other details need to deploy a very good amount of data analysis, retrieval methodologies and above all, a security mechanism to take care of the complexity and enormity of the data.

Big Data Security Analytics: A system that captures and stores an organization's Big Data sources relevant to information security for the purposes of uncovering cyber threats by interpreting data displayed within tables, charts, and graphs especially in big data fraud prevention, enterprises have to move from the traditional post incident forensics to a technology-driven predictive and proactive approach resulting from incidents and event logs, to fight frauds.

Know Your Progress

Software Development Life Cycle is a series of steps in software development beginning from the first step of software design and then on to development, testing and implementation. There are many models of SDLC like the waterfall model, prototyping etc. Depending upon the nature of software and the customer's requirements an appropriate model is chosen. Security in software should be part of software development life cycle irrespective of the particular model of SDLC adopted. User sometimes may not be aware of the security implications of a particular requirement. Still it would be the duty of developers to apprise the user of security implications of every object in the software and ensure all security initiatives are in place.

In the case of in-house software development too, security concerns still exists, though with a little different ramification. Security of source code, upkeep and maintenance of such code and utilising the best security features of the OS should be the main points for consideration of security managers without compromising on the OS features. Security features available in the RDBMS and those which are part of the application software that are used at the front-end and/or the application servers which may be part of the back-end or data centre should also be studied. An ideal mix of all features taking into account ease of use, utilisation of resources like bandwidth, processor etc. should be deployed. Version Control and Documentation should be well in place.

Whenever modern areas of technology like cloud computing are deployed care should be taken to ensure that security is not compromised. Especially, in cloud computing when the infrastructure and the software are provided by a third party called the cloud providers, care should be taken to see the security of data in storage or in transmission is not compromised and data integrity is maintained. Cloud Security is a complex area since it rests on the firm which provides the could services as well as the customer or user firm which uses the cloud and whose data is stored in the cloud.

Big Data is an emerging concept these days, especially in the case of major banks dealing with a huge amount of data. Security in big data is getting more and more complex wherein specific tools have to be deployed.

Key Words

CBS	ODBC	COTS	Prototyping
Waterfall Model	SDLC	EDI	VAPT
Software Escrow	Alpha Testing	Beta Testing	Regression Testing
White Box Testing	Black Box Testing	Cloud Computing	Virtualization
OWASP	Design Flaw	Vulnerability Scanning	Big Data

Questions

1. Which of the following is not a factor that influences the level of security in software?

   a. Expected use of the software like critical, non-critical, confidential, etc.

b. Capability of the software and the OS, RDBMS, front-end applications, etc.

c. Return on Investment of security initiatives

d. Level of user awareness and requirement

2. The main security concern in the case of procuring COTS kind of software is ________.

a. being a readymade tool, its integration into the existing data is to be verified

b. being a readymade hardware, its compatibility with the RDBMS should be studied

c. almost nil since such software will easily get integrated into the existing data

d. very insignificant since such software is a free utility and does not have any security implications

3. Which of the following may not be a cause for frequent failure of software?

a. Lack of user awareness and understanding of the feature of the software.

b. Improper testing at the user site or by the user.

c. Lack of proper key responsibility areas and role function definition.

d. Inadequate independent testing of the software.

4. In software development, version control is important because (*i*) the software is identified with the version of release to help in case of trouble shooting (*ii*) it enables testing and results identified with version which was tested (*iii*) it enables ensuring that only one version of the software is available (iv) it deletes all other versions from the developers' view (*v*) it enables the latest version to be put to use for testing or other further course of action—

a. All except (*iv*) are correct

b. All except (*ii*) are correct

c. Only (*i*), (*ii*) and (*iii*) are correct

d. Only (*i*), (*iii*) and (*v*) are correct

5. Escrow Arrangement with a third party organisation ensures that the software ________.

a. is kept safe for use and on payment by the third party

b. is kept safe to be made use of in times of need as per contractual obligations

c. can be deployed by the third party and maintained by the third party in case the developer is not able to maintain it

d. will ensure proper copyrights and cannot be used by any one else in an unauthorised manner

6. In the case of cloud service providers, which of the following is not normally provided by them?

a. Hardware Infrastructure

b. Storage

c. Application software, interfaces, etc.

d. Data

7. As part of software documentation, the development team provides the screen-wise outputs, inputting methods, data entry options, etc. in simple language as an open document is called—

a. System Manual

b. User Manual

   c. Documentation Manual

   d. Screen-wise Manual

8. Cloud Service providers normally provide services like PaaS, SaaS, etc. wherein PaaS means ________.

   a. Payment as a software

   b. Providing application as software

   c. Platform as a service

   d. Payment as a Security

9. Nessus is a widely deployed tool to check which of the following functionalities?

   a. Vulnerability and Penetration in network.

   b. Vulnerability in the software development.

   c. Network related application testing.

   d. Network enabled software security user level testing.

10. After a major software code change has been incorporated, the type of testing normally done__________.

   a. Unit Testing

   b. System Testing

   c. Regression Testing

   d. Alpha Testing

11. Integration testing seeks to verify the interfaces between components against a software design. (True/False)

12. Cloud computing is known for its security initiatives in place and handling data rather than for providing software application impacting the user needs. (True/False)

13. One of the major influencing factors in the case of outsourced software development is the Service Level Agreement entered with the developers. (True/False)

Answers

1. *c*	8. *c*
2. *a*	9. *a*
3. *c*	10. *c*
4. *a*	11. True
5. *b*	12. False
6. *d*	13. True
7. *b*	

C

MODULE

IT SECURITY THREATS

14

CHAPTER

Security Threats Overview

OBJECTIVES

After reading this chapter, readers will know the meaning and definition of a threat, what constitutes a major threat to an IT system, different types of threats, their criticality and their impact on different software and hardware assets in the IT system. The chapter also highlights the emerging threats of modern day IT systems, namely Cyber espionage and Cyber Terrorism and the steps that are to be in place to tackle them to minimize their impact.

14.1 Threats

The word 'threat' is itself alarming. Organisations will naturally try to get rid of them or will be least willing to face them.

We have previously discussed in Chapter 3 that 'threat' can be defined as an 'act of coercion proposed to elicit a negative response, a statement of an intention or an act to inflict pain, injury, damage or loss to another person or an asset and is often criminal in nature'. Hence in this chapter, we will be focusing on the different types of threats in the IT and Information Security environment and the impact every threat may have.

Like any other crime or offence, cyber threats too are human in origin though they are technical in execution and delivery. Hence to measure the gravity of an attack, it is essential that the behavioural assessment along with the technical aspects of the threat has to be measured. It is because of the human nature of the origin of the attack that quite often, companies with very strong information security initiatives in place, may become victims of an attack whereas companies even with many existing vulnerabilities may remain free too. And, sometimes the victim be it a company or an individual may not even immediately know about the victimization. Because of this paradigm in a cyber-threat, a cyber-attack is considered unique and cannot be easily compared with a traditional crime.

Threat, we have already noted, is an external event which causes or may cause harm to any information asset. Study of threats is closely associated with the study of risks and is a prelude to Business Impact Analysis and Risk Assessment. Threat is normally an event a trigger or a happening. It could normally be–

- An external event affecting the IT System
- An internal event affecting the system

- A Human element
- A natural incident or a serious natural disaster
- A foreseen incident or an anticipated and feared accident
- An Unforeseen event wholly unprepared

Issues concerning physical assets have already been discussed in detail earlier in Chapter 5. We will now have a brief look at the threats that impact physical assets in the organisation. It has generally been a point of debate and an ambiguous area in most organisations, especially in banks, on who should take care of threats to physical assets in the organisation - the Physical Security Department or the Information Security Department.

Though it is reasonably clear that the security of all information assets and their physical upkeep comes under overall charge of Chief Information Security Officer at the apex level, the ambiguity exists mainly at a lower level. Down the hierarchical ladder, there seems to be some lack of clarity on who would take care of maintenance, upkeep of small electronic gadgets the I.T Dept. or the Security Dept. or the user department itself. Hence there needs to be in place, a dependable co-ordination between the Physical Security Department and the Systems Department (or the IT Department) with regard to issues concerning threats to physical security.

There are of course, some technical issues in facing the threats, often as a result of improper interpretation, inadequate knowledge of and understanding of the electronic outputs. For instance, physical threats in an ATM cabin can best be addressed and studied by looking at the CCTV clippings recorded or by the ATM logs printed and stored at the ATM. In practice, however, most of the functional managers or even the security officers are not trained to interpret the ATM logs and find out the trail that the ATM transaction has left and it becomes the duty of the systems manager to interpret the log and find out the trail of events.

Social engineering and Impersonation: The threats that result from getting the confidence of users and getting their user information including passwords, gaining access into others' systems through gaining the confidence of such users and thus defrauding the actual users or owners of data and information is known as Social Engineering. In this context, it is worthwhile to note that the Indian Information Technology Act in Sec 66D has stipulated punishment for the offence of cheating by Impersonation.

Vishing which is a combination of voice and phishing. The *modus operandi* in such frauds is that someone calls the victim, often posing as if from the bank or other such known source, with some information about the victim and then engaging the victim/user/customer with some kind of conversation and getting some vital information about the bank account or an email account, ultimately gets the confidential information like username and password for the same.

Besides such instances, in a nation known for free communication in public transport system or free sharing of information and chatting freely even with strangers treating unknown persons too as 'guests' and 'acquaintances' in a public place, it is not uncommon that a social networking site is full of information including lot of personal details, Social engineering and impersonation in the electronic world has become very easy more so with criminal on the prowl hunting for data with 'information harvest' from any site available in the net.

Social engineering is just one of the methods of cyber-attacks or threats to information. There are so many methods and ways by which an information may be attacked. The manner through which a threat reaches the target *i.e.* the method or the *modus operandi* adopted is called a threat vector. Therefore, threat analysis or threat management presupposes a study of the threat vector.

A threat vector is different from a vulnerability in the sense that the latter is an existing weakness in the system whereas the threat vector is the manner or the method through which the threat will attack. Like threat, threat vector may be an external thing, plugging which may not be within the purview or capability of the security system whereas a vulnerability is an existing weakness in the system, which may be eliminated well within the organisation itself.

We have already seen the security controls in a networked environment. Now let us look at some of the threats to network.

DoS

Denial of Service popularly abbreviated as DoS attacks are among the most harmful threats from network.

We may have to study the DoS attacks along with DDoS attack *i.e.* Distributed Denial of Service Attack. As the name itself suggests, this is an attempt to make a computer or network resource unavailable to its intended users. There are many methods to achieve this, some are pure technological, some are absolutely illegal, unlawful and punishable and some are beyond the comprehension of ordinary technical people. But the motive anyway is harmful, illegal and malicious. Basically, it prevents an internet site or a web server or similar kind of service from functioning efficiently and keeping it temporarily or sometime indefinitely not available to genuine users.

When a DoS attack comes from more than one computer or the fraudster sends the attack through more than one system in a network by taking control of those systems or a network, then it is a Distributed Denial of Service attack. In reality, the DDoS attackers are not aware that they are engaging in a DoS attack against a site and that it is their systems that are used (technically and physically) to spread the attack. Perpetrators of DoS attacks normally target banks' sites or similar services or other critical servers like credit card payment gateways or such other financially sensitive servers.

Other than computer networks, sometimes DoS also refers to some critical resources like access to data or clogging the CPU with thousands of millions of requests to render it unavailable for genuine application based processing. Such attacks usually lead to a server overload which is also a form of DoS attack only. DoS attacks are certainly illegal as per the provisions of Information Technology Act in India and as the contractual obligations with the Internet Service Providers and other laws of the land, either in India or elsewhere.

In the context of DoS and DDoS attacks, we should know about Zombies. Though the word zombie means a corpse or a lifeless or completely unresponsive person, in computer parlance, zombie is a computer connected to the internet, that has been compromised by a cracker or a fraudster by a virus program who takes the system under his control and the system performs as per his wishes under remote direction like spreading a worm, spreading a virus or other malicious attacks on other systems. Besides being party to the malicious spreading of virus unintentionally, the owners of those systems also fall prey to the desires of such malwares otherwise also, since the bandwidth of their systems is consumed and all logs report their systems as the rogue mail senders and not the original sender.

More on Zombie and botnets in the next chapter on "Malware".

Of late, zombies are used in Pay Per Click kind of activities also *i.e.* an online advertising payment model in which payment is based solely on qualifying number of clicks. The advertiser only pays for clicks to the destination site based on a pre-arranged per-click rate. Zombies are used to perform such routine clicks, sometimes also referred to click frauds.

What is interesting to note is that DoS attacks, which once started as a technology and practiced by tech-savvy misguided youth has now become a profession. Now there are professionals who write DoS code with specific intention to create havoc in networks as a result of corporate or professional rivalry or other unlawful considerations, illegal intentions and malicious activities.

As depicted in the picture below, the attacker may send the malicious program from his system to another system which is compromised (called a compromised system or a master system which may be more than one) to spread the malicious program to the targeted or victim's systems. The slave systems

are acting as zombies without knowing what they are doing and simply obeying the instructions of the attacker in the network to the targeted victims of the original attacker, as per his plan.

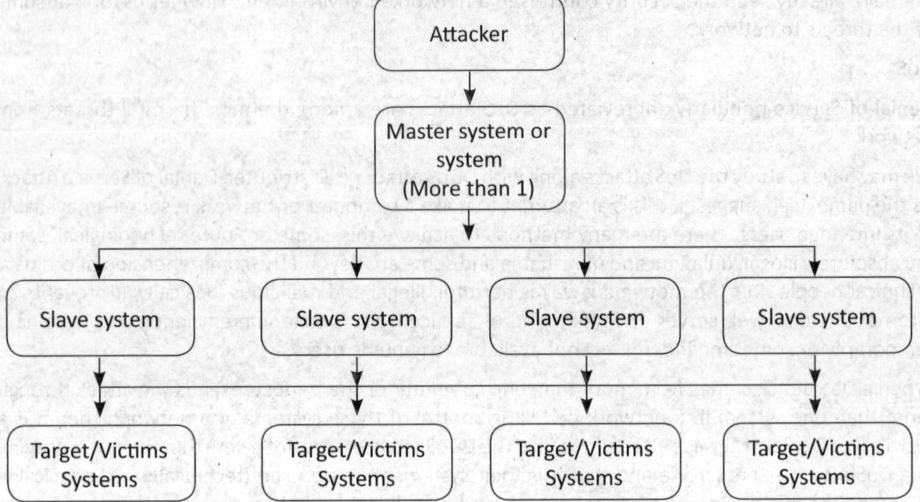

Fig 14.3.1 DoS Attack

Beside the DoS attacks there are many other threats that a network may face should be adequately addressed. One such attack is Man in the Middle Attack. It is a kind of eavesdropping in which the attacker has a separate connection with the victims and relays messages making them believe that they are talking directly to each other whereas the attacker has intercepted all messages between two victims and inject new ones. Such Man in the Middle Attacks are more pronounced in the case of WiFi connection and wireless access points.

Encryption though not a threat in a network is often construed as a threat when the encryption is used for illegal purposes and the service providers do not share the encryption algorithm with the regulators or the government agencies in times of need. What is a technological feature for use by one can always become a threat to the other if used for illegal or an unauthorised access purposes.

Authentication mechanism, unauthorised access in a network and illegal access privileges in a networked environment, improper configuration of network equipment, inadequate security in a network gadget etc. are all threats to a network.

14.2 After the network related threats, let us have a look at some of the software related attacks.

SQL Injection: An attacker enters an SQL (Structured Query language) statement into a web page with an intention to make the form permit an unauthorized SQL command in the database. If the penetration is successful, he gets a full access to the database and can get the data desired like financially critical or otherwise confidential data stored in the database.

In this context, the other phrases that are gaining in usage are **APT and Zero Day Threat**. APT short for Advanced Persistent Threat, one of the most dreaded threats these days is an attack coming from various threat vectors and multiple ways and attempts to stay undetected too. Normally difficult to understand for a general user and complex enough for a security professional to decode and know the impact, APTs are always quite advanced in technology and programming language and hence the normal target for APTs is financial or otherwise data critical organisations or any firm which has highly confidential data.

Zero Day Threat is a threat that existed on the day the software is released *i.e.* much before the user comes to know of it. It is otherwise called a zero-day vulnerability also since basically it is a weakness in the software application which the developer or the seller is either not aware or pretends to be unaware since there is no patch ready for it and still delivers the product (so that by the time the user reports it, the patch would be ready).

Cross-site scripting (XSS): is a complex vulnerability in web applications enabling to inject a malicious or other code or script into a web page owned by other users. Since these codes are surreptitiously injected, they bypass the normal controls and checks in the software. XSS may be written for data access, data theft, or a simple nuisance like a DoS attack right upto the serious threat of data theft itself.

Since the code is injected from one site to another, the attacker normally studies the vulnerabilities in the target system and attempts an easy access exploiting them. Sometimes the attacker gets a proper and enhanced access privilege in the victim's system and comfortably does the code injection or ports the malware. Originally started with a javascript, now XSS has become common and generic to denote a stealthy code injection into any web application including non-java applications.

Buffer overflow: Though buffer overflow is basically a vulnerability in the system, any intruder or an attacker will exploit the vulnerability and attack the system through it. To put in simple terms, buffer overflow is putting too much information into a space in a computer's memory. Without going deeper into any programming language and how memory allocation is made typically in any computer program, let us understand that a computer allocates some memory space for storing some information and in that space, some variable with larger space comes, resulting in overflow of the space rendering the last byte or the last few bytes not getting stored. This portion called stack is exploited by the attackers to store the information by overwriting the return address to point at the stack containing the instruction placed by the attacker.

Cross-Site Request Forgery (CSRF): Attackers trick users into performing unintended actions on a website where they are authenticated. This can lead to unauthorized changes in user settings or data.

Insecure Direct Object References (IDOR): Attackers exploit flaws in an application's access controls to gain access to unauthorized resources or sensitive data.

XML External Entity (XXE) Attacks: Malicious XML input is used to exploit vulnerabilities and disclose internal files, execute remote code, or perform denial-of-service attacks.

Sniffer is a program which monitors and analyses network traffic, detecting bottlenecks. Though a technology, sniffer can be deployed legitimately to capture network traffic or monitor traffic to enhance smoother flow of network traffic or maliciously to perform the same task. A network router actually reads data packets and determines the route to the destination. Therefore, when a sniffer is used illegitimately or in an unauthorised manner, it becomes a malware.

There are many issues that are pure technologies but when used for the purpose of committing a crime with criminal intention, come under the ambit of cyber-crime. What is a technological feature for the tech-savvy software people may be exploited by the fraudsters for furtherance of their criminal objectives.

One such attack to a network is steganography. Having its origin from the Greek word steganos meaning 'covered' and graphie meaning 'writing', the word steganography literally means covered writing. It finds a place in the study of attacks based on software and technology, because it can be (and has been) used to hide an encrypted message inside a file normally a jpeg file so that any unsuspecting viewer will take it as a picture and the intended recipient will decrypt and extract the message at the destination. Many terrorist outfits have used this technology to convey secret information often brief texts by email by sending harmless pictures of popular film personalities or other general photos, so that even in case the system is seized by the investigators, they may take it as a harmless transmission of some pictures only.

Threats may sometimes be purely on non-technological grounds and those not relating to information systems or technology also. For instance, in areas like Human Resources, there are many threats that

organisations face. Such threats often posed by employees are referred to as internal threats that result from disgruntled employees, dissatisfied work-force, HR related factors etc.

Besides such generic threats, there may be specific threats from human resources in the organisations like non-cooperative work force, an unwilling and non-dedicated contribution, inadequate commitment, etc. Many research studies worldwide have stated that disgruntled workforce are among the major threats in any organisation. Especially in the banking industry, where much critical data and financially sensitive information is handled, disgruntled work-force or other forms of insider threats is something which management can ill afford. We have already noted that pre-hiring verification and antecedent checking should be scrupulously followed to guard against insider threats to a considerable extent.

SCADA systems (Supervisory Control and Data Acquisition Systems) are used generally in key areas like power, Oil & Gas, water and waste management and sometimes in process industries like petrochemicals, cement, etc. These are also comparable to PLC systems *i.e.* Programmable Logic Controllers which are also the targets for a cyber-terrorist attack. With more and more key areas coming under computerization (like automated and unmanned Metro rail, etc. in the metros and urban centres) protection of such critical sensitive information asset is certainly going to be a major cause for concern in the years to come.

Improper upkeep of printers and lack of control of computerized print-outs do often pose a great threat to the organisation. Print-outs generated from the computers, improper upkeep of printers, inadequate control of printers especially a network printer to which printing instructions can be given over a network are all sources of major threats to information security.

Computerised print-outs do often carry much significance, especially in these days of more and more ogranisations and banks resorting to the misplaced phrase "This is a computerized print-out and hence needs no signature". Inadequate control over computer print-outs often read with the standard phrase as above may pose a great threat to the organisation, because in practice and in law, computerized print-outs *per se* are not exempt from signature. Perhaps organisations, certainly including banks, can slightly rephrase their sentences like "this is a computer generated and routine information print-out and hence is not signed" instead of mentioning "and hence needs no signature" thereby giving a meaning that a computerized a print out *needs no signature* which is an absolute misunderstanding of the legal position and misleading.

Just like the print-outs, the logs of transactions and the enormous trail that every transaction leaves is also very important since it serves as a record of immense evidence value in times of any dispute.

Threats maybe in the form of spying devices. Of late many spying devices come in small sizes, miniature formats some with the capability of transmitting data (as a GSM device) which can be fixed to even very small objects like a hand-bags, purse, wrist-watch, sun-glasses etc. Pictures of some of the spying devices that cannot catch human attention normally are given below:

Spying Camera Pen with Transmitter

Spy Key Chain with camera

Spying Shoe with camera and transmitter

Spying miniature camera

Detection of these spying devices is basically a physical control, but still there are also network devices and connectivity gadgets since these have transmitting capability. For instance, a button sized camera fixed on to an ATM was capturing the ATM PIN while the same was being entered by the user and was transmitting it to the fraudster receiving the transmission from a nearby place, a few metres away.

Drones and robotics: Unmanned Aerial Vehicle (UAV) or Remotely Piloted Vehicle run by a remote device individually or as part of a network, popularly known as 'drones' may also sometimes become a weapon for spying and a tool enabling attack at a later date.

Role of Vigilance Department, Disciplinary Action Cell or Department or the Risk Containment department or the Fraud Mitigation department is very significant to address the various threats to an organisation. Proper threat analysis should be conducted by all the concerned department so that it serves as a deterrent as well as a preventive step.

14.3 Cyber Espionage

In the context of data protection, it is relevant to study Cyber Espionage as a threat to organisation's data. Espionage basically means 'the practice of spying'. The electronic variant of spying is cyber espionage. All kinds of attempts to spy someone else's data or information *i.e.* getting the data without the permission of the owner or the custodian of the information can be called cyber espionage. It is a threat to computers, often a pure hardware gadget like a hidden camera, a button sized camera or a hidden voice recorder or a transmitter from a prohibited area will all come under this.

Normal acts of impersonation, shoulder surfing, social engineering or volunteering help to a stranger with a motive to spy the data like credit card details, etc. are all different variants of cyber espionage. Of late, a disturbing factor in corporate circles is that cyber spies are hired by corporate to attack the rival's system or by any other means reach the critical infrastructure of the rivals and get classified data and confidential information.

In the recent past, many cases of corporate data theft have been reported. The infamous case of the Sony attack, which saw the release of confidential data of employees and their families in November 2014, resulted in a huge reputation loss, like many other cases resulting in a loss in revenue due to movies being leaked, sensitive employee information disclosed, and executive emails were publicised, etc.

Espionage is often global and trans-border too, in which case nabbing the culprits becomes an arduous task. Though technically, national and international acts of espionage are almost the same, so long as they are going to occur as a result of a compromised network, investigation and detection makes it very difficult in the case of a trans-border attack. As it was said earlier, what is basically a technological feature (like a miniature camera, a mini voice recorder and transmitter or a virus attack) has now become a weapon to spy classified information and commit a cyber-crime.

Stuxnet, infamously called the 'first digital weapon' is a computer worm which was spoken about first in late 2010. Unlike any other virus, it did not simply steal the data but was programmed to attack modern PLCs (Programmable Logic Controllers). A much dreaded virus, Stuxnet functions by targeting machines using the popular MS Windows operating system and networks, then seeking out its targets.

Embezzlement refers to dishonestly appropriating assets or the fraudulent appropriation of funds properly entrusted to one's care but actually owned by someone else. In a computerized environment, the threat of embezzlement comes in the wake of systems wherein there are vulnerabilities in the system or there are causes prone to result in the attack of embezzlement. Attacks of embezzlement could be due to misguided employees or evil minded work-force acting as a result of greed for money or trying to capitalize on an existing vulnerability in the system.

14.4 Cyber Terrorism

Technology is most abused and misused by criminals as an 'enabler' in terrorism: Technology is a multi-edged tool like a swiss knife and can make or mar things. In this age of Internet of Things, with every information available in the Net, any data can be legitimately used, abhorrently abused, menacingly misused or deliberately disused too. Sometimes, the difference between a pure technology and an illegal use get blurred.

For instance, IP Tracing, IP Spoofing, Email Spoofing, Fastflux, Dumpster Diving, Scavenging, Steganography or even writing a DoS query generator program are all pure technologies which can be legitimately taught and learnt by anyone passionate about such technological know-how but, such knowledge when caught in the hands of misguided youth, may be grossly misused for solely terrorist purposes with dire catastrophic consequences.

Cyber terrorism is a terrorist activity in cyberspace. The most dreaded threat of modern days, Cyber Terrorism may be defined as the *premeditated use of disruptive activities, or the threat thereof, in cyber space, with a criminal intention to further social, ideological, religious, political or similar objectives, or to intimidate any person in furtherance of such objectives*. Just like physical attacks, a cyber-attack too is normally targeted against an individual, a community, a society or a nation at large. Hence cyber terrorism includes the use of electronic weapons like attacks to network, a DDoS attack on a nation's critical network. It often puts the public or any section of public in fear and normally not targeted against any individual but a group or a society or a nation. However, there is still some lack of clarity on how cyber terrorism can be defined. Suffice, safer to state that any incident that can create terror in the networked world or cyber space can be called cyber terrorism.

Cyber terrorists are often reported to have used many advanced technologies too like sophisticated DDoS attacks, cryptographic communication, proxy servers, hate websites, session hijacking, snooping. Today, we have a 'cyber army', an army not of guns and rifles and combat vehicles but of keyboards and mouse and network and servers. There is state sponsored terrorism, state trained cyber army, rogue nations and hate-policies. Tomorrow's wars will be fought not with guns but keyboard and remote controllers half the globe away that are capable of triggering a major attack to annihilate the power grid, destabilize a metro rail set up or obliterate an oil supply completely and sabotage critical infrastructure.

Cyber terrorism has been a growing concern globally attention on cyber terrorism increased after the 9th September, 2001 attacks on the World Trade Centre followed by the attack in Indian Parliament the same year on Dec. 13th and many other threats and attacks in different parts of the globe and in India too subsequently.

A cyber terrorist is a person who uses the computer system as a means or ends to achieve the above objectives. Combating cyber terrorism is not just an organisational call, but it is the combined responsibility of a society, industry bodies and the nation including all its wings in investigation, crime prevention, intelligence, etc.

For this study, it would be sufficing to know the implications of cyber terrorism in the society or in any industry in particular. It is the public sector industry and the mission critical infrastructure that are normally at a greater risk in cyber terrorism. Cyber-crime is generally a domestic issue, which may sometimes have international consequences but cyber terrorism is basically a global concern, which has domestic as well as international consequences. The common form of these terrorist attacks on the Internet is by distributed denial of service attacks, hate websites and hate emails, attacks on sensitive computer networks, etc. Strengthening the security networks, monitoring the web traffic and enhancing access control initiatives and above all, strict compliance with regulatory mechanism of the nation will all go a long way in facing the cyber terrorism attacks.

Cyber terrorism is already a fact. In future, battles are going to be fought not on battle-fields but in cyber space, strikes are going to be not from physical weapons but from networked systems and the attackers are not going to be physically present or traceable but are going to be obscure, hiding behind computers and other gadgets.

It would be relevant to note that the recent amendments to Information Technology Act called the IT Amendment Act, 2008 effective from 27 Oct. 2009 has addressed the issue of Cyber Terrorism calling it as affecting the sovereignty of the nation and stipulating Life Imprisonment as punishment, *vide* Section 66F.

In combating threats, organisations have to be fully aware of their corporate security policy, the risk management practices in vogue in the organisation, the compliance and regulatory requirements in dealing with threats and the user level requirements as part of threat management. Threat has to be properly analysed, studied in depth as to its origin, the damage occurred, the potentiality to further damage, lessons learnt, follow up action and the corrective and preventive action with review for the action taken. All these together form part of Threat Intelligence.

A proper threat intelligence action will

I. identify malware-infected files.

II. locate the botnet infected systems

III. take steps to isolate the infected ones, take steps to prevent further recurrence of the damage from the threat.

While it is well known that there is nothing like Threat elimination (since threats and attacks being external factors can never be eliminated), it is always possible, rather it should be possible, to take steps in minimizing the impact of any attack as part of Threat Mitigation exercise or a threat containment model.

Threat Management

Broadly, an attack may be (a) Targeted attack or (b) Opportunistic attack. Be it a virus, hacking, malware or some other attack, at the time of creating the malware or virus program, the code writer will decide whether he wants a targeted attack or a general opportunistic attack. Corporate espionage, spying of data, specific attempts of data theft, insider threats, extortion, cyber-squatting, impersonation etc. are all normally targeted and specific attacks, particularly made to work under specific systems with the IP address or the hardware address or the network identified earlier.

On the other hand, opportunistic attack may be targeted like wolves waiting on the prowl, looking for a prey, seeking vulnerabilities in a network or any unprotected servers or session hijacked data etc. wherein bank user id or other critical session or a PoS Terminal data is compromised and capture. Ultimately, this too may end in data loss, financial loss, extortion and other forms of financial or social or psychological victimization only. In both the cases, the attacker knows when, how and whom to attack.

Sometimes the *modus operandi* adopted may be changed so quickly that what was tried in one session may not hold good in the next session in a matter of few minutes or what was tried for one user may not hold good for another. Hence, under such a scenario, mitigation and remediation too will not be the same for all kinds of attacks. Mitigation or combating a threat always differs upon the threat vectors. Similarly, remediation efforts too will differ according to the nature of attack and naturally, there cannot be a hundred percent protection against any attack, be it a virus attack, malware attack or any other kind of threat.

A recent global study of malware and other attacks revealed that attackers actually recycle many of the same attack components. Though observed as new, in reality, however the attacks could be a combination of some of the components of fraudulent attacks that have been earlier tried and proved successful (for the attackers). In practice, most of the anti virus programs and the organisations utilizing them, are often a little behind the attackers technologically and in innovation and hence even if the attackers use the most proven and already tried forms of attack, they are more often successful, if only they change the manner or the threat vector a little.

Besides being updated about the Threat management and the various threat vectors, organisations have to improve on the following fronts, to enhance their security:

I. Inspect all data at the incoming stage
II. Scan the overwhelming volume of alerts
III. Apply manual processes wherever needed
IV. Analyse the effective security products designed for singular functions
V. Correlate information to identify infected systems
VI. Identify the weaknesses throughout the network, cloud etc.
VII. Execute protection across the network, devices and data.
VIII. Reduce the gaps between detection, analysis, and protection
IX. Be prepared for new threats with new tools, technologies, and vectors

To enhance threat management, understanding of different stages of a threat and identification of the threat vector is a must. The following are generally considered to be the different stages of an attack:

I. Plan and Delivery of the attack
II. Exploitation of the system
III. Installation of the target victim system
IV. Installation and implementation of the malware
V. Command and control of the target victim system
    - Get the benefits or data and leave no trace of the attack

Know Your Progress

Threats are external events that cause harm or have potential to cause harm to an information asset. Any natural calamity, a natural disaster, man-made attacks, insider threats, deliberate acts of data theft, etc. all come under this category. Some of the common controls in the information system to combat a threat are Video Surveillance, deployment of CCTVs, physical protection through barriers, etc. Denial of Service and Distributed Denial of Service attacks are those deliberate attempts to flood a critical server with heavy volume of queries and other kinds of network so that genuine users of the services are denied access to it. There are many technologies related threats like steganography. The technology of hiding a text message in another file say an audio file or a jpg file so that any normal viewer of the file cannot see the text message but only the recipient by entering his password will be able to read the message.

There are many threats to the information assets in the form of weaknesses in the system and software that emerge right on the day the software is written and even before they are released for public use, called Zero Day vulnerabilities. Cross Site Scripting are threats essentially in a web-site targeting the data in a stealthy manner.

Cryptography is another popular form of threat to an information in transit Data and information should be handled with care and with the best security in place. The practice of spying into another person's data is called Espionage. Of late, corporate espionage has become a cause for concern among corporate circles. Cyber Terrorism is another dreaded threat targeted against a society, a nation or a whole community and normally not against an individual. It is a war fought with technology as the main weapon as against guns and missiles and nations have to gear up technologically stronger to fight against cyber terrorism.

Understanding a threat, its route, its technological arsenal and the target, are all very essential to combat a threat successfully as part of Threat Management. The nature of attack and the methodology deployed has to be understood and analysed very carefully, so that any weakness in the system that the threat focuses on, can be eliminated.

Key Words

DoS	DDoS	Buffer Overflow	APT
Sniffer	Steganography	zombies	Zero Day Threat
Pay Per click fraud	Encryption	Man in the Middle Attack	SQL Injection
Espionage	Cyber Terrorism	Trans-border attack	Cross Site Scripting
Vishing	Information Harvest	Threat Vector	Threat Intelligence
CSRF	IDOR	XXE	

Questions

1. What are the essential elements of cyber terrorism?

(*i*) Involvement of a computer or a network in committing a crime.

(*ii*) The crime is normally against a nation or a community or society.

(*iii*) The crime is some spying activity like corporate data theft.

(*iv*) The act may be a crime in some nation but may not be so in other nations.

(*v*) The act involves some terrorist activity and use of physical weapons with computers.

a. Only (*i*) and (*iii*) are correct

b. All except (*iii*) are correct

c. All except (*iv*) are correct

d. Only (*i*), (*ii*) and (*v*) are correct

2. In the case of Pay Per Click fraud, the fraudsters__________

a. gives a link which when clicked goes to a duplicate or a fake website of a bank.

b. pays for the links which he provides and when you click it so that the website will not be reachable for genuine users.

c. pays for the number of times the websites is clicked by the users or computer systems and pays for the number of times the computer clicks the site.

d. pays for the number of times the users click the website so that the number of hits will give an escalated figure.

3. Which of the following is a common form of Cyber Espionage?

a. A crime between two individuals when they exchange mails or other e-communication

b. A corporate entity whose data is targeted and accessed in an unauthorised manner

c. Cyber crimes involving old age people

d. Any cyber crime wherein the data and not the people are the target

4. Zombie is a word used in computer parlance used to denote a ________________.

a. Computer systems that are used by attackers who take these systems under their control

b. Victims PCs or network systems targeted by attackers whose data is stolen when they act like dead systems

c. Attackers who spread malicious software and virus through a network to many systems taking those systems into their control

d. The Network used by fraudsters to spread virus and worms to other computer systems over a huge network, without the knowledge of the host systems

5. In a Distributed Denial of Service Attack in a network__________.

a. The attacker attacks many computers in a distributed fashion targeting all at random

b. The victims are also the attackers and do not know that they are the attackers

c. The victims are aware that they are the attackers but the attacks are distributed and they are denied access to the servers

d. The attackers target only banks and deny access to the users of internet banking systems

6. The sentence "This is a computer generated letter and hence needs no signature" is:

a. correct as this is the general practice followed by most organisations including banks

b. is misleading since no legislation in India gives a blanket permission to authorise any computer generated letter to go without an authorisation signature

c. is illegal since the Indian laws do not authorise any computer generated letter without an authorisation signature

d. is correct because the Indian I.T Act recognised electronic records as legally valid documents

7. Which of the following is FALSE in the case of encryption?

a. It uses some algorithm and a technology to ensure that the message cannot be read by unauthenticated persons.

b. It is a technology that is used to ensure that the message reaches safely ensuring proper integrity.

c. It is a threat which network managers should strive to avoid while communicating messages.

d. It can be used for legal transmission as well as for illegal communications since it is only a technology and by itself not illegal.

8. In a Distributed Denial of Service attack, another name for Zombie system is:

a. Master systems

b. Host systems

c. Slave systems

d. Compromising systems

9. A software or a device which monitors and analyses network traffic is called __________.

a. Sniffer

b. Novell Netware

c. Netware Tool

d. Network buffer

10. Buffer overflow in software programs can best be explained as:

a. threat in the program that should be immediately faced and plugged

b. vulnerability in the program with a potential to become a risk

c. additional hard-disk space which can be used by the attackers to store malicious information

d. an unused space in the hard disk which will be known to the programmers and can be exploited by attackers to store malicious software

11. Which one of these was called the 'first digital weapon'?

a. Fastflux

b. Stuxnet

c. Spy Drone

d. Root kit

12. Steganography is a cyber-crime. (True/False)

13. The Indian Information Technology Act does not address cyber terrorism adequately. (True/False)

14. Investigating a cyber-espionage case involving transborder occurrences often proves more complex. (True/False)

Answers

1. *d*	8. *c*
2. *d*	9. *a*
3. *d*	10. *b*
4. *a*	11. *b*
5. *b*	12. False
6. *b*	13. False
7. *c*	14. True

15
CHAPTER

Prevention and Detection of Software Attacks - Viruses and Malwares

OBJECTIVES

After reading this chapter, readers will get a clear knowledge about the software program-based attacks like virus, spyware, adware and all kinds of malicious software. Besides the technology involved in such software and the havoc they can create, we will also discuss the different types of attacks in the form of software, various methods to combat them, the steps to be taken to minimise the impact and the effective preventive controls to be put in place, whatever possible.

15.1 Introduction

A study of malwares should start with the study of virus and all other related software programs such as spyware, adware, trojan, worms, etc . We may, therefore, begin with virus. The word 'virus' though not a computer jargon basically, has now become popular as a computer term. Virus actually means 'an infective particle which is able to multiply within the cells of a host organism'. A computer virus, therefore, means a piece of software code or a software program surreptitiously (*i.e.* in an unauthorised manner) introduced into a computer system in order to corrupt the system or the data therein.

Hence, virus is basically a computer program or a software code written with an intention to inflict some damage. The intention is what distinguishes it from a software bug or a software that is malfunctional. Though the word 'virus' is not an acronym, it was later logically thought out to make it an acronym with the expansion of the word VIRUS as "Vital Information Resources Under Siege"

The earliest versions of virus codes were written with mostly the intention of proving technological supremacy that the code writer wanted to exhibit with his technological prowess and spreading it and of course introducing it in a host computer without the knowledge of the owner of the system. However subsequently, as we have already seen and discussed in the earlier chapters, virus writing or similar malicious code writing has become a profession with more and more hired professionals engaging in it out of personal vendetta or professional rivalry or corporate espionage.

Computer virus is a computer program. Just like any other program, it has a design, a functionality and an objective. Virus attaches itself to a program or file enabling it to spread from one computer to another, leaving infections as it travels. The severity or criticality of a computer virus too differs in degree like a human virus.

Some viruses may harmlessly keep sending spam mails, or displaying unwanted advertisement or other innocuous and sometimes irritating texts on the screen while others may be devastating enough to crash your hard-disk or infect your files and delete all data. The effect of a virus could be from simple irritating effect for a few minutes upto the disastrous effect of occupying your processor not letting it do other processing or deleting vital data from your hard-disk or consuming enormous memory. Viruses mostly attach themselves to executable file and get executed when you open the infected file or execute the command.

Though the words 'virus', 'worms' and 'Trojan Horses' are often used interchangeably, there is a subtle and technological difference in their characteristic features. Unlike a virus or worm is a piece of code that has the capability to travel without any human action, taking advantage of the transmission or transport available already in the system. In other words, worm has the capability to replicate itself without the user's action of executing any file and automatically replicates itself as hundreds of or thousands of copies of itself and sends them to say all the addresses in the address book stored in the system.

Since worm does not attach itself to any file and waits for an executable file being run, and then replicates itself, it occupies more resources like memory. Because of heavy memory consumption or other resource utilization like bandwidth, they too can cause havoc, and can halt the network or the system to come down with alarming speed and disastrous effect.

Trojan Horse is another malicious software. It is named after the mythological Trojan horse referred to in the War of Troy in which soldiers are said to have concealed themselves in the hollow wooden statue of a horse and entered the City of Troy as wooden horses and after a few hours broke open it and captured the city to end the war. In computer terminology, Trojan Horse refers to a computer program designed to breach the security of a computer system while apparently performing some innocuous function.

We download an audio file or a game executable file from the net, into our system. While the audio or other file gets executed, or the video game keeps playing, the hidden program will execute itself and keep doing its function like accessing your mail box or accessing your web history to record the last viewed web pages or other parts of your system. Trojan apparently will claim to be a useful software but actually will cause damage immediately after we install it on our computer. Like virus files, Trojans too have different functionalities ranging from simple nuisance of adding some silly information in our computer up to the more serious damage of deleting the files or compromising some confidential information.

15.2 Malware

Malware is a generic word, short for malicious software. Malware is a software that is designed to disrupt computer operation, gather sensitive information or unauthorised access to computer systems and indulging in any or all such malicious activities. It is normally a general term describing any kind of software that exploits or affects a computer without the consent of the owner.

Malware is often embedded in or attached to a spam email or in a pop-up message or advertisement that appears in the browser suddenly. Sometimes it comes as an attachment or as a link in a mail (from untrusted source or sometimes from a trusted source but which acts as a zombie or a bot, without the sender's knowledge) or sometimes even without opening the attachment or clicking the link, just opening the mail itself may start its malicious function.

Though the term malware is quite generic in nature and even viruses and worms can be put under this category, by their functionalities, viruses and worms are normally handled separately. Almost all malwares can be brought under the category of Trojan Horses by definition. However, we give below some of the popular variants of malware, as an illustrative and not exhaustive list.

I. Spyware
II. Adware
III. Botnet
IV. Trojan Horses
V. Rootkits
VI. Hijackers

Spyware is a piece of software that is often advertised as a free software which the user is tempted to install or sometimes installed without the user's knowledge itself and collects data about the user like the websites he accesses, games he plays in the net, the personal data sometimes confidential information like payment card details etc. and then sends the same to the creator of the website's server. By definition and functionality, spyware is a very harmful software and is becoming a growing menace which the security professionals are finding difficult to combat. Some spywares even search the hard drive and report back what are the programs installed, contents of address book etc.

Sometimes, while browsing we see a pop-up about some product and give an option "Know More" or some words to that effect. Aware that it could be a spyware, we close the small pop-up window without clicking anything there, satisfied that we have avoided a spyware. Unfortunately, not. The very fact that a pop-up window appears on a particular product of your choice by itself means that a spyware *already exists* in the system. It would be interesting to note that in the case of some malwares or junk mails, there would be a column "Unsubscribe" and the users would be tempted to click this column with the fond intention of avoiding such spam mails in future. What the users forget is that the very fact that "unsubscribe" is clicked sends a message to the sender (or the server who has originated the spam) that the email id is correct and thus gets validated.

Adware is a lesser harmful variant of spyware. It is less harmful because it collects data from the browsers you choose, the websites you visit and the kind of data entry you type or sometimes collects all these informations from your Network Service Provider (NSP) or the Internet Service Provider (ISP) himself and then displays a particular kind of advertisement that you would be interested in, as per the profiling built about you. There is a legal angle of sharing of confidential information involved in it, since NSPs, ISPs and globally popular mail service and search engine providers offer the information of sites often searched or websites often visited.

Sometimes we wonder how an advertisement on products of our tastes pops-up when we open our mail service and entirely different advertisements of products of other category pops-up when a teenager opens his or her mail box suiting his or her interests. All these could be based on the information shared, based on the frequent sites visited or the search engine queries given by the user.

Botnets: A botnet is a network of private computers infected with malicious software and controlled as a group without the owners' knowledge, e.g., to send spam. It is a collection of compromised computers, each of which is known as a 'bot', connected to the Internet. When a computer is compromised by an attacker, there is a hidden or underlying software code within the malware that commands it to become part of a botnet. The "botmaster" or "bot herder" controls these compromised computers *via* standards-based network protocols. The compromised computers act like zombies and perform as per instructions received from the attackers.

Computers are recruited into a botnet by running malicious software. This is done by exploiting some vulnerabilities, or by tricking the user into running a Trojan horse program, possibly in an email attachment. The software so downloaded controls the computer and can do anything by installing modules which allow the computer to be commanded or controlled by the attacker *i.e.* the botnet owner.

Stuxnet is a computer worm discovered in June 2010. As already stated in the last Chapter, it initially spread *via* Windows operating systems, as reported, widely and targeted against industrial and software equipment, as specifically programmed. Different variants of Stuxnet targeted various nations with specific objectives, later. It is still regarded as one of the worst because of the devastation that it caused.

Fast flux is a DNS (Domain Name System) technique used by botnets to hide phishing and malware delivery sites behind an ever-changing network of compromised hosts acting as proxies. A recent discovery often used in many sci-fi tech-savvy films and other thriller fictions. Fast flux also refers to the combination of peer-to-peer networking, distributed command and control, web-based load balancing and proxy redirection. In other words, when a call is traced the IP address and thereby the server will denote one place and in the next minute when another call comes, that address may refer to entirely different location thousands of miles away. It is used to make malware networks more resistant for discovery and counter-measures.

The basic idea behind Fast flux is to have numerous IP addresses associated with a single fully qualified domain name, where the IP addresses are swapped in and out with extremely high frequency, through changing DNS records, thereby confusing the security professional who attempts to trace the call and its origin. That is why fast flux is often used in phishing attacks by criminals and tech-savvy fraudsters.

Though we have studied an illustrative and small list of some malware, it should be noted that there can always be a combination of different features of malware. Malware gets its name based on its features and functions. What is a Trojan Horse can also be adware or spyware. What is adware can also be spyware, and so on. Malware is the functional and basic characteristic of all such software.

Prevalence of malware saw a huge rise during the year 2011 to such an extent that many security firms called the year as the "Year of Data Breaches". Most nations were conscious of data criticality, information security increasingly and India too defined "sensitive personal data or information" during this year, as a part of and sequel to the I.T. Amendment Act, 2008. Subsequently, however, data breaches and information theft at the corporate level grew to such a great extent every year that almost every year end, the security companies and info sec managers tend to call the year as the worst so far!

This was the period when dreaded malware called "zeus" and "SpyEye" were introduced, widely feared and spoken about. "Zeus" is a much dreaded malware capable of defeating common methods of user authentication adopted by banks. Fraudsters steal webmail logins by modifying anonymous attack tool with a hidden Trojan with the features as above. Originally feared few years ago, this malware is reported to have revised with more 'capabilities' to hide itself, in January 2012. FBI has recently gone on record warning about the characteristics of this virus and banks worldwide are taking steps to combat this.

Crime ware is a type of malicious software designed to carry out or facilitate illegal online activity. Earlier, malicious software or malware was written for glory or just for the heck of it, but of late, crimeware is specifically written, designed for spamming, data theft, or extortion or other criminal activity. It is not just a piece of software or a particular programme but a class of software program with "*mens rea*" or the criminal intention being the basis and a common fraudulent objective like extortion, etc.

Like cybercrime itself, the term crimeware covers a wide range of different malicious, or potentially malicious software programs.

Rootkits: It is a stealthy type of malware designed to hide the existence of certain software programs from normally accepted methods of detection. It gives the privilege access of 'root' typically as applicable in Unix operating system and kit refers to the software tool as a kit that implements the program to run it. Though the program name does not carry any negative connotation (*i.e.* root and kit), the term is often used to denote a malware that runs an auto installed software or one installed by an attacker mostly with root access to maintain the Access Privileges.

With such root and privileged installation with administrative powers, the attacker takes control of the system (which is now a compromised system) and does any settings change or configuration change in the system including disabling any anti-virus kind of detective software that may already be installed in the system. By virtue of this nature of root kit (to disable or circumvent any detection software), rootkits are considered to be very dangerous. However, rootkit detection can be successful if it deploys techniques like virus signature scanning, OS behaviour, memory dump analysis, etc. (The word signature scanning is not to be confused with the scanning of customers' signature used in branches).

Hijackers take control of various parts of the web browser, including the user's home page, search pages, and search bar. They may also redirect the user to certain sites, if the address is wrongly typed and sometimes prevents the user from visiting a website known for anti-malware capabilities or malware detection features. Earlier versions of Internet Explorer were considered to be prone to attack by Hijackers.

Spam or junk email, is a free advertising technique. It takes a toll on Internet users time, their resources, and the resources of Internet Service Providers (ISPs). The existence of malware in the system actually makes junk mail or spam land in the system flooding the mail box. According to a recently concluded private sector survey, around 85 billion spam email messages are sent every single day.

Cyber criminals are not interested in money but in data because of reasons like:

I. Stolen money is fixed and static whereas stolen data is dynamic and can be used any time to get converted as money.

II. Stolen data is an incidence of technology and hence may be replicated any time to be used in similar acts in any other instance or institution.

III. Stolen money will be detected instantly by the victims whereas stolen data will be used gradually and hence detected gradually.

IV. Data theft has a cascading effect since one account stolen may lead to other details, other accounts too.

All these drive the system security managers to take the data theft in financial institutions very seriously. They should be taking this as a clarion call for action and prepare themselves for more of this. Data breaches are so high and so prevalent in the recent years to such an extent that the new expression 'data is a digital currency' gathered momentum. The value of information and data was gaining importance in corporate circles and especially financial industries.

In the case of banks, it is not just the money or the data but it is question of trust that the customer has in it that their data is safe and secure. If this trust is broken, be it because of a technological goof, security flaw or a sheer non-compliance or because of a cost-saving measure, ultimately banks will find it extremely difficult to get back to the position where it was prior to the attack. That is why, banks are going in for more and more dependable controls and security measures like–

- encryption of data at various levels,
- multi factor authentication,
- access privileges,
- external audits,
- third party accreditation,
- ISO and ISMS certification and
- all kinds of compliance without any compromise.

15.3 Controls

Detecting of computer malware is sometimes quite difficult. If the malware is to get activated at a particular time or in a particular day or lies in a particular executable file then it cannot be detected until the date or time arrives or the exe file is executed. Even in such a case, one may notice some strange functioning of the computer system and may suspect some kind of malfunctioning but may not grow suspicious to call it a malware.

Before actually going into the technology of malware detection and controls, let us briefly study one of the earliest controls for virus: Anti-Virus software.

Almost all anti-malware suites carry anti-virus features in them. An anti-malware tool must identify known and previously unseen malicious files with the goal of blocking them before they can cause damage. Though tools differ in the implementation of malware-detection mechanisms, they tend to incorporate the same virus detection techniques.

Anti-virus software as a software technology has evolved over the years. Anti-virus program was written almost from the day one, a virus was written.

Signature based detection

This technology used important aspects of a file taken up for examination and detection to create a static fingerprint (mark) of known malware. This would denote a pattern, a series of bytes in the file or a cryptographic hash of the file. Similarly, 'signatures' are collected and recorded and patterns of all known malwares and viruses are maintained. This method of detecting based on 'signatures' is the oldest and in the years to come, may become obsolete or difficult to maintain too, because millions signatures are to be maintained and compared.

Until a 'signature' is developed for a particular type of malware, this method cannot detect the malware. Nevertheless, this method still continues to be quite popular, reliable and widely used. Taking advantage of this difficulty in this method, modern attackers frequently mutate their creations to retain malicious functionality by changing the file's signature to avoid detection of 'signature'.

Heuristics-based detection

It is a technology which aims at generically detecting new malware by statically examining files for suspicious characteristics without an exact signature match. For instance, an anti-virus tool might look for the presence of rare instructions or junk code in the examined file. The tool might also emulate running the file to see what it would do if executed, attempting to do this without noticeably slowing down the system. A single suspicious attribute might not be enough to flag the file as malicious. However, several such characteristics might exceed the expected risk threshold, leading the tool to classify the file as malware. One major disadvantage of heuristics detection method is that it can inadvertently mark legitimate files as malicious.

Behavioural detection observes how the (suspected malware) program executes and not merely emulates its execution, and attempts to identify malware by looking for suspicious behaviour, such as 'viewing' the malicious code or modifying the hosts file or observing the key strokes. The anti-malware program algorithm takes many such features together to indicate a malware. Because of such features, some anti-malware or anti-virus tools resemble Host Intrusion Prevention Systems (HIPS), which have traditionally existed as a separate product category.

Cloud-based detection identifies malware by collecting data from protected computers while analyzing it on the provider's infrastructure, instead of performing the analysis locally. In these days of abundant availability of bandwidth and network resources, this is a practice followed by some anti-malware software. The software captures the relevant details about the file and the context of its execution on the endpoint, and providing them to the cloud engine for processing. The local anti-virus agent only needs to perform minimal processing. Moreover, the vendor's cloud engine can derive patterns related

to malware characteristics and behaviour by correlating data from multiple systems as against other anti-virus components, based on their decisions mostly on locally observed attributes and behaviours.

Though the above are various techniques and methodologies in detecting a malware, in practice, however, the distinction is often blurred. Most of the processes adopted by any anti-malware tool is normally a combination of features from all these and these names are also used interchangeably sometimes. To keep with the pace at which malware writers continue to flood the market, anti-malware software writers too should be always ahead and be updated with the latest things in malware. As is said often, "you have to keep running even if you want to maintain your position", anti-malware should be a constant attempt in studying, detecting and preventing any kind of attack, by whatever name it is called spyware, adware, malware of just a virus!

Other than anti-virus software, there are now programs available exclusively to detect malware with specialized anti-malware features.

Malware and related attacks should be covered under the Information Security Policy of the organization. Besides the policy, the guidelines and procedures should address the issues clearly defining how a malware should be reported and how it is treated and the persons responsible thereof. Attackers are of late using more and more sophisticated technologies like "Attack-and-leave-no-trace" kind of attacks and sheer evidence destroying techniques making the job of investigators more complex. These anti-forensic techniques are getting deployed by professional hackers as more advanced methodologies of attacks on information assets. Security managers continue to learn from these attacks and every attack is an incident.

Incident Reporting mechanism dealing with malware and viruses is being dealt with separately in the next chapter.

Organisations should always procure latest anti-virus software and have an elaborate SLA with the anti-virus vendor to install periodic updates and upgrades at regular intervals. Such an installation should be automatic, constant and periodic and be with the capability to detect new viruses and worms and capture their signatures.

In the eagerness to procure anti-virus software, instances have been reported wherein organisations have actually purchased rogue software or a fake that would only display lots of faked warnings without actually checking the site or disk or sometimes detecting an old virus itself.

Malware and other attacks on OS: On an OS based analysis, it is commonly felt that Unix as an OS (and its closer cousin Linux) are generally less prone to virus attack than Windows. Linux, and Unix like OS are generally regarded to be better protected from virus though one has to accept that Linux malware includes Virus, Trojans and Worms too.

One major reason why Windows is attacked the most could be its widest usage and popularity and the vulnerabilities often publicised. The mail utility of Windows 'Outlook Express' has often been prone to viruses and has been charged to spread virus. Running Windows in admin mode or always logging as admin, usage of macros in MS Office suite, usage of older versions of Internet Explorer are all considered to be vulnerabilities that an attacker can exploit. Besides, some of the security features of Unix like running a program from a folder and disabling it to be run from any other folder etc. are not available in Windows. There also differences in these two OS on the way the OS takes input in the form of TSR (Terminate and Stay Resident) and related features from the OS design stage itself.

Preventive controls include using the latest and updated anti-virus, anti-spam, anti-malware or firewalls or anti-spyware software with a licensed usage with provisions for updating and upgrading too whenever necessary. Besides, downloading of unauthorized software, unlicensed software or untrusted games or any utility or music from an untrusted website is always dangerous and may often result in a Trojan acting as a malware. So, all of these should be avoided.

To sum up, an illustrative list of Dos and Don'ts with reference to malwares are given in the table below:

Dos	Don'ts
Scan all your attachments before sending them through email	Don't click on links inside pop-ups in the browser
Delete spam mails and unsolicited mails without opening them	Don't click on links in spam mails or from unsolicited mails
Delete junk mails and pop-ups even without clicking "Unsubscribe" or other options	Don't trust any spam message claiming itself to be an anti-spyware or anti-virus
Delete mails from untrusted sources offering anything free without selecting any option	Don't download any freeware or opt for any free software unless you know the source
Update the browser with licensed versions and paid upgrades, wherever available	Don't install plugins (ActiveX) if you are not certain what it is or why you need it
Wherever possible, secure your email by digital signature or other means of encryption	Don't download any additional feature while watching a movie or listening to an audio file
Run anti-spyware, anti-virus etc. periodically preferably with an arrangement with the software vendor	Don't open attachments from any unsolicited mail or an untested source/sender
In the case of known malware from your contacts, bring it to the knowledge of such sender preferably from another mail id	
Use strong password and insist this on your users too. Permit special characters in passwords. Use ftp-SSL wherever available and feasible.	

Know Your Progress

Virus is basically a computer program or a software code written with an intention to inflict some damage. The intention is what distinguishes it from a software bug or a software that is malfunctional. Viruses may of different types, ranging from innocuous ones (not stealing any data) just occupying your memory or flooding you with mails like spam mails upto the most dreaded ones of formatting the hard-drives or removing all data from your systems etc.

Virus mostly attach themselves to executable file and get executed when you open the infected file or execute the command. Worm does not attach itself to any file but simply replicates itself into hundreds and thousands of copies of itself, occupying much of resources like memory or network bandwidth. Trojan Horse refers to a computer program designed to breach the security of a computer system while apparently performing some innocuous function.

Malware is a software that is designed to disrupt computer operation, gather sensitive information or unauthorised access to computer systems and indulging in any or all such malicious activities. It is normally a general term describing any kind of software that exploits or affects a computer without the consent of the owner. Spyware, adware, Trojan, rootkits, hijacker are all examples of malware with varying features and with distinct characteristics of each.

There are many controls that should be in place to fight a virus attack and a malware attack. Anti-virus and anti-malware or anti-spyware are all software tools of varying characteristics working on different principles and methodologies like scanning the existing characteristics type or 'signatures'

of viruses and preventing them or looking at the purpose and functions of the programs etc. Anti-malware software should be in place as part of the controls to guard against all malware attacks. Many anti-virus products come as a suite of different products bundled into it like anti-spyware, anti-spam, anti-malware etc.

Besides all these controls, user should carefully guard his system by observing all Do's and Dont's in browsing like not clicking any link inside an untrusted mail, not clicking any pop-up window, not responding to a spam mail and by having the latest updated and licensed versions of anti-virus, anti-spyware and anti-malware software.

Key Words

Malware	Spyware	Trojan Horse	Anti-virus
Fast Flux	Rootkit	Anti malware	Botnet
Spams	Signature detection		Adware

Questions

1. Which of the following is a tool in anti-virus techniques?
   a. Signature scanner
   b. ActiveX controls
   c. Botmaster
   d. MalBuster
2. Which of the following is not a malware?
   a. Trojan
   b. Root-tools
   c. Botnet
   d. Spyware
3. Stealing information from systems is not an attribute of which of the following?
   a. Spam
   b. Botnet
   c. Trojan
   d. Rootkit
4. Which of the following is a technology of malware detection?
   a. SpyEye
   b. Botnets
   c. Cloud based detection
   d. Toolbars
5. The IT Amendment Act, 2008 effective from 27 Oct, 2009, referring to confidential information uses the phrase—
   a. "personal and confidential data"
   b. "sensitive personal data or information"

   c. "personal, sensitive and private information"

   d. "private and confidential data"

6. When you receive an unsolicited mail as an advertisement from a stranger, clicking "Unsubscribe" button in the mail__________________.

   a. is always advisable so that you do not receive such mails in future

   b. should also not be done and it is better to delete such mails

   c. is preferred after verifying whether the site or the link provided is genuine

   d. may be advisable only if you do not want to receive such mails

7. Which of the following is FALSE?

   a. Malware is sometimes bundled along with tools like with Anti-virus software.

   b. Anti-virus and Anti-spyware can be bundled along with Anti-malware software.

   c. Anti-spyware and Anti-adware are always part of Anti-virus.

   d. Anti-virus with signature detection works for Anti-spam also.

8. __________ should never be opened nor the link clicked, unless one is sure of the security risks involved.

   a. Window ads in the top of browser screen

   b. Virus in a screen of a browser

   c. Pop-ups in any part of browser window

   d. Spams in a mail screen browser

9. Use of macros in _______ is considered to be a vulnerability for virus to exploit and attack the system.

   a. MS Office

   b. Unix Operating System

   c. Windows NT Server

   d. Oracle database

10. When you trace the IP address from the same sender in a series of mails in a few minutes and the sender's location appears changed swiftly in every communication it could be____________.

   a. Stuxnet

   b. Trojan

   c. Fast flux

   d. Botnet

Answers

1. *a*	6. *b*
2. *b*	7. *d*
3. *a*	8. *c*
4. *c*	9. *a*
5. *b*	10. *c*

16 CHAPTER

Incident Management

OBJECTIVES

We often come across various incidents in life, be it our social life or office or otherwise. In this chapter an attempt has been made to define the incident that affects our computer system, the seriousness and features of various incidents, the steps to deal with various incidents and finally, on the issues that we learn from such incidents. Learning about all such incidents will pave the way for balanced handling of the systems and ensuring better management of the resources towards optimum growth of the organisation.

16.1 Introduction

What is a computer incident**?** The word 'incident' means an occurrence of an event especially something unwanted or unexpected. The word often refers to a minor event that may be subordinate to something major as opposed to a disaster (*about which we will be seeing in detail in chapter 18)* or a catastrophe. A computer incident normally denotes any unlawful, unauthorized, or unacceptable action that involves a computer system or a computer network.

Computer security incident is often a violation of some public law, or an organizational security policy or procedure (part of an IS Security Policy already discussed by us in chapter 3) and the perpetrator of such incident is often liable for criminal proceedings or other departmental punitive action.

Nature of computer security incident

No two computer security incidents are identical. For instance, take three distinct incidents *viz.* the CEOs getting spam mails in their systems, some failed attempts from a remote location into the public access system and the main server throwing error messages and failing to boot after a shutdown. Though all these three are broadly called computer security incidents, the impact, treatment, lessons learnt, corrective and preventive action for all these are grossly different. Having said this, we should not be unaware to the fact that all these three are nevertheless, computer security incidents, with varying degrees of impact and varying circumstances and accordingly deserving attention.

Though the procedure to deal with a security incident may vary from incident to incident, breaking down the procedure into logical steps will make the incident manageable efficiently with which an effective methodology can be evolved that is commonly acceptable.

Incidents which are business critical in nature such as breach of security or access violations or deviations from the desired path are expected to be anticipated, reported, needs to be rectified and normalcy restored at the earliest possible time causing least inconvenience to the stakeholders.

As we have already seen in the earlier chapters while dealing with Risk Management, Threats and Vulnerabilities, it is an accepted truth that threat can never be eliminated and can be mitigated, managed and always awaited too! Incidents get reported almost every day, every hour and every minute worldwide. In a SANS White Paper published in August 2015, it was reported that in the recent widely reported Sony data attacks as well as the US Office of Personnel Management attacks, around 10 million intrusion attempts were thwarted almost every month. Figures, such as million attempts, etc, sound like enormous and devastating if the remedial measures are human, but the IPS are all software driven, and programmatic, and therefore, if well configured, preventing even a million attempts is not all that difficult.

The same report also speaks about proper and well-designed Incident Response Management system and lists three main strategies:

I. Manual Forensics involve analysis of history and incidents, study of indicators of compromises systems in different variants of malware.

II. Basic forensics means the normal steps of complete analysis of the logs and trails left by the attacker involving the route, patterns, threat vectors, etc .

III. proactive incident management involves the follow-up and review of the action and studying their effectiveness and efficiency.

In legacy systems, organisations used to notice the path where there was a deviation, and acted upon it. In modern day computing and excessive dependence on zero tolerance systems with Service Level Arrangements promising 99.99 or 99.999 percentage of uptime with High Availability at all levels, every security incident should be noticed, watched and recorded, taking action like defining the deviation from the expected path, identifying the level of criticality and agreeing on the role to be played by the SLA.

No incident should be trivialized. Even normal testing failures should be treated like an incident and be reported to the functional head for follow up action. Otherwise, Trapdoors *i.e.* the security checks that are normally disabled during a testing phase (to avoid recurring blocks and constraints in the resources while testing other functions) if not enabled subsequently at the implementation stage do certainly become a cause for major concern and constitute a critical incident.

16.2 Objectives of Incident Response

An Incident Response should be based on specific objectives, on what is going to be achieved after such response. Understanding of the goals of Incident Management is therefore, necessary to evolve suitable plan for Incident Management. Ideally, the goals or objectives for Incident Response should be:

I. Confirm whether an incident has actually happened.

II. Assess the seriousness or criticality of the incident.

III. Establish controls for proper retrieval and handling of evidence.

IV. Minimise disruption to business and network resources.

V. Allowing criminal or civil action against perpetrators.

VI. Provide proper reporting with accurate facts to the concerned authorities.

VII. Protect the organisation's reputation and all information resources.

After an incident occurred, the response should be systematic and yet swift and be part of some laid down procedures.

16.3 Pre-Incident Preparation: Anticipating the unanticipated or expecting the unexpected event or adverse mishap, may sound rather pessimistic. Pre-incident preparation is all about learning from the

system policies and practices and be prepared for any eventuality. This step is based on the fact that in computer security nothing is beyond our scope or imagination. Though the time of occurrence of any event is always unanticipated, the cause that lead to an event or the circumstances can always be gauged and prudence lies in effective preparedness.

Detection of Incident and identification of the event as an incident is the first and significant step. Here, lies the basis of classification and the first step in the journey of Incident Response and Incident Management. This phase involves in identifying the event as a security incident distinguishing it from (*a*) a disaster or sounding like a major crisis with deadly impact and (*b*) treating it as too trivial not warranting an action at all. An improper definition of responsibilities at this stage or inadequate knowledge about the system leading to no-detection or incorrect detection of incident will lead to disastrous results.

Initial Response deals with the stage of responding to the incident by taking immediate action to escalate it as may be necessary as per the Information Security Plan in force and the extant regulations. The initial response is of paramount importance. Enough information should be gathered and 'knee-jerk' reaction should be averted. Calling an incident as a disaster putting a Disaster Recovery Plan into action is as dangerous and avoidable as terming an incident too trivial and neglecting it.

Here, right form identifying the incident, classifying the incident, and rushing for a response and steps like who should report, whom to report, how to report etc. are all considered. Classification of incident and the reporting mechanism are all part of the information systems security policy of the organisation and there should, naturally, be no confusion on who to report and to whom to report and the format.

However, much be the exhaustive nature of Information Systems Security Policy and however efficient be the security managers, it would be impossible to enlist all incidents and give a categorical classification of everyone in the list. Incidents are unpredictable in nature and there can be no cent percent listing of all incidents. Besides, what is critical in one environment or in one particular time of the day may not be critical during other times in other environments. Hence, classification is not a static concept but a dynamic one, that takes into account the entire gamut of circumstances that caused the incident.

Automated procedure of reporting as part of Incident Management has been found to be very useful and fool-proof especially for the purpose of analysis and for a corrective and preventive action. This system is called a Trouble Ticket System or a Computer Ticketing System or simply an Incident Ticketing System or in some other variant in organisation, but essentially it is a software that records the nature of incidents without missing out on any detail and used in trouble shooting.

By using such a system, the organisation can ensure that the service staff receive all required information of an incident without much human intervention and without giving room for miscalculation or the 'knee-jerk' reaction that was referred to earlier. Data analysis like time resolved to close a call, list of 'open' calls, nature of calls and details of recurrent calls, etc. can be done easily with such a software. There are ticketing software tools available which can be customized to suit the varying specific requirements of the organisation.

Deployment of such a tool ensures proper acknowledgement of every call registered, categorization, notice of follow-up action taken and details of closure. Often email ids of important stakeholders or the contact numbers like mobile numbers of team leads or project directors are associated with such software so that the moment there is an incident, such heads are notified electronically of developments without manual intervention.

In a ticketing system, the alerts or messages will be monitored by the ticketing server which will keep getting messages and the messages based on the configuration and settings will be sent to the respective stakeholders' PC or mobile by message or email or other means of communications to facilitate their early and immediate action. The input alerts or communication or alerts or triggers

could be from a server or a PC or a database kind of server or just some network equipment and the output from the ticketing software will be based upon the design and requirement.

Since such a system will contain complete details of trouble shooting calls, particulars of failures in hardware or software a proper analysis of calls received will help building the Business Impact Analysis and from thereon to Risk Matrix. Usage of a dependable system in ticket management will, therefore, go a long way in building the Business Continuity and Disaster Recovery Plan.

16.4 Action Methodology

As soon as the incident is reported, action to be taken is planned, formulated and immediate action is initiated. Collection of data that led to the incident or which is part of the incident is made. Depending upon the nature of incident, such data is collected either concurrently as part of the methodology of action, or before the action (*i.e.* preceding the action taken) or sometimes immediately after the incident.

Data collection stage should be done with utmost care. Some data especially in a live computerized environment are highly volatile and if not collected, will cease to exist or can be easily obliterated with almost nil or the least amount of trace and trail.

Computer evidence or digital evidence and evidence gathering is by itself a highly technical subject and not everyone goes for it. It needs system experts with specialization in cyber forensics to identify where the evidence lies and involves sieving through heaps of data available and picking the most useful ones. Evidence gathering in computers or from networks, requires the usage of some software tools and the human resources with expertise to handle such tools, collect, combine and then preserve for use by the authorities concerned.

However, there are some basic lessons in evidence gathering which have to be studied meticulously. Volatile evidences are those that are temporary and will go off, when the system is powered off. Data in Random Access Memory, sites that are being watched, access that is current and running etc. for a PC user and in the case of a Unix user, such volatile data will depend upon whether the person is a Unix user, an RDBMS user and again a user from dumb terminal, or from PC workstation or from a PC with front-end processor without storage etc.

Digital Forensics is a methodology in studying the evidence gathered, analyzing the trails and logs, taking out the hardware, network and software trails will be very useful in building up a strong digital evidence in Incident Management. Going into all such minute details of data gathering and evidence collection may be beyond the scope of this chapter but nevertheless, as part of Incident Management. Basic knowledge of where the evidence lies and how to pick it to serve the purpose of corrective and preventive action including investigating purposes, is absolutely essential.

In the context of Digital Forensics and incident response system, it is relevant to know about "baiting". Baiting is a social-engineering attack in which physical media containing malware is deliberately left in proximity to a targeted organization's facilities, where it may be found and later accessed by curious victims.

Like what is the data to be collected, system managers should also know from where the data is to be gathered. Information may be in the computer systems and such host based information may be like the system data and time, applications current running on the system, users logged in, number and details of open ports, applications running currently, history of recently opened files, data in the recycle bin, cookies, browser favourites, etc. As against this, data may be lying in the network spread across the network equipment and such information include the router details, firewall details, IDS logs, authentication server details if any, details of other network equipment used if any.

16.5 Processes Running

It is always critical and important to take a snapshot of all the running processes in the case of Unix or Linux (or for that matter even in a Windows multi user environment). The features available in the OS should be utilized for the same, for instance, if it is Windows with Active Directory enabled or otherwise configured, the type of configuration, users logged in etc. may be studied.

If it is a sniffer attack in a Unix network that is ticketed and reported, that should be handled swiftly. Sniffer is an attack (like Denial of Service already seen earlier) which essentially steals information travelling in a network, irrespective of the protocol of the network. Sometimes, as a prelude to run a sniffer the fraudsters may place the network in a promiscuous mode *i.e.* a state in which the network listens to all traffic not simply its own as against the normal (non-promiscuous mode) when the network traffic should listen to its own traffic and packets intended for it. In such a case, change of mode to promiscuous mode should itself be treated as a security incident and be treated accordingly. For instance, in a polymorphic threat, *i.e.* an attack wherein a malware modifies its own code, making it more difficult for some signature-based antimalware or antivirus programs to detect, the network managers have to be additionally cautious and technologically alert to study the actual threat vectors, trace the same and take remedial action.

Remote Administration Tool (RAT): A program that allows a remote operator to control a system as though he/she is physically in close proximity to the system. RATs are commonly used as a very effective device in fighting attacks in a huge network especially in organisations with a huge connectivity and access from across a big network, facing all kinds of APT attacks.

Some organisations have the Network Management or Monitoring Tools running. In such a case, the ticketing system synchronizing with such a monitoring tool will also throw the report, from where the attack came, along with location or port details or whatever, according to the nature of the tool configuration. There are open vulnerability assessment tools like Open VAS which can be deployed that will keep monitoring the network and sending alerts on the performance of target hosts scanning them concurrently, running the Network Vulnerability Tests, with Secured Socket Layer Support and with their own database to record the data for retrieval and analysis purposes.

If the incident is of a serious nature, the corrective action and bringing the system back to normal and mitigating the impact should be on a parallel basis taken up concurrently along with the steps of detection like from which system the attack came and which vulnerability was exploited.

The last stage is the Reporting Stage. This stage is different from the incident reporting stage, since the incident reporting is for taking immediate action and this stage with detailed reports is essentially for corrective and preventive action purposes only. This is a crucial stage because whatever be the nature of incident and the nature of follow-up and rectification action taken on it, unless proper reporting is done with all necessary data in the report, such incidents are bound to occur again and with the same amount of impact or probably a greater impact.

Depending upon the criticality of the incident, incident reporting may encompass different stages of Incident Management and parallel reporting will often be resorted to, to keep the management apprised of developments in tackling the situation.

A parallel step in all these stages will be the recovery mechanism, resolution steps and implementation of security controls in the stage as applicable. Information Security Policy may encompass all the stages of security management and there may be controls or measures to be taken for different stages of security management. Hence, it would be better to show the implementation of security measures as an action to run concurrently throughout the security incident response process.

16.6 There are some significant aspects of Incident Management that are part of the Information Systems Policy and the regulatory compliance. For instance, the regulator like the Reserve Bank of

India(RBI) may stipulate that all bank frauds involving more than Rs.1 lakh should be reported to the top management and to RBI as per laid down procedures and cash embezzlement involving theft of cash say more than Rs. 5,000/- should be reported to the police and network attacks in the form of DoS attacks in critical servers should be reported to the System Administrators and from them to the national nodal agency CERT-In etc. In all such cases, the Incident Management Systems whether automated or manual should incorporate all such guidelines in place and ensure that reporting mechanism is adhered to.

It is common practice among undertakings and especially public customer centric organisations like banks and telecom providers to underplay any security incident and try to trivialize the nature and criticality for fear of adverse publicity and public criticism about the security environment. In such cases, the Incident Reporting mechanism should also be subject to audit and the procedure adopted in reporting should ensure compliance with regulatory norms and procedures.

Reporting to in-house team of Risk Containment or Vigilance Department and an Inspection Department should also be done simultaneously, in tune with the policy and procedures in place. Any effort to wrap up the incident and conceal with deliberate intention to underplay the criticality or innocently not realizing the seriousness of the incident, should be dealt with deterrent punishment and firmly handled.

Dealing with an incident strictly from a regulatory compliance angle will enable

I. Identifying the incident as whether a civil or a criminal act.

II. Paving the way of further reporting and follow-up.

III. Fixing responsibilities on different layers of authority.

IV. Identification of the severity as an act of innocence or criminal breach of trust.

V. Identification as a violation of HR policy or other serious violation.

VI. Further preventive action like assessing the need for revising the HR and other policies

It is not just good business prudence but also in tune with best practices that organisations maintain a repository of 'lessons learnt', or 'common incidents' in its archives. It is common practice in organisations to have a separate committee functioning as 'Defect Prevention Committee' or in some other name acting as part of Incident Management Team normally headed by an experienced and senior professional.

The committee analyses the repository for potential incidents applicable to the project on hand, analyse the incidents reported and presents a report that includes a report on the effectiveness of action taken as a preventive methodology and corrective step. This committee will function under the overall umbrella of Information Systems Security Policy and be subject to Information System Audit procedures and be subject to audit accordingly.

While deploying the pattern based security incidents or signature based security solutions, it should be very well borne in mind that many unknown threats and malware cannot be detected. In fact, as was already seen in the earlier chapter on Threats. Some of the threats though based on the same methodology as the earlier ones, may come camouflaged in different form, to specifically deceive the signature based solution, such that the anti-malware will leave it and it would be passed off as a new threat or reported as a new incident. Because of such reporting as a new incident, it will again go through the rigours of getting reported, recorded, analysed and followed-up consuming all the systems resources.

In tackling such kinds of new incidents, or at least those incidents that are perceived as new, organisations have to efficiently correlate information to not only identify infected systems and weaknesses throughout the network, cloud, and endpoints but also execute protection across the entire system encompassing all the network gadget, devices and data. As the next step, they have

to reduce the gaps between detection, analysis, and protection while keeping up with new threats composed of various tools, technologies, and vectors.

16.7 Awareness

The success of Incident Management lies to a great extent to the level of awareness about the criticality and seriousness of various information systems, the nature of incident and the incident classification. Hence, awareness initiatives should be in place so that right from noticing of the incident, treatment of incident and the final reporting, all efforts are handled in a co-ordinated and well connected manner.

Know Your Progress

Incidents happen almost in every walk of our lives. Any event often unlawful or unanticipated occurrence or event in the computer systems or the network is termed as computer security incident. Though computer security incidents normally refer to events that impact a computer not in the category of a disaster and are by definition mostly unexpected or unanticipated, organisations will always do well to be prepared for any security incident and put all the security controls in place.

Objectives of Incident Management team include mitigating the impact of any attack, paving the way for a better Business Continuity Plan and Disaster Recovery Plan, recording the post-incident action taken and verifying the effectiveness of such action taken. The stages in Incident Management include pre-incident stage *i.e.* preparing for any untoward incident like sudden unexpected network outages, classification of incident as critical or major, etc., taking action to mitigate the impact, reporting the incident etc.

Taking action on the incident depends upon the nature of incident and the classification. Critical incidents should be acted upon immediately on two fronts namely the corrective action to put the system back to normal and the second, taking steps to identify the cause and take evidences for investigation purposes.

Evidence gathering is an essential part of Incident Management from the point of view of taking action as well as from the view of post-incident analysis. Finally, the reporting phase should include the nuances of preparing the report, usage of some tools for generation of reports and a clear unambiguous report analysis that will lead to identification of root cause, verification of effectiveness of action taken like corrective steps and preventive steps.

Key Words

Incident Management	Digital Forensics	
Sniffer	Promiscuous Mode	Knee Jerk reaction
	Incident Reporting	Evidence gathering
Ticketing System	Polymorphic Threat	Remote Administration Tool

Questions

1. Volatile Data as part of evidence gathering in Incident Management____________.
   a. will be in the system only when the network is on
   b. is normally a temporary data lying in the RAM and should best be collected before the system is turned off

   c. is not as important as non-volatile data since it is difficult to prove by virtue of its being volatile in nature

   d. is more important than the non-volatile date since more evidence lies here only.

2. Reporting an incident is normally done_______________.

   a. immediately after the incident occurs to enable action, without any further loss of time

   b. after the action methodology is formulated and action is taken and as the last step in Incident Management

   c. sometimes on a parallel basis in different phases of Incident Management depending upon the nature and criticality of incident

   d. by the affected party to the top management at any stage in the Incident Management where it is felt that the top management should be kept informed.

3. When compared to Business Continuity and Disaster Recovery Plan, Incident Management is often___________________.

   a. considered to be part of the BC-DRP itself since output from Incident Management forms part of the BC-DRP

   b. which helps in getting the BC-DRP approved by the top management since effectiveness of Incident Management initiatives depend on the Plan formulation.

   c. not connected with BC-DRP since that is a separate step which consists of various initiatives including Incident Management

   d. considered to be a part of the Business Impact Analysis which is the basic step towards formulating an effective BC-DRP.

4. To ensure that incidents are properly classified and handled effectively, the Incident Management Team will take care to________________.

   a. incorporate legal compliance initiatives in addition to the requirements of the organisation's own Information Systems Security Policy

   b. ensure that follow-up action is taken on all incidents like reporting to external agencies

   c. incorporate reference to external investigating agencies for all incidents as part of an automated process so that no incident is left out unreported

   d. mention all incidents and their classification in their policy and tell functional heads to go strictly as per that list

5. Incident should be reported by______________________________.

   a. the person who is affected by the incident in some way and directly concerned

   b. the network or supervisor or the functional head who is responsible for rectification

   c. the functional head whose carelessness caused the incident

   d. anyone who is part of the information systems environment and on whom lies the responsibility to report, as per the policy

6. Data like user logged in sessions, time logged in, sessions in use etc. in any OS, are normally obtained from______________________.

   a. Network logging sessions like router and switch and similar equipment

   b. Active Directory which keeps all user related information

   c. Access Privilege table in the OS as maintained in the RAM

   d. User management related information in the OS of the individual systems

7. Resolving the issue and putting the recovery process in place should ideally be______________________.

a. part of all the stages of Incident Management

b. done at the end of all the stages of Incident Management

c. the first step in the Incident Management system even before the classification

d. immediately after the classification of incident

8. For fear of adverse publicity, many security incidents are generally sought to trivialized or are left to unreported. (True/False)

9. A major advantage of Ticketing System is that it will ensure adequate automated rectification action. (True/False)

10. Round the clock network monitoring system will enable some of the network based incidents to be reported in an automated manner. (True/False)

Answers

1. *b*	6. *d*
2. *c*	7. *a*
3. *d*	8. True
4. *a*	9. False
5. *d*	10. True

17

CHAPTER

Fault Tolerant Systems

OBJECTIVES

In this chapter we will discuss the strength of information systems especially on how they face an attack and withstand the various types of attacks. Faults in the system normally refer to systemic deficiencies (as opposed to an external attack which has already been discussed in earlier chapter), an inherent vulnerability of a serious nature and the susceptibility to fail in the event of an attack. We will also discuss the various measures that can be taken to enhance the strength of systems and to ensure better fault tolerance.

17.1 Introduction

The strength of any information system, be it a hardware gadget or a software program lies in its strength to be of use, when required. A weak system and undependable system will be shunned and never liked. Fault-tolerance or graceful degradation is the property that enables a computer-based system to continue operating properly in the event of the failure of some of its components. The fault may be a result of inherent weakness inside the system which exposes the system's lack of ability to withstand failure in the event of a mishap or a similar event.

A basic characteristic of fault tolerance of a system is not the ability to completely avoid any attack or to prevent it but the ability to gracefully or slowly show the impact in such a manner that it is not seriously felt and the system does not come to a standstill suddenly. That is why "graceful degradation" is another term normally used in the context of fault tolerance. Fault-tolerance enables the computer-based system to continue operating properly in the event of the failure of or one or more faults within some of its components.

Organisations normally do have multiple central processors, peripherals, and system software and a huge network with convergence of different technologies and integration of various devices. Fault Tolerant systems are typically those which are able to continue operations even if there is a major hardware or software failure or a serious failure in a communication device or in the hard-disk or in a part of the network architecture, that will otherwise seriously impact the business of the organization.

To cite a simple non-computer and biological example, human beings having two legs, two ears, two eyes are all nature's gift on fault tolerance. If the vision is impaired temporarily in one eye or hearing is affected in one ear, human beings manage with the capability of the other functional parts and the system does not come to a grinding halt. Similarly, often prudent architecture designers in computer

systems go in for an extra provision of hardware or an additional capability for processing to be of use in case the actual requirement gets exhausted or is otherwise impacted.

The purpose of fault tolerance is to increase the dependability of a system. A complementary but separate approach to increasing dependability is fault prevention. This consists of techniques, such as inspection, whose intent is to eliminate the circumstances by which faults arise.

Fault and error

A failure occurs when an actual running system deviates from specified behaviour. The cause of a failure is the error. An error represents an invalid system state, one that is not allowed by the system behaviour specification. The error itself is the result of a defect in the system or fault. In other words, a fault is the root cause of a failure. It means that an error is merely the symptom of a fault. A fault may not necessarily result in *one* error, but the same fault may result in multiple errors. Similarly, a single error may lead to multiple failures.

17.2 Within the scope of an individual system, fault-tolerance can be achieved by anticipating exceptional conditions and building the system to cope with them, and, in general, aiming for self-stabilization so that the system converges towards an error-free state. However, if the consequences of a system failure are catastrophic, or the cost of making it sufficiently reliable is very high, a better solution may be to use some form of duplication. In any case, if the consequence of a system failure is so catastrophic, the system must be able to use reversion to fall back to a safe mode. This is similar to roll-back recovery about which we will discuss in the later part of this chapter.

A good fault tolerance system presupposes that there is–

- No single point of failure
- Fault isolation to the failing component
- Fault containment to prevent propagation of the failure
- Availability of reversion modes

The system has to ensure that there is adequate redundancy and no single point of failure. When a failure occurs, the system must be able to isolate the failure to the offending component. This requires the addition of dedicated failure detection mechanisms that exist only for the purpose of fault isolation. Proper categorization or classification of fault is essential.

Fault containment involves the steps in mitigating further damages from the fault. For instance, when there is a 'rogue transmitter' or a 'malware' that can swamp legitimate communication in a system can cause system failure, immediately steps should be taken to protect the system from further damage.

Fault Tolerant System is a subset of Business Continuity - Disaster Recovery Plan (to be covered in detail in the next chapter), and a prelude to it, over which, among other things, is the BCP-DR Plan normally built. Redundancy, backups, avoidance of single point failures, etc. are all the areas to be strengthened for building a dependable and strong BC-DRP. *What exactly constitutes a disaster and when to call a disaster and when to move to a Disaster Recovery Centre will be dealt with in detail in the next chapter*. But before such a situation and to prevent the impact of a disaster itself, the computer system should basically have an inherent strength or the wherewithal, *i.e.* the systemic resources to withstand the impact of the attack and the ability to continue with normal operations. This is the essence of Fault Tolerance.

Sometimes, Fault Tolerance Management can be treated as an extension of Threat Management since threats normally attack the systems and end in reported faults in the system. However, fault tolerance systems per se may not be related to threat or an attack itself and may be independently arising out of a vulnerability in the system or other kinds of system failures resulting a fault. Hence it is logical and proper to study fault tolerance system as an aftermath of incident reporting mechanism and just before the disaster recovery and business continuity plans.

Fault Tolerant Systems are different from BC DRP in the sense that while the BCDRP focuses on the entire gamut of providing continuity in the event of any threat, fault tolerance in the systems is only the system's ability in a limited extent to withstand the impact.

17.3 Building redundancy is a major pre-requisite for fault tolerance. Redundancy refers to the superfluous state of being, or the repetition or overlapping or the provision of additional or duplicate systems, equipment etc. that function in case an operating part or system fails, especially in mission critical areas. In our normal day to day life, we often meet much redundancies like in a car there is a mechanical brake in case the hydraulic brake fails and in computer systems, the backup data is kept safe for use in case the main server crashes resulting in loss of data etc.

Redundancy in information systems may be anyone of the four types: Hardware, software, Time redundancy or Information redundancy. However, in practice, such redundancies are not water-tight arrangements, because software redundancy or a network redundancy will depend upon the hardware capability, and the architectural redundancy in hardware like server duplexing or mirroring will depend upon the software capability to exploit the feature from the hardware. Hence these four are shown as overlapping in some part of their availability in the diagram below. Functional redundancy may be part of the software or the program source but should be supported by hardware to enable it.

Redundancies may also be passive redundancy or an active redundancy. For example, if against the estimated requirement of a 8 mbps line, the organisation goes in for a 16 mbps or much higher bandwidth, then it is passive redundancy, built to ensure against any sudden requirement for additional bandwidth. Error detection and such software controls are examples of active redundancy that will be active and monitoring the performance of the software or the network or the communication continuously.

Dual Core Execution is an example of redundancy and fault tolerance adopted these days. In dual core, the program is executed twice by two processors, normally called the front and back processors with the front processors executing the program and the instructions getting re-executed in the back processor to provide redundancy, like chip-level redundancy. The entire hardware fault tolerance systems is on a single die.

17.4 High Availability (HA)

HA is another popular term often used with redundancy and fault tolerance. HA is a system design approach and associated service implementation that ensures a pre-arranged level of operational performance ensuring fault tolerance and against the impact of any attack. It is a system for ensuring that the service is available at any time, without break with no downtime *i.e.* the time when the service is not available.

When HA is built in say hardware by a Redundant Array of Inexpensive (or Independent) Disks commonly known as RAID or server duplexing or such technology, it will guard against the server level availability alone. If the RDBMS fails or the OS fails or the network device fails or the network card or other interface card fails, then this HA will not do. Hence there should be co-ordination in design that the high availability in one will overlap and will deliver fail-proof service taking the available resources from the other.

HA is, therefore, a culmination of availability of people (associated with hardware, software and the entire gamut of HR), processes (network, software, systems, data, communications, etc.) and the technology (hardware, software, remote access if any and all other systemic resources). HA is normally measured in terms of percentage like 99.99% or 99.999% etc. and is often made a part of the outsourced vendor's SLA insisting that such percentage of uptime of connectivity (or the server or other resources availability) has to be ensured. Ensuring HA will go a long way in building a strong

Business Continuity and Disaster Recovery Planning. HA is not a standalone concept that building redundancy in one will suffice.

Another term associated with Fault Tolerance and HA, is latency in communication. In a computer system, latency is used to mean any delay or waiting that increases real or perceived response time beyond the response time desired. Latency is used as a synonym for delay, denoting how much time it takes for a packet of data to move from one designated point to another. Avoiding latency or minimizing is a primary concern in building HA and ensuring scalability in operations.

The term latency in a packet-switched network is measured either one-way (the time from the source sending a packet to the destination receiving it), or round-trip (the one-way latency from source to destination plus the one-way latency from the destination back to the source). Round-trip latency is more often quoted, because it can be measured from a single point. 'Ping' is a term often used almost in common usage too, to measure round-trip latency. Ping performs no packet processing; it merely sends a response back when it receives a packet and thus it is a relatively accurate way of measuring latency.

Transmission media (like optic fibre or VSAT etc.), the capabilities of network device used (router, bridges etc.), the data packet size, the technology used in communication are all the main factors that contribute to latency in communication. Where precision is important, one-way latency for a link can be more strictly defined as the time from the start of packet transmission to the start of packet reception.

Error correction and multi threading are all some of the techniques to improve latency and check network latency errors avoiding time delay in communication and thus improve the fault tolerance in systems.

Fault-tolerance is implemented not only in hardware and software but is also made available by protocols by the rules by which the computers communicate. For example, the Transmission Control Protocol (TCP) is designed to allow reliable two-way communication in a packet-switched network, even in the presence of communications links which are imperfect or overloaded. It does this by requiring the endpoints of the communication to expect packet loss, duplication, reordering and corruption, so that these conditions do not damage data integrity, and only reduce throughput by a proportional amount.

Data formats may also be designed to degrade gracefully. HTML for example, is designed to be forward compatible, allowing new HTML entities to be ignored by Web browsers which do not understand them without causing the document to be unusable.

17.5 Now, let us have a look at some of the hardware based fault tolerance techniques.

Disk Mirroring is the first line of protecting the data. It protects against hard disk failures by simultaneously writing over the same channel in two disks. If one disk fails, the other automatically comes up and immediately efforts should be on to replace or repair the first disk.

Disk duplexing is one step ahead of disk mirroring, an advanced feature. It involves redundant controller, power supply cable and both the channels are used to write the data, so that even if one channel fails, the other seamlessly keeps the system going uninterrupted.

Server duplexing is one more step in this design, which ensures that there are two separate servers, providing for complete redundancy. This technique guards against failures in Random Access Memory, server crash, network adapters in the servers, server performance failures etc. Here, servers can be placed in two different locations and software applications can be loaded in one server while the other is running and operational. When the upgraded server is brought online, it will synchronize with the other.

RAID (abbreviated for Redundant Array of Inexpensive or Independent Disks) is a storage technology that combines multiple disk drive components into a logical unit. Data is distributed across the drives in one of several ways which are called "RAID levels", depending on what level of redundancy and performance is required or planned. Storage Virtualization is an implementation of RAID technology. Here data striping *i.e.* the technique of segmenting logically sequential data, is adopted helping multiple segments accessible concurrently by enabling access from a processing device rather than from a storage device. There are six levels of RAID and depending upon the nature of data handled, criticality of access, the kind of hardware that can be deployed etc., the particular level of RAID is used.

Direct-Attached Storage (DAS) is computer storage that is directly attached to one computer or server and is not, without special support, directly accessible to other ones. For an individual computer user, the hard drive is the usual form of direct attached storage. In an enterprise, providing for storage that can be shared by multiple computers and their users tend to be more efficient and easier to manage.

Although Storage Area Network (SAN) and Network-Attached Storage (NAS) technologies *(discussed below)* are gaining in popularity, Direct-Attached Storage (DAS) is still the most common kind of storage, especially in small organisations. In fact, the simple technology of storage will suffice the requirements for small enterprises.

However, as the volume of data and the number of users grow, DAS becomes harder to manage. That is when companies start looking at the next step in storage. While some of those companies go directly to a SAN, the next most common step is to add storage to the existing network in the form of NAS.

Network Attached Storage

NAS follows a client-server approach. In NAS, there is a central file server consisting of a PC typically with a Network Operating System supporting the controlled file sharing Hard disks installed in the system providing adequate space for storage with sufficient scalability and capability to attach tape drives. It is considered to be the easiest and least expensive way to add storage to a network.

Storage Area Networks

Client systems access the NAS server through an Ethernet Systems often as part of the LAN. As against this, Storage Area Network (SAN) took the storage device away from the server connecting them directly to the network. SAN typically is a separate network of storage devices, physically removed from but still connected to the network. File sharing is operating system dependent and managed by the servers whereas in NAS allows greater file sharing across disparate OS also. SAN is most commonly implemented in a technology called fibre channel.

In NAS, almost any system can be connected whereas in SAN, only server class devices like SCSI devices can be connected. However there are designs where both are used with a SAN box with a Disk Array and a Tape Library connected to a NAS server which connects to different clients. Network and storage designers may plan a specific model taking into account factors such as the level of redundancy required, HA needed, cost implications etc.

In general, the more network-centric is the operation, the more will be the need to consider NAS or a SAN. It should be conscious and technological decision whether to add storage to a bunch of systems or add a single, more efficiently utilized chunk of storage to the network. NAS, even with simple NAS appliances, costs more per gigabyte than adding a new disk drive. But the higher utilization and ease of allocation can easily cover the added cost. One of the biggest advantages of low-end NAS is simplicity. Most NAS vendors, like NetApp, offer inexpensive NAS appliances that can be brought up on a network in less than an hour by staff with minimal training.

SAN Storage Server:

Network Attached Storage (NAS)

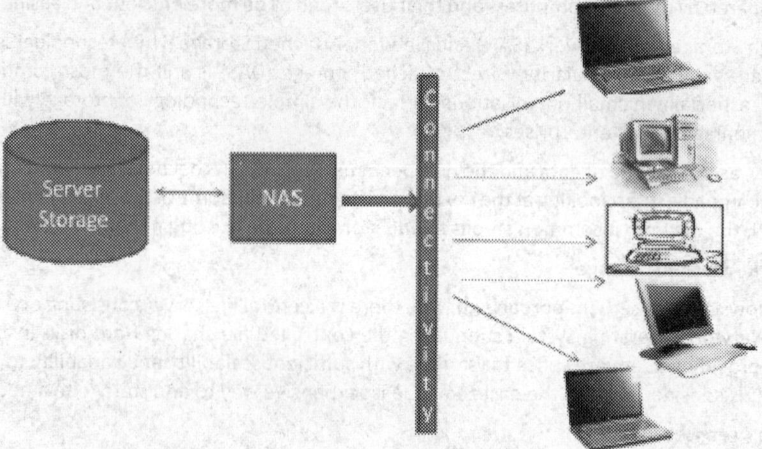

17.6 Software Fault Tolerance is deployed and ensured by proper testing of the software, immaculate implementation and proper synchronization with the network and hardware ensuring compatibility. All forms of failures and attacks in software are normally addressed and provided for before implementation and during the implementation also. Different tests such as User Acceptance Test, Beta Test phase etc. when properly conducted will reveal the vulnerabilities and exhibit the tolerance level of the software. However, there could still be some residual software faults.

The residual software faults are normally taken care of by proper software tolerance controls like recovery blocks and N-version programming.

Recovery blocks are used in the backward error recovery method. By this method, software is reset and restored to the point already pre-determined, as part of damage recovery process. This method envisages establishing a point of time during execution of a process called the recovery point to which the recovery is made. In the case of software design faults, it may not be possible to accurately determine which parts of the system state may change. Hence it is designed to record the current state as and when the object is to be changed monitoring all changes and accumulating the recovery data. The recovery data is accumulated for the most recently recorded recovery point by constantly monitoring the system changes.

Fault tolerance is a measurement of a device's or computer's ability to handle errors. Something that is not fault tolerant will fail immediately as soon as an error is encountered.

Fault Tolerant computing was earlier the essential pre-requisite in highly mission critical industries like aeronautics, electric trains and other such modes of transport where human lives depended on the computer systems driving the vehicles, where 100% safety was the norm with absolute zero fault tolerance. With more systems getting computerized and with an advent of Core Banking Solution involving storage and processing of millions of records of data in a single data centre getting accessed from across the globe, CBS kind of software also is equally mission critical though not involving the lives of people or, perhaps it does, as the lives of many investors or customers could be on their bank balances lying secure.

Hence it is but natural that telecom providers, banks and stock exchanges and all such organisations also are thinking of fault tolerant systems these days. However, in software, fault-tolerant computing is extremely hard, involving intricate algorithms for coping with the inherent complexity of the physical world. To face the bare truth, just as it was said that there is no "100% security in any system, nor 100% safety anywhere" there is similarly no 100% fault tolerance too. No matter how hard we try, there is always a possibility that something can go wrong. The best we can do is to reduce the probability of failure to an "acceptable" level. Unfortunately, the more we strive to reduce this probability, the higher the cost.

17.7 Services Oriented Architecture (SOA)

Service-Oriented Architecture (SOA) is a software design approach that structures applications as a collection of loosely coupled, interoperable services. These services are self-contained, modular units of functionality that can be accessed and invoked over a network, typically using standardized communication protocols such as HTTP, SOAP, or REST. SOA promotes reusability, scalability, and flexibility by decoupling services from the underlying implementation details and allowing them to be composed and orchestrated to meet various business needs.

17.8 The primary aspects of Service-Oriented Architecture:

Services: Services are the fundamental building blocks of SOA, representing discrete units of functionality that encapsulate specific business processes or functions. Services are designed to be self-contained, reusable, and interoperable, allowing them to be easily composed and orchestrated to fulfil complex business requirements.

Loose Coupling: SOA promotes loose coupling between services, meaning that services are designed to be independent of each other and communicate through standardized interfaces and protocols. Loose coupling reduces dependencies between services, making it easier to modify, replace, or update individual services without impacting the entire system.

Interoperability: SOA enables interoperability between heterogeneous systems, platforms, and technologies by using standardized communication protocols and data formats. Services can be accessed and invoked by clients regardless of the underlying technology stack, enabling integration and communication between disparate systems.

Service Contracts: Service contracts define the interfaces, operations, and data formats exposed by services, specifying how clients can interact with the services. Service contracts promote consistency, clarity, and interoperability by establishing clear expectations and guidelines for service usage.

Service Composition: SOA allows services to be composed and orchestrated to create higher-level business processes or workflows. Service composition involves combining multiple services to achieve a specific business objective, such as order processing, customer relationship management, or supply chain management.

Service Registry and Discovery: Service registries and discovery mechanisms facilitate the dynamic discovery and invocation of services within a distributed environment. Service registries store metadata about available services, while discovery mechanisms allow clients to locate and access services based on their functional capabilities and properties.

Message-based Communication: SOA relies on message-based communication between services, where interactions are facilitated through the exchange of messages containing structured data. Message-based communication enables asynchronous, decoupled interactions between services, improving scalability, reliability, and flexibility.

Service Lifecycle Management: SOA involves managing the entire lifecycle of services, from design and development to deployment, monitoring, and retirement. Service lifecycle management includes activities such as service identification, specification, implementation, testing, deployment, versioning, and retirement.

Governance and Management: SOA governance encompasses policies, processes, and tools for managing and controlling the design, development, deployment, and operation of services within an organization. SOA governance ensures compliance with architectural standards, promotes best practices, and aligns service-oriented initiatives with business goals.

Scalability and Flexibility: SOA architecture is inherently scalable and flexible, allowing organizations to adapt and evolve their systems to meet changing business requirements. Services can be easily scaled horizontally or vertically to accommodate changes in workload, user demand, or system requirements.

Efficiency in Delivering Business Solutions: Service Oriented Architecture (SOA) offers a modular, flexible, and interoperable approach to building distributed systems, enabling organizations to achieve agility, scalability, and efficiency in delivering business solutions.

Know Your Progress

The strength of any information system be it a hardware gadget or a software program lies in its strength to be of use, when required. Fault-tolerance is the property that enables a computer-based system to continue operating properly in the event of the failure of some of its components. The fault may be a result of inherent weakness inside the system which exposes the system's lack of ability to withstand failure in the event of a mishap or a similar event. It is the graceful degradation of the system and not the sudden outage or non-availability.

Fault Tolerance is enabled by proper redundancy, backup and other such factors. Wherever possible, proper redundancy has to be built to ensure that if one fails, the other automatically is enabled and serves the purpose. A good fault tolerance system presupposes that there is no single point of failure and fault isolation and containment.

Fault Tolerant System is a subset of Business Continuity - Disaster Recovery Plan and a good fault tolerance will pave the way for a better and dependable BCP. Redundancy is to be built not just in hardware by going for technologies like disk mirroring, disk duplexing, etc. but also in software also by ensuring proper controls are in place like backward error recovery, N-version programming etc.

High Availability and latency are some of the terms associated with fault tolerance. High Availability means making the information resources available to near 100% with the minimum acceptable downtime. Latency is the delay in communication that impacts availability of communication and data transmission across network.

Key Words

High Availability	Latency	SAN	NAS
Ping	Disk Duplexing	RAID	Disk Mirroring
Recovery Block	DAS	Dual Core	Recovery Block

Questions

1. Latency is a term used to—
   a. ensure better High Availability in network without loss of data packets
   b. measure the speed for the data packets to move from one designated point to another
   c. denote the loss of data packets resulting in delay for the packets reach destination
   d. mean any delay or waiting that increases real or perceived response time beyond the response time desired
2. The protocol that has fault tolerance feature inbuilt is—
   a. TCP
   b. FTP
   c. HTTP
   d. Telnet
3. The term used to describe the design ensuring a pre-arranged level of operational performance against the impact of any attack with no or the least downtime is called—
   a. Zero Fault Tolerance System
   b. Zero Latency in network
   c. High Availability
   d. BCP-DR
4. An example of fault tolerance in programming, using the resources of two processors is—
   a. Dual Core
   b. Core 2 Chips
   c. Dual Processing
   d. Twin mode processing
5. To measure round-trip latency without processing any packet of data _______ is used
   a. TCP
   b. Ping
   c. Packet Switched Network
   d. Router
6. Which of the following is wrong?
   a. In disk mirroring, data gets written into two disks simultaneously over the same channel
   b. In disk duplexing, data is written into disks simultaneously over the same channel
   c. In disk duplexing, data is written into two disks simultaneously with redundant channels
   d. In disk mirroring, there is no redundancy of channel over which data travels.
7. Fibre channel technology is used in—
   a. SAN
   b. DAS
   c. NAS
   d. RAID

8. Recovery blocks and N-version programming are two methodologies used in—
   a. Hardware Fault Tolerance
   b. Software Testing for user acceptance
   c. Software Fault Tolerance
   d. Dual Core processing
9. This is often measured as 99.99% or 99.999% in normal practice—
   a. Fault Tolerance in Hardware
   b. Network bandwidth
   c. High Availability
   d. SAN Storage optimization
10. SAN is generally costly and resorted to by big business houses True/False
11. Cent percent redundancy is a reality if organisations can spend money True/False
12. A good BCP-DR is essential and the basis on which a fault tolerant system is built. True/False

Answers

1. *d*	7. *a*
2. *a*	8. *c*
3. *c*	9. *c*
4. *a*	10. True
5. *b*	11. False
6. *b*	12. False

18
CHAPTER

Business Continuity and Disaster Recovery Management

OBJECTIVES

After reading this chapter, the readers will know the meaning and significance of Business Continuity and Disaster Recovery Planning especially from the IT perspective, factors that influence the DR Management, the criticality and seriousness of the various constituents of DRM and how and why organisation should be prepared for a DR Management at any time. Measures to put proper DRM initiatives in place and to review the success of a DRM will also be discussed.

18.1 Introduction

We have already seen in earlier chapters that the meaning of a threat, vulnerability and risk and have gone in depth about the various threats to an organisation's infrastructure and other resources. Definition of risk has also been discussed in detail. In this chapter, we will be discussing the concepts related to risk and risk management like disaster recovery, business continuity, etc.

Why Business Continuity?

The ultimate objective of any organisation is to deliver customer centric products to the customers' satisfaction at an optimal cost and continually enhance it. No organisation would like the business to be affected because of any expected or unexpected or unforeseen incident. The underlying principle should be: *at any cost, the business should continue.* It is with this objective that the entire concept of BC-DRP has evolved.

What is Disaster and DRM?

Disaster may be defined as a sudden event, such as an accident or a natural catastrophe, that causes great damage or loss of life, a phenomenon that causes huge damage to life, property and destroys the economic, social and cultural life of people. In business language and for organisations, disaster is that incident or an accident that greatly affects the business environment to such an extent that the business actually stops for a temporary period of a few minutes or hours or cannot continue at the normal pace.

Disaster may be of many types:

- Man-made like originated by human beings, attacks and insider threats
- Technological like server crash, software crash, etc.

- Natural like cyclone, floods, fire, earthquakes
- Terrorist attacks (9/11 in US, Mumbai 26-11-2008, Indian Parliament attack 13-12-2001)

Though the preventive controls for these are entirely different and no control can apply to the other, the DR mechanism in all these attacks are almost the same and the objective is simple: restoring normalcy at the earliest time ensuring resumption of service to customer with minimum loss of time and minimum dislocation.

Implementation of all preventive controls will certainly ensure that the impact of threat could always be mitigated, risk could be well managed and disaster could be averted. However, in a practical and real life scenario, there is nothing like 100 percent risk containment or complete disaster prevention. By the very nature, disaster is something which is not foreseen and therefore cannot be avoided. Hence, Disaster Recovery is a significant management concern.

DR Management or DR Plan (DRM or DRP in short) refers to the study of different disasters that impact business, the organisation's preparedness to face such disaster in the worst eventuality of its occurrence and the plan to manage the business continuously uninterrupted despite the disaster (though often with reduced facilities and resources ensuring customers' basic and essential needs). Thus BC-DRP is the systematic planning of the organization to resume business in the event of any major incident or a mishap without any serious break in service to its customers.

In short, BC-DRP normally involves the following steps like identification of the information assets, classifying them on the basis of criticality, identifying the critical areas including single point failures and then finally drafting the IT BC DR Plan.

18.2 Downtime

In these days of increasing competition and globalization, organisations especially banks can ill afford a situation when due to excessive dependence on technology, a small technological failure has impacted business. There can never be a down time in customer service. No bank can afford to tell the customers that due to server failure or other maintenance issues, their CBS server will not be available for a few hours. Why hours, a few minutes of outage of such critical servers like CBS or ATM server will adversely impact the bank's reputation and can never be allowed. It is in this context the study of BC-DRP assumes importance. After the Basel II norms were introduced and complied with by banks in India, BC-DRP has become an integral part of Risk Management study and BC-DR initiatives are being closely monitored by top management.

Though BC-DRP by itself is a broader area encompassing various business units and functions, it is normally referred to in the context of IT only. However, the BC DR Plan in a general sense covers the BC DR of all functions including Premises, HR and other areas. In other words, typically a sound BC DR Plan will talk about the BCP for HR activities (so that excessive dependence on one individual or a team is avoided and that there is always a secondary level back up personnel), BCP for Premises or other non-IT equipment and BCP for all other areas which cannot afford to have a downtime.

By virtue of these features in the BC-DRP, it is often considered to be a subset of IS Security Policy and referred to in that policy also, though it is a separate document by itself exhaustively written with the sole purpose of business continuity and disaster recovery.

BCP-DR in Cloud: Cloud providers do have BCP and DR, since they handle enormous amount of data, on behalf of various customers, with the details of their DR and BCP sometimes shared with the cloud users and sometimes not. Sometimes, when the details are shared with the customers and users, it has to be in sync with or merge with the continuity plans of the customers. Period of preservation of records, retrieval issues therein etc. are all to be discussed with the cloud users and customers and should be in conformance with their requirements and as per the legal or mandatory guidelines if any. The BCP and Data Centre infrastructure, network access, data storage arrangements should be in compliance with the regulatory norms. This is a very important requirement, especially in view of the fact that sometimes the cloud owners may maintain the data in an entirely different environment, different nation or in the cloud of an entirely different jurisdiction.

In a broader sense, the steps involved in BC DR Plan are summarized in the following manner in different phases as under:

Phase I drafting a BC-DR Plan.

- Information Asset Identification and Classification
- Vulnerability Assessment in the servers, network and all applications
- Threat Assessment and Incident Reporting Mechanism
- Business Impact Analysis
- Risk Management and Risk Matrix
- Backup Policy identifying the RPO and RTO
- Fixing of roles and responsibilities: Calling a disaster personnel to act and to contact, personnel in the Secondary centre if any and in DRS etc.
- Backup Policy: Off site, On-site and issues relating to Backup
- Identification of key personnel - Contact details
- Approval of the policy at the Top Management or Board level

Phase II Implementation of BC DRP

- Procurement of necessary hardware for redundancy
- Procurement of necessary backup software and other utilities
- Procurement of network equipment and other devices
- Ensuring backup being taken as per the policy
- Mock BCP Drill and review of results
- Steps involved in coming back to the normal PDC

Phase III Reviewing and Monitoring

- Periodic (scheduled or unscheduled) meetings on BCP
- Results of BCP Drill - Review
- Post DR activities: Back to normal server, HR and technology issues
- Reporting mechanism - RBI and other regulatory reports
- Continual improvement - Preventive and Corrective action
- Updating the Plan whenever any new hardware or software is procured
- Updating the Plan whenever a change is incorporated into the infrastructure

Though typically the DR mechanism starts with identifying critical areas and ends with the step of monitoring and review of the steps involved, in practice it is not a one linear approach like this. After every review and monitoring, the process of identifying newer areas and recently introduced processes or procured hardware starts and the cycle starts again. This process is replicated, in fact, every time a new hardware is procured or a new process is introduced in the organisation.

18.3 Phase I

In phase I, the steps relating to Asset Classification, criticality assessment for information assets, Vulnerability Assessment, Threat Analysis, Business Impact Analysis and finally the Risk Management have all been covered in earlier chapters. We may, therefore, begin from the Backup Policy. As part of the Business Impact Analysis and Threat Assessment or Threat Monitoring, businesses will study the single point failures, SPF in short. SPF basically means the area in IT infrastructure where there is no backup. Wherever there is dependence on one single equipment or on one communication line with no backup, such connectivity or equipment or infrastructure causes concern as SPF. For instance, a typical backup policy (or redundancy) should cover a second level (or a backup) for all the hardware and software associated with it, right from the server, hard-disks, (to protect against disk crash), software (copy of software), network (redundancy lines), router and other network peripherals (spare router and peripherals etc.) upto the last mile of connectivity.

'Last mile' connectivity is often used in telecom circles to denote the final leg of delivering connectivity from a telecom provider to a customer finally in his system. A typical redundancy should cover the entire connectivity upto the point of last delivery *i.e.* last mile connectivity where the system provides the service. SPF of any kind should be minimal and be part of residual risk well within the knowledge of management.

Redundancy or Backup should cover the entire area, the entire network or the whole connectivity thinking in terms of providing a proper backup for the server, for the software and the connectivity etc. In real world, sometimes this may not be possible or may be obtained with a high cost since this involves a backup line from another provider for the entire connectivity and a backup at the communication equipment level too. Managements will always strive to avoid or eliminate SPF completely or wherever it cannot be eliminated 100%, take steps to minimize it. Such residuary SPF will be the primary concern of BC DR Manager who will constantly be monitoring such SPF equipment or communication channels only.

There are two other concepts related to the Backup and Redundancy policy part of BC DRP called RTO and RPO.

Recovery Time Objective (RTO) is used to dictate the use of replication or backup to tape or disk. It denotes the time that the system can be down *i.e.* the tolerable or acceptable down time of system. In other words, if the RTO as planned is say 4 or 5 hours, then backup in tapes would suffice. With around 4 hours as the RTO, any time the server is down, the off-site backup can be brought back and loaded and the server or a backup server with the data from off-site backup, can be made to work in less than 4 hours. Thus RTO as planned is achieved here. However, if the RTO panned is zero, *i.e.* no downtime for server, then the organisation will go for completely redundant infrastructure with data getting replicated to off-site and with capability for the off-site server to come up instantly when the main server fails.

Recovery Point Objective (RPO) is slightly different. This dictates the allowable data loss *i.e.* how much data can an organisation afford to lose in the event of a disaster. If the backup (to an offsite location or the Disaster Recovery Site) is done say once in three hours and say the last backup was done at 4 PM, then if the server goes down at 6.50 PM, the data upto 4 PM alone will be in the backup which can be uploaded when the server comes up. In such a case the data entry made from 4 PM upto 6.50 PM would have been lost and may have to be re-entered. Typically, in a bank, the RPO will be zero. That is, backup will be continuous and be done bit by bit online so that when the server is down and data entry is stopping, the server when it comes up will do so with no loss of data. This is an ideal and perfect data protection solution that organisations would require.

So both, RTO and RPO, really influence the kind of redundancy or backup infrastructure and will have a bearing on the kind of backup the organisation will go for. Before discussing the other components of a BC DRP, let us discuss some backup related issues.

Backup assumes a significant part of BC DRP. In the earliest days of bank computerisation when bank branches had an ALPM system (Advanced Ledger Posting Machines) which were mainly standalone systems with one PC handling one particular function like an SB PC, a Current A/c PC or a Loan PC or a End of Day like Day Book and General Ledger PC, backups were taken in respect of such individual PCs in floppy disks and stored in safe vaults or in the strong rooms in branches.

With the advent of client-server architecture in which branch data were stored in a server connected to the entire branch by a LAN (Local Area Network), backups of the servers were taken in DATs (Digital Audio Tapes) as part of a backup menu provided to the branches. Thus the backup of the entire branch was also stored in the same premises. To overcome the impact of any disaster in the entire branch in the branch server as well as the backup disk also kept in the same premises, the concept of an off-site backup was introduced. Branches were advised to move the backup tape in another branch or other trusted location nearby so that in the worst event of entire branch getting struck by a disaster the off-site backup data can be uploaded in a spare server and data protection can be ensured.

However, this concept has now become obsolete and outmoded in banking industry in India, with almost all banks switching over to Core Banking environment with the data maintained at a central place namely Primary Data Centre and branches containing no data at all, except some minor front-end processors or tools.

18.4 Backups

On the technology side, backup can be either an external media backup or backup in the same server in another location or directory which can be retrieved in the event of data corruption. There are many backup techniques involving both hardware and software like data compression, mirroring, replication, server duplexing, remote backup, etc. On the systems side, backup can be any one or more of the following which the system managers will decide depending upon the requirement and criticality related factors.

- data backup (backup of the data alone is taken)
- incremental backup (backup of those that were added after the last backup)
- system backup (involving all data and system files and complete backup)
- OS backup
- RDBMS backup.

Backups may again be a manual backup when the system administrator gives a backup command in command line prompt or as part of a menu driven access or sometimes a scheduled one. Scheduled backups are normally an additional backup especially running at nights or during the non-peak hours so that the strain on the processor will be minimal.

In the context of different types of backup, ROBO backup, also known as remote data backup, is a concept that is gaining in popularity these days. It is the process of copying and archiving the data created by remote and branch offices (ROBOs) and storing it securely. Sometimes, systems managers in the remote centre handle the backup which may not be a primary responsibility for them. But better still, ROBO backup could be made part of a centralized backup itself, so that it is made dependable and recovery and restoration made easier.

Cloud backup is another remote backup and recovery solution which is being resorted to these days. With more and more organisations going to the cloud, backup of data too often becomes part of the cloud arrangement, which serves as a secondary storage so that the most recent backups are kept at on-site and the older ones in cloud storage, to be of use when required.

Now with the Core Banking Solution in place in all banks in India (with the exception of a few banks in regional rural bank category or in the co-operative sector), many concepts like Hot Site, Warm Site and Cold Site, Secondary Site and DR Site have gained significance.

Primary Data Centre (PDC) is the site wherein actually all critical servers like application servers, database servers etc. are located (*as shown in the diagram in Chapter 11 on Software Security Control).* This is a highly critical area wherein the infrastructure and physical security in the location plays a very important part. This room should be physically well designed to accommodate all the servers, a 24 x 7 monitoring, an absolute fail-free power and lighting, a 100% reliable cabling and AC provisions etc. Most of the banks have outsourced maintenance of data centre to (or hired a data centre from) professional data centre management companies. The exhaustive SLA with the companies provide for a 24 x 7 power, backup by inverter, backup by a generator, physical 2-layer or a 3-layer access control, redundancy in LAN equipment, cabling, etc.

Most banks have another data centre with almost the same capability in the same city and sometimes in a nearby location, called 'Secondary Site' which will have the servers almost the same as in PDC with the data getting written into these servers simultaneously with the former. In the event of the Primary Data Centre going down on a disaster, the system will seamlessly move to the Secondary Centre and data to all locations will flow from there.

As against this, thanks to the initiative taken by RBI and the worldwide awareness triggered by 11th Sep., 2001 terrorists' attack destroying the World Trade Centre, the concept of an Off-site back gained momentum. After the WTC attack with the collapse of entire structure of twin towers, only a few companies who had already a system of off-site backup of data (stored in a distant location like some servers in other cities or nations) recovered immediately back to normal business with data protection.

BCP-DR as a concept and as a matter of subject for serious study and implementation was spoken about subsequently and world woke up to the gravity of situation of deadly disaster striking. BCP-DR was later given utmost significance in banks and RBI in their repeated circulars as part of Risk Management initiatives especially under Operational Risk Management under technology risk took up the initiative.

Thanks to global awareness on the relevance and indispensability of a DRS, many institutions could withstand disaster worldwide subsequently like the Tsunami in eastern coastal parts of India, earthquakes in Japan and the floods in Mumbai, which would have otherwise, had a devastating impact on data protection.

As against the Secondary Site which is often in the same city of PDC or in a nearby location itself, the DR Site by its very definition should be in an entirely different city in a non-seismic zone. For this purpose, the seismic zone classification of India assumes importance. Banks are well advised to have the DRS in a different seismic zone from the one in which the PDC is located.

It would be a conscious decision of the management to have an exact bit by bit replication of data at the DRS perfectly in sync with the PDC (which would technologically involve a huge cost of having an identical set up of the entire infrastructure as in the PDC) or a DRS wherein the data gets written with a minimum time gap and 'sync' of a few minutes that would involve lesser cost. However, secondary data centre by definition is always in sync with the PDC as far as data is concerned and be ready to come up instantly and seamlessly when the PDC goes down.

Other terms associated with DRS and Secondary Data Centre are 'Hot Site', 'Warm Site' and 'Cold Site'. A hot site is one wherein the data gets written concurrently and is always ready with the necessary infrastructure with connectivity, LAN and WAN set-up with all network gadgets, to get connected to branches and remote locations, the moment the PDC is down. A warm site is one wherein the infrastructure is reasonably ready with the network gadget available but to be configured and brought up with some efforts and data to be updated say in a few minutes to make it connect to branches and remote locations. On the other hand, a cold site is just a site identified as an alternate data centre with the network equipment yet to arrive and the data replication issues yet to be tested.

Basically the entire process of selection of all such sites involves a perfect co-ordination among the various layers of top management of organisations especially banks like the Premises or Administration Department giving clearance for the physical locations and centres, Technology Department going ahead with the technology infrastructure, the software department or the outsourced software vendor ready with the software and RDBMS capability to 'sync' the data in the DRS locations, the HR department providing the necessary skilled personnel and above all, the approval from expenditure department giving financial clearance for all the expenditure.

The next major step under Phase I will be identification of key personnel forming part of the IT BCDR Plan or the BCDR Team. Typically the team would consist of representatives from key areas of technology department, network department, hardware department (or Infrastructure department), Audit or Inspection Department, HR and other important functional areas in the organisation. All these persons will be made aware of their key responsibility areas in the event of a disaster. Contact details of all these will be made available in multiple copies, with a copy preferably as a print-out, other than those in the data centre or other critical areas.

18.5 Who Should Call 'Disaster'?

Identification of a disaster is itself a task to be done by the designated official. Not that anyone in the organisation can call a disaster and arrange for moving the database to the DRS. Calling a disaster is the responsibility of a senior person who should swiftly set the ball rolling involving the technology, network, operations, infrastructure and all other concerned departments. The need for calling a disaster is dependent on the time of outage, anticipated length of outage, definition of disaster in the organisation and other points as per the BC-DRP of the organisation.

Besides all these, the other factors that must be considered for a BC-DRP design include:

- Probability of unplanned events, disasters like hurricanes or bio-chemical disaster
- Security threats planned, unplanned, feared, dreaded
- Increasing infrastructure and application interdependencies
- Regulatory and compliance requirements, becoming increasingly complex
- Failure of key third party arrangements
- Globalisation and the challenges of operating in multiple countries.

Taking all these into account, the BC-DRP is drafted and top management approval is obtained.

18.6 Phase II

Phase II of the BC-DRP involves in actually implementing the plan as approved and mentioned above. The first part in this phase will be to procure the hardware and software assets to put the backup in place, to ensure DRS is functional, to go for redundancy in network equipment, to ensure that network bandwidth is sufficient enough to carry the full load of data to the DRS and from thereon to all remote sites (as the PDC was doing).

After procurement of all the necessary infrastructure, a Mock DRS Drill will be conducted and repeated periodically at regular intervals or any time required. Conducting a DRS drill is very essential because it only gives the organisation confidence that in a real time event, when the PDC is down, data can seamlessly be moved over to the DRS from where all remote locations can be served. Conducting a

DRS drill and reporting to RBI is now a regulatory requirement as mandated by the country's regulator Reserve Bank of India.

Observations during the drill have to be noted very carefully like the volume of data handled, bandwidth available and the network capability, database capability, number of remote centres logged in and serviced, etc. Wherever the result is not satisfactory or there is a down time or a problem impacting the processor resources or network resources, such constraints have to be addressed immediately.

During the period of disaster, when the remote centres are accessing the DRS (and not the PDC) some organisations feel it is advisable to keep the remote centres posted of the development, so that the processor and other server or network resources will be conserved during the period and minimum transactions will be put through. However, of late due to security constraints and confidentiality of information many organisations and banks do not prefer disclosing to remote centres that the data is being made available from DRS and not from the PDC. In fact, there is a growing concern on whether the location of DRS itself, the nature of connectivity and other infrastructure there are all to be disclosed or not openly.

18.7 Phase III

Phase III of the BC DRM is the review and monitoring phase. Incident Management has already been discussed in detail in chapter No.16. Periodic reporting of incidents, review of action taken on such incidents, results of drills, efficiency of the systems during such DRP drills and the need for special attention or enhancement of resources if any, will be taken care of in this phase.

As BC DRM is itself a dynamic concept, the BC-DRP will be subject to review at periodic intervals as provided for in the plan or immediately after every disaster. Such review meetings will focus on the strength of the existing BCDRP and the need if any to enhance the existing infrastructure or have additional resources.

A very significant point to be noted is the need for constant updating of the BC DRP. Though the plan itself will normally provide for updating and review once in say six months, the task of updating should not be a routine one without proper application of mind. The plan should be updated immediately when there is an addition to existing infrastructure or when there is a change in hardware or network equipment procured or when there is a change in identified human resource in the BC DR Team.

If such constant updating is not done, the entire process of BC-DRP is bound to fail, as in the event of a disaster, the contact persons may not be available or there will be a major gap between the available resource and the recorded resource. Such a scenario will annoy the DR managers making the problem more complex and worsening the situation adding a disaster to disaster.

To conclude, the essence of BC-DRP is identification of threat as a disaster *i.e.* knowing the enemy called 'disaster' and to be prepared to face the challenges. To quote from the words of the famous Chinese thinker of 3rd century BC Sun Tzu:

"Know your enemy and know yourself and you can fight a hundred battles without disaster"

Know Your Progress

The ultimate objective of any organisation is to deliver customer centric products to the customers' satisfaction at an optimal cost and continually enhance customer satisfaction. No organisation would like the business to be affected because of any expected or unexpected or unforeseen incident. The underlying principle should be: *at any cost, the business should continue.* It is with this objective that the entire concept of BC-DRP has evolved.

Disaster may be defined as a sudden event, such as an accident or a natural catastrophe, that causes great damage or loss of life, a phenomenon that causes huge damage to life, property and destroys the economic, social and cultural life of people. Disaster may be a man-made event like terrorist attack or a technology based or a natural one like floods, earthquake, etc. A sound BC DR Plan will ensure that the organisation is well equipped to face any threats even a disaster. Drafting a good BC DR Plan involves a series of steps right from identification of information assets of the organisation, conducting a Business Impact Analysis and Risk Management, getting approval for the plan from top management, procuring the necessary hardware and software for implementation of the plan, conducting a DR drill like a real time scenario, studying the result and efficiency of steps taken and conducting a review.

There must be proper redundancy and backup for the entire infrastructure including telecom lines, software, hardware gadgets, etc. There should be nothing, as far as possible, without a backup, which would become a single point failure. Backups should be routine and preferably automated. The type of backup depends upon the management requirements based on factors like data criticality, accessibility, volume of data handled etc. An ideal design will be to go for a secondary data centre in the same centre with the data in perfect 'sync' with the live updates of primary data centre which would come up seamlessly in the event of the primary data centre failing and a DR Site in another city preferably in another seismic zone wherein data gets written with minimum delay say a few minutes.

Recovery Time Objective and Recovery Point Objective are all management decisions on the acceptable down time for the server and acceptable loss of data in the server when it comes up, after loading a backup. Factors influencing BC DRP include the backup policy, data criticality, regulatory guidelines, nature of data handled, top management commitment in technology based products and delivery.

Key Words

DRS, Primary	Data Centre	Secondary Data Centre
Single Point Failure	redundancy	Offsite backup
RPO	RTO	Last mile connectivity
DR drill	Seismic Zone	Incremental Backup

Questions

1. What is the correct order of steps in drafting a BC DR Plan?
   a. Planning for procurement of hardware for backup, Doing the backup, Checking for proper internal controls, acting at the DR Site to conduct a DR drill
   b. Asset classification, Business Impact Analysis, Risk Management, Approval for BC DR Plan, procure necessary infrastructure whenever necessary, conduct a drill, review.
   c. Plan for the BC DR Site, identify areas for the site, classify the network as critical and non-critical, procure backup network lines, conduct a DR drill, ensure backups are working, perform review
   d. Phase I for drafting the BC DR Plan, Phase II for procurement of all hardware and conducting a drill, Phase III for involving all staff members and Phase IV for review
2. Disaster is often the result of—
   a. Vulnerability in the system
   b. Deficiency in Business Impact Analysis

c. Unmitigated risk in Risk Management

d. Threat that is foreseen or not foreseen

3. A Disaster Recovery Site should normally be located in a different city—

a. in another state

b. in a far off from the coastal area and the Data Centre

c. in a different seismic zone

d. with safe and secure infrastructure preferably with outsourced management

4. Recovery Time Objective is the time—

a. the server can be down without affecting the business of the organisation

b. the management feels it can survive without a server and do the operations manually

c. the management feels acceptable as down time, before a backup restoration is done

d. for the DR Site server comes up and provides data to remote centres

5. When a tape backup (in an external medium) is sent daily to another location, it is called—

a. an offsite backup

b. remote secondary backup

c. DR Site backup

d. Digital Tape Remote Backup

6. When connectivity between two major cities is taken from one telecom service provider and the connectivity for such lines inside the premises is given by one router only—

a. it is a Dual Point Failure since there are two single point failures with no backups

b. it is a Single Point Failure for the router only since telecom provider will be one only

c. it is network redundancy for the telecom lines and single point failure for the router

d. it is a single point failure in both, since there is no backup in both the lines and the router

7. If a data centre has an offsite (or a DR site) which has got the necessary infrastructure with all hardware equipment and software in place and the data is to be uploaded to make it function as a data centre, then it is called—

a. Hot Site

b. Warm Site

c. Secondary Data Centre

d. DR Site

8. Which of the following is not a factor to be considered in designing a BC DRP?

a. Human resources available to man the centre

b. Probability of unplanned events, disasters like hurricanes or bio-chemical disaster

c. Security threats planned, unplanned, feared, dreaded

d. Globalisation and the need to operate from multiple locations

9. BCDR Plan is sometimes considered to be a—

a. subset of IS Audit Policy since IS auditors conduct audit of DRP infrastructure also *b.* a subset of IS Security Policy since points like Risk Matrix etc. evolve from there

c. a separate outsourced activity that will align itself with the functions of IS Security, IS Audit, HR and Inspection functions

d. flagship policy that includes the Security Policy, Audit Policy, Backup Policy, etc.

10. Which of the following features describes the functionality of BCDRP in brief?

a. Vulnerability Assessment

b. Preparedness

c. Backup Policy

d. Data Criticality

Answers

1. *b*	6. *d*
2. *d*	7. *d*
3. *c*	8. *a*
4. *c*	9. *b*
5. *a*	10. *b*

D

MODULE

IS AUDIT AND REGULATORY COMPLIANCE

19

CHAPTER

Information Systems Audit

OBJECTIVES

This chapter presents the meaning and definition of Information Systems (IS) Audit, its specific role in any organisation, the different types and methodologies of an IS Audit and their relative importance. An attempt is also made to present to the readers, the steps involved in conducting an IS Audit, the meetings involved in it, the kinds of reports and the follow-up action that organisations should take after an audit.

19.1 Introduction

The word 'audit' literally means official inspection of an organisation's accounts typically by an independent body and IS Audit means the process of inspecting Information Assets and their internal controls in the organisations. Auditing succeeds accounting and is always considered a step after accounting is completed, maybe in different stages of writing accounts.

It would be interesting to note that the concept of audit is not new and has been spoken about in many ancient literatures also. The importance of internal controls and audit and the independence of audit roles and functions have been underlined and described in the famous work "Arthashastra" written around 350 BC by Chanakya (Kautilya). Considered to be an administrative discourse, the book speaks about the internal controls of a kingdom, the roles and functions of a king, the segregation of duties, the writing of accounts and someone independently verifying them. Thus, the independence of audits is not a newly introduced phenomenon, nor is the application of internal controls to top management.

While the word 'audit' refers to inspection of accounts or verification of accounts of an organisation, normally by an independent body, an Information Systems Audit is a review of the controls, their adequacy and effectiveness, within an organisation's IT infrastructure. An IS Audit basically refers to an audit of the IT environment in the organisation.

Information Systems Audit was earlier referred to as EDP Audit (Electronic Data Processing Audit) in the early days of computerisation in banks. With extensive computerisation and almost the entire banking industry keeping all its data in computer systems the term Information System Audit gathered momentum and has come to stay now. However, the words 'IT audit' and 'computer audit' are also being used interchangeably these days to denote an IS Audit. The term IT Audit specifically refers to techniques using computers, including software, as a tool to independently test computer data

of audit interest and computer audit is a broader term denoting an audit of the entire computer infrastructure, hardware, software and all resources connected to it.

The only other term that is quite specific is "Information Security Audit" or" Computer Security Audit". Some firms resort to this kind of audit particularly for their IT departments or other data critical departments or networks. In a security audit, the focus will be on the controls with particular reference to data confidentiality, integrity, availability and other associated areas like authentication, access privileges, etc. In this chapter, however, we will be broadly referring to Information Systems Audits with specific reference to Security Audits wherever the context warrants.

Before we go into the other aspects of IS Audit, let us discuss some of the concepts that are closely associated with IS Audit, like frameworks, policies, charter planners, etc.

Framework refers to a structure or a support used as the basis for something being constructed. Hence, the IS audit framework is the mandatory requirements for the audit. It is called a framework typically because it is often a broad statement of auditor's responsibilities, ensuring that they have competence, integrity, objectivity and independence in planning, conducting, and reporting on their work. The guidelines supporting the professional standards assist the auditor in applying the standards and provide examples that an IT Auditor might follow to meet these standards.

A well-drafted framework involves everything from defining the scope to going through the audit process, assessing the controls and submission of reports and ultimately the evaluation of the audit procedures themselves.

The next term associated with IS Audit is Policies. Every organisation will have its own IS Audit Policy, as described in detail later in this chapter.

There are many guidelines associated with an IS Audit Policy, like the Policy for the assignment of audit functions, the policy for the selection of auditors, the policy for review and post-audit functions, etc. Typically, this policy will cover the 'why', 'what', and 'how' of an IS Audit. In other words, this policy will discuss the reason and purpose of conducting the audit, the scope of the audit, the selection of the audit area, the choice of audit functions, the selection of auditors, the definition of their roles and responsibilities and the actual methodology of conducting the audit.

The Audit Charter is the next important document associated with IS Audit. The Audit Charter is the actual mandate to perform the IS audit function and contains the four main areas related to the IS Audit:

I. Purpose of audit
II. Responsibility of auditors
III. Authority of auditors
IV. Accountability of auditors

The Audit Charter discusses the purpose of the audit, the role played by auditors and auditees, the scope, and objectives of the audit, etc. Responsibility here includes the tasks associated with auditing like ensuring the independence of the audit, accessing key performance indicators, risk assessment, etc. The Authority of auditors refers to the right of auditors to access relevant information, access functions, understand the scope and seek records within the scope, etc. Accountability refers to the responsibility of auditors to report to senior management the audit functions, findings, and appraisals of performance, etc.

In addition to IT auditing standards, IT auditors need to be alert to other laws, regulations, or other authoritative sources that may impact the conduct of an IT audit.

19.2 History of EDP Audit in Banks

The risks and control systems in computerized banks were earlier analysed by Coopers and Lybrand (U.K.) under the Technical Assistance Project funded by the Department For International Development (DFID) in the U.K. An inspection manual was prepared in 1997 with the assistance of the said international consultants for the guidance of the Reserve Bank officers inspecting banks in a computerized environment. Based on the consultancy report, the Department of Banking Supervision of the RBI issued in 1998 a detailed guidance note to banks apprising them of the risks in a computerized environment and suggesting associated controls to address the specific risk.

An assessment of the system of computer audit in banks as of March 31, 2000 was made based on the findings contained in the inspection reports of banks for the years 1998-99 and 1999-2000 and other specific feedback received from banks. It was found that in many banks, there was no formal EDP audit manual available. An audit sub-committee was formed, which later submitted its report in the form of the EDP Audit Checklist in April 2002. Since then, the evaluation of EDP audits in banks has become an integral part of the Annual Financial Inspection of banks.

Now the recent Gopalakrishna Working Group on Information Security, Internet Banking, and Related Areas in its report has taken into account the report of this as well as other working groups and committees and has submitted its report in January 2011, circulated by RBI to all banks in April 2011.

19.3 IS Auditor

It has often been a point of interesting debate whether an IS auditor should be from the technology department or the Inspection or Audit Department. Though an IS auditor need not be a technically qualified person to become a software engineer or a hardware specialist, the person should nevertheless, be a tech-savvy person with reasonable knowledge of various Operating Systems, the hardware and software issues in the organisation, the type and nature of information systems prevailing in the organisation and the general areas of concern in information security.

The relationship between an auditor and the auditee is very important. It is not a combative role, not a complementary role (though both may sometimes complement each other) since they do not complement or supplement the roles of each other. It should be more co-operative than adversarial. It is quite often that a well-informed auditor (out of enthusiasm) will want to demonstrate the smartness and exhibit the knowledge to the auditee, which might border on intimidation to the latter who may, as a result, hesitate to respond to even the normal queries of the auditor.

It is this relationship that is of the utmost significance. A non-responsive auditee or a misleading auditee, either out of lack of communicative skills, coercion, or sheer lack of knowledge, will ultimately derail the purpose of the audit. Hence, it is often the responsibility of the auditor to bring out the best in the auditee and complete the report.

Another point of debate often raised is: Should an auditor do the work of a consultant? Quite often the answer is no. Unless it is an internal audit and the audit objective itself is to conduct an audit, find out the gap, suggest ways to improve the system, etc. Under normal circumstances, the auditor will restrict the findings to remarks about the controls, their effectiveness and efficiency, implementation issues, the corrective action taken on the earlier audit reports, and all other issues relating to the audit alone.

Providing consultancy, based on audit findings and reports is not the entitlement of a typical auditor. The auditor stops with the findings, focusing on the gaps being identified, benchmarking them wherever necessary and comparing them with the best practices wherever applicable, and remarking on their compliance with the organisation's own policies and procedures wherever relevant. The auditor can go into the root cause analysis for such non-conformance and make that part of his report.

Auditor's qualities and qualifications: Having noted that a successful IS auditor need not be a fully qualified software systems specialist or an engineer, we can now have a look at who constitutes a good IS auditor. A good IS A or is always a discerning, professional, normal auditor with a reasonable software and systems background, preferably with a formal qualification in audit like CISA (Certified Information Systems Auditor) from ISACA. Of late, banks go in for empaneled auditors from CERT-In with whom there is a procedure for empanelment for IS auditors and IT auditors.

Chartered Accountants with an interest in technology and systems or software engineers and systems administrators with an interest in auditing may obtain CISA qualification. In either case, it is to be noted that a successful IS auditor will have the qualities and qualifications of both - audit and technology.

An IS auditor need not look at every computer with suspicion or with a magnifying glass and look at all the print-outs, logs, or trails. A discerning auditor will certainly know the areas to be audited, the controls to be in place and the action to be taken on such controls.

19.4 External *v.* Internal IS Auditor

In these days of outsourcing for most banks, it is quite common for banks to engage the services of audit professionals with CISA or other professional qualifications for conducting the audit. If audits are outsourced, banks engage the services of audit firms that are on the CERT-In panel or on their own approved panel taking care to ensure that empanelment is based on regulatory compliance like CISA qualification, experience and other eligibility criteria.

Since external auditors come from different organisations, it opens up the audit area giving a broader vision to the audit environment so that the organisation or bank can look forward to getting educated by the auditors and getting to know the best practices followed elsewhere.

On the other hand, a major disadvantage of engaging an external auditor is that some of the security issues that are quite confidential in nature may not be openly discussed with the auditor and the auditor may be left to think that there are no controls in place. Especially in the cases of undertakings dealing with sensitive and personal data of customers, some of the security initiatives may not be openly discussed with external officials and the external auditors would have to get at the facts with persuasion and difficulty.

In the case of an in-house team of auditors, it is better to engage CISA or other similarly qualified persons from the organisation's HR itself and train them in the audit area. On one hand, the in-house auditor may not be taken seriously by the auditee team and the process may get diluted. There may also be constraints like the auditor's inhibitions to comment on the functions of a colleague, or the ineffective implementation of a control or non-compliance with any regulatory procedure etc.

In any case, awareness and training are essential ingredients for a successful IS audit. Awareness initiatives should be taken by the organisation about the audit scenario, the audit methodologies, and the functions of auditors, auditees, and all other stakeholders. Such an awareness initiative should cover the entire gamut of the information system environment in the organisation.

After awareness, training should be imparted to the auditors and auditees on the methodologies of audit, audit procedures, and mainly report writing.

19.5 Audit Methodologies

Let us discuss IS audit processes and the methodologies being adopted. The series of activities involved in an IS audit is called the IS audit process which is depicted later in this chapter. The Auditor can commence auditing after understanding the organisation's requirements and preparing his own format to study, analyse, and then report. As opposed to this free-flowing type of audit, based on a broader understanding of audit requirements, etc., checklist-based audits are easier to adopt and hence more popular.

Checklist Based Audits

The Inspection or Audit Department prepares the checklist for conducting the audit with every chapter or every part of it focusing on specific areas, so that the auditor can go with the checklist to the audit area and get answers to all the questions in the checklist or himself verify the answers and complete the audit formalities. Gradation can also be done based on the negative answers to the checklists. It is a good practice to classify the questions (*i.e.* answers) on three or four grades of criticality like Very High, High, Medium, and Low. Thus, the number of negative or unsatisfactory answers to the high-critical areas alone can be discussed and focused for immediate attention.

There are some distinct advantages to a checklist-based audit, like

I. It ensures no critical area is left out.

II. It acts as a well drafted plan, helping with time management.

III. It can be provided to the auditee ahead of the on-site audit.

IV. It will ensure complete coverage of the audit area and scope.

V. It will help in collecting evidence wherever required.

VI. It provides a permanent record for future use, customisation, or improvement.

There are quite a few disadvantages to the checklist-based audits. With such a questionnaire, the auditor may sometimes, tend to go routinely with answers to the questions without proper application of mind, resulting in unreliable results. He will not go beyond the checklist and will cease to think on his own. If there is anything critical in the area that warrants immediate attention but is not provided for in the checklist, it may escape the auditor's attention. Besides, there are some questions for which a clear "yes" or "No" may not be possible as an answer and the real position could lie somewhere in between, with a 'No' with some adjectives or perhaps a qualified 'Yes'.

Nevertheless, checklist-based audits continue to be popular. To overcome the disadvantages mentioned above, some auditors have scope for such improvements in the checklist itself. Anyway, it should be borne in mind that a checklist is certainly not a static document and it will be ideal to keep revising it as and when necessary, taking into account the comments and qualities of answers that auditors get, taking care to ensure that only the latest version of the checklist is always used.

19.6 Types of Audits

There are generally two types of IS Audits, based on the use of computers in the audit, *viz*. (i) Auditing Around the computer and (*ii*) Auditing Through the computer.

Auditing Around the Computer is a simple auditing technique that does not involve the use of a computer in conducting the audit. It focuses on checking input controls and verifying accuracy in the output. This type of auditing does not utilize auditing computer tools or software. Security initiatives and controls, such as data integrity, confidentiality in upkeep and retrieval, etc., are verified form the user's perspective by inputting data and checking output accuracy.

In this kind of audit, the scope is simple for the auditors to understand, carry out, and report. Any auditor with a reasonably good knowledge of auditing and computer systems can conduct an audit successfully and come out with sensible reports. Since this audit does not involve verification of the technology of computers like source code verification, efficacy and efficiency of software, functionality of hardware, etc., the auditor will rely on reports for all these aspects (without conducting an audit for those areas) and will simply refer to them in the report.

Auditing Through the computer, on the other hand, means conducting the audit with the help of computers using auditing tools like the popular technique Computer Assisted Auditing Technique (CAAT). In this methodology, audit tools are used, the input controls are checked by inputting data and then the software is verified for its efficiency, speed and reliability with the help of auditing tools, and sometimes the report itself is generated.

This technique is quite useful in those circumstances when the program logic is complex and it may be impossible for a team to read the source code and understand and then audit, or, when the controls are so many that it would be difficult to individually verify them for their efficiency and reliability, etc. Since audits are conducted with the help of a tool, extensive audit trails and logs are available for interpretation.

One major disadvantage of this type of audit is that it requires a good knowledge of systems, the use and knowledge of audit tools available, the knowledge and experience to select the best audit tool for a particular organisation and the expertise to interpret the output and present it. Because of this feature, this process also includes the technique known as 'auditing with the computer' *i.e.*, conducting an audit with an audit tool running, either a readymade tool or a customised tool or going to a menu and selecting the audit functionalities as provided in the menu and taking the reports.

19.7 Planning Phase

The Planning phase in IS Audit phase involves a study of the audit objectives, focusing on areas of importance. The nature and type of audit may be any of the following:

I. An external routine audit, like a periodic one.
II. Audit for specific security purposes.
III. An internal team's routine.
IV. Second-party audit for a specific purpose (*i.e.*, an audit conducted by a supplier or a purchaser associated with the organisation).
V. Audit for looking into an incident that has been reported.
VI. Investigative audit with a purpose not openly divulged.

Study the audit areas

This step involves a visit to the areas of audit either physically or with logical access as part of an audit menu. The specific areas that are to be audited are studied, and the plan is drafted accordingly. The HR required is deployed, and a checklist is prepared accordingly in tune with the audit objectives.

At the time of the commencement of the audit, in the case of certification audit like ISO, there are structured procedures to be followed, like fixing the audit schedule, audit area, convening an Opening Meeting, mentioning the Non-Disclosure Agreement, etc. In the case of other audits, like the company's own IS Audit or an external IS Audit, the following steps are recommended:

I. Fix the audit schedule, and time, define the scope, and finalise.
II. Convene the Opening Meeting or talk to the functional head to be audited.
III. Apprise audit objectives (unless confidential where the purpose is not to be revealed).
IV. Discuss the areas to be audited, papers to be seen, systems to be verified, etc.
V. Give advance information in case a visit to any other data centre is warranted.
VI. Inform the other functional heads who may have to be audited during the day.
VII. Proceed with the audit after finalising the other infrastructure needs for the audit.

Evaluate the internal controls

Every organisation has its own internal controls like hardware controls, network controls, and software controls (*already discussed in the earlier chapters*). A list of all such controls is studied and their effectiveness is analysed. In the case of new applications or a new environment, that has not been covered so far by existing controls, the exact audit requirements and security criticality based on the asset classification are to be noted, and the check-list is to be revised or introduced accordingly. In the case of existing applications and existing information assets, the efficiency of existing internal controls is to be studied. In the case of an audit for specific security purposes, the existing security scenario, coverage, and adequacy of the IS Security Policy and its implementation, etc. are all audited.

This step of evaluating the importance of internal controls assumes great significance, especially in the case of an audit into a specific investigation or such confidential assignment when the audit objective is to conduct an inquiry into a security incident suspected or reported. Availability of internal controls, adequacy of the procedures in such controls, effectiveness of implementation, and incident reporting mechanism (*already discussed in the earlier chapter*) are all the key areas that would be focused on in this kind of audit.

The next significant part of the audit program would be to identify the deficiencies or do a Gap Analysis. Deficiencies may be due to inadequate IS policies, ineffective implementation, or careless monitoring, and other related factors. A prudent auditor will be able to identify all such factors, based on the response to the checklist or questionnaire-based interview methodology and based on the response and implementation of the requirements of earlier audit reports.

Deficiencies or the Gap Analysis can be against a benchmark, or the best practices, or the framework as required in the scope or as per the audit objectives. If it is an audit for certification against a specific standard, say ISO 27001, then the gap will be the Non-Conformance Report or Observation in a formal and structured manner. Otherwise, during the course of the audit itself, the auditor would have noted the deficiencies and the gaps and discussed them with the auditees.

19.8 Report Presentation

The success of an audit lies as much in its presentation as in the actual conduct of the audit itself. For certification audits of ISO and other bodies, there are proper formats in which the report is prepared and submitted. There are also Closing Meetings in which it is customary to involve the top management or the Information owners and apprise them briefly about the findings, if not reading out the entire report, and then formally present it to the Head of the Auditee team.

However, whether there is any structured format or not, it would always be better to do the following steps as part of this phase of the audit:

I. Convene a meeting of all important functional heads.

II. Mark the attendance in the meeting and discuss the issues.

III. Discuss the findings before preparing the report (unless it is an investigative audit in which the report is to be submitted only to a designated person confidentially).

IV. Involve the team and give them an opportunity to rectify the deficiencies at the stage of audit report preparation itself.

V. Listen to the views of auditee team members about the audit report.

VI. Offer clarifications in brief as to why such a remark or comment was made in the audit.

VII. Conclude the meeting with a reference to the Non-Disclosure Clause signed already, present the report, (and in the case of any certification audit give some reasonable time for rectification).

Conducting regular audits is one of the controls and security practices to be followed by banks, according to the recent report of the RBI's Gopalakrishna Working Group. The report further adds

"Bank's management and RBI, need an assurance on the effectiveness of internal controls implemented and expect the IS Audit to provide an independent and objective view of the extent to which the risks are managed. As a consequence, the nature of the Internal Audit department has undergone a major transformation and IS audits are gaining importance as key processes are automated, or enabled by technology. Hence, there is a need for banks to re-assess the IS Audit processes and ensure that IS Audit objectives are effectively met."

19.9 Audit Policy

Every organisation be it a bank or other critical financial sector, will have its own IS Audit Policy or Internal Inspection guidelines that comprise IS audit. The IS Security Policy and IS Audit Policy are both closely inter-twined and related to each other, though functionally and responsibility-wise they are absolutely independent areas.

As we have already seen in the earlier chapters on Organisational Security and Corporate Security, the IS Security Policy will speak about the broader areas of Information Asset Classification, Identification of criticality, Business Impact Analysis, Risk Management from a security point of view, Information System Security architecture, the CIO, ISO, their roles and responsibilities, Incident Reporting mechanism, implementation of security initiatives (right from physical up to the network and logical or software security ones), deficiencies in security etc.

As against this function, the IS Audit Policy will speak about the infrastructure to verify whether all those mentioned in the IS Security Policy are being adequately taken care of and implemented, with a team of auditors assigning them specific roles functions and providing them the necessary tools if any are required. The IS Audit Policy will therefore consist of the following essential areas:

Criticality of assets and classification from an audit point of view

I. Periodicity of the audit to be conducted
II. Classification of branch/business units for the purpose of audit
III. Audit criteria, scope-definition, and description
IV. Nature and methodology of the audit to be followed
V. Panel of auditors
VI. Follow-up procedures after completion of the audit
VII. Review mechanism for effectiveness of audit (Define roles of people involved)
VIII. Review mechanism for rectification of audit findings (Define role functions)

19.10 Cobit and Framework

The Control Objectives for Information and Related Technology (COBIT) are a set of best practices (framework) for information technology (IT) management created by the Information Systems Audit and Control Association (ISACA), and the IT Governance Institute (ITGI) in 1996. COBIT is an IT governance framework and supporting toolset that allows managers to bridge the gap between control requirements, technical issues, and business risks.

COBIT enables clear policy development and good practice for IT control throughout organizations, emphasizing regulatory compliance, helping organizations to increase the value attained from IT, aligning and simplifying the implementation of the COBIT framework. The latest version scheduled

to be released in 2012, COBIT 5 will consolidate and integrate the existing COBIT 4.1, and Risk IT frameworks and also draw significantly from the Business Model for Information Security (BMIS) and related areas.

19.11 Audit Reports

We have already seen that in the case of ISO audits, the report and the contents are always structured. Audit Findings are the remarks jotted down by the auditors during the course of the audit. Presented in a structured format, they become an Audit Report, often supported by audit evidence in the form of references, statements, or statistics.

After the completion of every audit, the last and most significant stage is 'Audit Findings'. The auditor should take care to present his findings to the auditee especially the top management or the officer responsible for the audit. Such findings, in the form of a formal report, should give proper reference to the observations recorded, be based on facts, and be empirical. Inferences based on opinion, any pre-conceived notions, ideas, or opinions - should be thoroughly avoided.

Findings should always match the terms of reference or benchmarks or the particular clause of the standard as per which the findings are a deviation or a non-conformance.

It is a good audit practice to categorise non-conformance reports based on criticality and the level of deviation, as major, minor or just observations. Some auditors also prefer to record and include in their reports any praiseworthy points or accomplishments as a matter of positive notes and motivational observations.

If, during the course of the audit or just before the audit closure procedures, the non-conformance has been rectified, the auditee may remove it from the report. Auditors normally give time for rectification of the non-conformance, do a verification report within the time stipulated, and satisfy themselves that corrective action has been taken. Some audit findings may involve only preventive action, and corrective action may not be possible. In such a case, the auditor may insist on preventive action and a root cause analysis for the non-conformance.

Before we conclude, it is relevant to study the meaning of the term "Audit Risk". We have already seen in the chapter on Risk Management, the different kinds of risks including residual risk. Audit risk is a term that is gaining in usage often referring to 'residual risk' as well. Audit risk is the risk that the auditor expresses as an inappropriate opinion when the financial statements presented to him are materially misstated. It indicates the auditor's willingness to accept that the statements may not be correct, after the audit is completed and an unqualified clean opinion is issued.

With the increasing penetration of IT and IT enabled services in common man's life and ever-growing dependence on information systems, the volume of IT-based transactions and electronic records is increasing at an alarming pace of growth. Hence, it would be highly difficult, if not practically impossible, for the auditors to verify all the e-transactions either in the system or their print-outs, accompanied by a certificate to verify their correctness. Auditors, therefore, adopt a risk-based approach.

While studying the role of auditors in an organisation, especially an external team of auditors, the story of Satyam Computers in India, is the earliest case that can be taken up for study. It is what is called the biggest corporate accounting scam in India in which the Chairman Shri B. Ramalinga Raju was convicted in 2015. As the chairman of Satyam Computer Services, he confessed in 2009, to a massive fraud exculpating most senior executives, independent directors and his own family members, with just two exceptions, *viz.,* the Chief Financial Officer and statutory auditors, M/s. Price Waterhouse Coopers. Our study here is mainly with regard to the role of auditors. For auditors, what is their responsibility, how far and how deep? Are they investigators, a fact-finding team or a team to run some software tools and report the output? These were all the points of debate in all knowledgeable circles for many months after the Satyam failure came out.

Let us confine ourselves to the fact that the role of the IS auditor is mainly with respect to the examination of internal controls in the information systems infrastructure of the organisation, their adequacy, effectiveness, implementation and the nature of corrective and preventive action wherever required. The success of any organisation is, therefore, dependent on the nature of the data handled, confidentiality, security initiatives in place, controls implemented and lastly, the role of IS auditors in verifying whether the controls are effective.

Know Your Progress

An Audit refers to an official inspection of an organisation's accounts, and an IS audit refers to the process of inspecting information assets and the effectiveness of internal controls implemented, commenting on their adequacy, effectiveness, efficiency, and monitoring mechanisms.

Audits should always be independent, as has been emphasized from time immemorial. IS Audit was earlier referred to as EDP Audit. Of late, terms like Computer Audit, IT Audit are also used interchangeably to denote IS Audit. The RBI has formulated detailed checklists that have been subsequently revised and is closely monitoring the IS audit mechanism in banks.

An IS Auditor should basically be a good person with an acumen for information systems and good knowledge of computers. He should have all the qualities of a good auditor. An Audit can be done based on a questionnaire in the form of a checklist, in which case the auditor will go with the checklist and get answers to all the questions. This process ensures that no significant point is left in the audit scope. Regarding the methodologies, there are two types of audits: namely **Auditing Around the computer,** meaning audits will be conducted without going into the software and other technical points of information systems and based on inputs and output controls only. The other methodology, namely **Auditing Through the computer,** means that audits will be done with the help of audit tools and the running of audit-related software by auditors who have reasonably good proficiency in software and systems skills.

The IS Audit Process involves steps like planning, identifying the audit areas, evaluating the internal controls, identifying the deficiencies and finally the report presentation. IS Audit Policy deals with the rules and procedural guidelines for IS Audit in the organisation. COBIT is a framework discussing good practices for effective IT controls in organisations. Audit risk is the risk that the auditor feels arises out of some mis-statement that the auditor notices in the submissions made by the auditee organisation.

Key Words

EDP Audit	Computer Audit	Auditing Around the computer
Checklist audit	Auditing Through the computer	Audit Findings
Audit Policy	Audit Risk	Internal controls

Questions

1. In Auditing through the computer, the auditor ______________.
   a. need not have a good knowledge of computers but should know the work process
   b. should be a good programmer and software professional but does audit on special assignments

c. should be basically an auditor with reasonably good skill-set in computer systems

d. does the audit only through a computer and does everything online without the help of any print-outs and checklists

2. In auditing around the computer ________________.

a. auditing is done with the help of all peripherals like printers placed around the computer

b. auditor has good knowledge of computer systems and programming skills and uses the same in auditing

c. audit is done with the help of a checklist which does not contain any software of system related questions

d. audit is done with input and output process controls without going into the software source code

3. RBI's Committee on Internet Banking and related areas which has dealt with at length on IS Audit recently is called ________________.

a. Narasimhan Working Group on IS Audit

b. Gopalakrishna Committee on IS Audit

c. Gopalakrishna Working Group on Information Security, Internet Banking, etc.

d. Ananthakrishna Working Group on IS Audit

4. One of the disadvantages of a checklist-based audit is ________________.

a. it provides answers to predetermined questions and has no scope for further enhancement

b. an auditor may tend to go mechanical and give answers without application of mind

c. an auditor may not add his views and will himself tick the answers

d. an auditor may give answers without going to the audit area and in absentia

5. Audit Risk is often associated with which one of the following risks ?

a. Residual Risk

b. Accounting Risk

c. Operational Risk in Accounting

d. Risk of mis-statement

6. In a typical IS architecture, IS Audit will be ________________.

a. a subset of IS Security and will be supervised and monitored by the IS Security Committee

b. an independent set up with powers to audit even the top management including the apex level Information Security Committee

c. a separate independent function not belonging to the organisation to ensure its unbiased approach

d. the overall function to draft, monitor, review and audit even the IS Security architecture

7. COBIT is often associated with ________________.

a. Framework of IT related functions

b. Framework of IS Security

c. Benchmarking and Standards to prepared for ISO certification

d. Objectives for IS Audit and IS Security and related controls

8. The Independence of IS Audit is a new concept being introduced globally ever since the massive use of computers started. (True/False)
9. Audit Findings and Audit Report are independent functions and not part of the audit process. (True/False)
10. A successful IS Audit does not require a good IT consultant. (True/False)

Answers

1. *c*	6. *b*
2. *d*	7. *a*
3. *c*	8. False
4. *b*	9. False
5. *a*	10. True

20
CHAPTER

Regulatory Mechanism in Indian Banks

OBJECTIVES

After reading this chapter, the readers will know the meaning and significance of regulatory bodies; in the banking and financial sectors, especially in areas concerning banking functions, telecom, and other related areas. Compliance issues on specific regulatory guidelines, the need and importance of various supervisory controls initiated by the regulators, particularly on information systems and information security, and related areas are also dealt with. Besides the main regulator for the banking industry, *viz.*, the Reserve Bank of India, the functions of other regulators that impact the banking industry, like TRAI, SEBI, IRDA, etc., are also briefly discussed in this chapter.

20.1 Introduction

Banks are the backbone of a country's monetary system and hence play a significant role in the economic growth of a nation. Especially, in a developing and growing economy like India, banks' role in nation-building is quite enormous. Thanks to the advent of globalisation and the thrust on privatisation that started in the mid-1990's there has been stiff competition among banks, and the banking industry in India has seen enormous change. Just like any other system, the banking system in the country is susceptible to weaknesses, and risks, which should be managed well by individual banks and regulated well by the monetary authorities. The Preamble to the RBI describes its functions as regulating the issue of bank notes, keeping reserves with a view to securing monetary stability in India, and generally operating the credit and currency systems of the country to its advantage. The RBI Board was reconstituted in 2006, with members like Azim Premji and Kumar Managalam Birla forming part of the Central Board, besides the Local Boards in the Northern, Eastern, Southern, and Western areas. On completion of their term, Y.C. Deveshwar, the noted industrialist, was inducted into the board in September 2012, along with representatives from the IAS, academia, etc.

20.2 RBI as the Regulator

Banking in India is mainly governed by the Banking Regulation Act, 1949, and the Reserve Bank of India Act, 1934. The RBI and the Government of India exercise control over banks from the opening of banks to their winding-up by virtue of the powers conferred under these statutes. The RBI, as the regulator for the banking industry in India, has enormous responsibility and a role of paramount importance in the financial system of the nation.

All the regulatory provisions are not uniformly applicable to all the banks in the country. The regulatory purview of the Reserve Bank extends to a large segment of financial institutions, including commercial banks, co-operative banks, non-banking financial institutions, and various financial markets. Application of the whole or part of any regulation, enactment, or guideline is decided by the RBI, taking into account factors like the nature of ownership of the bank (private or public sector, foreign or Indian, co-operative or commercial bank, etc.), the nature of such regulation, and other significant areas.

The RBI was constituted under Section 3 of the RBI Act, 1934, to take over the management of currency from the Central Government and carry on the business of banking in accordance with the provisions of the Act. Besides being the sole authority for the issue and management of currency in India, the RBI is also a banker to banks, a banker to government, and a supervisor of the banking system in India.

This main role of the RBI as regulator of the banking sector is interesting, by virtue of the powers conferred on it by the Banking Regulations Act. As the regulator, RBI has the following powers:

I. to issue a license.
II. to control credit, including collecting all credit information.
III. to monitor and supervise the entire banking system relating to moratorium, amalgamation, and winding-up.
IV. to impose penalties regarding developmental activities in the banking system.
V. to resolve disputes among banks, if required.

This supervisory role of RBI, has of late, had wider technological ramifications, and RBI has been playing this role diligently, donning the cap of the technology and systems security captain in the banking industry and guiding all banks in the nation.

Probably time has come when RBI performed its role at a higher level than as a regulatory body, and served as an institution to guide the netizens, protect the net-savvy customers, monitor the banks, and evolve a pro-active approach in this cyber-security landscape.

To quote the words of Shri G. Padmanabhan, Executive Director, Reserve Bank of India, in his lecture on Cyber Security on 28 February, 2015, "One might argue that we already have RBI-issued directives currently in place today to protect the customers' interest. Besides, institutions such as BCSBI, set up by the Reserve Bank, have also been very active in setting up codes for protecting customer interests. These are largely in the regulatory domain, and the common person is not well aware of them, nor are they seen as the basic rights of customers. The point that we are trying to flag is that all customers must be legally protected from suffering losses when they become a victim of a cyber-crime, as a matter of right. As we have seen, security is a function of four parameters: governance, policies, systems, and awareness. Of these, the real challenge for the Indian financial system is awareness. The Cyber threat is real and is constantly evolving. No organisation is immune or can claim to be fully secure against a cyber-attack. Preventive measures are a must in this scenario. Where prevention fails, make up for it with quick detection and a decisive response. Every organisation should have an IT Governance Policy as a subset of its cyber-security policy."

(Source: https://rbi.org.in/scripts/BS_SpeechesView.aspx?Id=945 retrieved on 17 Nov. 2015)

20.3 RBI'S Regulatory Initiatives Taken so far

The RBI has so far set up various committees and working groups on different subjects in Indian Banking industry, and the regulatory mechanism has been evolving over the years. Follow- up action on such committee reports, as may be necessary, is being taken, like circulating them to banks in India for information in general, revision of checklists if any, and specific compliance wherever necessary, based on such committee reports.

Sometimes further detailed guidelines circulars are also issued by the RBI, and periodic meetings are convened either at the top management level or at the functional executive level so as to ensure that the guidelines actually percolate down to the lower level to the field officers or the functional executives who may have to follow the guidelines.

Jilani Working Group on internal controls and inspection/audit system in banks 1995 identified key risks associated with IT systems, mainly performing an assessment of inspection of EDP activities. Banks were advised to bring the entire domain of EDP activities under the Inspection Department. Computer auditing was still in the developmental stage in banks. An assessment of computer audits in banks as on 31 March, 2000 was made. A sub-committee was constituted with Shri A.L. Narasimhan, Chief General Manager, as the convener. The Classification of risk in the IS environment as a serious subject evolved.

Subsequently, a working group was formed for information systems security in the banking and financial sectors, headed by Dr. R.B. Burman, E.D. The working group prepared a document on checklists for the IS Audit Committee on Computer Audit and Information System Audit Policy in 2001, and the document has for long served as the basic document for banks on IS Audit and IS security issues. Of course, until the recent Gopalakrishna Working Group submitted its report.

20.4 Gopalakrishna Working Group

Under the chairmanship of Shri G. Gopalakrishna, Executive Director, RBI, a working group was established following the announcement in the April 2010 Monetary Policy Statement, which recommended enhancing RBI guidelines relating to the governance of IT, information security, and related areas. The report circulated to all banks through an RBI letter dated 29-4-2011, covers various areas mentioned below:

1. IT Governance
2. Information Security
3. IS Audit
4. IT Operations.
5. IT Services Outsourcing
6. Cyber Fraud
7. Business Continuity Planning
8. Customer Awareness programmes and
9. Legal aspects.

The exhaustive report submitted takes into account the significant points in all the earlier committee reports, recommendations, and serve as a one-point reference on IT Security and related issues from a regulatory compliance angle. This report is a significant step and a milestone in the regulatory and supervisory roles played by RBI.

The Group felt that there was a need for banks to follow a consistent approach in each focus area, to minimize differing interpretations. As recommended in the report, the RBI has asked all Indian banks to setup their respective committees to tackle the rise of cyber-crimes. Under these guidelines, banks are required to have their IT Security policies framed by a CIO and reviewed annually. The working group also felt the need for a forum for CISOs to interact, so that they could exchange knowledge on security threats.

As a preventive measure against cyber-crimes, the group felt the need for increased authentication while banking online. The guidelines have asked banks to audit applications and check for penetration and vulnerability before rendering them live. Additionally, the use of spreadsheets is no longer advised for critical applications. Banks have been asked to proactively test for vulnerabilities in critical applications and also take charge of data security - for data residing in electronic form, data warehouses, databases, and data archives.

The guidelines have also laid emphasis on reporting cyber-attacks and cyber-crimes to CERT-In. On other aspects of security, like personnel security issues, the working group has advised the banks to conduct profound background checks, especially for those who monitor sensitive data and also for people who have access to mission-critical applications.

The Working Group has given an illustrative Information Security checklist covering various areas in its Annexures. The checklist given under "Security Policy: Governance, Implementation, and Review" will be very helpful for banks to read, follow, and conform to. Some of the checklist points on the periodicity of the IS Security Policy Review, the ownership and the powers vested with it, for the security policies of banks, etc. are all very vital and have to be followed scrupulously. For a detailed check-list, the readers are advised to visit the RBI website and the detailed Gopalakrishna Working Group report.

One of the things that the Gopalakrishna Working Group has mentioned but the banks have yet to catch up on is in the area of cyber-crime insurance.

Over the years, while the definition of risk has remained the same, its perception and presence have changed. Now insurance for the virtual world is being spoken about. Already, in the West, cyber-crime insurance has come to stay. In India, cyber-crime insurance policies are being offered by very few companies. It is at a very nascent stage. Now there is no benchmark, standards or yardstick for cyber-security.

There are many regulatory compliance rules, for ISO Certification (for its 27001 standards), but there are no benchmarks to state that this is THE BEST. Some industry bodies were discussing the feasibility and acceptability of proposals to award banks for their best performance in IT products and the adoption of the most secure IT practices. However, in the absence of a proper yardstick, such efforts could not be carried out in a massive and popular manner.

Besides, cyber-crime insurance claims or cyber-crime complaints too cannot be taken as a yardstick, for reasons like ambiguity on the definition of a crime, nature and classification of complaints, nature and level of grievance provided, etc. In the case of cyber-crime insurance, experts also take time to understand the risk, reward, and implications of selling cyber-insurance. Added to all this, is the fact that no bank will be willing to openly express the nature of complaints (like the amount involved, *modus operandi*, complainants' details, etc.) for fear of adverse publicity to the bank that it is weak in security practices.

If a pre-insurance audit is mandated, the norms for an audit to qualify a bank to be given a cyber-crime insurance policy have to be properly designed and defined. This is another ambiguous area. A mere ISMS certification as per ISO 27001 or compliance with RBI regulations, or even a PCI-DSS compliance or any other compliance may itself not be adequate for a bank to qualify itself for cyber-crime insurance by the insurance company.

Even assuming that the bank is fully compliant or is ISMS certified by one certification firm, the question of acceptability by another ISMS certification firm is still open, which will again question its eligibility for cyber-crime insurance, and when the policy is questionable, the settlement of the resultant claim hangs in doubt.

It is reported that even in the West, in the first few years of cyber-crime insurance, the insurers have not noted this as a profitable business. Under these circumstances, in the absence of coordinated efforts on the part of insurance companies, regulators from the banking and insurance industries and the user's representatives, the concept of cyber-crime insurance may take a longer time than planned to take off, though there are signals indicating an awareness of its usefulness and necessity.

20.5 Compliance in Banks

Compliance on the part of banks in India is closely associated with the regulatory guidelines of the RBI, besides compliance with the bank's own Information Security Policy, the local government's policies, the municipal and civil rules and regulations, especially employee-related, work-environmental, welfare-related and other similar guidelines. However, we will confine our study to the compliance-related guidelines, acts, and rules on the system front, especially the system security-related areas.

To ensure better compliance and to inculcate in the banks a sense of seriousness about compliance with regard to the various rules and regulations of the regulatory body and the state, the Reserve Bank of India has instructed banks to identify a top executive of the bank as the Compliance Officer. The term 'compliance risk' is also gaining in importance these days, especially among banks and Public Sector undertakings in India. "The impact that non-compliance and ineffective compliance can have on the banks' business, its profits, its reputations, etc. can be referred to as compliance risk" (IIBF book on Compliance in Banks, 2023). The compliance officer will be vested with the rights and duties to co-ordinate the various compliance issues and assist the top management in effectively managing the compliance risk faced by banks.

Banks have been advised to have a clearer and top-management approved compliance policy. The policy will broadly focus on the compliance structure and compliance philosophy of banks and define the hierarchy of the compliance function in the bank. The relationship between the Chief Compliance Officer and the functional heads of compliance functions of various departments is normally discussed in this policy document, including the monitoring mechanism, the review structure of compliance functions, and the areas of responsibility for non-compliance.

From an IT Security perspective, the compliance functions have a great impact on the system security at the bank. Whenever a new product is introduced, especially a technology or network-based product, the compliance area of the product has to be checked and confirmed. After designing the product, the software is ready and perhaps the marketing team is ready to launch it. If the product does not comply with any particular regulatory norm of RBI, is non-conformant with any particular guideline of local rules and regulations, or even if the product software cannot generate a particular MIS for reporting mechanisms for compliance, it will become a waste of resources.

The compliance department and the IS Security Department have to work in close unison with each other at the stage of the design of any new product and any innovative service or scheme to be launched by banks.

Compliance functions have assumed greater significance these days, with more and more technology-based services being thought of at the regulatory level and at the state level too. For instance, taking Financial Inclusion to the next step, the Government recently launched the Jan Dhan Scheme (2015) with many ramifications, including for the social, financial, and economic sectors, envisaging the equitable growth that comes with it.

Dr. C. Rangarajan, former Chairman of the Economic Advisory Council to the Prime Minister and former Governor of the Reserve Bank of India, has stated that "Financial inclusion has two dimensions: (a) providing deposits and payment facilities to the disadvantaged and underprivileged and (b) providing credit facilities to such people. Technology has facilitated improved facilities for depositing and withdrawing cash." (*Source: The Indian Banking System: Some challenges by Dr. C. Rangarajan, in IOBOA Crusader, Special Issue, September 2014*). Thus, the impact of technology on today's banking is immense, and technology is the basis of banking today.

More so, with the sudden popularity and growth of payment banks with non-banking institutions, *i.e.*, non-lenders vying with traditional banks in the banking business of dealing with small payments and deposits, banking itself is seeing a new paradigm. Under such a milieu, the entire gamut of compliance has to be redefined, as a corollary of redefining banking. The RBI and other regulators have to devise new means, new laws and new regulations to bring the non-lending bankers, or NBFCs, whose presence is going to be a force to reckon with in Indian banking, into the gambit of regulatory banking in India.

The RBI has to perhaps increase the weapons in its arsenal, to regulate banking with all its arms and wings (Banks, NBFCs, Payment Banks, Card-related institutions, PoS establishments, etc.) and the cap of a strict regulator exercising its penal and punitive powers too, besides acting as a facilitator of banking and encouraging innovation and technology in banks. Though superficially acting as a facilitator of technology, and enabler of innovation in computerization may not appear to go in sync with the role of a regulator insisting on security in these products, RBI has to, nevertheless, perform the role adeptly, in view of the enormous responsibility it has shouldered upon itself.

In India, the regulator, the RBI, also performs a role in the grievance redress mechanism in its capacity as the Banking Ombudsman, though it is not directly related to the compliance function. Perhaps it could be argued that the Banking Ombudsman gets a complaint because of some 'non-compliance' *i.e.*, a bank not performing its duty and thereby defaulting in its service, giving way for a complaint and the need to contact the Banking Ombudsman.

20.6 Penal Powers of RBI

As the regulator of banks in India, the RBI has some penal powers, *i.e.*, the powers to levy penalties on banks for specific acts of omission and commission. RBI fined 19 banks, including the country's top private and foreign banks, for violating its guidelines on derivatives, specifically on offences reportedly like selling unsuitable products to corporations, selling products without verifying the underlying exposure, and selling derivatives to companies that do not have risk management practices in place.

The RBI is empowered to give directions to Non-Banking Finance Companies (NBFCs) and even prohibit those that do not adhere to a set of prudential norms, from accepting deposits and imposing penalties under the provisions of the RBI Act. Submission of any wrong information, any inconsistency, or any inaccuracy in reporting can invite the imposition of penalties specified under the Banking Regulation Act.

20.7 RBI's Regulatory Mechanism Already in Place

The Reserve Bank continues to build a regulatory and supervisory architecture in line with international best standards, adapted to suit domestic conditions. The objective has been to make the Indian banking sector more competitive, efficient, sound, and dynamic. Foreign banks and domestic banks with an overseas presence successfully migrated to Basel II on March 31, 2008. Policy measures initiated by the Reserve Bank are generally aimed at enhancing the prudential standards of the banking system in order to make it more resilient and aligning these with international best practices while ensuring customer protection.

The RBI has also issued guidelines strengthening the internal controls in banks in an endeavour to align the vigilance function in the private sector and foreign banks with that of public sector banks. Detailed guidelines have been issued so that all issues arising out of lapses in the functioning of the private sector and foreign banks, especially those relating to corruption, malpractices, frauds, etc., can be addressed uniformly by the banks for timely and appropriate action.

As the regulator of the nation, RBI has been issuing guidelines and circulars on areas other than IS Security and IS Audit, like Anti-Money Laundering, Know Your Customer guidelines, Payment of claims in respect of deceased depositors, guidelines on deposit accounts, etc. However, such guidelines and circulars (on areas other than IS Security) are beyond the purview of discussion in this chapter, and we will focus on IS-Security related areas alone.

Guidelines for fraud prevention

In a study made across banks on fraud detection, it was observed that there was a lack of consistency in the treatment of transactions with characteristics of fraud as well as in the reporting to the competent authority. The banks have been advised to suitably modify their policies and streamline the operating framework. In order to ensure close monitoring and tighter controls so as to thwart frauds, especially in housing loans, export finance, loans against fixed deposit receipts, etc., the banks have been asked to structure their operating framework on three tracks: namely, (*i*) Detection and reporting of frauds; (*ii*) Corrective action; and (*iii*) Preventive and punitive action.

In the case of close relatives who find it difficult to furnish documents relating to place of residence while opening accounts, banks can obtain an identity document and a utility bill from the relative with whom the prospective customer is living, along with a declaration from the relative that the said person (the prospective customer) wanting to open an account is a relative and is staying with him/her.

Banks were required to review the risk categorization of customers at a periodicity of not less than once every six months. Banks were also required to introduce a system of periodic updation of customer identification data (including photographs) after the account is opened, which should be not less than once every five years in the case of low-risk category customers and not less than two years in the case of high/medium-risk customers.

In cases of variance in home and host country KYC/AML regulations, the overseas branches/subsidiaries were required to adopt the more stringent regulations of the two. Banks were required to put in place adequate screening mechanisms as an integral part of their recruitment and hiring processes.

Some guidelines were issued to Recovery Agents too, like following a due diligence process, verification of verifying the antecedents to be done by agents, obtaining due authorization for the agents, which should be carried out by them, posting on the bank's website the up-to-date details of the recovery agency firms, etc.

Role of the RBI in Micro finance Institutions: The government has proposed to bring all micro finance institutions (MFIs) under the ambit of the RBI, with powers to formulate policies for the sector and regulate it. It is proposed to empower the RBI to issue directions to MFIs on issues like tenure of loans, repayment schedules, processing fees-related instructions, interest, and life insurance premiums.

20.8 RBI

The RBI's vision document (IT Vision of Reserve Bank India - 2011-17 dated 28th February, 2011, https://rbi.org.in/Scripts/PublicationVisionDocuments.aspx?Id=629) for the period 2011-17 envisages commercial banks moving forward from core banking solutions to enhanced use of IT in areas like MIS, regulatory reporting, overall risk management, financial inclusion, and customer relationship management. It also dwells on the possible operational risks arising out of adopting technology in the banking sector, which could affect financial stability, and emphasizes the need for internal controls, risk mitigation systems, and business continuity plans.

Besides, as the regulator is ever-concerned about the threats in the IT landscape in the country's banking domain, the Reserve Bank of India announced in May 2015 that it has plans to set up a new IT subsidiary responsible for strengthening cyber-security in the Indian banking sector in the form of a cyber-security arm to supervise and formulate policies for information security and IT- related issues in banks in India. The precise nature of the subsidiary is yet to be formulated. In the Press

Conference, the Governor of the RBI said that the entity will attract people from the IT sector to focus on issues affecting the information security area in banking and equip the sector with the tools necessary to face any attack.

Taking the issue of creating awareness on the part of bank customers in India on cyber-crimes and related areas, the RBI has been issuing warning messages and notifications in the public domain, including in many private electronic media, cautioning people against phishing frauds, revealing their user name and password, accessing their bank accounts from untrusted and unauthorised apps and devices, and all such frauds. These are all very commendable and appreciable efforts for a regulatory body to pro-actively guide the public and banks, which will go a long way in crime prevention. RBI has also set up, though not exactly in the area of cyber-crime awareness, The Depositor Education and Awareness Fund Scheme, 2014, with the operational guidelines getting notified to all banks in 2015.

The RBI is not the only regulatory body, though it is the most powerful as far as the Indian financial system is concerned, shouldering the responsibility of supervision and control of the entire banking system. It is to be recorded that, but for such independence, administrative capability, and supervisory mechanisms creating a level playing field, allowing the private sector to grow along with the public sector in a competitive manner, and at the same time exercising control wherever necessary, India could not have remained unaffected by the economic meltdown of the US and other economic crises of the Western nations.

Just a few years ago, the US economy was struggling with excessive usage of credit card borrowings, sub-prime lending, banks failing, etc., and is gradually recovering from the aftermath. It was due to sound financial policies that the Indian economy showed remarkable resilience and remained grossly unaffected by the US downturn on the economic front. The RBI certainly deserves full credit and appreciation for its effective monitoring and close observation to maintain the Indian Banking industry with the least adverse impact.

Before we go into the roles and functions of other regulatory bodies like SEBI, TRAI, and IRDAI, let us briefly look at the ongoing debate on the role of the RBI and the co-ordination among all regulatory bodies in the nation.

Quite often, there has been criticism that better co-ordination among all the regulatory bodies in the nation will pave the way for a smoother implementation of various government initiatives, especially in the IT, ICT, and IS Security fronts. What is seen as a liberalised regime encouraging private sector players by one regulator should not be seen differently by others. The information, especially on security-related areas, should not be withheld by one regulator without sharing it with others since, in a developing economy, no regulator can work in a water-tight compartment.

The idea of a super-regulatory body was mooted by the Raghuram Rajan Committee in 2008 (who has since become the Governor in September 2013) which went into the financial structure reforms and the regulatory architecture in India. Some other countries do have a system of a super-regulatory body with oversight powers, especially to ensure better co-ordination among the various regulators. A case in point is the Financial Stability Oversight Council in the US. Drawing parallel with such a council and other such bodies in other countries, the Government of India constituted an apex-level body, the Financial Stability and Development Council, with the objective of strengthening and institutionalising the mechanism of maintaining financial stability, financial sector development, and enhancing inter-regulatory coordination, under the chairmanship of the Union Finance Minister.

RBI expressed its concern about the powers of regulation and supervision vested with it so far exercised by it single-handedly. It is important to understand that FSDC will not breach the autonomy of the RBI in the financial sector as a regulator. It is to be seen in the days to come, whether and when FSDC will act as a super regulatory structure with overriding powers or a better coordinating agency involving regulators like RBI along with the Finance Ministry with the overall governance responsibilities.

20.9 SEBI

The Securities and Exchange Board of India (SEBI) was established in 1988, by the Government of India through an executive resolution and was subsequently upgraded as a fully autonomous body (a statutory board) in the year 1992 with the passing of the Securities and Exchange Board of India Act (SEBI Act) on 30th January, 1992. It is a statutory and autonomous regulatory board with defined responsibilities, to cover both the development and regulation of the market and independent powers. Perhaps, this was a welcoming development and a positive outcome of the Securities Scam of 1990-91.

The basic objectives of the Board were:

I. to protect the interests of investors in securities
II. to promote the development of the Securities Market
III. to regulate the securities market and
IV. for matters connected therewith or incidental to it.

Since its inception, SEBI has been targeting securities and attending to the fulfilment of its objectives with commendable zeal and dexterity. The improvements in the securities markets, like capitalization requirements, margining, the establishment of clearing corporations, etc., reduced the risk of credit and showed a healthy trend in the capital market.

SEBI has introduced comprehensive regulatory measures, prescribed registration norms, eligibility criteria, a code of obligations, and a code of conduct for different intermediaries, like, bankers to issue, merchant bankers, brokers and sub-brokers, registrars, portfolio managers, credit rating agencies, underwriters, and others. It has framed bye-laws, risk identification and risk management systems for clearing houses of stock exchanges, a surveillance system, etc., which have made dealing in securities both safe and transparent to the end investor.

Two broad approaches of SEBI are, to integrate the securities market at the national level, and to diversify the trading products, so that there is an increase in the number of traders and the markets provide a level playing field adhering to all statutory norms and ensuring compliance.

20.10 TRAI

The Telecom Regulatory Authority of India is the regulator of the telecom industry in India. Though not directly dealing with banking and the financial system, telecom regulations have a bearing on the financial and banking regulations in the country, and hence TRAI as a regulator and RBI as another have much to share and contribute to nation-building. TRAI was set up with its administrative set up as per the Telecom Regulatory Authority of India Act, 1997.

The National Telecom Policy was first formulated in 1994, later, a new revised policy came into being in 1999. The Broadband Policy was framed in 2004. The mission of TRAI is to ensure that the interests of consumers are protected and, at the same time, nurture conditions for the growth of telecommunications, broadcasting, and cable services in a manner and at a pace that will enable India to play a leading role in the emerging global information society.

The main objectives of TRAI include providing a fair and transparent policy environment that promotes a level playing field and facilitates fair competition. In pursuance of these objectives, TRAI has been issuing a number of regulatory guidelines and directions for strict compliance, which will evolve the telecom market as an efficient player in a multi-operator, multi-service open market environment from the state-run monopoly that it was, years ago.

On the security and technology front, some of the steps taken by TRAI as the regulator are quite significant. For instance, in view of the continuous complaints from credit card subscribers and the

observations of some High Courts in public interest litigations, TRAI framed the Telecom Unsolicited Commercial Communications Regulations, 2007 for curbing Unsolicited Commercial Communications (UCC). The Department of Telecommunications (DoT) issued further guidelines for telemarketers and stipulated that all the telecom service providers should set up a mechanism to receive requests from subscribers who do not want to receive such unsolicited calls and maintain and operate a 'private do not call' list.

Nowadays, with more and more crimes being committed with a computer, a network, or a mobile as a tool, investigators are relying heavily on evidences from mobile tracing the communication tower as a means to trace the culprit or secure evidences. In all such cases, the contribution of TRAI as a regulator stipulating the period of preservation for e-records by telecom providers, the details to be kept in the Call Details Record (CDR) and other relevant records, and the mandatory requirements will go a long way not only in effective regulation but also in reliable crime detection and efficient crime prevention.

CDR contains details such as the called number, the number that placed the call, the date and time that the call was started, the time that it connected, and the time that it ended. Call management records (CMRs, or diagnostic records) also contain details such as the jitter, lost packets, the amount of data sent and received during the call, etc. CDR data comprises CDRs and CMRs collectively. A single call can result in the generation of several CDRs and CMRs, which are normally very helpful for their forensic and evidentiary value.

Interestingly, there is an administrative set up to serve as a watchdog for TRAI. Called the TERM Cell, the Telecom Enforcement and Resource Monitoring Cell of the Department of Telecommunication, and set on 5 August, 2008, replacing the earlier Vigilance Telecom Monitoring Cell (VTMs) of the DoT, the TERM Cell has a three-fold function, namely:

I. Vigilance functions
II. Monitoring functions
III. Security functions

Empowered with the monitoring function, TERM conducts subscriber verification audit functions, which has since resulted in enhanced compliance with subscriber verification by the service providers, from around 60% reported earlier to more than 85%, according to statistics released by DoT. TERM Cells have offices in 34 centres in the country.

20.11 IRDAI

The Insurance Regulatory and Development Authority of India (IRDAI) was set up, by an Act of Parliament in 1999, with objectives to protect the interests of the policyholders, to regulate, promote, and ensure orderly growth of the insurance industry, and for matters connected therewith or incidental thereto, like reinsurance schemes, including issues relating to pensions forming part of such insurance schemes. Subsequently, the Pension Fund Regulatory and Development Authority (PFRDA) was established by the Government of India in August 2003 to promote old age income security by establishing, developing, and regulating pension funds, and to protect the interests of subscribers to pension funds schemes.

IRDAI and the Pension Fund Regulatory and Development Authority (PFRDA) crossed swords over the issue of commissions. Once again, tension is rising between both parties. The latest point of contention is PFRDA's act listing life insurance companies to furnish annuities to subscribers of the National Pension System. The National Pension System (NPS) is governed by PFRDA.

NPS collects savings from monthly annuity payments for government employees after retirement and the unorganised sector. However, as per law, the transition of the collected savings into a monthly income stream can solely be done by a life insurer. At a recent insurance summit, J. Harinarayan, Chairman of the IRDAI, said that life insurance companies were not obliged to act as intermediaries for third parties. In 2009, a panel led by former pension regulator D. Swarup advised that the commission for agents be completely disposed off and all agents be converted into independent financial advisers under the Financial Well-Being Board of India (FINWEB).

With effect from January 1, 2012, life insurance companies were asked to withdraw all pension products that did not meet the revised guidelines. In December 2011, the life insurers filed 21 revised pension products and also sought further clarification on the guidelines from the IRDAI. In response to the queries raised, the regulator said that the guidelines do not apply to Group Gratuity and Group Leave Encashment products.

20.12 Legal Enactments

The significant legislation in the field of Information Security in India is the Information Technology Act, 2000, and the subsequent Information Technology Amendment Act, 2008, which came into effect from 27th October, 2009. One major contribution of the I.T. Act of 2000 was to give legal recognition to electronic records. Of course, the procedures relating to authenticating an electronic communication, electronic evidence, etc. were also discussed in the Act. Besides dealing with the civil offence of data theft and the procedures relating to adjudication for such offences, the Act also dealt with some cyber-crimes of criminal nature, like hacking, e-publishing of obscene material on the net, child pornography, cyber terrorism, etc.

The Act amended certain provisions of the Indian Penal Code, the Bankers' Books Evidence Act, the Indian Evidence Act, and the Reserve Bank of India Act, 1934, introducing the concept of electronic records, electronic evidences, electronic communications, etc. Procedures relating to digital signatures were also presented in detail in the Act. The word 'digital' signature was since replaced by 'electronic' signature, subsequently enacted by the Amendment Act, 2008.

As far as the banking industry is concerned, the I.T. Act is a significant step in the right direction, since for the first time in India, an attempt was made to legally recognize electronic data and preserve evidence in an electronic form. A print-out of material accompanied by a certificate stating that the same is a print-out of a record of data stored in the system that is securely handled, with adequate backup procedures and in a non-tamperable state, etc., will constitute a valid electronic record and electronic evidence for the purpose of Bankers Books Evidence and other Acts.

Hence thanks to the passing of the Act, there is no need to carry the bulky and heavy bank ledger to court or investigators in the event of any fraud or crime happening in the branch as evidence; and instead, just a print-out along with a certificate in the prescribed format would suffice. In fact, this is one provision of the IT Act (recognizing the electronic evidences as shown in print outs) that has most often been misunderstood and misinterpreted, including by banks, prompting them to take a print out of a letter or a statement and send it to the public with the signature column left blank at the bottom and with a Post Script stating that "This is a computer-generated print out and hence needs no signature".

Similarly, the Indian Evidence Act has been amended by the IT Act, recognizing electronic records as evidences. The Indian Penal Code has also been amended to include cheating by electronic means, cheating by personation electronically, forgery of electronic records, etc. as offences. The RBI Act was amended to recognize electronic cheques and electronic payment modes among banks and the status of payment settlements like RTGS, NEFT, etc. Thus, the I.T. Act paved the way for digital evidence, or evidence in electronic form, in India.

On the compliance side too, the IT Act is quite significant for banks in India. There are sections in the Act on due diligence and 'reasonable security practices' to be followed by "body corporate"

dealing with or handling any personal data and any act of negligence arising out of not following the reasonable practices, as referred to in Section 43-A of the IT Amendment Act, 2008.

Especially in view of the phrase 'sensitive personal data' used in the same section, banks dealing with public bank account-related data, have an added responsibility on the compliance side itself. If any data breach happens on the bank's server, banks are legally liable for the data loss to the owner of the data, namely the customer or the third party, whichever is the owner. Besides, there is also a provision (in Sections 72 and 72A, supra) on data breaches and due diligence practices while dealing with "breach of confidentiality and privacy" and access without consent and "disclosure of information in breach of a lawful contract".

These provisions have a huge impact on the roles, functions, and security practices of third- party intermediaries dealing with public data, which also includes banks, and hence the compliance initiatives of banks have to take these into account. To be precise, the CTOs, CISOs, and CEOs of banks are liable unless they prove that reasonable security practices have been adopted and followed in the bank.

Besides the major legislation, the I.T. Act and the I.T. Amendment Act, there are other legislations that have a bearing on the legal compliance side, especially in the electronic arena, like the amendment to the Negotiable Instruments Act recognizing the cheque truncation system, the Anti-Money Laundering Act, and other similar enactments.

To conclude, the strength of the nation is often derived from the strength of the three pillars, *viz.* the Legislature, the Judiciary and the Executive. Regulatory bodies like the RBI have a pivotal role to play in the executive functions of getting the rules in place, supervising the implementation, and penalising wherever necessary. On the development side, the regulators do play a proactive role by offering suggestions and feedback to the policy makers with the broader objective of taking the country on a safer and more secure path towards economic self-sufficiency and global supremacy.

Know Your Progress

Banks have a significant role to play in nation-building. The Financial System needs a regulator to ensure the industry's adherence to all statutory obligations and compliance with regulations. The RBI, as the regulator for the financial system in India, especially the banking industry, has many distinct functions, like issuing currency, serving as the bankers' bank, serving as the government's bank, and above all, acting as the supervisor and monetary authority.

The important regulatory powers of the RBI include the powers to monitor and supervise banks right from licensing upto the closing or winding-up of banking companies, as enshrined mostly in the Banking Companies Regulation Act as well as in the RBI Act. RBI has been discharging its duties as an effective regulator by constantly updating the systems and procedures, especially in the Information Systems arena, IS audits and related areas. Many committees have been set up on such subjects as IS Audit and Internet Banking, whose recommendations have been circulated among banks and necessary follow-up action, including changes if any are required in the checklist for conducting audits, etc. Recently, the Gopalakrishna Working Group of RBI submitted its report on Internet Banking, IT Governance, IS Audit, and other related areas, and the detailed report was circulated among banks by the RBI in April 2011.

Recently, the Financial Stability and Development Council was set up under the chairmanship of the Union Finance Minister, which will, besides having regulatory and supervising powers, also act as a coordinator among regulatory bodies.

Besides the RBI, SEBI, as the regulator, is for the capital market, enforcing discipline, free and fair play in the stock market, and regulating it. TRAI, as a regulator, takes care of the telecom industry in India, taking care of the subscribers' interests and regulating the network and telecom service providers, enforcing discipline, uniformity, and encouraging competition for the overall benefit of the subscriber. IRDA is the Insurance Regulatory and Development Authority, which protects the interests of policy holders for the orderly growth of the insurance industry.

Key Words

Regulation	Compliance	Monetary Authority	TRAI
IRDA	SEBI	TERM Cell	FSDC
Digital	evidence	electronic signature	CDR

Questions

1. Who was the industrialist inducted into the board of the RBI Central Board, in 2006?
   a. Shri Nandan Nilekani
   b. Shri Azim Premji
   c. Shri Ratan Tata
   d. Shri Anil Ambani
2. The Standardised checklist for IS Audit was introduced by RBI in 2001, on the recommendations of the Working Group under ________________.
   a. R.B. Burman
   b. Jilani
   c. Gopalakrishna
   d. Narasimhan
3. As part of regulatory mechanism, RBI has got the powers to levy ________________ on ________________.
   a. Penalty, public sector banks
   b. Punishment, all banks
   c. Penalty, all banks in India including private sector banks
   d. Penalty, private sector banks only
4. Which one of the following is not one of the 9 topics in the Gopalakrishna Working Group?
   a. IT Operations S Audit
   b. IT Services Outsourcing
   c. Data Manipulations by insider threats
   d. Business Continuity Planning
5. When it was set-up, ________________________ was considered to be a super regulator with monitoring powers and control and equipped with better co-ordination among all regulators.
   a. Financial Supervision and Development Committee
   b. Financial Stability and Development Committee

   c. Financial Supervision and Development Council
   d. Financial Stability and Development Council

6. Which of the following is not an objective of SEBI?
   a. To protect the interests of investors in securities.
   b. To promote the development of Securities Market.
   c. To regulate the securities market, integrate the securities market at the national level.
   d. To protect the interest of the government by ensuring there is no evasion in revenue.

7. A mechanism to receive requests from subscribers who do not want to receive such unsolicited calls and maintain and operate a 'private do not call' list TRAI framed the ________________.
   a. Telecom Do Not Disturb Registry Regulation
   b. Telecom Unsolicited Commercial Communications Regulations, 2007
   c. DoT Do Not Disturb Regulations, 2007
   d. Telecom Unsolicited and Do Not Disturb Regulations, 2007

8. In telecom circles, the term CDR refers to ________________.
   a. Call Divert Register when the companies register the calls received and diverted
   b. Call Diagnostic Records for the diagnostic details of calls lost packets, the amount of data sent and received during the call etc.
   c. Communication Details Register *i.e.* contains the subscriber's name and number and the mobile device identification number etc.
   d. Call Details Register with particulars like when started, connected and the time that it ended and other such management records used for call diagnostics.

9. Issues relating to insurance schemes are only regulated by IRDA. (True/False)
10. The FSDC will have the RBI Governor as its Chairman. (True/False)
11. The TERM cell is like a regulatory body under the Reserve Bank of India. (True/False)
12. The I.T. Act legally recognizes the truncation of a cheque (electronic form). (True/False)

Answers

1. *b*	7. *b*
2. *a*	8. *d*
3. *c*	9. True
4. *c*	10. False
5. *d*	11. False
6. *d*	12. False